Leisure and popular culture in transition

THOMAS M. KANDO

California State University, Sacramento
Sacramento, California

Leisure and popular culture in transition

with 31 illustrations

THE C. V. MOSBY COMPANY

SAINT LOUIS 1975

Cover photograph by Rick Vanderpool

Library of Congress Cataloging in Publication Data

Kando, Thomas M   1941-
    Leisure and popular culture in transition.

    1. Leisure. 2. Recreation. 3. Popular culture.
I. Title. [DNLM: 1. Leisure activities. 2. Recrea-
tion. 3. Social change. QT250 K16L]
GV171.K36   790'.0135   74-14775
ISBN 0-8016-2616-1

TS/CB/B   9   8   7   6   5   4   3   2

For ATA

❦ Foreword

The United States emerged from World War II as the most powerful nation in the world. A population that had suffered the deprivations of depression and war had to be resettled, retrained, and rewarded for loyal service. Outside the United States a world shattered by war had to be reconstructed. However, the American industrial machine, recently retooled at public expense as a byproduct of war, was equal to the task. Americans in the 1950s were about to make the acquaintance of a type of society they had not known for thirty years—not since the 1920s had Americans suspected the potential of scientific-industrial technology when implemented by access to enormous natural resources, including fossil fuels, for creating a world of unprecedented material affluence.

Already in the early 1950s some students sensitively attuned to the winds of change realized that the world arising after World War II had permanently transformed the significance of work and its relation to leisure.

America's traditional work ethic had been strongly influenced by ascetic Protestantism. The devoted Protestant had conceived of his work as his "calling," as the place in day-to-day affairs where God tested his worthiness for salvation. From this point of view a man's work was the primary basis of his identity. Leisure was secondary to work and was legitimately employed in restoring mind and body to the state of effectiveness his work required. Personalities formed around the Protestant ethic were described by David Riesman as inner-directed—under the control of the individual's conscience, which in turn was shaped by his position in the generational system.

However, in Riesman's view, while inner-directed personalities were still to be found in the post World War II world, a new type of personality was arising in response to changed conditions. Riesman described this new personality configuration as other-directed, for its control mechanism was not a generationally located conscience, but a set of peer group norms. The other-directed personality manifested its properties not so much in an individual's work life as in his consumption patterns. For this new type of personality leisure time pursuits had replaced work patterns as the decisive sphere where selfhood was realized.

As the 1950s wore on and despite some ugly international cold war developments (the Berlin airlift and Korean conflict) and despite political witchhunting at home (by the House Un-American Activities Committee, by Senator Richard M. Nixon, and by Senator Joseph McCarthy), the most impressive process in America was the emergence of the United States as an affluent mass society. Before the decade of the 1950s was over the sociology of leisure and its various subdivisions (the sociology of sports, of popular culture, of art and of play) had taken shape as major subdivisions of the field of sociology.

However, despite the shortening of the workweek and increasing amounts of free time at the disposal of the great mass of Americans, despite the material affluence and the elaboration of an array of institutions that implemented the consumption orientation, despite the enormous growth of almost all forms of the entertainment industry, despite all these things, by the 1960s an increasing number of Americans, and not simply an insignificant minority of "beatniks," began to display signs of disillusionment. For one thing the new consumption practices implemented by credit arrangements, installment buying, and the like could turn into a form of entrapment. Millions of persons bought so many things on time that they were forced to spend some of the free time made possible by the shortened workweek moonlighting on second jobs to keep up with the payments. Ironically, at times it appeared that enslavement to work had been replaced by enslavement to leisure.

Moreover the very affluence of the 1950s brought to the fore old problems. Who could deny the goodness of a society that provided such material affluence to so many millions? But it soon appeared that all sections of the population did not participate equally in the material benefits of the mass society. The apparent affluence of the many exacerbated the sense of injustice of the deprived few. Underprivileged minorities were politically activated to demand their share.

Furthermore a new generation was coming of age, a generation that had never known first hand any other world than one of great affluence. To this new generation material well-being was taken for granted and could hardly be viewed as other than spiritually barren. To idealistic youngsters the fact that some minority groups did not share in the material well-being they took for granted, could only appear as hypocrisy on the part of their elders. Some joined the civil rights movement, further helping to legitimize it and, incidentally, gaining some experience in the techniques of civil disobedience, which they were later to employ in the interests of the youth, women's, and gay protests.

To some persons there seemed to be a message in such developments for the problem of leisure. Before one rejoiced at the vista of endless material prosperity and reorganized the world to achieve self-realization in the sphere of leisure, perhaps social and economic injustice should be attended to. Nor was the end in sight to developments that were giving the phenomena of material prosperity and leisure an ambiguous mien.

While the civil rights and poverty protests were occurring in the early 1960s the country was getting bogged down in the Indo-China war. Though the older generation more or less reluctantly accepted the war at first as a patriotic duty, it was never really popular even to them; the war was even less popular to young people of draft age who faced disruption of their lives by war service. From the beginning many of the poor and blacks saw the war as a distraction from the injustices at home. To many young people facing service in an unpopular war and already used to challenging the apparent hypocrisy in the inequitable distribution of material affluence, the war seemed like a self-evident additional example. Meanwhile the leaders of the United States appear largely to have forgotten a principle as old as Machiavelli: one cannot fight an unpopular war in a democracy without first corrupting the democracy. As involvement in the war deepened, millions of young people did everything possible to avoid war service including, eventually, mass protest activities employing various techniques of civil disobedience, draft dodging, expatriation, and desertion.

Meanwhile, since the war was never really popular and because a pay-as-you-go plan might well have forced home its implications on the society at large, Presidents Johnson and Nixon resorted to deficit financing of the war. This resulted in inflationary pressures on the domestic economy. While the elders of the persons of draft age by and large remained patriotic and at least neutral toward the war, they were under increasing economic pressure from war-induced inflation. The members of the respective generations, thus, did not generally see that their respective problems arose from the same source: the young saw the war as a threat to their life plans for questionable reasons; their elders found it increasingly impossible to make ends meet while they were plagued with unpatriotic children. The estrangement of the generations was an added component in the alienation that each day seemed to grow more widespread.

As disillusionment spread, more and more people were inclined to give ear to the studies of special groups who had been led to question the very future of contemporary society. The ecologists and demographers were making dire predictions. The ecologists were pointing to the possibility that if contemporary industrial production continued on its course unmodified, it could well destroy the environment essential to all higher forms of life; the demographers were pointing to the possibility that the worldwide population explosion could well result in major disasters before the end of the twentieth century. And always in the background was the fact that the major world powers continued to stockpile atomic weapons although each already had enough to kill every man on earth from twenty to fifty times.

In view of all such developments in the 1960s the vision that had begun to emerge at the end of the 1950s of the leisure society resting on almost inexhaustible material prosperity and offering every man an almost endless vista of free time for creative self-realization began to appear rather superficial. Moreover, if developments in the 1960s were such as to raise questions of the implications of the changing ratios between work and leisure for Americans, developments in the 1970s (the energy crisis, the crisis of confidence centering on Watergate, the continuing spiral of inflation) would appear to invite wholesale reevaluation. This is precisely what Dr. Kando has undertaken.

In *Leisure and Popular Culture in Transition* Dr. Kando places the problem of leisure in a perspective of world history. He reviews the interrelated terms "leisure," "recreation," "play," and "the game," he details various contemporary positions on "high" and mass culture, and he outlines the notion of the leisure society that emerged toward the end of the 1950s. These tasks accomplished, Dr. Kando undertakes an encyclopedic review of the history and current status of the various forms of high culture, mass culture, mass leisure, and participant and spectator sports in America. He pays particular attention to variations in leisure time activities by age, sex, race, ethnicity, geography, religion, education, occupation, and social class.

According to Dr. Kando, the counterculture of the late 1960s was one of the most promising postwar developments with respect to both forms and interpretations of leisure. Dr. Kando appraises the state of high culture in America and comes to the conclusion that it is relatively poor. Nor does he see much value in most commercial forms of mass culture. By contrast the counterculture revolution of the late 1960s, in his view, represented a profound spiritual experience and, ideally, a first step toward the true leisure society. The counterculture has, of course, been an attack upon what remains of the Protestant ethic toward work and the Victorian ethic toward sex. Kando argues that the movement has meant, at worst, licentious nihilism but, at best, a constructive new value system that may, in his view, provide the first building blocks for the only viable alternative for the society of the postindustrial age. He ends on this note:

We thus arrive at a prognosis and an ideal. It seems probable that work and nonwork will become increasingly integrated, and that this will be the key to many current problems in both spheres. Our leisure ideal borrows from de Grazia's Aristotelian concept and from the counterculture. Ideally, the future society will provide freedom for creativity. The work-leisure distinction will vanish, and so will that between audience and performer, between passive spectatorship and active participation. Music, games, and entertainment will become *happenings,* permitting the free democratic participation by all. Art will become public once again. Education, too, will become a creative participatory process involving all, not merely the teacher. Such freedom will not preclude learning and growing, as gurus, teachers, coaches, and facilitators will continue to gently and firmly show the way to greater perfection. As Davis (1967) predicted, some day we shall all be hippies.

Dr. Kando has made his personal preferences quite clear. He not only advocates leisure, but a specific conception of leisure. He has reviewed the entire field and stated all the current points of view. His text will be of value to all students of leisure, whatever their persuasions.

Don Martindale
University of Minnesota

✿ Preface

The aim of this book is to provide a more or less comprehensive text for the emerging field of leisure and popular culture. As the title indicates, the conceptual area carved out differs somewhat from such established subfields as the sociology of leisure, the sociology of sport, mass communications, recreation studies, and popular culture. It straddles and covers portions of each of these areas because it is felt that there is an underlying unity to the subject matter of those disciplines. The book attempts to bring together material that is currently dealt with in a variety of college courses in a variety of departments. While the book is essentially sociological, as is my background and most of the research used, the more important claim is that it is interdisciplinary. The subject matter of this book is, in one word, culture, with a prime emphasis on leisure.

Leisure is a modern sociological problem, evolving out of certain historical conditions. Furthermore, it is a highly controversial problem that may be expected to become even more crucial in

future years. Hence, to deal with the problem of leisure adequately a book must do at least the following three things: (1) discuss the background history of leisure as a modern problem, (2) provide information about currently dominant recreational behavior in our society, and (3) deal with the philosophical issues involved and point to likely forms of imminent social change in this area. Past, present, and future. This, essentially, is the framework of the book.

The first four chapters are theoretical. Chapter 1 provides an overview of the book's two major themes: the history and changes in our attitudes toward work and leisure, and current changes in our national consciousness and lifestyle. Chapter 2 reviews four key concepts in the sociology of leisure—leisure, recreation, play, and game. Chapter 3 addresses itself to the central controversy raging in this field: What do Americans do in their spare time, what are their cultural predilections, and is it true that these leave much to be desired? After a conceptual discussion of popular culture and related terms, the various positions vis-à-vis the issue are presented. The conclusion reached is that whereas an elitist rejection of popular culture may be misplaced, a melioristic policy attempting to uplift the quality of cultural, intellectual, and recreational life in America is nevertheless called for. Chapter 4 examines the related question of the alleged "leisure boom." While technology has vastly increased our productivity, our purchasing power, and the potential amount of free time at our disposal, in the end, as de Grazia has stated, Americans have failed to achieve true leisure. Technology's promise was a better quality of life. The causes for the failure of that promise are examined.

The second part of the book is substantive. Chapter 5 covers high culture, Chapter 6 deals with the printed media, Chapter 7 discusses cinema, and Chapter 8 covers sports, outdoor recreation, and travel. For each of these activities, data are provided on the following sociological correlates: sex, age, race and ethnicity, geography, religion, values and tastes, education, occupation, and social class. In addition, each area is treated historically, and the most important issues encountered in the pertinent literature are discussed.

The final chapter of the book addresses itself to the question of cultural change, attempting to formulate both the most likely and the most desirable forms of leisure, culture, and lifestyle toward the end of the twentieth century. An ideal typical depiction of the youth culture of the 1960s is offered, identifying that movement's major innovative contributions for leisure and culture. Also appraised are the potential for both positive change and sinister retrogression inherent in the so-called counterculture. It is argued that the generally questionable outcome of the experiment begun by the under-thirty generation in the 1960s

should not cause us to question the validity of the *ideals* that had inspired that youth movement. As for the immediate future, the energy shortage, inflation, and the other rampant economic problems of the seventies suddenly show that, in a poor, overcrowded, and interdependent world, the affluent society is not all that affluent after all. It therefore becomes all the more imperative to reappraise our values, our lifestyle, and our conception of good leisure and good culture. While earlier critics like de Grazia did not foresee the ecological crisis and the resurgence of the scarcity principle due to population growth and a wasteful growth economy, their message becomes all the more prophetic: more than ever, we must cease equating leisure with material consumption and mindless hedonism, redefining it, instead, along an Aristotelian ideal. The respiritualization of leisure and lifestyle—the advent of a true leisure society—is not incompatible with the current crisis of Western civilization. It is *demanded* by it.

Finally, in acknowledging the help and support from which this book has profited, I can, alas, mention only a few of the many kind people who directly or indirectly contributed to the project during the three or four years of its incubation and execution: colleagues Bob Gliner, Jeff Hubbard, Worth Summers, and Geoffrey Watson, and reviewer John Loy all helped with ideas and criticism. Graduate assistants Jim Spencer and Tom Wilson did valuable research; secretaries Lois Hill and Caroline Schaefer's help was heroic and selfless, particularly in view of the ongoing assault on academic research, staff, and facilities. But most of all, there is no doubt that the book would not have been written without the support of my wife, Anita.

Thomas M. Kando

❦ Contents

**Leisure and popular culture
in transition**

chapter 1

 # The work society

Since the dawn of history man has understood that survival is to be earned, not taken for granted. Whether by hunting, gathering, preying, tilling the land, or mass producing with machines, he has had to laboriously provide for himself or perish. Malthusian economics correctly appraise the species' past condition as being characterized by limited resources but unlimited desires, thus ensuring the perpetuity of a subsistence life dominated by conflict and unfulfilled needs. The scarcity principle, then, has been at the foundation of human existence.

Man's struggle for survival has taken increasingly complex forms in terms of technology and social organization. On the one hand this has been necessitated by increasing population size and density, and on the other hand it has resulted in a geometric increase in productivity. It is not clear, of course, whether the margin safeguarding species' survival has thereby become increasingly comfortable; today's ecology movement argues that man's relationship to nature is as precarious as ever, if not more so.

Although variations in survival have successively taken the forms of hunting, gathering, fishing, slavery, agriculture, feudalism, industrial capitalism, and socialized economies, its theme has remained essentially the same—individual and collective survival in the face of scarce resources.

For tribal man, as for all subsequent generations, a necessary condition for survival was the successful mastery of nature. Here, it could take such relatively simple forms as the collection of enough vegetables, catching enough fish or wildlife, or successfully preying upon other groups of men. In any one of these cases there was, at the core of the group's social life, a set of activities that centered around survival, subsistence, making a livelihood, in sum, work.

The Neolithic revolution is the term that has been given to the advent of agriculture. Approximately seven thousand years ago in Mesopotamia, and again, independently, three thousand years ago in Mesoamerica, man learned to domesticate plants and animals. This enabled him to move on from a nomadic existence based on hunting to a sedentary way of life dependent on agriculture. The size and density of human groups increased. Villages replaced bands and camps. Some energy could now be devoted to activities other than food getting. For the first time some members, supported by a farming majority, could develop into full-time specialists as religious, medical, political, and crafts experts. The division of labor was thus under way. The terms of the equation were altered, but not its basic format. The technological and organizational forms that collective survival took became more complex, but collective survival remained the guiding principle: each member remained in charge of a function vital to the collectivity. Most members' energies were devoted to food production, but to some, work had already assumed a new form.

The division of labor took another enormous step with the advent of urbanization. The Bronze Age, which began in the Near East about five thousand years ago, ushered the rise of the preindustrial city. As technology progressed, man organized himself in larger and more complex ways, thereby not only perpetuating his existence but also accumulating knowledge and culture. A necessary condition for cultural accumulation was writing, the invention of which had occurred during the Neolithic revolution. The preindustrial city embodied the growing segment of the population that did not have to solely devote itself to food production. Supported by the surrounding rural population, urbanites were freed to engage in political, educational, administrative, military, artistic, religious, scholarly, trading, and manufacturing activities. Through trade or war, large geographical areas sometimes became unified around preindustrial cities. The proliferation of the division of labor often produced a complex social stratification, with a high degree of correspondence between caste or class on the one hand, and occupation on the other. Stratification generally ranged from the slaves and outcastes, who were mostly in charge of lowly manual tasks, to a hereditary nobility, whose functions were governmental, military, and religious. Pooling the energies and resources of large populations and the efficiency resulting from the division of labor accounted for and were necessitated by the highly sophisticated forms collective survival began to assume. In vast portions of the world, particularly in Asia, the exploitation, regulation, and distribution of water resources led to what has been called the hydraulic society[1]: this is a highly centralized social system whose

---

[1]See Karl Wittfogel's (1957) ideological but incisive theory about the emergence and maintenance of hydraulic societies.

despotic political character is a response to the need for the disciplined regulation of water utilization by large populations over large geographical areas. In plain words, when a vast area is dependent upon a single river, dikes, terraces, and irrigation works must be constructed and safeguarded; this, then, produces a centralized and at times despotic government. In addition, the ruling urban strata were now able to extract from other segments of the population the surplus labor that produced such massive monuments as the Egyptian pyramids, the manpower to wage war against neighboring states, and, for the first time, the economic support for the sumptuous lifestyle of a leisure class.[2] Thus a fundamental feature of the urban revolution was a tremendous increase in the division of labor. Collective survival now became a sophisticated process characterized by functional interdependence and the type of social bond Durkheim called "organic." For the first time the anomaly of leisure even became known.

In ancient Greece, leisure became a recognized possibility. Mastery of nature has been the central and burdening theme in man's history. However, the Greek philosophers, Aristotle in particular, transcended that. Greece was a preindustrial, seafaring urban society. On the basis of colonies, conquest, and slavery, some Greek *poleis* supported a number of citizen-philosophers who formulated ideals of a leisure society. This is the birth of the theme around which this book is written. Most of the following chapters deal, in effect, with the Aristotelian leisure ideals and their applicability two thousand years later.

Ancient Rome epitomizes the preindustrial society at its apogee. Here, collective survival assumed extreme imperial-

istic form, to the point where humanity became synonymous with Roman humanity. Competing civilizations such as Carthage had to be destroyed, literally plowed under. The dominant values of Roman society included power, productivity, growth, and hard work. As Cato the Elder typically admonished the Roman farmers: "When it rains, look for something that can be done indoors. Do not lie around, but clean up, for cessation of work is not accompanied by cessation of expenses. . . . Bear in mind that a field is like a man: however great the return may be, little remains, if there are lavish expenditures" (quoted in Guinagh and Donjahn, 1942:165–166). Thus, Roman civilization was the first far-reaching elaboration of the principle of human survival through mastery of the environment.

Western antiquity was followed by a millenium during which the division of labor came to a temporary halt. During the Middle Ages, individual and collective survival became perhaps more precarious. It is perhaps precisely because of this deterioration in the quality of life that man remained, during that era, very much a *homo faber,* not a *homo ludens.*

The Renaissance signaled the full-scale resumption of the trends we have been dealing with—the proliferation of the division of labor and the assault upon the environment. The culmination of these trends in our times is related at least to the following phenomena: empirical science, capitalistic commerce, and the Industrial Revolution.

The epoch immediately following the Renaissance has been called the Age of Reason. It is during this period that Western man first combined logical, deductive thought, a habit inherited from Greek antiquity, with inductive experimentation, thus producing empirical science and technology. At about the same time, Western man's explorations

[2]The classical work addressing itself to the emergence of the leisure class is, of course, Thorstein Veblen's *The Theory of the Leisure Class.*

also led him to the development of trade and the exploitation of various regions of the world to a level of commercial and colonialist activity far surpassing those in antiquity. Furthermore, the resulting favorable balance of trade was not used to initiate a lifestyle of sumptuous leisure but was plowed back into economic enterprise, producing the beginnings of Western capitalism. Capitalism as a form of behavior represented a further step toward mastery of the environment. It derived spiritual support from such religious doctrines as Calvinism (Weber, 1958) and was made possible by the new technology.[3]

Scientific technology led to the Industrial Revolution. During the successive stages of a revolution that has yet to be concluded, handcraft was first superseded by mechanical production of commodities; subsequently machines were built that build other machines; finally machines were built that regulated themselves. As mechanization, automation, and finally cybernation succeeded each other, man's role could be expected to be reduced, or elevated, to that of decision maker rather than operator.

Thus the rise of scientific technology, its application in industry, and an economic system emphasizing and maximizing production rather than consumption are the three facets of man's final assault on the environment in the modern era. Underlying and supporting this enterprise are the major Western ideologies, be they Marxian socialism, the Protestant work ethic, or the individualistic

ethos of self-made Horatio Alger. The scarcity principle, valid as it applied to primitive man's relationship to nature, continues to dictate modern man's approach to his environment as well. It has become the *excuse* of scarcity.[4]

Nowhere perhaps does the excuse of scarcity find more adherents than in our own affluent society. America, per capita as well as absolutely the wealthiest society at the present time, operates as if individual and collective survival were as problematic as they have been for the nomadic hunting band.[5] The underlying assumption still seems to be that man and society must overcome nature to survive, and that to this end they must work, produce, and exploit. At this point, material consumption becomes the adjunct of the production ethic. Under advanced capitalism the single most important ramification of the production ethic underlying Western civilization has been the necessity to consume in order to maintain an expanding economy. Thus, advertising, the media, and the literature should not obscure the fact that, in terms of causal and logical primacy, postindustrial society remains first and foremost the producing society, secondly and only adjunctively the consuming society, and last as well as least the leisure society.

We have cursorily traced the survival theme through history, from the Neolithic era to modern America. We must now ask ourselves in greater depth what man's *feelings* have been toward this necessity. We saw for example that some Greek philosophers already formulated a

---

[3]While Marx, as we shall see shortly, emphasized the causative influence of technological developments upon the emergence of an industrial value-orientation and Weber focused more on the reactive effect of values and ideas upon economic behavior and economic structure, to set up a "Marx versus Weber controversy" is to set up a straw man. The theories of these two men with regard to work, work ethic, and capitalism are complementary rather than contradictory.

[4]The term comes to us from Roszak (1969) paraphrasing Marcuse (1962).
[5]While species survival is indeed once again problematic, as it was at the dawn of prehistory, the *causes* for this are exactly the opposite of those that threatened the continued existence of *Homo sapiens* two million years ago. Man's worst enemy now is man himself, not his natural environment. Species extinction is now likely to be the result of overexploitation and ultimate environmental destruction, not scarcity of survival resources.

leisure ideal, an ideal that primitive societies cannot afford and advanced societies, for some reason, reject. Let us now delve briefly into this aspect of man's cultural development—his feelings about work.

Tribal man, living at a precarious subsistence level, must have had a low level of consciousness about his condition. The concept of work may not have existed for him, much less a work-leisure polarity and the evaluation of these two alternatives. Effort and exertion for sheer physical survival must have seemed as inevitable as death itself, at best leading to such metaphysical speculations about his origin as the theory of original sin. In general, work must have been so natural as to be invisible. Primitive man was no more able to objectify his condition than fish can conceptualize water. When man took the first steps toward the division of labor and the development of surplus productivity, however, differences emerged. Some men produced the means of subsistence to support others, who in turn provided various services for the collectivity. In addition, some individuals were supported by the workers for no immediately apparent reason, being merely "in power." Finally, differential wealth accumulation began to take place, and this, too, led to inequalities in power. In sum, society got under way, with its stratified social structure.

Cultural attitudes toward work have varied greatly through the ages. With social differentiation, at least two fundamental ways of making a living are conceivable: productive work and the predatory exploitation of others. The early American sociologist Thorstein Veblen (1899) pointed out that in many societies predatory exploitation of men by men has been considered more meritorious than labor—the utilization of nonhuman resources. While labor has frequently been viewed as odious and relegated to the lower strata, arms and slaughter, as well as the fine arts, have been considered honorable and the prerogative of a leisure class or of some other elite. This cultural outlook, according to Veblen, emerged during the stage of lower barbarism as a result of the institutionalization of private property. In modern industrial society, Veblen argues, this fundamental human trait has led to the conspicuous consumption of wealth as the primary way to gain the esteem of others and to invidious distinctions between the different social strata of society. Veblen (1914) posited in man an instinct of workmanship. Because of this, man has developed technology, civilization, and productive economic systems such as capitalism. Man is a creator and a producer. Even as he engages in conspicuous and nonproductive consumption as a member of the leisure class, he is engaged in a pecuniary struggle, if only as a parasite or exploiter. As predators on their fellowmen and exploiters of the natural environment, the elite, too, are making a living. Furthermore, far from formulating an Aristotelian leisure ideal that would undermine the existing social structure, preindustrial societies, leisure class and workers alike, showed a deep appreciation for material wealth, if not the drudgery that is involved in its acquisition. Thus, while preindustrial societies may not have extolled the virtue of hard work, their product, wealth, has been universally appreciated. Asceticism as a widespread and positive ideology is rare among primitive, barbarian, and feudal societies. It is subscribed to mostly by small religious sects and philosophical schools, gaining ascendency in such rare instances as the spread of Christendom over medieval Europe.

Aldous Huxley (1923) wittily traced some of the subsequent developments in man's attitudes toward work: In antiquity, men were periodically plagued by the *daemon meridianus,* attacking mostly in the heat of the day. The demon, better referred to as Accidie, of course represents sloth, idleness, laziness, boredom, inactivity. Ancient Rome thus personified idleness into an evil deity, giving testimony to its basic cultural orientation. During the Middle Ages the demon acquired the name Acedia and became one of man's eight principal sins. The prospects of idleness and sloth remained as frightening as ever. Subsequent to the Renaissance, Accidie became a disease entity, sometimes called melancholy, sometimes referred to as the spleen, later among the romantics described as the *mal du siecle.* Thus, throughout Western history prior to the Industrial Revolution, idleness was either a sin, a demon, or a disease. Apparently, man's central function was taken to be, somehow or other, production. For the vast majority this meant making a living at a subsistence level. For some, the accumulation of wealth resulted in sumptuous consumption. Small elite societies at times extracted sufficient support from subordinate populations to be able to extol and engage in the benefits of leisure. It should be noted here that true leisure is not necessarily dependent on affluence. While a minimum productivity is necessary to stay alive, the man of leisure need not be wealthy. Diogenes realized leisure through contemplation and meditation, living in a tub. King Croesus and his modern-day equivalents have not, in spite of their gold.

If the seeds of a leisure society were present in preindustrial society, they were effectively weeded out during the subsequent era. In the first place, a true and egalitarian leisure society was never a real possibility. For that, collective survival remained too precarious, technology too backward, productivity too low. The survival margin remained narrow, and the existence of a small leisure class, which sometimes blinds historians into biased descriptions of entire societies, should not obscure the fact that most men worked, worked very hard, and saw no possible alternative, except in heaven. Thus, there were four slaves for every free Athenean, and furthermore, the vast majority of the free citizens of Athens were workers, not philosophers. Second, the developments that began in the sixteenth century, while ultimately enhancing the *potential* for a true leisure society, resulted mostly in a vast increase in work.

In the sixteenth century, technology was once again on the move. A millenium of relative stagnation in this area of Western development came to an end. As pointed out earlier, scientific technology may be said to date back to this period. In addition, the rigid social structure of medieval Europe also came loose. A growing urban minority was now able to enhance its social position through commerce. Upward mobility through work now became a possibility, and at last the bourgeois revolutions of the eighteenth and nineteenth centuries opened up upward channels altogether. America, blessed with virgin natural resources, became the scene of the most massive upward mobility through economic activity. Now the other-worldly asceticism embodied in medieval Catholicism and reflecting a static social system lacking opportunities for upward mobility was called into question. Less quietistic alternative religious doctrines emerged, more conducive to economic behavior. Calvinism, in particular, was a belief system that enhanced work orientation, for it postulated predestination for salvation and thus implied that man, through his works and through simultaneous frugality, could detect the signs of divine selection. Thus Calvinism was among the ideas that led men to work hard and to reinvest the fruit of their labor rather than leisurely enjoy it (Weber, 1958). Whereas medieval man's life had been ascetic of necessity and oriented to the afterlife and possible salvation therein, the seventeenth century Protestant merchant developed an *inner-worldly* asceticism—frugality combined with a here-and-now orientation.

Nowhere were the new work ethic and the spirit of capitalism more pronounced than in northwestern Europe and North America, areas that had gone Puritan Protestant as a result of the Reformation. New England was a model of early capitalist society, and such early Americans as Benjamin Franklin epitomized the spirit. "Remember that time is money," admonished Franklin, adding that "after industry and frugality, nothing contributes more to the raising of a young man than punctuality," and "he that sits idle . . . throws away money" (Weber, 1958), herewith, incidentally, reminding us of some of Cato's formulations two thousand years earlier.

The spirit of capitalism led to rapid upward mobility for many in societies that were circumstantially well endowed. All too often, however, it maximized social and economic inequalities, particularly as the Industrial Revolution got under way. Now a new ideology was called for, a doctrine concurring with capitalism in its emphasis on work and production, but differing from it insofar as it was collectivistic rather than individualistic.

Marxism's role in the evolution of the work ethic is interesting. It is true of course that Marx envisioned the ultimate achievement of true human freedom once the realm of necessity, that is, production for the satisfaction of material wants, had been taken care of. In his own words: "the shortening of the working day is [the] fundamental prerequisite . . . for the development of human potentiality for its own sake" (1964:255). However, this does not mean that Marx viewed all labor as either alienating or as soon to become superfluous. In the first place, much of contemporary labor is alienating, Marx argued, not because of the inherent nature of work, but because of its specific organization under industrial capitalism. "The division of labor," he explained, "only becomes a real division from the moment when the distinction between material and mental labor appears." As a consequence, "enjoyment and labor, production and consumption devolve on different individuals, coming into contradiction" (1964:92). It is therefore "the detail-worker of today, the limited individual, the mere bearer of a particular social function, produced by large-scale industry" (1964:252) who is, above all, engaged in alienating labor. Therefore, the "final aim (of the revolution) is the abolition of the old division of labor" (1964:253), not labor per se, for labor can, as one of man's natural tendencies, be a process of self-actualization. In Marx's own words: "At the end of every labor-process, we get a result that already existed in the imagination of the laborer at its commencement. He not only effects a change of form in the material on which he works, but he also realizes a purpose of his own" (1964:88). Thus labor can, ideally at least, be "something that gives *play* to one's bodily and mental powers" (1964:89, italics added).

Second, "just as the savage must wrestle with nature in order to satisfy his wants, to maintain and reproduce his life, so also must civilized man, and he must do it in all forms of society and under any possible mode of production" (Marx 1964:254). Thus the true freedom that lies beyond the work society is not clearly explicated in Marx's writings, and there appears to be, according to the philosopher, a form of labor so meaningful as to make it undistinguishable from play. Meanwhile, it is of course the "revolutionary transformation period which lies between capitalist and communist society" (1964:256) that seems to have become fixated in the iron curtain countries, where true freedom has been permanently postponed in favor of the "temporary" work society.

Today Marxism functions in developing socialized societies much as the Protestant ethic functioned in developing capitalist countries earlier. Both ideologies extol the virtues of hard work, motivating the individual and contributing to collective economic growth. The functional parallel between early Protestant Puritanism and current socialist Puritanism is further highlighted by the fact that in present day Russia and China, various forms of leisure and hedonistic activities are labeled "bourgeois" and "decadent," be they modern dance, music, or sexual activity. The point is that societies, early capitalist societies in the West and modern-day socialist societies in the East, realize the functional incompatibility of rapid economic development and leisure. Today socialist societies live in accordance with a belief in hard work, in salvation through work and in solving human problems through work. For example, Marxists still feel that the primary solution to poverty must be economic development rather than birth control. Curiously, Marxists thereby find themselves on the same side of the fence as Roman Catholics when it comes to the population control controversy. For, as a Soviet representative to the United Nations once said: "Overpopulation is nothing but the fruit of capitalism; with an adequate social regime, it is possible to face any growth of population. It is the economy that must be adapted to the population, not the reverse" (quoted in Merton and Nisbet, 1961:319). Thus at the present time the work ethic, coupled with a fundamental faith in economic expansion, prevails both East and West.

In the United States the culture's work orientation has been caused by a number of factors. In the first place, Puritan Protestantism was the cultural context in which the foundations of the new nation were laid. It has been said that our society was born "in detestation of idleness" (Dulles, 1965). It was New England, of course, that carried the enforcement of work and the prohibition of all amusement to its greatest extreme. In Massachusetts, for example, the devil was held responsible for all dancing, especially "gynecandrical dancing or that which is commonly called Mixt or Promiscuous Dancing of Men and Women" (1965:6). In general, ruling powers both North and South, Puritan or Anglican, found it necessary to enforce continual work. For example, the Virginia Assembly decreed in 1619 that any person found idle should be bound over to compulsory work (1965:5).

Quite apart from the Puritan culture, which happened to prevail at the time of America's inception, natural conditions constituted an additional factor demanding hard work and proscribing leisure: the early colonists in the East and the later pioneers on the western frontier both faced harsh circumstances, a strange and unfamiliar wilderness, starvation, disease, and a hostile aboriginal population. Thus, in the history of America individual and collective survival were more precarious than in contemporary Europe. The added challenge resulted in a response characterized by increased achievement motivation. The age-old struggle between man and nature was enacted more fully in North America than elsewhere, producing ultimately the former's most unequivocal and eventually self-defeating victory over the latter.

We may mention separately a third factor conducive to America's work culture: the coincidental presence of huge natural resources and untapped territories at a time when Western technology was becoming ready for the final assault on the environment. Thus while the North American natural setting provided formidable challenges to prospective settlers, at the same time it also offered unprecedented promises, once nature was overcome. As a result of an environment that was simultaneously hostile and promisingly attractive, American man was motivated both positively and negatively to become working man par excellence. He lived both on the rugged frontier of Western civilization and in the land of opportunity.

At the level of social structure the land of opportunity produced a fundamental departure from the older, European setup. The single most distinctive feature of American social structure has been its exceptional rate of social mobility. The rapid upward mobility of millions was made possible by abundant natural resources and a liberal political system; it made the work ethic meaningful and ensured continued adherence to it by many. American social stratification became characterized mostly by *status politics*. Indeed, as the sociologist Lipset (1963) has argued, status politics can be distinguished from *class politics* in that status politics prevail in prosperous, mobile, middle-class societies while class politics are typical of more stagnant societies with large lower classes. Thus, Lipset implied elsewhere (1964), whereas European stratification featured mostly class politics, American social structure was typified by status politics because here, prosperity and rapid upward mobility of many de-emphasized the purely economic component of social differentiation. Thus it was possible at times to think of America as a classless society. For a long time American sociology did not feature the subfield of social stratification, and when Lloyd Warner finally began to focus on our society's social stratification after all, he merely studied status, not class. Stereotypically at least, America has been a middle-class society. To say this is to say that the dominant value system has centered around upward mobility achieved through individ-

ual effort. Indeed, studies have repeatedly shown, and recent statements (Banfield, 1968) again argue, that it is neither the lower class nor the upper class but the middle class that stands for deferred gratification, future-orientation, and hard work.

This leads us to the level of social psychology. Just as American social structure has been the object of numerous analyses, so the American national character has been the subject of an enormous amount of theorizing. While most theories are impressionistic, they generally concur in their essence, thus lending each other credibility. Going back for example to Frederick Jackson Turner (1920), the hypothesis, essentially, is that the rugged frontier conditions have created the toughness, resourcefulness, individualism, and versatility that made the American character. Along similar lines, David Riesman (1950) coined and dealt with the now famous notion of the inner-directed early American, pointing out that nineteenth century social and economic conditions in this country led to inner-directedness, and its success. The rugged individualist, the self-made man, the Horatio Alger, the strong and self-determined individual, and above all the hard worker typified the inner-directed man, an eminently nineteenth century product of cultural and economic conditions more prevalent in America than elsewhere. A recent and widely popularized statement in the continuing characterization of American man is Reich's (1970). Horatio Alger is now labeled "consciousness I." In Reich's words (1970: 21): "Facing a new and vast land, a new freedom, and seemingly limitless riches, [consciousness I] centered on the truth of individual effort. America would prosper if people proved energetic and hard working." Consciousness I held that nature is beautiful but must be conquered and put to use. It was the American Dream shared by the colonists and the immigrants, by Jefferson, Emerson, the Puritan preachers, and the western cowboy. Thus, historically, America has been the work society, as a result of cultural, natural, and economic conditions.

But what about today? While most discussions of the American national character concur on its basic features during the nation's formative years, the same sources also agree about its subsequent development. What the nearly consensual view of scholars, historians, sociologists, and other commentators boils down to is that our national character has gradually turned away from the "Horatio Alger" individualism just discussed in order to develop the opposite traits of conformity, softness, sociability, adaptability, and submissiveness. As with the earlier type, most theories are economic-deterministic, attributing changes in the national character to changing technological and economic conditions.

As far back as 1893, Turner viewed the closing of the frontier and its potential consequences with misgivings. Turner's fears as to the type of man and type of society that industrialization and urbanization might produce anticipated, prophetically, the jeremiads of scores of social critics half a century later.

For example, the central thesis of Riesman's (1950) work on this subject is that inner-directed man has been replaced by *other-directed* man. Along with other contemporary social critics, Riesman feels that as a result of technological and socioeconomic changes, the twentieth-century, urban middle-class American has become soft, pliant, shapeless; he is no longer imbued with a purely private ambition but is group oriented. Riesman's work, as several other evolutionary theories of social character, is actually an ideal-typology. It consists of contrasting types, which include early inner-directed and contemporary other-directed man.

Quite parallel is Reich's (1970) theory,

already introduced earlier: Reich's "consciousness II" is nothing but Riesman's other-directed type. In the author's own words: "Consciousness II people are tremendously concerned with one another's comparative status" (1970:76), and "the satisfactions, the joy of life are to be found in power, success, status, acceptance, popularity, achievements, rewards" (1970:90). As in Riesman's theory, consciousness II is somewhat the polar opposite of another type, consciousness I.[6] The typologies of these two authors are quite similar, in content as well as in form. In fact, the similarities go further, and they are shared by other culture critics as well. Reich points out that consciousness II "came into existence as a response to the realities of organization and technology" (1970:90), and "the consciousness II man thus adopts as his personal values the structure and standards and rewards set by his organization" (1970:77). This merely paraphrases such earlier statements as Whyte's *Organization Man* (1957), Mills' *White Collar* (1951), and Wheelis's *The Quest for Identity* (1958).

Organization Man is a study of the new American middle class. According to Whyte the former ideology of individual effort, while still rendered lip service, has in fact been superseded by a new social ethic. This bureaucratic ethic "makes morally legitimate the pressures of society against the individual. Its major propositions are three: a belief in the group as the source of creativity; a belief in belongingness as the ultimate need of the individual; and a belief in the application of science to achieve the belongingness" (paraphrased in Martindale, 1960:428).

---

[6]Both theories include additional types. Riesman also has a tradition-directed character, preceding inner-directed man, and Reich describes a "consciousness III," presumably future man. Reich's consciousness III, incidentally, has been so severely criticized and ridiculed by social scientists (see, for example, Nobile, 1971, and Berger and Berger, 1971) as to make one question their motives.

Mills' critique of middle-class America follows similar lines. Again the middle class (the white-collar groups, as opposed to the wage-workers) is said to be prestige oriented and to exercise an authority that is organizationally derived. The new white-collar pyramids "are youthful and feminine bureaucracies" in which such personality factors as social adaptability are the main qualification.

Allen Wheelis deplores the emerging social character for the same reasons: it is flexible and adjustable rather than strong and committed. "The social character that is coming to prevail is not given to dedicated pursuits. Idealism is on the wane. . . .The social character of our time, being largely without goals, lacks a sense of meaning and purpose. . . . Modern man has no sense of direction. He watches those around him and sticks to the group" (1958).

While American social scientists such as Mills, Riesman, Wheelis, Whyte, Reich, and Turner signal a nation that is becoming self-conscious about some undesirable developments in its culture and personality, their message is echoed internationally as well: wherever industrial technocracies came to be what they are, there are pessimistic culture critics deploring the effects this has upon human character. Thus in France, Jacques Ellul warns against the dangers of *The Technological Society* (1964). Ellul argues that the application of technical criteria to all areas of human life, including education, leisure, and sports, will result in a "biocracy" in which man-the-machine becomes an adaptable organism devoid of conscience and virtue. Man thus becomes totally integrated in the group, truly a mass man. He lives in a state of technical anesthesia in which values, religion, love, and emotions are no longer felt. As a final integration, all feelings have become rationalized, everyone is "happy" in the Huxleyan sense of the term. Ellul's diagnosis is meant to

apply to all industrial societies, not merely to one specific nation.

Such disgust with the technocracy, be it East or West, in America, western Europe, or the Soviet Union, is shared by Herbert Marcuse (1962). Marcuse's critique of the technocracy follows neo-Marxian lines. This may partly account for his popularity with the New Left on both sides of the Atlantic. Like Marx, Marcuse is concerned with man's oppressive alienation from his labor, from his fellowmen, from himself. Furthermore, like Freud he views the evils of alienation and repression as caused, in part, by civilization itself, that is, by industrial bureaucratic civilization. The liberation from modern man's dehumanized condition advocated by Marcuse and his followers may have to be primarily "psychic" and individual, or by way of old-fashioned revolutionary class struggle against capitalist oppression.[7] In any event, Marcuse's appraisal of technocratic man is, in many ways, similar to that of the other contemporary critics discussed in this section.

Now, then, what does all this imply for our topic—the vicissitudes of the work ethic in society, particularly in the American technocracy? To summarize what has been said so far, the first stage of American culture and personality—inner-directed man, consciousness I—is said to have been superseded by a technological society epitomized by the other-directed, one-dimensional white-collar organization man. This shift in culture and personality, however, does not mean that American ideology has now relinquished work as one of its central values. It merely assumes a different form.

The Protestant ethic, of course, held hard work, thrift, and competitiveness as

---

[7]Roszak discusses the issue in the following terms: It is in Marcuse's writings, the counterculture of the late 1960s, and the liberation movement which they embody, that the ultimate "confrontation between Marx and Freud takes place" (1969:84).

its supreme social values. Now Americans have come to adopt a less individualistic and more social or even bureaucratic ethic (Whyte, 1957). Whereas for our grandfathers the key words were work, thrift, and will, in our time they are flexibility, adjustment, and warmth (Wheelis, 1958). Yet contemporary American culture cannot be understood unless we realize (1) that millions of individuals cling to "consciousness I" (Reich, 1970) and (2) that the new ethic also emphasizes work, to a very great extent anyway.

Indeed, upward social mobility through individual effort—the essence of consciousness I—is still the ideology of masses of Americans. Nowhere does this manifest itself more clearly than in the ritualistic, anachronistic, and brutalizing work schedule of some small-town lower-middle-class residents (Vidich and Bensman, 1958); individuals living, as Marshal McLuhan would say, in a never-never "Bonanza"-land of their own imagination. The gut-level reaction of silent-majority Americans to the welfare crisis is further evidence of their pathological aversion for idleness. Secondly, the new social ethic of the organization man still centers around work, albeit in a different form; now, it is believed that "the individual should do his best to fit himself into a function that is needed by society . . . or the occupation or institution or organization" (Reich, 1970:76–77). Achievement remains a key value and excellence becomes, in fact, even more emphasized. As a consequence "we have a kind of psychosocial inertia in operation that keeps us living in a discipline appropriate to scarcity even while abundance is available" (Roszak, 1969:111). Marcuse's *performance principle* apparently continues to regulate the behavior of contemporary Americans.

A true cultural revolution is envisioned by such utopians as Reich. His consciousness III would indeed represent a radical departure from the work ethic,

unlike consciousness II. Indeed, what the radical counterculture advocates is an ideology that would lead directly to the true leisure society. Roszak (1969:109) writes, "as the excuse of scarcity wears thin, as work discipline with the coming of cybernation relaxes, the performance principle and the dominating regimes it supports are called into question [and] work can become play." However, the furious reaction against Reich's book (e.g., Nobile, 1971) shows that America is not, in 1972, verging toward green. Quite to the contrary, as Berger and Berger (1971) show, the country is more likely to undergo a "blueing" process during the coming years, a process in which the technocracy, far from coming to a grinding halt as a result of the desertion of some of its children, will simply devolve upon the rising blue-collar working classes.

Thus the question is, why have automation, cybernation, and affluence produced the organization man rather than the hippie-philosopher on a massive scale? Why have they produced a technocracy rather than a leisure society?

One reason, of course, is the lingering Protestant ethic. It was noted earlier that millions of individuals still function according to "consciousness I" principles. Dulles (1965), in his history of American recreation, points out that even in the 1960s Puritan traditions continued to influence Americans in their approach to leisure. It is still felt that leisure ("pleasure does make us Yankees kind o' wince") should only be used for ultimately productive ends. "The one-time acceptance of a social responsibility in promoting work [is now] being translated into a new obligation in organizing leisure" (1965:391).

A second, more fundamental factor is the emergence of a new value system that continues to place a premium on work, emphasizes conspicuous material consumption, but fails to put a high premium on leisure. Work, in the new scheme of things, derives its worth no longer because of *survival value,* but from *status enhancement.* It has always been true that the *source* of income was as important in determining individual worth as the *amount* of it.[8] However, whereas *unearned* income (dividends, inheritance) was "better" than earned money (wages, salary, fees), the situation may currently be reversing itself; for example, money gotten through public assistance is, by middle-class standards, considered soiled. So is "easy money" obtained legitimately through gambling, illegitimately through theft, or either way through prostitution. Thus, while the new economics urge us to accept the facts of unemployment, welfare,[9] unearned money, idleness and leisure, we are, at the same time, more than ever competitively scrambling for work, jobs and second jobs, which are becoming ever scarcer.

Wilensky (1961) provides data to show that the distribution of work and leisure is becoming increasingly uneven. In a representative sample of a number of professional groups, he found that one third of the high income-men work at least fifty-five hours a week, compared to only about one fifth of the less affluent. "High income does not remove the drive to work; it slightly, but consistently, boosts the 55-hour rates . . . especially

---

[8]Ever since W. Lloyd Warner began the study of American social stratification, scales measuring class, status, and power have generally included indicators of income *source* as well as amount.

[9]In a cover story significantly entitled "Welfare— The Shame of a Nation," *Newsweek* (February 8, 1971) quotes the following figures: 13.5 million Americans on welfare as of early 1971, up 70 percent over five years earlier and up 41 per cent in the last fourteen or fifteen months. The total cost of welfare today is estimated at $15 billion, half of it carried by the federal government. In the major cities the proportion of welfare recipients to the population varies from one in five (Boston) to one in twenty-three (Dallas). New York City alone has a welfare population of 1,147,595.

for white-collar strata." Moreover, Wilensky argues, "long hours" men are a growing minority of individuals employed mostly in such vanguard occupations as professors and managers. Thus he estimates that the percentage of long-hours men (working fifty-five hours per week or more) goes up from 20.5% in 1950 to 26.9% in 1970. At the same time, the percentage of unemployed and underemployed is also going up. The point is that those who have increasing free time on their hands are the involuntarily retired, the poor, the unskilled, the chronically unemployed. Thus there is a growing category of men *condemned to leisure,* as well as a growing minority of men who, of their own volition, work increasingly hard.

Since our middle-class ideology is obviously not going to dignify welfare, even when the day comes that an hour of doing nothing earns as much as an hour of work, it seems that work's most important reward is becoming *prestige* rather than money. This may be why those who need to work least, often work hardest. We may envision a day when work will be among the scarce commodities granted to those most deserving of it, lending to them first and foremost status and secondarily perhaps income. In fact, many of us are frequently working for no remuneration at all, occupied in a variety of committee work or other organizational activities. The right to be occupied may yet become a purchasable commodity! One will compete for jobs, although it may be more lucrative to remain unemployed. At this time, it is possible to discern a status-bestowing function in gainful employment that represents the opposite source of prestige of, say, Veblen's leisure class, which derived its high status precisely from *inactivity!*

We have said that the new value system places a high premium on work, albeit less and less for its survival value and increasingly for its status-bestowing function. At the same time, material consumption is of central importance to "proper living." The importance of consumption is twofold: in the first place, it retains, to some extent, the status-bestowing function signaled by Veblen. More importantly, however, mass consumption has become a sine qua non of our economic system. The role of advertising in capitalism is fundamental. It has been treated innumerable times.[10] The point, here, is that lavish material consumption, rather than being the *privilege of an elite,* is becoming *the duty* of the masses. Such a situation has been envisioned in science fiction[11] and by at least one sociologist, who speaks of "a polarization between the toiling classes and the leisure masses" (Riesman, 1958: 375). A kind of Marxism in reverse obtains. The masses, rather than being made to work inhumanly hard to support the elite's expensive leisure life, are made to consume inhumanly much in order to keep the elite working. If our earlier assessment of the new value of work is correct, then indeed one of the ultimate funtions (not necessarily intended) of Keynesian economics is to keep the captains of industry, the professionals, and the sociologists at work, a work that they may not need from a pecuniary standpoint, but which most certainly sustains their stature in the overall society. Thus Marx and Veblen may be turned around: consumption is becoming the duty of the masses, work the privilege of an elite. This reversal is caused by the combination of our initial work-oriented ideology and the expansionary nature of capitalism—consumption for the sake of production.

To discuss the current state of American leisure under the conditions just outlined, we must now, belatedly, define some of our terms. *Work* will be used throughout this book in a variety of meanings, all having to do with effort and exertion that somehow are productive, either materially or otherwise. The term may be used synonymously with *labor.* Thus work goes beyond its everyday sense of making a living. *Leisure* is an ambiguous term. The *Encyclopedia of the Social Sciences* defines it as "freedom from activities centering around the making of a livelihood." The sociologist Smigel (1963:10–11) shows the ambiguity of the concept by pointing out that some authors use it to denote free time, while others mean certain (recreational) activities. Here, we shall tend to follow the philosopher de Grazia (1964:233) and conceive of leisure as neither time nor activity, but a state of mind of man, a state of freedom from everyday necessity, in fact as an ideal condition of man. Perhaps the most helpful distinction between work and leisure (and conceptual discussions of this polarity will recur throughout the book) is that work needs extrinsic justification while leisure is intrinsically rewarding. Thus a given activity, say playing football, may be work to one person and leisure to another, depending on its meaning.[12] *Consumption* is used in its economic sense of using up goods or services. Recreation, finally, will be used in its literal, hyphenated meaning: activity that re-creates man, restores his energy, rests him from work, and prepares him for it.

Equipped with these terms, we may now make some descriptive and explanatory remarks about American leisure. Contemporary American society has

---

[10]For a brief bibliography on the literature of advertising, see de Grazia (1964:490). A critical, much criticized, but still best-known work on the subject is Vance Packard's *The Hidden Persuaders.*

[11]For example, Huxley's *Brave New World,* where serious work is reserved for the ruling elite and hedonism relegated to the masses. Also, in a story by Frederick Pohl (1957) the upper classes are rewarded by being allowed to spend less time consuming voraciously and more time with work.

[12]On the necessity to distinguish between the *form* that a work or nonwork activity takes and its *meaning,* see Kando and Summers (1971).

mass consumption, mass recreation, but little leisure. This becomes clear when we realize that recreation in America has two functions. From the standpoint of the individual, it restores his energy for work. From society's standpoint, it fulfills a major functional prerequisite, namely that of sustaining the economic system.We have already dealt with the cultural and psychological reasons for the present nature of American recreation. They relate, in part, to the lingering Protestant ethic. What remains to be done at this point is to briefly characterize American mass recreation from a structural point of view.

The structural-functional analysis of leisure and recreation has been suggested by Ed Gross (1961). However, Gross, following Parsonian tradition, wished to establish the universal functions of leisure and recreation in society. We maintain that the nature of American recreation is specific and that it is caused by needs that are specific to our economic system. A useful distinction here was made by Stone (1955), who differentiated between play and display, or between the game and the spectacle. Play is free, spontaneous, unpredictable, and always somewhat courageous. Display, however, is show. The game is played, as were the Greek Olympics. The spectacle is a commercialized or otherwise exploitative display, as were the Roman gladiator shows or as is American football today. American recreation is now mostly mass spectacle and display, rather than free, active, playful participation in games. We have mass recreation but not leisure. As in ancient Rome, our welfare state provides the population with bread and circuses, now we have televised games on the moon, but no leisure. The reasons for this are ultimately structural-functional: mass consumption and costly mass spectacles fulfill imperative systemic needs.

What has been said in the latter part of this chapter is that the coming of au-

tomation, cybernation, and affluence would logically seem to produce the leisure society. However, this does not occur because of two developments. First, the society's value system is such that the new status hierarchy places an increasing premium on work; secondly, the society's economic structure—corporate capitalism—demands costly mass consumption and spectacular mass recreation rather than freedom in leisure.

If most of this chapter appears to be critical, it should be realized that it is merely the first chapter. Already the vision of such men as Reich, Roszak, and Marcuse has been introduced, albeit critically. These men sympathize, sometimes naively, with the counterculture. They envision an alternative society in which true leisure could prevail. In addition, the leisure ideal is also formulated by such philosophers as de Grazia who, while temperamentally far removed from the buoyant counterculture and closer to an Aristotelian *weltanschauung,* or world view, nevertheless endorses the same objectives. Finally, some appraisals of contemporary popular culture (Wolfe, 1966; 1968) and of modern mass media (McLuhan, 1964) also see therein the seeds of the development of true leisure, freedom, and individual expression. These, then, will be the more optimistic notes to be picked up in later chapters.

STUDY QUESTIONS

1. As long as man has existed, his survival has been precarious, predicated upon the successful exploitation of his environment. Explain Malthus's central theorem on this and show how the current "no growth" ecology and population movements are actually restating what Malthus said earlier. Is it true that the old scarcity principle has now become the *excuse* of scarcity? If so, then what recommendations does this suggest for capitalism, technology, work, and leisure?
2. Trace the theme of human economic survival through the following eight stages: tribal society, agrarian society, preindustrial urban society, ancient Greece, ancient Rome, the Middle Ages, the Renaissance, the Industrial Revolu-

tion. Use and define such concepts as the Neolithic revolution and the hydraulic society. Which of these eight stages have permitted the most leisure, and which have demanded the most work? Why?

3. Along with changing economic structures goes, always, a changing legitimating culture. Just as the theme of human economic survival can be traced through the consecutive historical stages, so try now to trace the changing cultural values and attitudes toward work and leisure through the following seven stages: tribal society, lower barbarism, Graeco-Roman antiquity, the Middle Ages, the Renaissance, the Reformation, Marxian socialism. What does Huxley's Accidie personify? What has been the role of Calvinism, at least according to Weber? Finally, getting back to the first sentence of this question, discuss the relationship between socioeconomic structure and culture. Does structure generally come first, as the Marxians argue, or can culture change before the structure does? What are the two positions' implications for the best way to accomplish social and political change in the United States today?

4. Discuss the place of work, leisure, and consumption in the history and culture of the United States. First, why have Americans traditionally been such exceptionally hard workers? Show how this was rooted both in the country's social structure and in its typical personality structure. Next, trace the major changes that have occurred in the American personality ("consciousness") in the last forty or fifty years. Mills, Reich, Riesman, Wheelis, Whyte, and many others seem to agree on the basic changes our national character has undergone during the twentieth century. What are some of these changes? Do most of these authors like or dislike

most of what they see? How about you? Finally, what are the "new American's" attitudes toward work, leisure, and consumption?

5. Reich saw the imminent *greening* of America, but Berger found that naive and argued for America's *blueing* instead. What did each author mean, and who do you think was more right? Why?

6. According to many contemporary culture critics, the trouble with America today is that it has become a technocracy, and this trouble is shared by many other countries as well. What, then, is wrong with the technocracy? Try to define this concept from what Ellul, Marcuse, Roszak, and others have written about it. Make sure you distinguish between technology and technocracy. And if the technocracy, as the critical sociologists argue, makes most people unhappy, what is the best way to remedy this? Which form or combination of forms must liberation and revolution take, according to the various sources?

7. Modern technology could have produced true leisure for all, but de Grazia and others argue fairly convincingly that it has merely created technocratic consumption and a certain amount of regimented recreation. First, define and distinguish leisure, technocratic consumption, recreation. Next, explain how work, while assuming a new meaning in the twentieth century, has nevertheless remained at the center of our value system. Work's primary reward in the nineteenth century was money. Today, what new reward seems to be overtaking that function? Can you see how capitalism might be moving toward a "Marxism in reverse" in which work will be the elite's privilege while consumption becomes the duty of the masses. Refer to such sources as Riesman and Wilensky.

REFERENCES

Banfield, Edward
    1968   The Unheavenly City. Boston: Little Brown and Company.
Berger, Peter L. and Brigitte Berger
    1971   "The Blueing of America." New Republic (April 3):20–23.
de Grazia, Sebastian
    1964   Of Time, Work and Leisure. New York: Anchor Books.
Dulles, Foster Rhea
    1965   A History of Recreation: America Learns to Play. New York: Appleton-Century-Crofts.
Ellul, Jacques
    1964   The Technological Society. New York: Alfred A. Knopf, Inc.

Gross, Edward
    1961   "A Functional approach to leisure analysis." Social Problems 9 (Summer).
Guinagh, Kevin and Alfred P. Donjahn
    1942   "Cato on agriculture." Pp. 165–167 in Latin Literature in Translation. New York: Longmans, Green and Co.
Huxley, Aldous
    1923   "Accidie." In *On the Margin; Notes and Essays*. New York: Harper Bros.
Kando, Thomas and Worth C. Summers
    1971   "The impact of work on leisure: toward a paradigm and research strategy." Pacific Sociological Review (Special Summer Issue):310–327.
Lipset, Seymour Martin
    1963   Political Man. Garden City, N.Y.: Doubleday and Company, Inc.

1964 in Daniel Bell (ed.), The Radical Right. Garden City, N.Y.: Doubleday and Company, Inc.

Marcuse, Herbert
1962 Eros and Civilization. New York: Vintage Books.

Martindale, Don
1960 The Nature and Types of Sociological Theory. Boston: Houghton Mifflin Company.

Marx, Karl
1964 Selected Writings in Sociology and Social Philosophy. New York: McGraw-Hill Book Co.

McLuhan, Marshal
1964 Understanding Media: The Extensions of Man. New York: McGraw-Hill Book Co.

Merton, Robert K. and Robert Nisbet
1961 Contemporary Social Problems. New York: Harcourt, Brace & World.

Mills, C. Wright
1951 White Collar. New York: Oxford University Press

Newsweek
1971 "Welfare—the shame of a nation." (February 8).

Nobile, Philip
1971 The Con III Controversy. New York: Pocket Books.

Packard, Vance
1957 The Hidden Persuaders. David McKay Company, Inc.

Pohl, Frederick
1957 "The Midas plague." In the Case Against Tomorrow. New York: Ballantine Books, Inc.

Reich, Charles A.
1970 The Greening of America. New York: Random House, Inc., and Bantam Books, Inc.

Riesman, David
1958 "Leisure and work in post-industrial society." Pp. 363–385 in Eric Larrabee and Rolf Meyersohn (eds.), Mass Leisure. Glencoe, Ill.: The Free Press.

Riesman, David, Nathan Glazer and Denney Reuel
1950 The Lonely Crowd. New Haven, Conn.: Yale University Press.

Roszak, Theodore
1969 The Making of a Counterculture. Garden City, N.Y.: Doubleday & Company, Inc.

Smigel, Erwin O.
1963 Work and Leisure. New Haven, Conn.: College & University Press.

Stone, Gregory P.
1955 "American sports: play and display." Chicago Review 9 (Fall):83–100.

Turner, Frederick Jackson
1920 The Significance of the Frontier in American History. Henry Holt & Company, Inc.

Veblen, Thorstein
1899 The Theory of the Leisure Class. New York: The Macmillan Company.
1914 The Instinct of Workmanship. New York: The Macmillan Company.

Vidich, Arthur and Joseph Bensman
1958 Small Town in Mass Society. Princeton, N. J.: Princeton University Press.

Weber, Max
1958 The Protestant Ethic and the Spirit of Capitalism. New York: Charles Scribner's Sons.

Wheelis, Allen
1958 The Quest for Identity. New York: W. W. Norton & Company, Inc.

Whyte, William H., Jr.
1957 Organization Man. New York: Simon & Schuster, Inc.

Wilensky, Harold L.
1961 "The uneven distribution of leisure: the impact of economic growth on free time." Social Problems 9 (Summer):32–56.

Wittfogel, Karl A.
1957 Oriental Despotism: A Comparative Study of Total Power. New Haven, Conn.: Yale University Press.

Wolfe, Tom
1966 The Kandy-Kolored Tangerine-Flake Streamline Baby. New York: Pocket Books.
1968 The Electric Kool-Aid Acid Test. New York: Farrar, Straus & Giroux, Inc.

Ata Kando

chapter 2

 # What is leisure, and what should it be?

The dual topic of this book is both controversial and ill defined in the literature. Leisure and popular culture have been defined in many different ways. Moreover, to some these terms mean good things, while to others they represent something bad. The main reason why we link the terms leisure and popular culture is that the two phenomena have, *in practice,* been closely connected. Much of popular culture takes place in the nonwork sphere of man's life, that is, in his leisure time.

Leisure has a multiplicity of definitions, the most prominent among these being derived from two schools. The classical, Aristotelian school, whose most eminent contemporary spokesman is the philosopher Sebastian de Grazia, conceives of leisure as cultivation of self, meditation, the development of true spiritual freedom, in brief an ideal that is far from accomplished in contemporary American society. The second school, which includes a majority of contemporary sociologists as well as laymen, simply uses the term leisure to describe, empirically, the various recreational activities that people engage in. Leisure, then, can be defined normatively and descriptively. Thus the controversy regarding leisure is not merely about how the term should be defined but, more importantly, about what leisure ideally ought to be. Although the classical school conceives of leisure as man's highest ideal, the "empirical" school implicitly views leisure as of secondary importance to work. Thus both schools' definitions are value biased, the empirical school still operating under the assumptions of the Protestant work ethic. This chapter discusses this dual controversy, in addition to distinguishing leisure from such related concepts as recreation, play, and game.

The debate about popular culture is similar to that dealing with leisure. There is, first, no consensus as to the proper meaning of the term (some would like to see it banned from the sociological vocabulary, cf. Wilkinson, 1971). Second, popular culture, too, may be either accepted or rejected. Bluntly, there are those who are *for* popular culture and those who are *against* it. Those who argue that current popular culture is base and vulgar may equate it with mass culture, advocating less of it and more high culture. Many among them indict the mass media for being socially and culturally harmful (cf. Rosenberg, 1971). Those, on the other hand, who view popular culture as an important and often creative phenomenon argue that contemporary cultural participation is certainly better than at earlier times in history (White, 1957) and that to dismiss such manifestations of modern popular culture as rock music, jazz, and the electronic media is mere snobistic elitism (Lewis, 1972; McLuhan, 1969). Chapter 3 deals with the various issues and positions in the great popular culture debate.

At the conclusion of this chapter I shall clarify my own position with regard to the two controversies at hand. Leisure, I shall argue, must inevitably be defined normatively; popular culture, I feel, must be embraced both as an important phenomenon and a useful concept. As a concept, it must be defined as broadly as possible. When this is done, it becomes the focal point where the following phenomena—each the subject of subsequent chapters—meet: high culture, mass culture (including mass media), mass leisure, "prole" culture, marginal subcultures, and the counterculture.

• • •

Few words in the vocabulary of students of society are as controversial and ambiguous as the term leisure. This is first the result of the existence of a number of related, overlapping, and ill-defined concepts. Among the words that have often been used in contradistinction to, as synonyms of, or as related to leisure, we find recreation, play, and game. Our first task, in this chapter, will be to define and distinguish these terms. A second reason for leisure's ambiguity is that it is used, broadly, with two different and incompatible purposes. Some simply use the term as an empirical concept referring to specific recreational activities. Others give to the word the normative meaning of an unaccomplished ideal. Although additional difficulties arise from the fact that some define leisure as a certain type of *activity,* others as *time,* and others as a *frame of mind,* it is the dual purpose with which the term is used—objectively descriptive on the one hand and normative on the other —which makes it so highly ambiguous. The second objective of this chapter is to discuss leisure's descriptive and normative uses.

LEISURE

The multiplicity of leisure's meanings is generally recognized. Kraus (1971) states that the word has at least four widely found meanings: the "classical" view, the view of leisure as a funtion of social class, the concept of leisure as a form of activity, and the concept of leisure as free time. Berger (1962) discerns two definitions, each with its own tradition. One tradition conceives of leisure as "free time" or time not devoted to paid occupations. The other, much older classical tradition conceives of leisure as cultivation of the self and a preoccupation with the higher values of life. Smigel (1963) also recognizes two definitions of leisure. One views leisure as "freedom from the necessity of being occupied"; the other simply equates leisure with free time. Most observers recognize at least a duality in leisure's meaning. Smigel and Berger, for example, refer essentially to the same cleavage in the literature. Berger speaks of the classical tradition, which views leisure as enoblement of self, meditation, and which goes back to Aristotle. Smigel notes that one conception of leisure is that it is a "freedom" of some sort. Both authors refer, in essence, to a classical and normative conception of leisure, which has been advocated primarily by philosophers, culture elitists, reformers, in brief by those who view leisure as an ideal. The alternative conception recognized by both these authors is the same—free time. Thus the second meaning of leisure is more prosaic. And, just as the classical conception is subscribed to by a certain school, so this prosaic definition of leisure, free time, is the one generally accepted by the other camp, a camp that includes not only most modern sociologists but probably a majority of contemporary Americans as well. Thus the most fundamental distinction to be made in any discussion of leisure has now emerged. There is a normative, or "classical," use of the term and there is a descriptive, empirical use. The latter usage evades philosophical issues and simply centers around what

people do in their spare time. This empirical use of the word leisure is, understandably perhaps, favored by more people.

Definitional difficulties with leisure do not stop at this point. While Berger and Smigel both recognize the broad distinction to be made between the classical view and the "other" view, they immediately fall out over whether leisure is *time* or *activity.* For this reason, Kraus's definitional discussion is one of several that are more complete. In addition to recognizing the classical conception of leisure and its ancient Greek philosophical tradition, Kraus distinguishes between the concept of leisure as a form of activity and leisure as free time. The view that leisure is nonwork *activity* is fairly prevalent. The Frenchman Dumazedier (1967), for example, defines leisure as "activity—apart from the obligations of work, family and society—to which the individual turns at will." When leisure is used to denote activity, it becomes more or less synonymous with recreation. Viewing leisure as unobligated *time* is, according to Kraus, the most common approach of them all, and the approach finally used by the author himself. To this author, then, leisure is a form of nonobligated, or discretionary, time. Earlier, Kraus also discusses a fourth concept of leisure—the view of leisure as a function of social class. This view goes back to Veblen's *Theory of the Leisure Class* (1899), where the author shows the relationship between status and the possession of leisure.

Thus far four meanings of leisure have been discussed, each supported by its own school of adherents. Clearer than the differences, however, is a similar realization among all sources that there is some sort of a normative, or classical, conception on the one hand and a conception of leisure as having something to do with free time and recreational activities on the other. Thus authors attempt to formulate the following type of all-encompassing definitions of leisure: "The complex of self-fulfilling and self-enriching values achieved by the individual as he uses leisure time in self-chosen activities that recreate him" (Miller and Robinson, 1963). Such a definition is as valiant as it is difficult to digest. It is essentially an attempt at incorporating in one and the same definition the normative classical tradition, the concept of free time, and the empirical description of recreational activities. In the following pages we shall deal with the concept of leisure in three ways: in a literal, semantic fashion, in a sociohistorical context, and, finally, in a normative manner.

Etymology of leisure

The word leisure originates from the Latin *licere,* meaning to be permitted. From *licere* came the French word *loisir,* whch means free time, and such English words as license, meaning permission. Thus literally, leisure means freedom of action. The *Oxford English Dictionary* defines leisure along these lines. According to that source (quoted in Larrabee and Meyersohn, 1958), leisure can mean (1) freedom of opportunity to do something specified or implied, (2) opportunity afforded by freedom from occupations, (3) the state of having time at one's own disposal, (4) deliberation.

Encyclopedias contain lengthy definitions of leisure, dealing not only with the word's literal meaning but also with the normative and conceptual difficulties alluded to in the previous section. According to the *Encyclopedia of the Social Sciences* (Craven, 1933) "leisure, the opportunity for disinterested activity," must be distinguished from amusement, recreation, and the like. "For purposes of social analysis," the author continues, "the concept usually means simply freedom from activities centering around the making of a livelihood." Furthermore, Dumazedier's definition of leisure in the

International Encyclopedia of the Social Sciences (quoted in Kraus, 1971) stresses that leisure should also be distinguished from "semileisure," that is, activities that have some utilitarian purpose, such as gardening or do-it-yourself hobbies.

All encyclopedic definitions of leisure point out that the Greek word for it is *schole,* which leads to the English *school, scholarship.* The significance of this is that it indicates that leisure, traditionally, has incorporated education, scholarship, and philosophy. Thus the very etymology of the word points to the classical Aristotelian conception, to the view of leisure as an ideal state of freedom and spiritual enlightenment.

Theories of leisure

The main source of difficulty in arriving at a consensual definition of leisure is that its meaning depends upon the cultural value-system of those that do the defining, specifically, upon the value placed on work and nonwork behavior. Thus by leisure the ancient Greeks meant one thing, the early New England settlers another, and a primitive tribe yet something else. Most discussions of the concept of leisure show an awareness of its culture-boundness, hence frequent references to, and comparisons of, for example, the ancient Greek leisure ideal, the Puritan condemnatory attitude toward it, and primitive man's total lack of its conceptualization.

Primitive man probably indeed failed to conceive of work and leisure as two distinct categories. Under conditions of scarcity and a subsistence economy to which all contributed more or less equally, the possibility of a leisure class or leisure time probably did not occur. Not that work was always the natural or most frequent activity. Early anthropologists have in fact posited that primitive man only produced the minimal amount of goods necessary for survival, thereupon always returning to his natural state, namely one of rest, play, or idleness, this being presumably the fundamental difference between him and modern industrial man. However, even if this were the case, leisure can only be conceptualized in contradistinction to work, and that polarity was no doubt either absent or only rudimentarily realized in the primitive mind.

Leisure was discovered in ancient Athens. Economic and social-structural conditions make this plausible. As a technologically relatively advanced state where the division of labor had proceeded further than in surrounding societies, and wealthy as a result of a vast maritime empire, Athens could, better than anyone else, afford leisure. As citizens of a "democracy" supported by slavery, Athenians enjoyed both the right and the opportunity to devote themselves to the higher things in life. Hence Greek philosophers, for the first time in Western history, formulated a leisure ideal that stressed not lavish material consumption (no doubt Darius, Xerxes, and other Asian potentates easily outdid their Athenian contemporaries in that respect), but the pursuit of spiritual enlightenment. Aristotle in particular stressed that meaning of the word *schole,* the Greek equivalent of *leisure* (de Grazia, 1964). The Greek leisure ideal was defined so rigorously by such men as Plato and Aristotle that not even artists and sculptors were regarded as leisured men, since to them, those activities were a continuous trade rather than a freely chosen interest (Craven, 1933). Classical Greece apparently came up with the most idealistic conception of leisure. And, as de Grazia (1964:12) points out, a common Greek word for work is *a-scholia,* which means the absence of leisure. Thus, significantly, Greek civilization defined work as a function (namely the absence) of leisure, whereas we do the exact opposite, defining leisure as nonwork. These two possibilities indicate

the diametrically opposite cultural emphases of the two civilizations. In Athens, leisure was primary and work derivative; with us it is the other way around.

In Rome the Greek leisure ideal was watered down. While the Latin words for leisure and business are *otium* and *negotium,* suggesting the same positive conception of leisure and negative conception of work as in Greece, Roman history and culture make clear that we have, here, the first manifestation of the expansionistic work society that culminates 2000 years later in the industrial West. Empire building and bureaucratic organization are Rome's legacy to the world. They developed out of hard and frugal rural work—the Puritan work ethic *avant la lettre!* As we saw in our introductory chapter, Cato the elder sang the virtues most central to the Roman temperament—hard work, frugality, clean living. Leisure to the Romans meant primarily rest from work.

The medieval conception of leisure was even narrower. On the one hand, Christian dogma stressed the importance of contemplation as a divine activity. On the other, however, economic conditions led to the formulation of a work ethic that accounts for leisure's secondary importance in medieval culture. On the medieval frontier, after Rome's collapse, life was once again rugged and precarious. As a necessity for the survival of the pioneer-monk, work, particularly rugged, manual, rural labor, became a virtue and, conversely, idleness became a sin. As St. Benedict said, "idleness is the enemy of the soul."

The further development of the work ethic and the concomitant deterioration of the Greek leisure ideal subsequent to the Middle Ages was traced in the previous chapter. The Renaissance ushered in the Age of Progress through technology. Protestantism led to the spirit of capitalism. The Industrial Revolution led to mass labor. The dominant ideology of industrial society defined work not only as necessary but also as salubrious and self-justifying. In other words, no longer was economic activity merely a means; it now became an end in itself. Accumulation of material goods and their productive reinvestment now had to proceed even beyond the point where an adequate level of living had already been reached. According to Weber (1958) the Calvinist in particular believed that such behavior was the only indication of God's grace. As we saw earlier, nowhere else has there been a greater use for such a totally negative conception of leisure than in America.

We now live in the postindustrial era, and observers have signaled the emergence of a new outlook toward work and leisure. The emphasis on material consumption first noted by Veblen (1899) among the upper strata of society has become the way of life of the broad middle class. Consumerism, then, has gradually replaced frugality. If we define, along with Margaret Mead, virtue as that in which pain precedes pleasure, and vice as that where pleasure comes first, then vice has become the American way of life, witness credit installments, enjoy-now-pay-later arrangements, and so on. It may be true that the focus of American life has become the home rather than work (Mead, 1958). New values and a new consciousness may be emerging. However, such a shift (presumably away from a rigid work ethic and back toward the Aristotelian leisure ideal) has been wishfully anticipated for at least 40 years (cf. Craven, 1933), and yet today, consumerism merely leads to demands for better pay, more jobs, second jobs, women's jobs. If there is a new concept of leisure in the postindustrial welfare state that was absent under early capitalism it is this: under pressure from political reformers and trade unions, man's need for *recreation* has been accepted.

Hence there is a fairly vigorous recreation movement today, emphasizing the healthful functions of sports and outdoor activities and demanding parks and other recreational facilities.

In sum, the concept of leisure is intimately related to the historical and cultural context in which it is used. It was discovered by the ancient Greeks, to whom leisure was a spiritual ideal. In subsequent civilizations—Rome, the Middle Ages, industrial society—leisure gradually began to embody idleness, then waste of time, finally sin. Huxley's demon, Accidie, symbolizes leisure's changing image well. Today, our culture defines leisure primarily as *recreation* because we have (re)discovered the utility of sports and other recreational activities. This is our cultural conception of leisure, still essentially utilitarian.

Normal approach to a definition of leisure

Bennett Berger (1963) correctly points out that a conception of leisure must be normative. "We are all," he writes, "compromised Greek citizens carrying the burden of compromised Protestant ethics." We have an opinion, not only about what the word leisure means but also about whether or not it is a good thing. To the extent that it is the Greek philosophical school that *advocates* a certain leisure ideal, this book sides with that school, along with such men as de Grazia, Dewey, Pieper, and Russell.

De Grazia (1964) defines leisure as "a state of being free, a condition of man." Pieper (1963) conceives of leisure as "an attitude of mind and a condition of the soul that fosters a capacity to perceive the reality of the world." Russell (1935) first humorously defines work as "either altering the position of matter at or near the earth's surface relative to other such matter (which is unpleasant and ill paid) or as telling other people to do so (which is pleasant and highly paid)." Contending that moving matter about is emphatically not one of the ends of human life, the British philosopher therefore advocates more leisure as the road to happiness and joy. Dewey's preoccupation with leisure was tangential to his life-long concern with education: "Education has no more serious responsibility than making adequate provision for enjoyment of recreative leisure; not only for the fact of immediate health but still more, if possible, for the fact of its lasting effect upon habits of mind" (1921:241). Thus Dewey's conception of leisure, as those of Russell, Pieper, and de Grazia, is close to the Greek ideal: a spiritual capacity for freedom. What is most significant about Dewey's contribution is that it brings back the Greek notion of *schole,* or education as a self-justifying process rather than as vocational training. Half a century later we seem as far from implementing Dewey's recommendations as ever, witness the renewed emphasis of colleges on the applied value of learned skills and the tendency to reduce institutions of higher learning to trade schools. It is no coincidence that these four men are all philosophers. One is German, one English, two are American. All are un-American in their outlook, even Dewey, the father of that eminently American school of thought—pragmatism.

As sociologists, we must account for our conception of leisure. If we define leisure normatively, it is because we feel that we have uncovered an important social need. One of sociology's tasks is to discover and formulate the major social problems. One such problem seems to be a growing cultural lag between our social system and our value system with regard to work and leisure. On the one hand, our technological and social infrastructure demand that we cease plundering the environment, that we come to our senses and begin to equitably enjoy our high material standard of living. Our cultural superstructure, on the other

hand, refuses to reward such an outlook, continuing to honor business, work, production, and exploitation. As Berger phrases it, "a culture which has not learned to honor what it is actually committed to produce creates an uneasy population" (1963:32). The social problem, then, is that the value system is unable to "honor the typical situations which the social system engenders." Specifically, while technological affluence inevitably forces leisure upon us, we continue to reject it as evil. It is therefore imperative to arrive at a socially more acceptable conception of leisure than the one currently in vogue, and this inevitably leads us back to the Greeks, who embraced leisure not as an absence of things to do, but as an opportunity to do things.

RECREATION

Like leisure, the word recreation is defined in many different ways. Unlike leisure, most definitions of recreation concur that it denotes certain activities rather than an ideal. Miller and Robinson, for example, define recreation as "the process of engaging in activities during leisure time, with a set of attitudes that makes possible the attainment of leisure values" (1963:7). The Neumeyers define recreation as "any activity pursued during leisure . . . that is free and pleasureful, having its own immediate appeal, not impelled by a delayed reward beyond itself or by any immediate necessity" (1958:22).

Etymology of recreation

The term recreation stems from the Latin *recreatio,* meaning restoration, recovery. The word's etymology therefore implies the replenishment of body energy expended on work, literally the *recreation* of energy. Although many sociologists emphasize the fun and play elements in recreation, the linguistic roots of the word remind us that it ultimately refers to activity that is subordinate to work. This is why, in our society, leisure and recreation are often used synonymously—both denoting nonwork activities that one engages in periodically as a necessary change from the routine and compulsion of work. However, as the next discussion will show, other cultures, by conceiving of leisure differently, have also given a different content to the word recreation.

Theories of recreation

Just as the Greeks invented leisure, so it can be said that Rome invented recreation. And just as the meaning of leisure has changed depending on the normative content given to the word by different cultures, so has the meaning of recreation, depending on its changing behavioral content through the ages.

Cursorily tracing the history of recreation, it is significant to note that anthropologists and archaeologists generally speak of the *play* of primitive man; historians write about the *leisure* of ancient civilizations and about the Roman *games;* and sociologists often discuss *recreation* in modern society. This suggests the culture-boundness of the modern recreation concept and the difficulty of applying the same word to the activities of tribal man, modern man, medieval man, and other men.

Primitive man, then, has always known play, and he has always created art. The singing competitions of Eskimos, the grim battle of the Kwakiutl's potlatch gift exchanges, the various bat and ball games of North and Central American Indians, the rich musical and rhythmic dance tradition of Africa, all these come to mind when thinking of tribal culture. However, to term such activities "recreational" would be a temporocentric fallacy—applying our time- and culture-bound concept of recreation to alien phenomena with entirely different meanings. Thus the Eskimo's

singing contest is, among other things, a duel, that is, an institutionalized legal phenomenon (Hoebel, 1964). The Vancouver islanders' potlatch is a complex political, economic, religious, ritualistic, and kinship phenomenon (Benedict, 1946; Mauss, 1954). The Africans' dancing and musical activities are as much religious and social as they are "recreational." Thus to attempt to isolate primitive man's recreational activities is futile, because recreation is a Western conceptual category.

In Rome, we have the first anticipation of the modern recreation concept. Unlike leisure, recreation connotes a fairly down-to-earth set of activities in which *many* participate, not merely the members of a leisure class or a philosophical elite. Thus, because the structure of Roman life was not unlike ours, it is there that mass recreation first became a possibility. The sheer size and complexity of Roman society—at its height an empire of perhaps 100 million population with a capital city of 2 million—engendered conformity, passivity, and massification in all areas of life. Hence the "bread and circuses" provided by the Roman rulers for the masses. The Roman games gradually expanded into spectacles the size of which have yet to be exceeded. The Circus Maximus at one time accommodated nearly 400,000, the Colosseum 90,000. Here, the public passively witnessed gladiatorial games, sea battles waged in artificial lakes, chariot races, vicariously enjoying bloodshed and brutality. The vulgarity of Roman recreation has often been deplored and contrasted with the nobility of the preceding Greek civilization, where men often engaged in active, fair, competitive sports. Mass leisure, today so often indicted for its appeal to man's basest impulses and for its unedifying character, first became a reality in ancient Rome. To that extent Roman recreation was not unlike ours today.

The modern concept of recreation did not develop directly out of the Roman tradition. First, a dark era in the history of recreation had to pass. The dark ages, in this case, were not the Middle Ages, but the first Industrial Revolution. Whereas medieval society merely abandoned the extravagance of Roman mass leisure (no great loss, historians might concur), nineteenth century industrializing society nearly saw the complete disappearance of recreation. This was the time when unfettered capitalistic expansion imposed subhuman living and working conditions upon the working masses. Life was harsh in the entire Western world. If conditions were perhaps somewhat better in North America than in Europe due to an abundance of space and natural resources (a debatable point in any event, as Charles Dickens would testify, cf. Dulles, 1965), this was vitiated by the presence of a virgin environment waiting to be tamed and thus engendering working and living conditions at least as rigorous as those east of the Atlantic. Therefore, in no part of the industrial world was recreation initially either a problem or a significant phenomenon. Twelve to fourteen working hours per day were common, child labor was general, and life expectancy was short. Whatever little nonwork time remained at a person's disposal, much of it was spent on basic biological needs—sleeping, drinking, eating, recuperating, reproducing. Although the stereotype depicting the nineteenth century proletarian as an animal stems from a social-Darwinistic ideology attempting to justify continued exploitation and repression of the masses, it is probably true that he did not have much time, energy, or motivation for the higher things of life. Thus, while *leisure* may have been practiced by a small upper crust (Veblen, 1899), recreation was not a widely recognized possibility at this time.

Only in the twentieth century does the concept of recreation become applicable in a widespread sense. In America, for example, the populace learned slowly during the nineteenth century how to play and to enjoy free time constructively (Dulles, 1965). Then, toward the end of the century, we have the emergence of the "recreation movement." This has gradually come to mean two things, primarily: an increasing public awareness of, and therefore governmental budgeting for the population's recreational needs, and a definition of that need primarily as one for sports and the outdoors. Thus part of the recreation movement in the United States has been the creation of national, state, and local parks and other public recreational facilities and the emergence of YMCA, YWCA, and other similar organizations. Internationally the trend has been parallel, with *Turnvereins* emerging in Germany in the nineteenth century and, as worldwide symbol of the recreation movement, the Olympic Games held nearly every four years since 1896.

Current meaning of recreation

Thus we arrive at the current conception of recreation. Kraus (1971) distills from a variety of definitions the following elements, which we also consider essential to the current meaning of recreation: (1) the element of free choice, as opposed to compulsion or obligation, as with work; (2) the element of intrinsic reward, as opposed to some such ulterior motive as money, as with work (a recreational activity may be reimbursed, but even then, money must be only secondary to the enjoyment of the activity itself, as for example, amateur rock musicians getting paid for performing at a party); (3) the fact that recreation, unlike leisure, is *activity,* not an ideal, or sheer idleness, contemplation, or rest; (4) the fact that almost any kind of activity can, *to someone,* mean recreation; it is not so much *what* one does as the subjective meaning of the activity; the same activity may be work to some but recreation to others (think, for example, of any sport in which both professionals and amateurs engage); this last element leads me to add one that Kraus overlooks; (5) recreation may be physically and mentally demanding, or it may be light and relaxing, but it is always conceived in some dialectical relationship to work. As we argue elsewhere (Kando and Summers, 1971), recreation may be a spillover from, or a compensation for, work; a recreational activity that compensates for a dull and easy job would be physically and mentally absorbing. Kraus also argues that recreation generally implies something constructive, for example, intellectual growth. I feel that this is more a connotation of leisure than of recreation. Instead, I feel that a final element of recreation is (6) that it frequently refers to sports and outdoor activities and almost never refers to activities that are intellectually strenuous. Thus I agree with de Grazia (1964:233) that "like the Romans, our conception of leisure is mainly recreative." De Grazia's conception of recreation enables us to distinguish it from leisure. Unlike the leisure ideal, recreation is non-normative, because it describes activities that are generally not edifying; unlike leisure, it must always be conceived in contradistinction to work; unlike leisure, it refers to that in which the average modern man engages, for example, sports and spectacles.

PLAY

Definitions of play are as varied as those of leisure and recreation. The sociologist Kaplan (1960:20), trying to assign play to children and recreation to adults, writes that play can mean either "a light, informal, make-believe action such as the play of children, [or] a more formal, stylized, intense and even serious presentation of some aspect of life on a stage." The psychologist Piaget attempts to establish a definition of play in terms of fundamental psychic processes. Having shown that human activity can range from *assimilation* (of environmental stimuli) to *accommodation* (to the environment), he argues that "play begins as soon as there is predominance of assimilation" (Piaget, 1958:71–72). The historian Huizinga (1949) traces the play element through the ages, concluding sadly that this element has been on the wane and that it is increasingly neglected in contemporary civilization. Play, to Huizinga, is a cultural universal because it is essential to human nature—*homo ludens.* It is used by the author in its broadest sense, as the antithesis of serious activity. In the terminology of the social psychologist Goffman (1961) the antithesis of serious activity is called, among other things, "fun" activity, while play and playing are used in a narrower, game-theoretical sense—referring to the moves one takes when playing a game. The point of this unsystematic selection of definitions is that the meaning of the concept of play depends primarily on the analytical purpose for which it is used.

Etymology of play

The word play comes from the Latin *plaga,* meaning a blow or thrust, as when stroking an instrument or striking a ball. Other Indo-German languages derived related words for play. The German *Spielen* and the Dutch *spelen,* for example, are etymologically and semantically close to the English *play.* These words not only derive from the same root but also cover more or less the same meanings, for instance, the playing of sports, musical instruments, and games. There is, of course, some shift; for example, while our theater play does not translate literally as *Spiel* or *spel* in these Germanic languages, those words, on the other hand, cover the meaning of our word *game.* Thus in English, play must be distinguished from game, a difference that we shall discuss in a moment.

Theories of play

Just as in the case of leisure and recreation, play may be said to have been invented at a given historical and cultural junction. While Huizinga writes of the "natural" playfulness of man and anthropologists view play as a cultural universal, the conceptual category of play as primarily the domain of children or at least childlike behavior did not emerge in the West until the early seventeenth century. This is because, as Aries (1962) shows, the conceptual category of child itself did not appear until then. As paintings by Giotto, Durer, and Breughel show, the Middle Ages had two types of people only—adults and *homunculi,* (little adults). The facial traits, attire, and functions of children in medieval paintings are frequently those of little old men. The childhood socialization of royalty and nobility were ruthlessly adultlike. Lower-class children were not excluded from adult spheres such as tavern, bedroom, or workshop. And, while men played then as they always have, this was not perceived as being play or being childlike. As Stone (1970) nicely shows, both the social identity, "child," and child's play, like all other social phenomena, are creatures of history.

Theories of play were therefore not formulated until the eighteenth century. By the nineteenth century, however, much theoretical, social-scientific speculation about play began to take place. At least six early theories of play, summarized by Kraus (1971:238–245), can be discerned.

1. The surplus-energy theory, according to which play is primarily motivated by the need to burn up excess energy. This theory was advanced by the English philosopher Herbert Spencer and

by the German author Friedrich von Schiller, among others.
2. The recreation theory, according to which play, rather than burning up excess energy, conserves or restores it. This theory was advanced by the German philosopher Moritz Lazarus.
3. The instinct-practice theory of play, according to which both animals and men need a period of protected infancy during which they can play, that is, practice and perfect the instinctive skills that will be seriously needed later in life. This theory was put forward by the Swiss philosopher Karl Groos.
4. The catharsis theory, which states that play often serves as a safety valve for the expression of bottled-up emotions. This theory, related to the surplus-energy theory and subscribed to by several modern psychologists, goes back to the ancient Greeks. Aristotle already saw play as a means of purging oneself of aggressive feelings.
5. The recapitulation theory advanced at the turn of the twentieth century by the American psychologist Stanley Hall, which suggests that each child, through play, relives the history of the human race. The reasoning behind this theory was the same as that behind the belief that the development of the individual human fetus recapitulates the entire evolutionary process of the human race: ontogeny repeats phylogeny. Thus while Groos's instinct-practice theory states that play is an instinctive process of practicing for the future, Hall's theory says that play is an instinctive way of rehearsing the past.
6. The relaxation theory of play, finally, is an extension of the earlier recreation theory, stating that modern man, if he is to function healthily, must find active outlets in play so as to compensate for deprivations from work. This theory was advanced by

the American psychologist G. T. W. Patrick, among others.

From these six theories a distinction between two types of play begins to emerge, a distinction essential to a contemporary theory of play. There is the play of children, whose primary function according to most psychologists and educators is anticipatory socialization into adult roles and skills; and there is the play of adults, which serves as relaxation, release, or compensation from work.

Modern theories of play build upon this realization. The countless modern theories can best be discussed in categories. One such category consists of physiological theories. A second category examines play from the point of view of aesthetics, creativity, self-expression. Third, there are the theories proposed by psychologists and educators. A fourth category consists of theories advanced by sociologists, anthropologists, and historians.

Going back to John Dewey's point of view that *activity,* rather than rest, is the organism's natural state, "modern physiology has established the value of vigorous play activities in developing and maintaining muscle tone, organic vigor, and vitality of body functioning" (Miller and Robinson, 1963:125). Thus one area of play about which there is now agreement is that of participant sport and its healthful functions.

Aesthetic theories of play date all the way back to ancient Greek philosophy. Throughout the ages, philosophers have postulated man's inherent need for artistic and intellectual fulfillment and the perils of neglecting those needs. It is this aspect of play that I emphasize throughout the book when using the normative definition of leisure. One theory that fits under this heading is the self-expression theory of play, proposed by Elmer Mitchell and Bernard Mason. This theory states that man's play is a response to a

basic need for accomplishment and creativity. Another similar theory is implied in Abraham Maslow's famous hierarchy of needs. According to this psychologist the highest of man's needs is self-actualization. This means that man has a basic need to be creative and play, since artistically and aesthetically creative behavior is a way to accomplish self-actualization. As Miller and Robinson (1963:143) summarize the aesthetic theories of play, such theories stress that the function of play is to bring beauty into man's life with the purpose of encouraging in him self-actualizing creativeness.

Psychologists and educators have built upon the early theories discussed previously, distinguishing between the play of children, whose function is primarily pedagogical, and the play of adults, whose function is primarily cathartic. The former kind of play was emphasized, for example, by George Herbert Mead, whose distinction between play and game has become classic. Play, according to Mead, is what takes place when a child plays, for example, *at* being a mother, or a teacher, or a policeman; it is a simple imaginary enactment of roles that the child may, at some future time, have to enact in seriousness. The game is a more organized and more sophisticated form of activity, as, for example, when a boy participates in a game of baseball; now it becomes necessary to take on a whole variety of roles, understanding not only one particular role but the rules of the entire game of baseball. Thus as Mead views it, the child gradually learns to participate effectively in society, at first through play, later learning to take on the "generalized other" as in any organized game. The role of play in the learning process has been emphasized by a growing number of progressive pedagogues, including John Dewey and Maria Montessori, whose systems differ primarily from classical education in that they are less structured and more spontaneous, in short more playful. Piaget, the famous Swiss child psychologist, identifies six frequently used criteria of play—it is an end in itself, it is spontaneous, it is pleasurable, it is unorganized, it is free of conflicts, and it is "over-motivated" behavior (1958:69–72)—and then argues that play's fundamental characteristic is that it is assimilative behavior. That is, all human behavior may be either assimilative, incorporating new environmental stimuli, or it may be accommodating, adjusting *to* external stimuli. Play, Piaget suggests, is assimilative, and it is essential in human development, since it is the process of psychologically digesting new situations and experiences.

The other major psychological function of play, the cathartic release that is provided when *adults* engage in play, has been stressed by the Freudian and psychoanalytic psychologists. Erik H. Erikson (1950), for example, views play as therapeutic in the sense that it provides release of libidinal tension and frustration. Play, according to the Freudian view, is a means to mitigate the repressive effects of industrial civilization and to, at least partially, give vent to repressed instinctual needs.

A fourth category of theories is the sociohistorical interpretation of play. Huizinga, as we mentioned, traced the play element common to all cultures. Play, considered by the Dutch historian to be crucial to civilization, pervades all social institutions—war, law, religion, politics. The Frenchman Roger Caillois (1961) also focused on the relationship between play and culture. Using ancient Greek terminology, he distinguished between agonistic play (e.g., competitive sports), alea (games of fate and luck), mimicry (theater and other games involving role playing), and ilinx (play that involves vertigo and other sensory stimulation, such as drug use). The play element as

a cultural universal is, of course, discussed by a variety of anthropologists as well. Hoebel (1966:287) quotes Justice Holmes saying, "it is one of the glories of man that he does not sow seeds and weave cloth, and produce all the other economic means simply to sustain and multiply other sowers and weavers. . . . After the production of food and cloth has gone on a certain time, he stops producing and goes to the play, or he paints a picture." In sum, as Miller and Robinson state it, "sociology and anthropology have contributed to play theory the findings that play is a cultural universal, having a social function that produces institutional forms and social forces" (1963:138).

Our discussion of play has primarily been one of theories and perspectives. Before social scientists could theorize about play, it had to be discovered. While this took place some two or three hundred years ago in the West, our civilization has yet to accord to the concept the recognition it grants to, say, work, or religion, or law, witness the marginal place of play theory in the social sciences. Nevertheless, there is a growing awareness of the play phenomenon in society. Also, social scientists now distinguish between child's play and general play, and between the various functions of these two. Furthermore, sociologists and anthropologists are beginning to discern the existence of institutional arrangements centering around play, recognizing play as a truly social phenomenon, not merely as an individual human need. Finally, there is a distinction to be made between play and the game, or between theories of play as just discussed, and game theory, to which we now turn.

GAME

The difference between play and the game is intuitively realized when contrasting the word play with the recently famous title *Games People Play* (Berne, 1964) or with the label "game theory," both of which obviously imply highly serious activities. The term game seems to be applicable to just about any activity—war games, the money game, games people play, the status game, the game of life, or, more conventionally, a football game, a game of bridge.

Etymology of game

The etymology of game helps only slightly. Game is related to the old German *Gaman,* meaning glee. Thus the original meaning of game is not far from that of play, namely, fun, spontaneous, nonserious activity. For example, although a standard definition differentiates play from game by defining the former as a particular instance of the latter (Von Neumann and Morgenstern, 1944:49), Goffman and other sociologists tend to use the two words interchangeably. Play and game are seen as part of recreation, as fun, as the opposite of serious activity.

Nevertheless, social scientists have assigned to play and game increasingly divergent meanings. In general, game refers to a more highly structured, organized and regulated form of activity than does play, which in turn is more spontaneous, free, childlike. Mead's distinction between play and game has already been explained. Other sociologists have built upon that distinction. Stone (1962), for example, explains that the play of little children involves misrepresentation of self, that is, fantasy only, while the game later on involves the serious assumption of real new identities. What this all means is that game is generally considered to be more complex and more *intellectual* than play. Game theory reflects this most clearly.

Game theory

Over the past decades a new perspective has emerged among social scientists.

This perspective, game theory, was originally a mathematical technique devised between 1927 and 1944 by John Von Neumann and Oscar Morgenstern (1944) as a scientific aid to the task of decision making (Rapoport, 1962:2). Game theory was thus initially concerned with the logic of conflict, that is, with the theory of strategy. Used in that context, the word game means a competitive conflict situation in which each participant wishes, somehow, to win. The situation may be a game of tic-tac-toe or a world war. A "game" defined in this fashion can be formalized; that is, the rules regulating it can be formulated, the various possible moves hypothesized, and the outcomes calculated. Goffman, for example, suggests that certain gaming situations have *realized resources,* that is, can be treated as if the entire encounter, the game, is the outcome of potentialities given at the outset; "the elements of each encounter will be treated as if they constituted a full deck" (Goffman, 1961:28).

Of course, not all conflict situations can be treated as games. A dogfight or a human quarrel in which angry, random insults are exchanged is a fight, not a game. Furthermore, only some games are games of perfect information, games in which theoretically each player's best strategy can be specified in advance (e.g., chess, tic-tac-toe). Most games are not like that because they also involve secrecy, chance, luck, bluffing, psychological warfare, unpredictable coalitions among an unpredictable number of participants, sudden rule changes, and so on. Game theory, then, in its initial mathematical sense, refers to the effort at bringing techniques of logical and mathematical analysis to bear on problems involving conflicts of interest. It brings conflicts up from the level of *fights* to the level of *games,* where the intellect has a chance to operate. In sum, one word describes the very special meaning of game as used here: calculation. Ironically, this is the very antithesis of all the connotations of play, leisure, and recreation, connotations of random, spontaneous, free, emotional behavior.

From this point on, "game theory" has been used in an ever wider sense. To Goffman, a game-theoretical approach still means a conception of interaction as a series of moves, a model that is at least potentially a matrix of (quantitatively) specifiable outcomes. Yet beyond an initial explanation of this fact, Goffman's treatment of games is entirely impressionistic. Kraus's discussion of game theory emphasizes the utility of games and simulation techniques as teaching devices, both for young students and in the world of business, management, and decision making. Finally, there is the increasing number of psychologists and sociologists whose "game-theoretical" approach simply refers to a vague conception of all, or much, of human interaction as game-playing behavior.

Thus Eric Berne (1964) describes various types of interpersonal relationships that are quite common but which he terms "games" because they entail calculation and manipulation so as to accomplish some ulterior end. The games described by Berne include life games (games played sometimes as a lifelong career, such as playing the role of alcoholic), marital and sex games (played between marital and sex partners), party games (games played at ordinary social occasions), underworld games (played, for example, between policemen and law breakers, as when the criminal's objective is to toy with law enforcers, getting away while risking apprehension), consulting games (games played between patients and their therapists, for example) and good games (those that, even though they are games, do some good to other players). The main point is that Berne does not approve of games. The goals of human life should be, according to this psychiatrist, intimacy, autonomy, awareness, and spontaneity, thus transcending games. Thomas Szasz (1961), another humanistic psychiatrist, also feels that a great deal of everyday human interaction is game behavior. Mental illness, according to this author, results from playing socially inappropriate games. Berne, Szasz, and others of similar persuasion (e.g., Fromm, 1962; Maslow, 1954; Rogers, 1959; Shostrom, 1968) feel that true interpersonal actualization and mental health begin where game playing stops. However, nowhere do these normative reformers specify how "genuine" behavior differs from games. In fact, Szasz's writings suggest that all behavior is game behavior, so long as the individual is engaged in behavior whose goals and rules are meaningful to him. Thus one plays one's game in life, be it one's professional career, criminal acts, participation in ritualistic conformity, or in deviant subcultures, or in totally idiosyncratic behavior (the schizophrenic game).

Sociologists have recently contributed

to this brand of "game theory." Lyman and Scott (1970) propose a typology of games that consists of the face game (games we play whenever we are protecting identities), the exploitation game (played when we wish to obtain power over others), the information game (in which we seek information about others), and the relationship game (in which we either build or break down relationship₅). These authors also imply that games are pervasive. Their typology is implicitly held to be exhaustive.

What is nowhere clear in this entire body of literature is what *non*-game-playing behavior could be. It might be deduced that it is free, spontaneous interaction, since games always refer to *strategies* followed toward some ulterior goal. Be this as it may, game at this point stands for contrivedness and dishonesty, in opposition to freedom and spontaneity. Thus it is interesting that at least one connotation of the term lies entirely outside the leisure ideal and play concept embraced by those who view leisure, play, and recreation not only as desirable but as all that is beautiful in human existence. Perhaps more neutrally, game theory seems to refer to that position in social science which maintains that man is essentially a strategist, negotiating rules with others and attributing certain meanings to his behavior (i.e., enjoying the game). Game theory thus becomes a humanistic existential philosophy, stating that the meaning of man's life is in the existential games he plays and that he himself constructs those games.

SUMMARY AND CONCLUSION

This discussion has dealt, conceptually, historically, and theoretically, with (1) leisure, (2) recreation, (3) play, and (4) game. It was seen that *leisure* may be defined in a variety of ways, but that the definitional controversy with regard to this term in the end boils down to two positions. One uses leisure either as an empirical concept to describe existing recreational behavior, or one uses it as a normative concept, an ideal toward which people should strive. However, closer examination shows the "empirical" conception of leisure to also be normative, in the sense that it is based on the tacit cultural assumption that leisure, while necessary, is secondary to work. I argue that the "idealistic" conception has a place in sociology because one of the tasks of sociology is to discover and to formulate social problems and because, clearly, one of today's most threatening problems stems from a growing cultural lag between our economic structure (producing abundance) and our value orientation (implying scarcity). Hence I argue for a redefinition of leisure, one that would emancipate it from work and conceptualize it as an independent and primary social fact, as did to some extent the ancient Greeks.

The discussion of the other leisure-related terms revealed, first, that *recreation* is generally used in the "empirical" sense of the leisure concept, that is, to describe what most men do in their spare time, for example, sports and outdoor activities. *Play* was seen to have engendered a great deal of theorizing, particularly by psychologists and educators because of the apparent importance of the pedagogical and socialization functions of the play of little children. Adult play is often seen as recreation. *Games*, finally, are activities that are more highly organized than play. Furthermore, there has been a recent trend in psychology, psychiatry, sociology, and philosophy to apply a "game theoretical" approach to the analysis of interaction. When this is done, any relationship in which the participants apply intellectual reflection to their mutual moves so as to accomplish some personal interest may be termed a game. It is not clear from the literature whether all meaningful social interaction is to be considered game behavior, or whether there is, beyond games, some "pure" and transcendentally valid interaction.

STUDY QUESTIONS

1. Compare and contrast the major contemporary defintions of leisure presented in this chapter. I, along with sociologists like Berger and Smigel, have argued that most definitions can be classified as either empirical or normative. What is meant by this? Show how this is indeed the case.
2. Definitions of leisure fail to agree as to whether it is (1) activity, (2) time, or (3) a state of being free, and they also range from (a) normative to (b) empirical conceptions. Give examples of definitions emphasizing each of these possibilities. Show how some definitions therefore confuse leisure and recreation, other ones leisure and time, others leisure and nonwork. In this book, I argue for a normative conception of leisure because I feel—along with Berger and de Grazia—that leisure today is becoming a social problem. Explain why leisure is now a social problem and why this necessitates its reconceptualization along certain normative lines. Do you or do you not agree with this position? Why?
3. When tracing the etymology of the word leisure back to Greece and Rome, we come across such words as *schole* (school), *a-scholia* (work), and *negotium* (negotiation, business, work). This has interesting implications. Show, on this basis, what leisure meant to the ancients. Show also how their conception of the work-leisure relationship was the exact opposite of ours today.
4. Leisure, recreation, play, game, and childhood are, as all sociological concepts, culture bound. After defining each concept, show how leisure, childhood, and recreation were literally invented by specific cultures at specific times. Show also how play and game apply to different situations. Finally, what has happened to the use of the game concept in contemporary social science?
5. A distinction that is central to this book and to the whole sociology of leisure is that between what Stone calls play and display, what Mead in a different context calls play and game, what others have called game versus sport. Whatever dual concepts are used, the point sociologists wish to make is that leisure and recreational activities can range from a free, spontaneous form to a more institutionalized and often massified and commercialized form. Discuss these two possibilities with all their complex implications. Why do most sociologists feel that the latter type of leisure is bad? Can you see how the current professionalization of sport (even at the college and high school levels) constitutes an erosion of wholesome leisure? Why have both Roman and American societies been said to magnify this tendency, while the Greeks and perhaps the Europeans until recently still had more "true leisure"?
6. Discuss the six major classic theories of play, and show how most of them see two types of play—the play of adults and that of little children. Most generally speaking, what seems to be the single most primary function of adult play, and of children's play?
7. Modern theories of play try to specify the types, functions, and criteria of play. What typologies have been proposed by men like Mead and Caillois? What criteria of play does Piaget identify? What are the functions of play according to the Freudians, and what are they according to modern educators like Dewey and Montessori?
8. Show the evolution of game theory from a mathematical technique to an existential philosophy. What kind of mathematical technique was game theory first supposed to be? How is this still visible in the work of sociologists like Goffman? Then, what kind of "game theory" do we find in the books of psychiatrists like Berne, Shostrom, Szasz, and sociologists like Lyman and Scott? Give examples of what these men mean by games. Are games good or bad? Why? Can you think of any behavior that would *not* be considered a game, according to these authors? Show why game theory tends to deal with the very antithesis of true leisure.

REFERENCES

Aries, Philippe
  1962   Centuries of Childhood. New York: Alfred A. Knopf, Inc.
Benedict, Ruth
  1946   Patterns of Culture. New York: Mentor Books.
Berger, Bennett M.
  1963   "The sociology of leisure: some suggestions." Pp. 21–40 in Erwin O. Smigel (ed.), Work and Leisure. New Haven, Conn.: College and University Press.

Berne, Eric
  1964   Games People Play: The Psychology of Human Relations. New York: Grove Press, Inc.
Caillois, Roger
  1961   Man, Play and Games. New York: The Free Press.
Craven, Ida
  1933   "Leisure: according to the Encyclopedia of the Social Sciences." Pp. 402–405 in The Encyclopedia of the Social Sciences V. New York: The Macmillan Company.

de Grazia, Sebastian
1964   Of Time, Work and Leisure. New York: Anchor Books.

Dewey, John
1921   Democracy and Education. New York: The Macmillan Company.

Dulles, Foster Rhea
1965   A History of Recreation: America Learns to Play. New York: Appleton-Century-Crofts.

Dumazedier, Joffre
1967   Toward a Society of Leisure. New York: The Free Press.

Erikson, Erik H.
1950   Childhood and Society. New York: W. W. Norton & Company, Inc.

Fromm, Erich
1962   The Art of Loving. London: Unwin Books.

Goffman, Erving
1961   Encounters: Two Studies in the Sociology of Interaction. Indianapolis: The Bobbs-Merrill Co., Inc.

Hoebel, E. Adamson
1954   The Law of Primitive Man. Cambridge, Mass.: Harvard University Press.
1966   Anthropology: The Study of Man. Third Edition. New York: McGraw-Hill Book Co.

Huizinga, Johan
1949   Homo Ludens: A Study of the Play Elements in Culture. London: Routledge and Kegan Paul Ltd.

Kando, Thomas and Worth C. Summers
1971   "The impact of work on leisure: toward a paradigm and research strategy." Pacific Sociological Review (Special Summer Issue):310–327.

Kaplan, Max
1960   Leisure in America. New York: John Wiley & Sons, Inc.

Kraus, Richard
1971   Recreation and Leisure in Modern Society. New York: Appleton-Century-Crofts.

Larrabee, Eric and Rolf Meyersohn
1958   Mass Leisure. Glencoe, Ill.: The Free Press.

Lewis, George H.
1972   Side-Saddle on the Golden Calf: Social Structure and Popular Culture in America. Pacific Palisades, Calif: Goodyear Publishing Co., Inc.

Lyman, Stanford M. and Marvin B. Scott
1970   A Sociology of the Absurd. New York: Appleton-Century-Crofts.

Maslow, Abraham
1954   Motivation and Personality. New York: Harper & Row, Publishers.

Mauss, M.
1954   The Gift: Forms and Functions of Exchange in Archaic Societies. New York: The Free Press.

McLuhan, Marshall
1969   "Playboy interview: Marshall McLuhan." Playboy:53–56, 59-74, 157-158.

Mead, Margaret
1958   "The pattern of leisure in contemporary American culture." In Eric Larrabee and Rolf Meyersohn (eds.), Mass Leisure. Glencoe, Ill.: The Free Press.

Miller, Norman P. and Duane M. Robinson
1963   The Leisure Age. Belmont, Calif.: Wadsworth Publishing Co., Inc.

Neumeyer, Martin H. and Esther Neumeyer
1958   Leisure and Recreation. New York: The Ronald Press Company.

Piaget, Jean
1958   "Criteria of play." Pp. 69-72 in Eric Larrabee and R. Meyersohn (eds.), Mass Leisure. Glencoe, Ill.: The Free Press.

Pieper, Joseph
1963   Leisure, The Basis of Culture. New York: The New American Library, Inc.

Rapoport, Anatol
1962   "The use and misuse of game theory." Scientific American (December):108-118.

Rogers, Carl R.
1959   Client-Centered Therapy. Boston: Houghton Mifflin Company.

Rosenberg, Bernard
1971   "Mass culture revisited." Pp. 2-12 in Bernard Rosenberg and David Manning White (eds.), Mass Culture Revisited. New York: The Free Press.

Russell, Bertrand
1935   In Praise of Idleness and Other Essays. London: George Allen & Unwin, Ltd.

Shostrom, Everett L.
1968   Man, the Manipulator. New York: Bantam Books.

Smigel, Erwin O.
1963   Work and leisure. New Haven, Conn.: College and University Press.

Stone, Gregory P.
1962   "Appearance and the self." In Arnold M. Rose (ed.), Human Behavior and Social Processes. Boston: Houghton Mifflin Company.
1970   "The play of little children." In Gregory Stone and Harvey Farberman (eds.), Social Psychology Through Symbolic Interaction. Waltham, Mass.: Ginn/ Blaisdell.

Szasz, Thomas
1961   The Myth of Mental Illness. New York: Dell Publishing Co., Inc.

Veblen, Thorstein
1899   The Theory of the Leisure Class. New York: The Macmillan Company.

Von Neumann, John and Oskar Morgenstern
1944   Theory of Games and Economic Behavior. Princeton, N.J.: Princeton University Press.

Weber, Max
1958 The Protestant Ethic and the Spirit of Capitalism. New York: Charles Scribner's Sons.

White, David Manning
1957 "Mass culture in America: another point of view." Pp. 13-21 in Bernard Rosenberg and David Manning White (eds.), Mass Culture: The Popular Arts in America. New York: The Free Press.

Wilkinson, Doris Y.
1971 Book Review of Toward a Theory of Popular Culture: The Sociology and History of American Music and Dance, 1920-1968, by Duane Braun. American Sociological Review (April):370-371.

chapter 3

 # What is popular culture, and is it good culture?

The purpose of this chapter is to provide a conceptual discussion of popular culture and related terms and to appraise the sociology of popular culture and the warring camps within this emerging subdiscipline.

When discussing popular culture, we may not have an exact definition at our fingertips, but we somehow generally agree that it has to do with high culture, mass culture and mass media, mass leisure and mass consumption, prole culture and prole leisure (the culture and leisure of the proletariat, the lower class), subcultures, and the counterculture. Each of these terms is, in turn, fuzzy and ill defined. Yet I shall argue in this paper that they have both heuristic and pragmatic value. For example, high culture and mass culture are useful when referring to the cultural activities of the upper and the lower social strata respectively. Also, these concepts have long been used in the literature to denote specific cultural phenomena. Thus we have little trouble assigning television and radio to mass culture, and football and baseball to mass leisure. It is therefore under these conventional headings that a discussion of many different cultural phenomena can take place, and it is under the umbrella of popular culture that they somehow all seem to tie together.

A second concern here will be the various ideological factions one inevitably encounters when delving into cultural phenomena. While the literature is rich in opinions about culture, writers essentially are divided into (1) those who feel that mass culture and popular culture are bad culture and (2) those who do not. The great popular culture debate generally features normative idealists pitted against empirical realists.

A CONCEPTUAL DISCUSSION

The conventional sociological meaning of culture is simply "the way of life of a social group" (Theodorson and Theodorson, 1969:95). Thus a typical old definition states that culture is "that complex whole which includes knowledge, belief, art, morals, law, custom, and any other capabilities and habits acquired by man as a member of society" (E. B. Tylor, 1871). On the other hand, the everyday meaning of Culture with a capital "C" tends to be "that which is excellent in the arts, manners, etc." Thus a cultured man is he who is well versed in classical music, poetry, the arts. The literature in the area of mass culture[1] and popular culture[2] does not use culture in either of these meanings. We feel that a third meaning of culture is implicitly shared by all students of mass culture and popular culture, namely, *the typical ways in which a society, or type of society, spends its time when not working.* Culture, here, means essentially *popular* culture. Note the word "typical"; we are concerned with the activities that typify, say, the American way of life as distinct from another culture. For example, typical features of American culture today are mass spectacles, television, and hot dogs; typical features of ancient Greek culture were dramas and political town gatherings. This conception of culture excludes such phenomena as laws, traditional politics, organized religion, work; on the other hand, in addition to covering high culture (e.g., symphonic music), it also encompasses mass culture (e.g., Hollywood), mass leisure (e.g., spectator sports), and counterculture (e.g., rock music).

Students of cultural activities have used a variety of classifications. Some distinguish between three levels of culture; some simply dichotomize; some use more than three categories. Shils (1964:5), for example, distinguishes between superior or refined culture (e.g., poetry), mediocre culture (e.g., most television shows), and brutal culture (e.g., boxing). Browne (1972:5) sees four areas of culture—elite, popular, mass, and folk. Others distinguish between high-culture and mass culture. On one point most sociologists seem to agree: culture reflects social stratification. Thus cultural classification can be traced to how we conceive of social stratification. Since American stratification has, at least since Lloyd Warner, generally been viewed as a trichotomy (upper, middle, and lower), culture is most frequently divided into three. An alternative view is provided by the Marxists, who see in capitalist society only two classes, and hence only two cultures.

Modern society is not merely a stratified series of social classes, each with its corresponding culture. In addition, there are a variety of subgroups, each with

[1] For example, Bensman and Rosenberg, 1963; Howe, 1948; Jacobs, 1964; MacDonald, 1953; McLuhan, 1964; Rosenberg, 1957; Rosenberg and White, 1957; 1971; Shils, 1964; White, 1957; Wilensky, 1964; Winthrop, 1965.
[2] For example, Braun, 1969; Gans, 1966; Lewis, 1972; Lowenthal, 1950; Riesman, 1950; Tumin, 1957; Warshow, 1970; Wilensky, 1961; Wilkinson, 1971.

their respective subcultures. Furthermore, culture is undergoing ongoing change. Thus culture, like society itself, may be compared to a kaleidoscope of ever changing and contrasting subcultures. Some of these represent society's stratification, for example, high culture and mass culture; other ones, for example, artists, western cowboys, urban sexual groupings, sectarian religious groups, have little to do with social class. Change, finally, is embodied by a phenomenon such as the counterculture of the under-thirty generation in the late 1960s.

Popular culture

While none of the classificatory concepts dealt with in this chapter is more elusive than popular culture, none has as broad an application. Gregory Stone's (1972) remarks about play apply to popular culture a fortiori: "the concept has been wrapped in so much toilet paper that it looks round; the cutting edges have been dulled and blunted." One finds at least three major uses of the term in the literature. One of these is illustrated by Nye's recent definition (1972:19), according to which "popular culture is the most visible level of culture, the one found between the extremes of elite and folk culture." Thus popular culture sometimes denotes middle-class culture.

Sometimes popular culture is distinguished from mass culture simply in the sense that it is the better of the two. It is implied that popular culture has an artistic commitment which mass culture lacks. For example, rock star Stephen Still's music could be said to have degenerated from popular culture into mass culture because of commercialization. Also, popular culture has been said to be the culture of the people up to, say, fifty years ago, whereas mass culture may be said to be the typical culture of modern mass society with its mass media (Handlin:1964).

In a different sense, popular culture also refers to the study of certain artifacts, folkways, and institutions which have often been overlooked by sociologists in the past. For example, the telephone, the bicycle, TV-dinners, roadside restaurants, or any other element in America's everyday life. Used as such a label for the study of everyday life (cf. Lewis, 1972; Truzzi, 1968), popular culture becomes an ethnology of American mores, folkways, and institutions.

Some of the ways in which popular culture has been used in the literature have been indicated, along with some of the concept's empirical referents. On that basis, popular culture may now be defined as the *typical cultural and recreational activities of typical segments of a society.*

High culture

Should high culture be included in a discussion of popular culture? Some authors (cf. Browne, 1972:10) feel that popular culture excludes elements that are narrowly intellectual or creatively elitist, that is, high culture. Yet we feel that high culture, as an important facet of a society's leisure life, deserves a place in the sociology of leisure and popular culture.

High culture has been used in at least four ways: (1) as the culture of the social elite, for example that of Veblen's leisure class; (2) as culture that is exploratory, creative, revolutionary; (3) as the repository of a society's great cultural tradition (the "classics"); and (4) as excellent culture. According to definitions 1 and 3, high culture conserves the past; according to definition 2 it explores the future, and according to definition 4 it is that which the observer prefers. To cut through this Gordian knot, we suggest a simple ostensive approach. Since high culture has generally referred to such things as classical music, theater, poetry, the fine arts, a practical definition can be

*the recreational, cultural, and artistic ac-
tivities traditionally not included in mass
culture, such as theater, ballet, classical
music, and the fine arts.* One advantage
of such a definition is that it permits
high culture to be popular. For example,
classical ballet, a form of high culture,
is also one of Russia's most popular
forms of entertainment.

Mass culture and the mass media

High culture's conceptual opposite is
mass culture. It, too, has had a multiplicity of meanings: (1) just as high culture may be used as the culture of the
elite, so mass culture is the culture of the
masses; (2) when high culture is viewed
as excellent culture, then mass culture
becomes inferior culture; (3) mass culture is simply the culture of the numerical majority; (4) mass culture consists of
"all elements of life which are generally,
but not necessarily, disseminated by the
mass media" (Lewis, 1972:19).

Again, what specific areas of culture
does the concept generally cover? Two of
the best known readings in mass culture
(Rosenberg and White, 1957; Rosenberg
and White, 1971) are made up of articles
that deal with radio, television, motion
pictures, the printed press, in sum the
mass media. Here, too, practicality would
suggest a somewhat ostensive definition:
*mass culture consists of cultural elements
traditionally not included in high culture,
and transmitted by the printed press, the
electronic media, or by other forms of
mass communication.* Such a definition
makes it possible to conceive of relatively rare mass cultural activities, for example, a one-time televised chess match
or T-lab.

Mass leisure and mass consumption

How does one distinguish mass leisure
from mass culture? The two are evidently related; witness the fact that the two
best known works in the field, *Mass Culture* (Rosenberg and White, 1957; 1971)

and *Mass Leisure* (Larrabee and Meyersohn, 1958) have been called "companion
volumes" (Larrabee and Meyersohn,
1958:ix).

To recite basic sociology and say that
leisure is behavior whereas culture is not
does not help very much. We know since
Marshall McLuhan that the distinction
between behavioral *content* and cultural
or technological *form* is epistemological
rather than ontological. Is the World
Series mass leisure or mass culture? Evidently both. So, just as the contents table
in *Mass Culture* enabled us to define the
concept, so the articles assembled in
Mass Leisure tell us what that term
means. They deal mostly with conventional recreational activities like sports,
camping, hobbies, travel. Thus, to Larrabee and Meyersohn, as to others, mass
leisure means no more and no less than
*the typical recreational activities in mod-
ern mass society.*

At times, we think of mass culture as
being more inclusive than mass leisure.
We do not necessarily think of fads, fashions, tastes, or political trends as leisure
activities, yet they are part of mass culture. Then again, as in the case of televised spectator sports, motion pictures,
or entertainment magazines, mass leisure and mass culture become identical.

Veblen would have thought of mass
leisure as a contradictory idea. Indeed,
leisure has historically been the prerogative of the elite. Do contemporary masses
devote their spare time to true leisure?
Certainly not, according to de Grazia and
like-minded philsophers, who argue that
modern leisure is merely *mass consumption.* Their point is this: modern technology and affluence promised the leisure
society but instead produced the consumer society; we seem to have transformed means into ends; that is, material
consumption, instead of remaining a
means toward a more leisurely life, has
become our guiding principle; our greed
seems insatiable, and the Protestant

work ethic, far from becoming obsolete, dictates continued hard work, overtime, moonlighting; in the face of plenty, we adhere to the principle of scarcity. Accordingly, the oft heralded leisure boom[3] and the growth of a multibillion dollar leisure market are merely more mass consumption. The purchase of second homes, land and lots, campers, and electronic equipment is economic rather than leisure behavior. In fact, such durable consumer goods may often be true investments that require work and produce no leisure.

Prole culture and prole leisure

Sociologists (e.g., Lewis, 1972) and popular authors (e.g., Wolfe, 1965) have now begun to write about "prole sports."

Prole sports include such activities as cycle racing, demolition derbies, roller derbies, and wrestling. Prole culture and prole leisure simply refer to *the cultural and recreational activities of the proletariat.* We introduce this category as an additional level in the stratification of popular culture.

While sociology can no longer be termed an elitist discipline as it was in the days of Comte and Spencer, it remains a bourgeois science. Thus, in the sociology of leisure and popular culture, mass leisure and mass culture may have gained a certain degree of legitimacy, but lower-class cultural and recreational activities are still largely ignored. Yet each year prole sports attract more spectators than professional football, and the national audience for such prole music as country-and-western is far larger than

that of rock, jazz, and classical music combined.

Subcultures

The concept of subculture is relatively old in sociology, particularly in its application to deviant behavior (cf. Bordua, 1961; Cohen, 1955; Miller, 1958). Here, we use the term in its more general meaning of *the culture of any identifiable segment of a society* (Theodorson and Theodorson, 1969:424). A comprehensive discussion of leisure and popular culture must recognize the existence of lifestyles and leisure activities that may not be the reflection of social class. Some activities, for example, those of artists, jazz musicians, or those of a sectarian religious colony, can only be located *outside* the core culture, not at its top, middle, or bottom. Other recreational activities, for example, mate swapping and the drag parties of the homosexual and tranvestistic communities, are, while perhaps mostly middle-class affairs, nevertheless so deviant that to classify them as mass leisure would be misleading and lack common sense. Hence, the sociology of leisure and popular culture must also deal with subcultures. Examples of what we have in mind are jazz, rodeo, poker, billiards, and a variety of alternative sexual lifestyles.

The counterculture and folk culture

Our final category is the counterculture. For a proper definition of this term, we must first ponder two related concepts —subculture and contraculture. From what was just said about subcultures, it appears that a contraculture is one kind of subculture. Indeed, as Yinger (1960) explained, "delinquency and drug addiction . . . political and religious movements . . . may *invert* the values of the dominant group." A subculture which stands, thus, in opposition to important aspects of the dominant culture is a contraculture.

---

[3] There are a great many naive dollars-and-cents approaches to leisure. These sources generally see Americans experiencing immense gains in leisure, discretionary spending, recreation, and culture, in sum a veritable leisure explosion. See, for example, *Fortune* (1958), Toffler (1964), *U. S. News & World Report* (1969, 1972). The realities of Nixonomics may be silencing such fantasies at this time. What matters here is that material consumption is irrelevant to a philosophical conception of leisure.

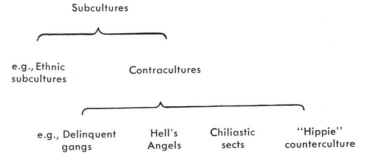

Fig. 1. Conceptual relationship between subculture, contraculture, and counterculture.

The counterculture may, in turn, be seen as one type of contraculture. It is clear from the rapidly expanding literature on this subject[4] that counter culture has come to mean the antiestablishment subcultural youth movement generally associated with the hippie phenomenon. It may be defined as *the retreatist-rebellious youth movement which emerged in the mid-sixties in affluent segments of affluent societies, and which has been called the hippie phenomenon.*

Fig. 1 makes it clear that the hippies are merely one case of contraculture (next, for example, to Hell's Angels) and that contracultures are merely one type of subculture (in addition to ethnic and other subcultures).

In a strange and novel fashion the counterculture mixes the latest electronic technology (musical instruments, light shows) with tribal elements. For example, its preferred mode of communication contrasts sharply with the depersonalized character of modern mass media. Because the counterculture borrows from and admires tribal culture,[5] strives

toward retribalization (McLuhan, 1964; Ragni, 1968), and advocates direct interpersonal contact, much of it may be characterized as *folk culture.* Indeed, folk culture can be defined as *culture which is shared and transmitted through direct, oral communication, as in tribal and folk societies.*

In line with its leveling orientation, the counterculture tries to erase the performer-audience distinction (Berger, 1971; Eisen, 1969), deemphasizing individual stardom and reintroducing the communality and anonymity of cultural and artistic production so typical of folklore and of medieval folk society. These trends are well illustrated by the jam session, the happening, the living theater, the guerilla theater, the be-in, love-in, and even the massive pop festival. In general, the counterculture favors direct communication over media mediation, and communal participation over a mass audience–star performer distinction.

In this discussion we have dealt with a number of concepts central to the sociology of leisure and popular culture. As I see it, they all somehow tie together under the umbrella of popular culture, although overlap and ambiguity are far from minimal. Fig. 2 summarizes visually the delineations suggested in the preceding pages.

HIGH CULTURE: THE CONTROVERSIAL ROLE OF THE CREATIVE ARTS

It may seem odd at first that high culture, too, would be a controversial topic.

---

[4] Cf. Belz, 1969; Eisen, 1969, 1970, 1971; Lewis, 1972; Lipset, 1971; Reich, 1970; Roszak, 1969; 1973; Roxon, 1969; Taylor, 1968; Ten Have, 1972; Wolfe, 1968.

[5] The movement has been described by innumerable observers as a neoromantic trend advocating a return to nature, tribalism, and primary values. One illustrative example, out of a myriad of possibilities, is the recently re-released motion picture *Billy Jack.* It presents American Indian culture—particularly its inherent animism—as a way out of the impasse reached by white civilization.

Conventional society, with pluralistic and mass characteristics					Alternative society, with folk characteristics	
Orientation: rational and purposeful (pragmatic) Values: materialistic					Orientation: affective Values: idealistic	
Work	Nonwork				Work-nonwork distinction vanishes	
		Popular culture			The counterculture	
		Upper class	Subcultures		Social classes vanish	
		High culture				
Mass production	Mass consumption	Middle class				
		Mass leisure	Mass culture		Folk culture	
		Lower class				
		Prole leisure	Prole culture			

Fig. 2. Areas covered by popular culture and related concepts.

After all, mass culture may understandably create apprehension among intellectuals, artists, sociologists, and purists in other quarters, but what disagreement could possibly exist about the desirability of creative art?

The truth of the matter is that, while it may be difficult to find anyone who is "against art," support for the arts often amounts to little more than lip service. Frequently a politician will speak out in favor of art. A clue to his sincerity is in whether he proposes substantial public assistance to the arts. When he does not, he generally couches his position in the argument that art means freedom and that governmental intervention in the arts reeks of totalitarianism.

What should art be?

The question of governmental art policy is part of the broader controversy regarding the proper role and functions of art and artists. What public policy toward the arts one advocates depends on one's conception of art's place in society. On the one hand, there are those who feel that art must be purely self-justifying in terms of aesthetics—art for art's sake—

and on the other those who feel that art's functions must be educational, social, and even political—*art engagé*. Hannah Arendt is a spokeswoman for the art for art's sake position. Using the words art and culture interchangeably, she phrases her position as follows:

An object is cultural to the extent that it can endure; this durability is the very opposite of its functionality, which is the quality which makes it disappear again from the phenomenal world by being used and used up. The "thingness" of an object appears in its shape and appearance, the proper criterion of which is beauty . . . . Thus the functionalization of the world which occurs in both society and mass society deprives the world of culture as well as beauty. Culture can be safe only with those who love the world for its own sake, who know that without art . . . all human life would be futile and no greatness could endure. [1964:51-52]

Some of those who consider art for art's sake a sterile ivory-tower position, advocating precisely the functionalization of art so deplored by Hannah Arendt, are artists themselves, for example, French filmmaker Jean-Luc Godard whose works represent an effort to synthesize art and social revolution. More frequently, the politicalization of art is imposed upon artists extraneously, by a social system or a state. This reaches its ultimate form in the two classic cases of Soviet socialism and fascism. In the USSR social realism and the persecution of such men as Solzhenitsyn show the ultimate perversion of an *art engage* policy. In Nazi Germany and fascist Italy the total subservience of art to propaganda did likewise, even though fascism lured the talent of futuristic painters and poets (d'Annunzio) and the misguided sympathy of an Ezra Pound.

A more acceptable conception of art's purpose than either *art engagé* or art for art's sake is quoted by Sir Herbert Read:

> The purpose of art is not to exist for its own sake . . . or to be utilitarian, or propagandist, or socialist realist; still less, of course, should it embellish life or invent forms of pleasure or produce artifacts for the market. The artist is a sacred vessel through which blows the spirit of his time and place and society; he is the man who conveys, as far as possible, a total human experience, a world. [1966:vi]

This is a conception of art to which many contemporary Western artists probably subscribe. As Lazarsfeld sums up the voice of the artist: "they all agree that the goal and task of the artist is to interpret human experience . . . . They have no doubt that life for everyone

would be much harder if art didn't help to make sense out of it" (1964:xvi). Indeed, British poet Randall Jarrell said that "art is primarily to enable us to get through our lives and to help us bear them" (1964:183). And James Baldwin added that the job of the creative artist is to discover "just why the lives we lead on this continent are mainly so empty, so tame and so ugly [and] to have a standard, to cling to it and to maintain it . . . whether or not it is followed" (1964:123). The point of view of the artist is well summarized by Sweeney: "the true artist, who by his essential nature is a seeker, an explorer, always apart and in advance of his fellows, provides what the mass media fail to give: standards of quality and integrity for our culture as a whole" (1964:96). Thus artists concur that "to be an artist cannot be a democratic thing" (Baldwin), that "the artist, qua artist, is an individualist, and the quality of his art lies in its individuality" (Sweeney), and that his function is neither to provide propaganda for the state, nor to produce that which will sell best, but to function as a cultural vanguard free from all influences that might deter from pure creativity.

Art and money

Judging from the way artists conceive of their role in society, the logical conclusion would seem to be a total laissez-faire policy toward the arts, meaning absence of public and even private subsidies. This is indeed the conclusion arrived at by Read, who writes: "I do not believe that the arts can be organized by state departments and I look sceptically on all our efforts to promote art by state patronage" (1966:v).

Let us examine the implications of a rigorous laissez-faire philosophy of art. Laissez-faire is always a double-edged sword. It maximizes freedom but minimizes economic security. What Read in fact is advocating is total freedom for the artist to do his thing, and to starve. Now there are those who argue that this is as it should be. An old misconception has it that artists, to be good, must be unhappy. This is the romantic stereotype of the alienated genius, outcast during his life and idolized posthumously. Van Gogh, Beethoven, Dostoevski and Baudelaire are among the many examples that give substance to the stereotype. Thus even a contemporary art director suggests that "it is difficult for the artist to function in a prosperous society. Many creative artists feel that way. Many are leaving for poorer countries" (Lionni, 1964:178). The truth of the matter is that van Gogh, Beethoven, Dostoevski and Baudelaire made their contributions *in spite* of the social and economic obstacles they had to face, not because of them. The argument that artistry flourishes under conditions of personal and social deprivation is probably an erroneous application of Freudian sublimation theory. It is most definitely used as a justification of economic injustice, and it has little empirical foundation. Quite to the contrary, art's golden eras have generally occurred at times of peace and wealth, as when Athens, Rome, Venice, Florence, Amsterdam, Paris, and London flourished so that artists were happy and well fed. The unhappy relationship between the artist and society that some assume to be a necessary one only goes back to the beginning of romanticism.

That artists are quite normal in their material wants is evidenced by what has taken place under mass capitalism. In the absence of governmental subsidies, artistic production, like everything else, is increasingly determined by supply and demand. As the poet Randall Jarrell notes, it is a fable to assume that the truly mature artist, the creative person, is always going to produce great works of art no matter what, and that he will never be corrupted or bent or warped or seduced. For, as Lazarsfeld points out,

there are now institutional temptations (foundation money, university positions) and popularizers (1964:xvii), both making it increasingly attractive for the artist to sell out.

The dilemma of capitalist mass culture, then, is essentially this: how to continue to produce good culture when there is little economic incentive to do so. It seems obvious that a continued laissez-faire approach to culture—under the guise of democracy—will further undermine quality art. Thus some form of national cultural policy is essential.

Arthur Schlesinger Jr. suggested, as far back as 1959 (1964:148-154), what elements of a federal cultural policy were already present and how these might be developed into a constructive governmental program.

Until the mid-sixties, the only public support for the arts in America was at the municipal level (and in one state, New York). No federal money went to the arts, except the approximately $2 million spent annually by the state department to export performing artists on foreign goodwill tours. By contrast, other major Western countries had long ago established a history of governmental support for the arts. For the performing arts alone the Austrian government spent, in 1961, nearly $40 million, $5.50 per capita. In Germany the situation is similar. In 1964 local governments in that country spent over $112 million on theaters and operas alone, $2.00 per person. The central French government's performing arts budget was $10 million in 1964. That of Italy was $8.5 million. That of Great Britain was nearly $10 million (Baumol and Bowen, 1966:361-364). Thus the United States was, until recently, the only major Western country without a governmental art budget.

Since, as Berger phrases it, "in America the prospect of government subsidy for the arts carries the aura of totalitarianism, while foundation money is considered more democratic" (1964: 118-119), we might expect nonpublic subsidy for arts to play the role that public funding plays in Europe. While private support for the arts in the United States is indeed substantial, it is not commensurate with either private support for other activities, or with public support for the arts in Europe. In 1964 total philanthropy in America amounted to approximately $12 billion, including gifts by individuals, corporations, and foundations (Baumol and Bowen, 1966:306). Out of this, approximately $100 million went to the performing arts, $0.50 per capita. Thus even when private sources of funding are considered, the performing arts are far more poorly endowed in the United States than in Europe.

In 1965 Congress finally took the first step in the direction of a national cultural policy by establishing the National Foundation on the Arts and Humanities and approving a three-year $21 million

budget. By 1971 the endowment had increased to $15 million per year. In addition, the states now spent a total of $27 million on the arts (the bulk of it in New York). Under the leadership of Nixon appointee Nancy Hanks, the National Endowment for the Arts was expected to increase to nearly $40 million by fiscal 1973 (Jacobs, 1972). While this progress was still modest (the United States government now spent nearly the same amount of money on the arts as did Austria, with a gross national product fifty times smaller), it was a step in the right direction.

Conclusion

The question, here, has been whether art should be a matter of total individual freedom and governmental laissez-faire, or an activity that is somehow "functional" as well as strongly backed by the government. The answer is not simple. In the first place, while *art engagé* has, historically, led to the excesses of social realism and fascist propaganda, it should not be

Ata Kando

completely dismissed. Second, while art for art's sake may seem an attractive proposition to some, many artists feel that theirs are the additional tasks of cultural education and standard maintenance in an otherwise mediocre society. Third, when it comes to financing the arts, a total laissez-faire philosophy turns out to be as nefarious as strict governmental regulation. Under the guise of freedom, or worse, the pseudoromantic notion that the artist must suffer in order to express his genius, the artist is let free to either be poor or sell his skill to the highest bidder in a free market economy. If I have argued in this section that an enlightened national cultural policy is necessary, it is because I see that as the only way out of the massification of culture. Let us now turn to this problem.

MASS CULTURE INDICTED

When approaching the popular culture debate, one first sees two camps: those who are for popular culture and those who are against it. The first tendency is therefore to give to each camp a name, for example, the "liberals," who accept popular culture, and the "elitists," who reject it. Being for popular culture may mean that one welcomes new cultural trends, and in this sense, this camp may indeed be termed liberal. Being against may mean being an old-fashioned purist who feels that classical music, concerts, and ballet are the only forms of good culture. In this sense, those against popular culture are the elitists, as is, for example, Herbert Read, who categorically dismisses all cinema and jazz as "entertainment."

But the debate frequently shifts its emphasis, moving on from an indictment of *popular* culture to an attack upon *mass* culture. When the protagonists argue about mass culture, being for it can become the conservative position, meaning an acceptance of a "bread and circuses" policy imposed by the elite upon the masses. Being against mass culture can, here, become a radical attitude which says that the common man has as much potential for high culture as anyone, if only in a just society this potential were permitted to flourish.

Thus to distinguish, in the popular culture debate, only between the liberals and the conservatives is insufficient. While Berger (1963:24), for example, writes that "there are two major ideological approaches to this problem . . . conservative intellectuals who see the social stratification of culture as inevitable . . . [and] liberal and radical intellectuals who accuse the suppliers of mass culture of catering to the lowest levels of popular taste in order to achieve the highest of net profit," we must extend this vision.

Elitist arguments against mass culture

The elitist's position is essentially based on the assumption that there is a necessary inverse relationship between the quantity and the quality of culture. Ernest van den Haag phrases the question as follows: "Is it possible to extend a higher civilization to the lower classes without debasing its standard and diluting its quality to the vanishing point? Is not every civilization bound to decay as soon as it begins to penetrate the masses?" (1964:55). To the first question, the elitist's answer is an unequivocal no; his answer to the second question is inevitably yes. Why? Because, to quote the same author, "the mass of men dislikes and always has disliked learning and art. It wishes to be distracted from life rather than to have it revealed; to be comforted by traditional (possibly happy and sentimental) tropes, rather than to be upset by new ones. It is true that it wishes to be thrilled, too. But irrational violence or vulgarity provides thrills, as well as release, just as sentimentality provides escape" (1964:59).

Interestingly, many an artist tends to

be an elitist. Randall Jarrell writes that "whenever the circle of consumers of art has been widened, the immediate result has been to debase the level of artistic production . . . today in consequence of the emergence of the lower middle classes and certain sections of the industrial workers as consumers of art, a phenomenon well known in past history is recurring" (1964:182).

Clive Bell (1928) suggested nearly half a century ago in England that there must be inequality in order for high culture to flourish. "If the community wants civilization," Bell argued, "it must pay for it. It must support a leisured class as it supports schools and universities, museums and picture-galleries. This implies inequality. On inequality all civilizations have stood." Since only "those who never had to earn money know how to spend it," culture and the arts can only flourish in the hands of an idle and wealthy leisured class. This class must be presumably state supported. It must definitely be parasitic. Bell argued that civilization has always blossomed in the age of tyrants and that it may be incompatible with democracy.

Thus in the end the elitist attributes the mediocrity of contemporary mass culture to the rise of liberal democracy, arguing that in an earlier and less egalitarian age, art had not yet lost its integrity. What Bell said in early twentieth century England has been reiterated more recently in America by conservative culture critics like Daniel Boorstin: in a general indictment of popular culture, Boorstin (1961) argues that the democratization of art has led to its vulgarization. This is because, beginning with the democratic revolutions of the eighteenth and nineteenth centuries and the graphic revolutions of the nineteenth and twentieth centuries, true art has become mass reproduced, abridged, digested, and popularized for purposes of mass consumption. "What the new public museums

were to works of art, the new popularizations were to works of literature . . . sculpture, painting, tapestries and objets d'art were taken out of context by being removed from monastery and palace to the public museum [and] much of the literature was expurgated, simplified." According to Boorstin, then, the availability of art has been bought at the cost of its integrity. The culprits are modern technology and liberal democracy. In his sweeping indictment of the age of liberalism, Boorstin leaves no stone unturned, mentioning even the King James Bible translation as contributing, ultimately, to cultural deterioration (1961:121).

Conservative arguments against mass culture

Elitist and conservative arguments against mass culture must be distinguished. Conservative means, literally, wishing to *conserve* the older culture and arguing that it is better than new culture. Boorstin is not only an elitist but also quite conservative, using a remote past as reference point for beauty and truth. There was a time when the task of newspapers was to report news, he argues, whereas today they fabricate it. Two centuries ago some men had god-given greatness; today, such heroes have been replaced by celebrities, the products of media and press agents. In olden days travel meant true adventure and experience of life; today, this has been replaced by tourism, a bland and sterile commodity within the reach of everyman's checkbook. These so-called pseudoevents are modern phenomena typical of mass society. Boorstin feels that modern life is artificial and that good culture is something of the past.

The deterioration and massification of culture is often attributed to modern technology. Handlin (1964), for example, feels that modern mass culture is inferior to earlier popular culture because it is more depersonalized. The depersonalization of culture is primarily attributed to the emergence of mass media. When communication media are evaluated in this vein, the newer the medium, the more harmful it is perceived to be. Thus the conservative argues that, while it is the graphic revolution that initiated the process of cultural deterioration, the printed medium is nevertheless preferable to electronic media; in turn, while all television is bad, color is a worse evil than black and white (Rosenberg, 1971); similarly painting is true art while photography cannot be; theater is inherently superior to motion pictures; black and white pictures are superior to color movies, which in turn are not as abject as Cinemascope and the other advanced techniques. The conservative, then, turns out to be suspicious of *any* novel communicative or expressive technology. This is not new, for Socrates already attributed Athens' ills to the invention of writing. And, no doubt when more advanced media emerge, television will take its place among the respectable art forms.

The conservative culture critic does not admit to rejecting the new per se, but claims to reject that which is depersonalized, commercialized, vulgarized, made functional and technical. However, value judgements are frequently ad hoc. Jazz and rock music are inevitably considered inferior to classical and other earlier music. This may take the form of sophisticated arguments (Read, 1966), or blunt partisanship, as when arch-conservative Los Angeles newscaster George Putnam claims transcendental superiority for a Rodgers and Hammerstein musical over *Hair.* Sometimes the overwhelming public recognition given to some modern cultural product gives it, at last, respectability. Thus not even Putnam, or Rosenberg (1971), attacks the Beatles. And, in another area of mass culture, baseball is considered by the conservative to be intrinsically superior to football (Howe, 1948). The argument, here, is that baseball is more refined than football because it is slowpaced and allows audience interaction, while football is a rapid, brutal, and dehumanizing spectacle. But ad hoc interpretations work both ways, as McLuhan (1969) shows. In that author's perspective, football is the fast, multidimensional game best suited to our age of television and total sensory involvement; unlike the linear, segmented and cerebral baseball experience, football is now said to offer a total sensual and esthetic involvement.

Radical arguments against mass culture

The motive for criticizing mass culture may also be a radical humanitarian one. The manifesto of the radical culture critics was written by Rosenberg on two occasions, both times as one of two introductory chapters to the main anthology in this area, *Mass Culture* (1957) and *Mass Culture Revisited* (1971). Both times, Rosenberg's radical critique of mass culture is followed by a liberal defense of it by David Manning White. These joint statements may be viewed as the prime position statements of the two camps in the great popular culture debate.

Rosenberg's argument is that to be against mass culture does not mean being against the masses but against *those who dehumanize the masses.* The real culprits are Madison Avenue, the mass media, irresponsible opinion leaders, and modern technology. Mass man is the victim. Rosenberg rejects Schlesinger's (1964) notion of an aesthetic quotient, which says that, just as with intelligence, men are *naturally* endowed with different levels of cultural aptitude. According to Rosenberg, anthropology shows that art is a cultural universal; the common man has the potential to understand true art; if the working class is underrepresented among the high culture audience, it is probably because concerts, operas, ballets, and plays are so often gala affairs in multimillion dollar cultural centers; on rare occasions Beethoven, Shakespeare, or Beckett have been brought to the working man's own arena, performed in inexpensive community settings, and they have caught on.

Marxist arguments against popular culture

According to the Marxist view, mass culture is not only supplied by the elite to the masses for financial profit, but it is also the opiate which prevents the emergence of revolutionary consciousness. Control is accomplished in a variety of ways: first there is, allegedly, mind-control; Marx, Lenin, and subsequent Marxists have argued that bourgeois democracy is not true democracy and that it provides no true political and cultural alternatives, because the downward flow of messages through the media is in fact a one-way indoctrination process. Second, the new media themselves, qua media and apart from the messages they carry, tend to contribute to passive nonresistance. Here, television is always the prime example given, with emphasis on its soporific effects. The third step toward the psychological emasculation of the masses is accomplished through the presentation of a great deal of violence in the media. By vicariously identifying with that violence, displacing dammed-up hostility in this fashion, the proletarian becomes less likely to act out in society.

In addition, the Marxist rejects popular culture because it merely reflects a decaying bourgeois culture and is essentially irrelevant, epiphenomenal. This is the meaning of communists' rejection of jazz, rock, and other hedonistic culture. Silber (1972), for example, in a review of *A Clockwork Orange,* argues that Kubrick's talent is misguided because it fails to grasp the basic causes of violence; the film, although admittedly made by a talented individual, is a symptom of a dying social system and therefore not worth very much. Furthermore, it follows that

to study popular culture, as many young sociologists now do, is a cop-out. It is radical chic rather than true radicalism.

MASS CULTURE DEFENDED

Just as with the critics of mass culture and popular culture, those who approve of these cultural forms range from conservatives to radicals. As Lowenthal (1964) pointed out, both camps have roots that go at least as far back as sixteenth-century France. There, Montaigne was among the first to argue that there is no point in denying the masses the gratifications of common entertainment. Human nature being what it is, the Frenchman seems to have felt, the public might as well be given superficial entertainment, which meets a universal human need. Today, business-oriented (Toffler, 1964), liberal (White, 1957; 1971), and other apologists of modern mass culture argue that cultural consumption has not only increased quantitatively but qualitatively as well. They answer culture critics with statistics showing that no other society in history has ever enabled as many of its members to enjoy good music, good art, and good culture; that the presumably culturally richer past for which modern culture critics long nostalgically is fictitious.

Elitist and conservative arguments for mass culture

Edward Shils (1964) sums up the conservative position vis-a-vis mass culture quite nicely, arguing that, given the inherent intellectual limitations of a majority of men, mediocre and brutal culture is indeed what the masses deserve and will continue to enjoy. Bread and circuses, then, is the proper cultural policy.

Arthur Schlesinger's *aesthetic quotient* idea has already been introduced. The historian feels that, just as with intelligence, individuals are *inherently* endowed with greater or lesser capacities for art and culture. Thus no amount of education would render Bach, Dostoevski, or Klee comprehensible to the masses.

Common to all such arguments justifying the existence of mass culture is the familiar box office notion that the public gets what the public wants, and an implicit elitism which assumes inherent human inequalities.

Liberal arguments for mass culture and the mass media

Foremost among liberal apologists of mass culture is David Manning White (1957; 1971). As indicated earlier, his retort to Rosenberg may be viewed as the position statement of this entire camp. If American mass entertainment today is not as refined as some would like it to be, White reminds us that surely the Romans' gladiators and Elizabethan England's bear batings were symptomatic of far more barbaric mores. For the remainder, White's arguments are mostly statistical: 80 million Mozart recordings sold since 1920, a tenfold increase in symphony orchestras, ten times more people attending concerts than baseball games, 400 million paperbacks sold per year. The implication, throughout, is that progress is not merely quantitative but also qualitative.

Other authors echo this line of reasoning. For example, Toffler's *The Culture Consumers* attempts to show that good culture and good business go together. Toffler uses financial data to show that America is experiencing a cultural boom.

It is often the modern mass *media* that apologists of mass culture feel called upon to rescue. Thus, James Sweeney (1964), former director of New York's Guggenheim museum, feels that the mass media are no threat to genuine art, since the artist is an individualist anyway. The media and high culture can coexist peacefully. Leo Rosten (1964) goes one step further, turning the table on the intellectuals. Blaming the mass media for most people's failure "to attain the bliss

of intellectual grace" is merely the latter-day intellectuals' brand of scapegoating. They should, instead, meet their own responsibilities. Frank Stanton (1964), former president of the Columbia Broadcasting System, feels that the media genuinely try to do a responsible job, although collaboration with the intellectuals would serve a better purpose than the mutual hostility so typical at this time.

Whether defending the mass media or pointing to quantitative cultural growth, many apologists of mass culture share an acceptance of modern cultural trends which the culture critics reject. Such authors as White have a "mod," "with it" outlook that makes them less likely to frown upon jazz, *Playboy,* and television than would many contemporary culture critics.

Radical arguments for popular culture and prole culture

Beyond the old-school liberals, we find radical young sociologists—they may be called pop sociologists—and such isolated figures as Marshall McLuhan and Tom Wolfe. This group not only accepts electronic mass culture, it actually elevates it as the mainspring of postindustrial creativity, as the potential source of revolutionary cultural change. In Rosenberg's derogatory words, "at peace in the electric wonderland, they celebrate what used to sicken them" (1971:3).

By pop sociologists, we mean the growing group of authors who focus on areas of culture largely ignored by establishment sociology. Good examples are the readings assembled by Lewis (1972), Stone (1972), and Truzzi (1968), in which one finds articles about high society, the black bourgeoisie, the New Left, the bicycle, the telephone, Beatlemania, nudist camps, sectarian cults, card games, pool, and a variety of sports. The subject matter of pop sociology is its distinguishing feature, for neither its methods nor its value assumptions need differ from, say, the sociology of large-scale organizations, or small group experiments. Today, pop sociology finds little acceptance in the profession's inner circles. One searches in vain in the indices of the *American Sociological Review* for articles about sports, leisure, and popular culture. Not even the *American Journal of Sociology* deserves the kindness, in this respect, granted it by Stone (1972:1–16). *Society* maybe.

Because Marshall McLuhan has been called the high priest of pop culture, let us first discuss some of his ideas.[6] McLuhan's central thesis is that all means of communication, apart from the content of their message, exert a molding influence upon both the individual and the social structure. As a particular instance of technological determinism, this thesis therefore falls in the same class of theories as Ogburn's cultural lag and Marx's historical materialism. The originality of McLuhan's contribution resides in his choice of *communicative* technology as history's independent variable.

Precivilized tribal man lived in harmony with nature, as he relied, in a balanced way, upon all his perceptual senses. Prior to the invention of writing, culture was oral and life more auditory. Without writing, knowledge could not be monopolized, hence the egalitarianism of most tribal societies. Tribal man lived in acoustic space which, unlike visual space, is without center or margin. As a consequence of these features, primitive man's experiences were experiences of total involvement, spontaneity, simultaneous multisensory stimulation and emotion.

Not all writing destroyed this idyllic situation. The pictorial cultures with their idiographic characters (for example, the Egyptian hieroglyphs) retained a certain correspondence between object and experience.

---

[6] The following discussion is primarily based on McLuhan (1964; 1969).

It was the invention of the phonetic alphabet that once and for all destroyed unity in human life. With the emergence of semantically meaningless abstract symbols, sight and sound were separated; the fragmentation of personality began; visual perception took precedence over all other senses; this fostered an atrophy of the unconscious; man no longer experienced gestalt. Thus phonetic literacy led to fragmentation, dissection, linear and analytic thought. Rationality superseded spontaneity; detached and unilinear experiences replaced simultaneity and gestalt; Western logic, with its sequential cause-effect reasoning, emerged. On the plus side of the equation, mankind gained technology and social organization, as exemplified by Roman, and later, American civilizations. On the negative side, we discovered mental illness, alienation, and the other concomitants of progress.

The invention of the printing press (Gutenberg, sixteenth century) further accentuated what the phonetic alphabet had already begun. Now, nationalism, industrialism, and war were also among the products of media change. A written language could now be disseminated over an entire linguistic area, thus unifying Europe's nation states; and the printing press became the model for all subsequent mechanization and hence for the Industrial Revolution.

The third major invention was the telegraph (1844). This led to the electronic revolution now under way. Finally, the visual supremacy established by the phonetic alphabet now comes to an end. Sensory balance will be restored; man's retribalization, a return to the global village, is under way, thanks to television and other electronic media, which once again provide total involvement and wholeness of being.

Thus the cultural revolution is toward the here and now feeling, togetherness, involvement, totality. McLuhan labels the medium most typical of, and responsible for this trend—television—*cool*. His argument is that it creates involvement in depth without excitement or agitation. In addition, he documents the trend in many other areas of leisure, consumption, and daily living. In sports, for example, while baseball (hot) may have been the appropriate national pastime in an individualistic, inner-directed, one-thing-at-a-time society, the age of television (cool) demands such team activities as football, basketball, hockey. Similarly, just as television's images are blurred, with mysterious contours, so the increasingly popular small foreign car provides a tactile experience (cool) quite different from the visual, enclosed space provided by the larger and better looking American car. Tactile sports like skiing are becoming enormously popular. All this represents a trend toward being "with it," "digging" from within, "putting it on." In architecture there is a trend toward nonspecialized, multipurpose space. The same trend exists in clothing. And in music, art, and speech, forms dissolve and blur into one another. Popular classical composers are now Bartok, Schönberg, Berg, and Stockhausen. Their music is the antithesis of such Renaissance composers as Bach and Mozart, whose work represents the bygone era of the Gutenberg galaxy. It is interesting to note that McLuhan welcomes the very same dissolution of distinct forms of expression which Boorstin (1961) so deplores, thereby clearly clashing with that man's conservatism. McLuhan also explains to us the nature of the successful modern television personality that Boorstin so abhors (the celebrity, the human pseudoevent). Consider, for example, presidents Kennedy and Nixon; McLuhan suggests that Kennedy was a shaggy, blurry identity; he could have been a doctor, a professor, a football player, or a grocer; he was the perfect television personality. Nixon is a sharp, intense personality, a definite *type;* television is not an appropriate medium for such a man. It might be interesting to speculate as to whether Nixon abstained from television appearances because of this realization. McLuhan suggests that there are appropriate television personalities (Johnny Carson) and appropriate motion picture (hot) characters (John Wayne). The latter must represent definite types, good, evil, strong, weak. Motion pictures give direction to the viewer; television leaves closure up to him, demanding imaginative reorganization; its image is a Seurat-like pointillistic mosaic. All in all, the Canadian author is the prime apologist for television and related phenomena, arguing that what television fosters is not passivity and "spectatoritis," but total involvement.

McLuhan views himself essentially as an outsider looking in and raising our level of consciousness about an environment in which we are so submerged that we cannot know it. Whenever a psychophysical system, for example, man, experiences an intensification of one of its senses, organs, or functions, the nervous system automatically counteracts with a self-protecting numbing of the affected area—*narcissus narcosis*—as an instinctive defense mechanism. Media, from the earliest modes of communication to the computer, are extensions and intensifications of our organs, senses, and functions. If, therefore, we are so unaware of the world in which we live and of the changes occurring around us under the impact of modern communication techology, it is because we are naturally unable to face the new media-induced environmental conditions which, at the moment that they become pervasive, become invisible. We can no more be aware of our immediate conditions as fish can know water. We live in the past, in a rearview mirror society, in "Bonanza" land. Every age romanticizes the era immediately preceding it, from which it derives its guiding ideals and values, values which are therefore inevitably obsolete. However, it now becomes imperative to wake up to reality. We must all become "artists," McLuhan argues, that is, become aware of what is going on, at the cost of greater sensitivity, effort, and perhaps pain, but with the promise of an end to the constant state of repressed anxiety and stupor so characteristic of modern mass man. If we do not, the environment and the technology we have created will control us. We must realize that the medium is the message, profoundly affecting our minds and our relationships. We must reassume control over our creations. As it is, there is the danger of reversing the order of things to a state whereby the cyberneticist will be a mere servomechanism to his computer, the businessman merely an extension of his clock, as the Eskimo could be seen as just the servomechanism of his kayak, in brief a situation in which the victors belong to the spoils.

In the final analysis, McLuhan urges us to wake up, to resensitize ourselves and to cease repressing our consciousness. As a foreigner and outsider, he claims privileged status and awareness of the conditions of American mass culture. It is difficult to estimate the enormous amount of vitriolic criticism as well as unadulterated adulation this man has elicited over the years. Good recent examples can be found in Rosenberg and White (1971) (for example, Widmer's article) and in Miller (1971). The important point is that in spite of fuzzy thinking, aggravating puns, ad hoc justifications of whatever popular cultural form he happens to like, and bad hypotheses, McLuhan remains an important figure in the continuing popular culture debate. His motives seem to be those of a humanist seeking to comprehend the consequences of modern technology so as to salvage man, his freedom, and his primacy.

More and more young sociologists consider popular culture and mass culture worthy of their professional attention. For example, George Lewis (1972) has assembled a number of articles that deal with cultural, recreational, and consumptive activities typical of a variety of social groupings, including high society, the black bourgeoisie, the revolutionary blacks, the New Left, the counterculture, the middle masses, and the working class. The originality of these and other similar contributions is that they focus on areas of culture that earlier sociologists did not deign to touch, namely the leisure patterns of the middle, lower, and marginal segments of our society. This is a new and radical sociological emphasis.

One source of inspiration for pop sociology has been novelist Tom Wolfe, whose books often deal with the subcultures of outcastes, outsiders, and their extravagances. The *Electric Kool-Aid Acid Test* is a sympathetic account of a hippie family; it may go down as the best documentation of the countercultural spirit of the 1960s, as did Kerouac's *On the Road* for the 1940s. In *The Kandy-Kolored Tangerine-Flake Streamline Baby,* Wolfe focuses on a variety of popular cultural happenings, including *prole* sports. As Browne (1972:5–6) points out, "Wolfe . . . thumbs his nose at the prejudice and snobbery that has always held at arms length all claims of validity if not esthetic accomplishment of the culture of the masses."

SUMMARY AND CONCLUSION

This chapter has dealt with some unresolved issues in the sociology of leisure and popular culture. In the first part I tried to delineate the concept of popular culture and a number of other terms central to the subdiscipline. The second part of the chapter zeroed in on the controversial nature of popular culture itself. Here, the question has been whether popular culture is essentially *good* culture, or *bad* culture. While both positions have advocates ranging over a wide ideological spectrum, most of the participants in the great popular culture debate have in the past belonged to one of two camps.

The optimists argue that contemporary America is better off than any other society in history. Americans are better off because they have more leisure time and less work (White, 1971:15). This increased leisure time often leads to refinement in taste and more good culture (Toffler, 1964). Ours is not a bland mass society, but a pluralistic one (Bell, 1960) in which individuals may freely choose from a variety of cultural offerings, from highbrow to lowbrow. If leisure can be viewed as either compensatory for deprivations incurred on the job, or, to the contrary, as a spillover of the features of one's job (Kando and Summers, 1971), then according to this view of leisure and popular culture, leisure should be primarily compensatory, easy fun and no more. And finally, whatever the quality of popular culture may be, it does not serve to complain about it, since man's cultural behavior is dictated by human nature. Thus we live in the best of all possible worlds.

On the other side are the pessimists, the critics, the malcontented philosophers, ranging from conservative romantics to left-wing revolutionaries. They do not see cultural progress. While material consumption has greatly increased, this has nothing to do with leisure, they argue, and actually we work harder than

ever, precisely for the sake of consumption (de Grazia, 1964). Modern popular culture and mass culture are vulgar and uniform (Rosenberg, 1957; 1971); ours is a mass society (Mills, 1956) with increasing uniformity; thus the great popular culture debate parallels that regarding leisure. A majority of those who accept current popular culture conceive of leisure prosaically and simply as recreation from work; on the other hand, many of those who are critical of modern mass culture are also those who define leisure normatively, idealistically, as a state or activity of creativity, effort, and excellence. These two related issues are summarized in Fig. 3.

Pop sociology attempts to pass between the Scylla of bland commercialism and the Charybdis of rigid criticism. It opposes the Ivy League conservatism of establishment sociology and the Marxian dogmatism of the critical school (cf. Marcuse, 1964), but also rejects the dollars-and-cents approach typical of much of the recreation movement today (see Kraus, 1971). It remains radical and critical. Its program is the study of popular culture as an independent variable (Lewis, 1972).

I concur that sociology should not ignore the importance of popular culture. To drop the concept from our vocabulary, as has been suggested (Wilkinson, 1971), because of its elusiveness is to miss im-

	Positions	
Issues	Idealists	Realists
Leisure	Those who define leisure as an ideal (e.g., de Grazia)	Those who define leisure as recreation (e.g., Kraus)
Popular culture and mass culture	Those who feel that mass culture is bad; the pessimists (e.g., Rosenberg); the snobs (e.g., Shils)	The optimists, the apologists of popular culture (e.g., McLuhan, Wolfe); the liberals (e.g., White); the spokesmen of media and business interests (e.g., Toffler); pop sociologists (e.g., Lewis).

Fig. 3. *Leisure and popular culture: two great controversies.*

portant phenomena. As we move deeper into the postindustrial era, phenomena which seemed relatively trivial only some years ago assume increasing importance. The well-documented shift in emphasis from work to leisure and from production to consumption is, of course, a case in point. Sociology must admit that sports, music, dance, recreation, sex, games, play, and consumption are central to our social system and that to describe these processes implies neither their necessary endorsement nor their rejection.

STUDY QUESTIONS

1. Discuss the concept of culture, the various levels of culture, and the various conceptual areas within culture. Make sure you show that culture often reflects social stratification but that there are also cultural phenomena which cannot be readily stratified. Then, discuss the casual relationship between culture and structure. Discuss the two schools of thought in this regard. Why can one school be associated with Marx and philosophical materialism, and the other with Weber and philosophical idealism? Can the two positions be reconciled? Where does the concept of cultural lag fit in? What position is taken in most of this book? Why? Which position makes the most sense to you? Why?

2. Compare and contrast the meaning of the following concepts: culture, popular culture, high culture, mass culture, prole culture, subculture, contraculture, counterculture, and folk culture. Give several examples of each. Then, appraise each of these cultural areas. Can judgments be made about their relative superiority or inferiority? In other words, is there such a thing as good culture and bad culture? What have been the main arguments for such value judgments? Which sociologists have voiced them? And what have been the counterarguments? Again, by whom? Finally, how do you feel about this whole business? Since we all agree that in areas like science and technology there is such a thing as truth and expertise, why shouldn't this apply to art, beauty and culture as well? Whatever your position, make sure you give it a good thorough argument!

3. Of the various cultural domains and levels discussed in this chapter, some have received far greater attention from sociologists than others. Discuss the prevalent attitudes among sociologists toward such areas as mass culture, prole culture, popular culture, folk culture. Why have, for example, prole culture and popular culture generally been deemed unworthy of the sociologist's attention? Who has finally had the guts to look into these areas?

4. Discuss the relationship between art, money, and government. First, what is meant by *art engagé* and art for art's sake? What is wrong with both these positions? What would be a better alternative than either of these positions? Then, as far as the money issue is concerned, what can we say about poverty and alienation among artists? Why is it silly to assume that artists are generally poor and alienated during their lifetime, and that this is perhaps proper? Why can art not thrive in a laissez-faire capitalist system? What should be done about it?

5. Arguments against mass culture and popular culture range from elitist to Marxist arguments. Discuss, after having defined mass culture, some of the criticisms which have been leveled at it. What, for example, has been said in this context by elitists like Jarrell and Bell, conservatives like Boorstin, radicals like Rosenberg, and Marxists like Marcuse and Silber? The mediocrity of contemporary mass culture has been attributed to one, several, or all of the following factors: mass society, the mass media, capitalism, America, and technology. How, precisely, are these five factors supposed to be responsible for cultural deterioration? Do you agree or disagree? Why?

6. Mass culture, popular culture, and prole culture also have many supporters. These range, again, from elitists to radicals. Define these types of culture and discuss the arguments made in favor of them by conservative elitists like Shils, liberals like McLuhan and White, businessmen like Toffler, and radicals like Lewis and Wolfe. What fundamental attitude do most supporters of mass and popular culture share? Do you share their view or not? Why?

7. In the final analysis, the great popular culture debate pits only *two* types of men against each other, be they radical or conservative, elitist or egalitarian, Marxist or capitalist, revolutionary or retreatist. What, essentially, are the two opposing attitudes toward contemporary culture and cultural change in our society? What are the implications for sociologists? My own attitude is somewhere between these two. Explain how I arrive at this position, both with respect to culture and leisure. Finally, what is your own underlying attitude toward contemporary popular culture in America, and why?

8. Many still consider Marshall McLuhan the high priest of popular culture. Discuss the Canadian's basic thesis and elaborations concerning the impact of communicative technology upon human behavior and consciousness. What kind of con-

sciousness has tended to follow from iconic script, the phonetic alphabet, print, and now finally the electronic media? Give examples of how, according to McLuhan, the whole culture

today is becoming less analytic and more gestaltist, less cerebral and more intuitive. Do you or do you not agree with McLuhan's thesis, and why?

REFERENCES

Arendt, Hannah
1951 The Origins of Totalitarianism. New York: Harcourt, Brace & World, Inc.
1964 "Society and Culture." Pp. 43–52 in Norman Jacobs (ed.), Culture for the Millions? Mass Media in Modern Society. Boston: Beacon Press.

Baldwin, James
1964 "Mass culture and the creative artist: some personal notes." Pp. 120–123 in Norman Jacobs (ed.), Culture for the Millions? Mass Media in Modern Society. Boston: Beacon Press.

Baumol, William J. and William G. Bowen
1966 Performing Arts—The Economic Dilemma. New York: The Twentieth Century Fund.

Bell, Clive
1928 Civilization. London: Chatto and Windus, Ltd. and Harcourt, Brace & World, Inc.

Bell, Daniel
1956 Work and Its Discontents. Boston: Beacon Press.
1960 The End of Ideology: On the Exhaustion of Political Ideas in the Fifties. New York: The Free Press.

Belz, Carl
1969 The Story of Rock. New York: Oxford University Press.

Bensman, Joseph and Bernard Rosenberg
1963 "Mass media and mass culture." Pp. 166–184 in Philip Olson (ed.), America as a Mass Society. New York: The Free Press.

Berger, Arthur
1964 "Notes on the plight of the American composer." In Norman Jacobs (ed.), Culture for the Millions?" Mass Media in Modern Society. Boston: Beacon Press.

Berger, Bennett M.
1963 "The sociology of leisure: some suggestions." Pp. 21–40 in Erwin O. Smigel (ed.), Work and Leisure. New Haven, Conn.: College and University Press.
1971 "Audiences, art and power." Transaction (May):27–30.

Boorstin, Daniel J.
1961 The Image: A Guide to Pseudo-Events in America. New York: Harper & Row, Publishers.

Bordua, David S.
1961 "Delinquent subcultures; sociological interpretations of gang delinquency." The Annals of the American Academy of Political and Social Science 1961 (November):119–136.

Braun, D. Duane
1969 Toward a Theory of Popular Culture: The Sociology and History of American Music and Dance, 1920–1968. Ann Arbor, Mich.: Ann Arbor Publishers.

Browne, Ray B.
1972 "Popular culture: notes toward a definition." Pp. 5-11 in George H. Lewis (ed.), Side-Saddle on the Golden Calf. Pacific Palisades, Calif.: Goodyear Publishing Co., Inc.

Cohen, Albert K.
1955 Delinquent Boys. Glencoe, Ill.: The Free Press.

de Grazia, Sebastian
1964 Of Time, Work, and Leisure. New York: Anchor Books.

Dumazedier, Joffre
1968 Pp. 250 ff. in International Encyclopedia of the Social Sciences, vol. 9. New York: The Free Press.

Eisen, Jonathan
1969 The Age of Rock. New York: Random House, Inc.
1970 The Age of Rock 2. New York: Random House, Inc.
1971 Twenty-minute Fandangos and Forever Changes. New York: Vintage Books.

Ellul, Jacques
1964 The Technological Society. New York: Alfred A. Knopf, Inc.

Fortune, the Editors
1958 "$30 billion for fun." Pp. 161–172 in Eric Larrabee and Rolf Meyersohn (eds.), Mass Leisure. Glencoe, Ill.: The Free Press.

Gans, Herbert J.
1966 "Popular culture in America: social problem in a mass society or social asset in a pluralist society?" Pp. 549–620 in Howard S. Becker (ed.), Social Problems: A Modern Approach. New York: John Wiley & Sons, Inc.

Handlin, Oscar
1964 "Comments on mass & popular culture." Pp. 63–70 in Norman Jacobs (ed.), Culture for the Millions? Mass Media in Modern Society. Boston: Beacon Press.

Howe, Irving
1948 "Notes on mass culture." Politics 5 (Spring):12–123.

Hughes, H. Stuart
  1964 "Mass culture and social criticism." Pp. 142–147 in Norman Jacobs (ed.), Culture for the Millions? Mass Media in Mass Society. Boston: Beacon Press.

Hyman, Stanley Edgar
  1964 "Ideals, dangers and limitations of mass culture." Pp. 124–141 in Norman Jacobs (ed.), Culture for the Millions? Mass Media in Mass Society. Boston: Beacon Press.

Jacobs, Jody
  1972 "Wave-maker behind U. S. arts program." Los Angeles Times (February 20).

Jacobs, Norman (ed.)
  1964 Culture for the Millions? Mass Media in Modern Society. Boston: Beacon Press.

Jarrell, Randall
  1964 "A sad heart at the super-market." Pp. 97–110 in Norman Jacobs (ed.), Culture for the Millions? Mass Media in Modern Society. Boston: Beacon Press.

Kando, Thomas and Worth C. Summers
  1971 "The impact of work on leisure: toward a paradigm and research strategy." Pacific Sociological Review, (Special Summer Issue):310–327.

Kornhauser, William
  1959 The Politics of Mass Society. New York: The Free Press.

Kraus, Richard
  1971 Recreation and Leisure in Modern Society. New York: Appleton-Century-Crofts.

Larrabee, Eric and Rolf Meyersohn (eds.)
  1958 Mass Leisure. Glencoe, Ill.: The Free Press.

Lazarsfeld, Paul F.
  1964 "Mass culture today." Pp. ix–xxv in Norman Jacobs (ed.), Culture for the Millions? Mass Media in Modern Society. Boston: Beacon Press.

Lewis, George H. (ed.)
  1972 Side-Saddle on the Golden Calf: Social Structure and Popular Culture in America. Pacific Palisades, Calif: Goodyear Publishing Co., Inc.

Lionni, Leo et al.
  1964 "Mass culture and the creative artist." Pp. 176–187 in Norman Jacobs (ed.), Culture for the Millions? Mass Media in Modern Society. Boston: Beacon Press.

Lipset, Seymour Martin
  1971 "New perspectives on the counterculture." Saturday Review (March 20):25–28.

Lowenthal, Leo
  1950 "Historical perspectives of popular culture." American Journal of Sociology 55 (January):323–332.
  1964 "An historical preface to the popular cul-

ture debate." Pp. 28–42 in Norman Jacobs (ed.), Culture for millions? Mass Media in Mass Society. Boston: Beacon Press.

MacDonald, Dwight
  1963 "A theory of mass culture." Diogenes 3 (Summer):1–17.

Marcuse, Herbert
  1962 Eros and Civilization. New York: Vintage Books.
  1964 One-Dimensional Man: Studies in the Ideology of Avanced Industrial Society. Boston: Beacon Press.

McLuhan, Marshall
  1964 Understanding Media: The Extensions of Man. New York: McGraw-Hill Book Co.
  1969 "Playboy interview: Marshall McLuhan." Playboy 53–56, 59–74,157–158.

Miller Jonathan
  1971 Marshall McLuhan. New York: The Viking Press, Inc.

Miller, Walter B.
  1958 "Lower class culture as a generating milieu of gang delinquency." Journal of Social Issues. 14 (3):5–19.

Mills, C. Wright
  1956 The Power Elite. New York: Oxford University Press.

Nye, Russell B.
  1970 The Unembarrassed Muse: The Popular Arts in America. New York: The Dial Press.
  1972 "Notes on popular culture." Pp. 13–19 in George H. Lewis (ed.), Side-Saddle on the Golden Calf: Social Structure and Popular Culture in America. Pacific Palisades, Calif: Goodyear Publishing Co., Inc.

Ragni, Gerome, Galt MacDermot and James Rado
  1968 Hair, the American Tribal Love-Rock Musical, RCA Record (LSO 1150).

Read, Herbert
  1966 Art and Society. New York: Schocken Books, Inc.

Reich, Charles A.
  1970 The Greening of America. New York: Random House, Inc. and Bantam Books, Inc.

Riesman, David
  1950 "Listening to popular music." American Quarterly (2):359–371.

Rosenberg, Bernard
  1957 "Mass culture in America." Pp. 3–12 in Bernard Rosenberg and David Manning White (eds.), Mass Culture: The Popular Arts in America. New York: The Free Press.
  1971 "Mass culture revisited." Pp. 2–12 in Bernard Rosenberg and David Manning White (eds.), Mass Culture Revisited. New York: The Free Press.

Rosenberg, Bernard and David Manning White (eds.)
1957 Mass Culture: The Popular Arts in America. New York: The Free Press.
1971 Mass Culture Revisited. New York: Van Nostrand Reinhold Company.
Rosten, Leo
1964 "The intellectual and the mass media: some rigorously random remarks." Pp. 71–89 in Norman Jacobs (ed.), Culture for the Millions? Mass Media in Mass Society. Boston: Beacon Press.
Roszak, Theodore
1969 The Making of a Counterculture. Garden City, N. Y.: Doubleday & Company, Inc.
1973 Where the Wasteland Ends. Garden City, N. Y.: Anchor Books.
Roxon, Lillian
1969 Rock Encyclopedia. New York: Grosset & Dunlap, Inc.
Schlesinger, Arthur, Jr.
1964 "Notes on a national cultural policy." Pp. 148–154 in Norman Jacobs (ed.), Culture for the Millions? Mass Media in Mass Society. Boston: Beacon Press.
Shils, Edward
1964 "Mass society and its structure." Pp. 1–27 in Norman Jacobs (ed.), Culture for the Millions? Mass Media in Modern Society. Boston: Beacon Press.
Silber, Irwin
1972 "Distorted vision of despair." Guardian (January 5).
Stanton, Frank
1964 "Parallel paths." Pp. 85–91 in Norman Jacobs (ed.), Culture for the Millions? Mass Media in Mass Society. Boston: Beacon Press.
Stone, Gregory P.
1955 "American sports: play and display." Chicago Review 9 (Fall):83–100.
1972 Games, Sport and Power. New Brunswick, N. J.: Trans-Action Books.
Sweeney, James Johnson
1964 "The artist and the museum in a mass society." Pp. 92–96 in Norman Jacobs (ed.), Culture for the Millions? Mass Media in Modern Society. Boston: Beacon Press.
Taylor, A. J. W.
1968 "Beatlemania—the adulation and exuberance of some adolescents." Pp. 161–170 in Marcello Truzzi (ed.), Sociology and Everyday Life. Englewood Cliffs, N. J.: Prentice-Hall, Inc.
Ten Have, Paul
1972 The counterculture on the move: a field study of youth tourists in Amsterdam. Paper presented at the 1972 ASA meetings, New Orleans.

Theodorson, George A. and Achilles G. Theodorson
1969 A Modern Dictionary of Sociology. New York: Thomas Y. Crowell Company.
Toffler, Alvin
1964 The Culture Consumers. Baltimore: Penguin Books Inc.
Truzzi, Marcello
1968 "The decline of the American circus: the shrinkage of an institution." Pp. 314–322 in Marcello Truzzi (ed.), Sociology and Everyday Life. Englewood Cliffs, N. J.: Prentice-Hall, Inc.
Tumin, Melvin
1957 "Popular culture and the open society." Pp. 548–556 in Bernard Rosenberg and David M. White (eds.), Mass Culture: The Popular Arts in America. New York: The Free Press.
Tylor, E. B.
1871 Primitive Culture, vol. 1. London: John Murray.
U.S. News & World Report
1969 "83 billion dollars for leisure—now the fastest growing business in America." (September 15):58–61.
1972 "Leisure boom biggest ever and still growing." (April 17):42–45.
van Den Haag, Ernest
1957 "Of happiness and of despair we have no measure." Pp. 504–536 in Bernard Rosenberg and David M. White (eds.), Mass Culture: The Popular Arts in America. New York: The Free Press.
1964 "A dissent from the consensual society." In Norman Jacobs (ed.), Culture for the Millions? Mass Media in Modern Society. Boston: Beacon Press.
Veblen, Thorstein
1899 The Theory of the Leisure Class. New York: The Macmillan Company.
Warshow, Robert
1970 The Immediate Experience. New York: Atheneum Publishers.
White, David Manning
1957 "Mass culture in America: another point of view." Pp. 13–21 in Bernard Rosenberg and David Manning White (eds.), Mass Culture: The Popular Arts of America. New York: The Free Press.
1971 "Mass culture revisited." Pp. 13–21 in Bernard Rosenberg and David Manning White (eds.), Mass Culture Revisited. New York: Van Nostrand Reinhold Company.
Widmer, Kingsley
1971 "Generator in our mass culture machine." Pp. 102–119 in Bernard Rosenberg and David Manning White (eds.), Mass Cul-

62   LEISURE AND POPULAR CULTURE IN TRANSITION

ture Revisited. New York: Van Nostrand Reinhold Company.

Wilensky, Harold L.
1961 "Social structure, popular culture and mass behavior." Studies in Public Communications 3 (Summer):15–22.

1964 "Mass society and mass culture: interdependence of independence?" American Sociological Review (29):173–197.

Wilkinson, Doris Y.
1971 "Toward a theory of popular culture: the sociology and history of American music and dance, 1920-1968." Book review. American Sociological Review 36 (April):370–371.

Winthrop, Henry
1965 "Leisure and mass culture in the cybernating society." Journal of Human Relations 13 (1):15–22.

Wolfe, Tom
1965 The Kandy-Kolored Tangerine-Flake Streamline Baby. New York: Farrar, Straus & Giroux, Inc.

1968 The Electric Kool-Aid Acid Test. New York: Farrar, Straus & Giroux, Inc.

1971 Radical Chic and Mau-Mauing the Flak Catchers. New York: Bantam Books, Inc.

Yinger, J. M.
1960 "Contraculture and subculture." American Sociological Review (October):625–635.

Herb Taylor/Editorial Photocolor Archives

chapter 4

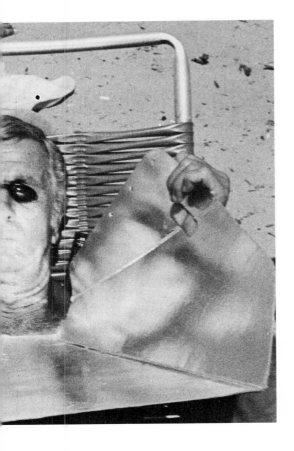

Toward the leisure society?

In Chapter 3 I contrasted the views of those who feel that Americans are well on their way to a leisure society with those of more pessimistic social commentators. It is therefore appropriate to consider the issue itself in some depth.

When speaking of the leisure society, we actually mean two different things, and much of the controversy about leisure in fact results from confusing the two. It is possible to point to the technological progress of the past few centuries and argue that this has partially freed man from work and given him free time and leisure. But one may also point out that man has not utilized this opportunity to enoble himself in the leisurely arts. Thus when the question is asked, "Are we moving toward the leisure society?" two matters are raised: have the *conditions* been created which make widespread leisure possible, and if so, has this opportunity been actualized? In this chapter, we shall see that the answer to the first question is yes, while the latter answer must be answered with a qualified no. We shall attempt to discover some of the causes for our failure, thus far, to take advantage of the opportunity provided by technology.

THE ROLE OF TECHNOLOGY

If one takes the dawn of history as baseline for an examination of man's gradual emancipation from the principle of scarcity, early technological revolutions such as the invention of fire, the Neolithic revolution (the domestication of plants, animals, and the invention of agriculture), and the fifteenth century commercial revolution (the emergence of a world economic market) must all be included as important contributing factors. However, it is mostly from the eighteenth century on that a Malthusian world view becomes clearly unnecessary; from then on, technology creates at least the preconditions and the potential for a leisure society.

It is customary to distinguish four industrial revolutions, the first of which began in eighteenth century England. In the 1770s, England began to apply water and steam power in manufacture. Textiles, for example, became an industry as a result of the introduction of such devices as the spinning jenny and the cotton gin. The factory began to replace the family-run workshop (Rose, 1969:509).

The second industrial revolution also began in England, in the late nineteenth century. Its chief contribution was the introduction of electric power, permitting more complex machinery.

The third industrial revolution began in the United States in the first part of the twentieth century. This revolution involved not so much technological innovations as changes in the forms of production. Henry Ford and other captains of industry introduced scientific management, so-called Taylorism, using the assembly line for greater specialization and mass production of cars and other commodities.

The fourth industrial revolution is the label customarily attached to the dramatic increase in productivity that is taking place in the United States and elsewhere in the Western world since the Second World War. The technological means of this latest revolution are (1) the use of such new energy sources as nuclear power and (2) automation (Rose, 1969:510). Automation goes beyond the earlier mechanization in three ways: it makes production into a continuous process through which the product moves "untouched by human hands;" it uses feedback control devices or servo-mechanisms which enable the production process to regulate itself; it uses computers for the recording, storing, and processing of information. Automation rests primarily on electronic technology.

The four industrial revolutions have had a profound impact on all areas of social life, including the structure of industry, the labor market, education, government, the family, the population, and the cultural and mental life of society. Automation is predicted to further revolutionize all areas of life in the next decades. Sociologists feel that technology can, over the long run, make for a happier people. The great increase in productivity can benefit the people in two ways: (1) real income and the standard of living may go up sharply and (2) working hours may be sharply reduced. This, in turn, leads some sociologists to predict that "there will be a great flowering of leisure-time activities for the common man" (Rose, 1969:515).

It is clear indeed that technology has produced a higher standard of living as well as shorter workweeks. William Faunce (1963) points out that output per man-hour has been rising by 2% to 3% a year over the past fifty years. In the non-govermental sector of our economy, productivity has approximately doubled over the past twenty-five years. This has raised the per capita buying power by approximately 60% and reduced the average workweek by 7.5 hours. In the past century the average workweek for nonagricultural workers has declined from about sixty-five to forty hours.

Despite such impressive statistics, however, many social commentators concur that the "flowering of leisure" predicted by such men as Arnold Rose has not yet materialized. In fact, the praise of technology's benefits is currently making place for a wave of skepticism. While the role of technology has been potentially a liberating one, many now argue that it has, instead, created new forms of bondage. Instead of making our lives richer all around, technology is often said to have contributed to a deterioration of the quality of life. We must now deal with this argument.

The case against technology

In recent years the literature indicting technology and its social consequences has been multiplying factorially. It ranges from poor journalism trying to pass for social criticism to profound philosophical scholarship. We mean such works as de Grazia (1964), Ellul (1964), Goodman (1960), Goodman and Goodman (1947), Marcuse (1962), Mills (1951), Reich (1970), Riesman (1950), Roszak (1969; 1973), Toffler (1970), Whyte (1956) and Zijderveld (1971). While these and many similar works vary widely in quality, outlook, and topic, they all have bearing on what I should like to call the new romanticism.

There is, in the latter part of the twentieth century, a new romanticism emerging in the Western world, particularly in America. The counterculture, with its short-lived rise and (perhaps temporary) fall in the 1960s, has been both its most vivid and most ephemeral manifestation to date. Much of the latter part of this book deals with the counterculture and with the possibilities it may offer out of the technological impasse. Here, we concern ourselves with the new romanti-

cism's more enduring representation in the writings of postwar culture critics. Unlike the hippies, who seem, at least for the time being, to have burnt themselves out, conforming thereby to the generalization that social movements' life span and intensity are inversely related, the modern school of cultural criticism is both older and still vigorously productive. Like the Jefferson Airplane, Gerome Ragni, and other exponents of the counterculture, most contemporary culture critics direct their attack at modern scientific technology and its concomitants in the areas of personality and social structure, in one word, the *technocracy.*

There is, then, a new romanticism in our age, a romanticism far more profound, enduring, and consequential for future history than the mere radical and hippie movements. More and more, Western intellectuals disaffiliate themselves from the scientific ethos; in the social sciences, humanistic schools are mushrooming; the call is for a return to empathy, community, and nature; ecology and conservationism mean, of course, the rediscovery of nature; in the writings of social critics, bureaucracy and dehumanization have become nearly synonymous; this surely is a far cry from that great initiator of organizational analysis, Max Weber. Thus, while admitting the uniqueness of any new social situation, we may nevertheless characterize much of the contemporary intellectual climate as partaking in an era of neoromanticism.

The term technocracy is convenient because it encompasses the totality of the neoromanticist's target. It covers, in the first place, the three areas which Jacques Ellul (1964) feels to have been invaded by technology—economic technique, organizational technique, and human technique. Economic technique—the application of mechanization, automation, and "scientific management" in agriculture and industry so as to increase the production of material commodities—is of course our most immediate referent when dealing with technology. This is where technology's benefits have been most frequently emphasized, as they have been the most obvious. Yet it is in this area, too, that technology's evils were first signaled. While Marx and the Marxists attribute the industrial worker's alienation from his labor more to the relations of production (capitalism) than to the forces of production (technology), today, workers' "alienation" generally means the boredom that results from assembly-line technology. The industrial revolutions, first mechanization and later automation, have so fragmented and monotonized the production process that work has become tedious and meaningless. This is the first argument against industrial technology. One sometimes also hears the corollary that the quality of mass production is inferior to that of handicraft, that quality is, in fact, on the way out. For example, great violins have presumably not been built since Stradivari's death; as an example from within modern industry, but with similar logic, one hears that with cars, for instance, the Volkswagen, recent models are inferior to older ones; the implication is, again, that the introduction of the latest laborsaving devices has further undermined the product's quality.

Ellul's critique of the technological society becomes more pronounced in the next two areas of technique. The second area that has fallen prey to technification since the first industrial revolution is social organization. It is an error, the Frenchman argues, to reduce the Industrial Revolution to the introduction of mechanical technique. Actually, it leads to the systematization of everything, from law to language, from measures to urban planning. Organizational technique is most evident in the massive modern state and its bureaucratized government.

What Ellul deals with at this point is, of course, echoed by many other contemporary social critics. This is the problem of bureaucratization, a major facet of technocracy. As early as 1950, David Riesman focused on the problem, soon to be followed by Mills (1951), Whyte (1956), and a continuing flow of subsequent contributors (for example, recently, Reich, 1970, and Roszak, 1973). Riesman attempted to show that the consecutive phases of the Industrial Revolution produce new breeds of men. For example, contemporary industrial society produces the typically other-directed new middle class. While consumption has replaced production as the primary concern of this new typical American, this has not led to true leisure. And, most central in Riesman's critique, individualism is rapidly disappearing. C. Wright Mills' description of the new middle class is even more severe. Due to industrialism, corporateness, and bureaucracy, the new professional and white collar workers are becoming "cheerful robots," automatons. William Whyte treats the same theme: the emergence of the "organization man" —that middle-class, group-oriented, managerial suburbanite—as a consequence of the bureaucratization of modern society. The theme is currently presented to us again, by sympathizers of the counterculture. Reich's three consciousnesses merely restate that early industrialism produced a hard working individualist, contemporary industrialism produces a bureaucratic conformist, and hopefully that the counterculture will lead us out of the technocratic impasse. Roszak, too, attacks modern bureaucracy on the grounds of its dehumanizing effects. The historian's emphasis is mostly on the scientific ethos, which presumably underlies, and is to be blamed for, the increasing systematization and objectification of human interaction, which then takes bureaucratic forms.

The third domain that is invaded by

technique is the human self. Ellul shows that man himself, at last, becomes the object of technique, a means to be manipulated through a variety of "scientific" procedures. We see the emergence of human technique everywhere, in education, work, propaganda, amusement, sport, medicine. The so-called "behavioral sciences" are its clearest example. As a result, the formula for the future is man-the-machine, with total emphasis on adaptation. The future is likely to be a *biocracy,* without place for such concepts as virtue and conscience. Man, Ellul argues, will be alienated not only from his work, but from his recreation as well, since that is also becoming increasingly technical. Furthermore, increasing flight from reality into illusory worlds through drugging and psychological repression will produce the triumph of the unconscious. Man will adapt totally, become an integral part of the group. Integration and adaptation, then, are the key words for an understanding of the future. Individuals will be anesthetized against such socially disruptive tendencies as values, religion, love, emotions, and prejudice. Mind and instinct will be integrated, and so will group and individual. Everyone will be equally happy—and bored.

Ellul's argument against human technique is the clearest case of humanism. It vehemently attacks the type of behavioristic brave new world proposed subsequently by Skinner (1970). In the age-old controversy, it sides unequivocally with free will and against determinism. As with the first two arguments against technocracy, the dehumanization argument also finds advocates in many different quarters. Rozak's recent book (1973) also indicts the "automatization of personality" under the impact of human techniques. Not only do we have the behavioral sciences, psychotherapy foremost, representing the authoritarian manipulation of man's mind, but we also have the "nihilism of the new biology," which tampers with nature itself, as it promises (or threatens) to produce test-tube humans. Roszak's voice is merely the latest addition to a tradition that in some ways includes such men as Herbert Marcuse and even Freud, the general point being that modern technological civilization fragments human personality, forces man to repress essential needs, deprives him of the experiential gestalt enjoyed by primitive man, and thus reduces him to a mechanized and dehumanized entity. Zijderveld's concept of "intellectual Taylorism" summarizes nicely modern man's intellectual predicament as perceived by many contemporary culture critics. Automation is taking place not only in industry, but in thought as well. It is a characteristic of modern science. As Western societies become automated, bureaucratized, and pluralized (i.e., fragmented), Zijderveld argues, they move away from what Dutch historian Romein called the *common human pattern.* Western man's experience, therefore, is becoming increasingly unnatural or *abstract.*

Today the major thrust of the neoromantic critical school is, perhaps, directed at a fifth target to be discussed here, the scientific ethos upon which the technocracy is founded. Roszak clarifies the relationship between science and technocracy as follows: "by technocracy is meant that social form in which an industrial society reaches the peak of its organizational integration" (1969:5) and "that society in which those who govern justify themselves by appeal to technical experts who, in turn, justify themselves by appeal to scientific forms of knowledge. And beyond the authority of science, there is no appeal" (1969:8).

The neoromantic rebellion, whether that of California hippies, French students, or disaffiliated historians like Roszak himself, is thus against empiricodeductive science. It rejects deductive logic as a criterion for validity, embracing value and experience instead. It rejects the ethos of objectivity and embraces subjectivity instead. It rejects positivism and embraces mysticism. Roszak's work contains demonstrations of modern science's dehumanizing practices. For example, the author describes how Herman Kahn's Hudson Institute plans to develop strategies to integrate hippies into the social system and how to exploit the possibilities of programmed dreams. An Appendix offers us such cases as a psychological study of death-row prisoners' responses to their pending execution, biologists' proposals for the creation of Frankenstein-like reconstituted live humans, and the use of computer simulation to *determine* what human behavior ought to be regarded as normal. A recent case that one would want to see included in Roszak's Appendix is the Tuskegee experiment, in which a study of the effects of syphilis involved the use of a control group (black prisoners) exposed to the disease and let to deteriorate and die for purposes of scientific observation. More generally (and apart from such gross but presumably relatively rare perversions of scientific practice), the argument is that the very nature of positivistic science—emphasizing objectivity, quantification, deterministic causality, detachment, and manipulation of variables, as well as study objects—reduces man to an object, to a means, and thus dehumanizes him.

A sixth point against modern technology was popularized recently by Toffler. The main argument, in his *Future Shock,* is that modern technology has speeded up the pace of life and the rate of social and cultural change to the point of strain. Future shock is the disease of change, the cancerous growth of uncontrolled and accelerating change. As Toffler sees it, "behind [this] lies that great, growling engine of change—technology" (1970:25). This trouble was, of course, identified much earlier by Og-burn (1922) and named cultural lag. Some segments of society (e.g., technology) change more rapidly and more easily than others (e.g., culture and personality). Toffler's original contribution consists in arguing that man's capacity to absorb change may be finite, and that to go beyond the overload point may cause massive social and psychological breakdown. The author's own position combines, totally unsatisfactorily, a warning against this particular technocratic danger, with technocratic solutions for it! Yet the social and psychological disorientation that may be one of technology's latest consequences is well worth noting.

A seventh negative feature of the technological society is now coming to the fore in full vigor as we approach final energy depletion and irreversible environmental destruction. When the neoromanticist advocates a return to nature, when the ecology movement urges us to save nature, when the megalopolis is perceived as the ultimate perversion of urbanism, we are not merely faced with an ideological alternative, but quite possibly with the only viable strategy for survival. As these words are being written, the Los Angeles basin is being hit by the first serious smog alert of the season. Parents are advised by radio to keep their children indoors, and some wise individuals have already begun to use their masks as they move about the city. Meanwhile, the federal Environmental Pollution Agency has just announced its permission to postpone the final application of pollution standards to the automobile industry. That the critical ecological point has been reached is evidenced in a different fashion as well. For the first time in history we are running out of a basic fuel. We shall undoubtedly purchase massive amounts of oil from the Middle East, but the more fundamental point is that the energy crisis has arrived. While it is thus far only the *unlimited* use of energy which has come to an end, it is from here on merely a matter of time and *quantitative* change before American society, its culture and lifestyle, are *qualitatively* altered. In its environmental aspect, our industrial civilization seems just to have reached the threshold of scarcity.

In conclusion, it should be clear that the neoromantic argument is much more than a mere attack against material technology in our own society. It is a sweeping indictment of technocracy everywhere, of today's entire world culture. As Roszak reminds us, technocracy is not the exclusive product of capitalism, but of accelerating industrialism. The "technological coalescence" (1973:19) has united the world into a technocratic culture initially exported by the West. Today, we may distinguish between suave technocracies (the U. S., Western Europe, Japan), vulgar technocracies (the socialist states), teratoid technocracies (Nazi Germany), and comic opera technocracies (the so-called developing nations). Economic and technological development have become the new world religion. Thus the neoromanticists, unlike Rousseau, Thoreau, Tönnies, and Jung, to mention but a few predecessors, have no place to go and nothing to do but to actively try to reform spaceship earth, in which they, as everyone else, are trapped. Since technology was initially believed to promise the leisure society, we may now reexamine that possible avenue out of the technological impasse.

What happened to leisure?

It is Sebastian de Grazia who, more than anyone else, is responsible for destroying the myth that technology has freed many from work, and for leisure. Throughout his now classic *Of Time, Work and Leisure,* the philosopher-social scientist argues and at times almost irrefutably demonstrates that more often than not the machine has led to a de-

crease in freedom, a decrease in free time, and a decline of leisure.

In the first place, even if we equate for a moment leisure with free time (an unwarranted procedure, as shall be seen in a moment), it is not clear that the machine has led to a shorter work week and to more free time. As far as the length of the work week is concerned, the familiar statistics that seem to indicate substantial gains over the past century (cf., Faunce, 1963; de Grazia, 1964, Appendix) are misleading. When corrections are made for such things as moonlighting, commuting, woman's work, and do-it-yourself activities, most of the alleged gain in nonwork time is frittered away. Whereas it is said that the average workweek has declined since the mid 1850s by more than thirty hours (from about seventy hours in 1850 to less than forty hours today), de Grazia demonstrates that the weekly gain is actually closer to 8.5 hours, and even that amount is not unambiguously "free," as much of it goes to such work-related activities as expense account lunches and moving to a new job. Thus de Grazia concludes that "comparisons in our favor are delusive. Since 1850 free time has not appreciably increased. It is greater when compared with the days of Manchesterism or of the sweatshops of New York. Put alongside modern rural Greece or ancient Greece, though, or medieval Europe and ancient Rome, free time today suffers by comparison, and leisure even more" (1964:83).

Second, let us consider what men actually choose to do with the extra time technology has supposedly given them. Faunce (1963:86) indicates that "the benefits of increased productivity have been distributed between income and leisure on roughly a 60-40 basis, 60% going into greater income and 40% for more leisure time." And "thus far a further reduction of the work week has not become an immediate collective bargaining objective of American trade unions generally"

(1963:87). What we are gaining, then, is primarily time to earn more money. And as far as the 40% that goes into "leisure," what most men actually think of doing with this "leisure time" is once again indicated by de Grazia: "When Americans are asked why they would like more free time, they answer typically that they could then get the shopping done, or get the children to the dentist, etc." According to a study by Matthew Arnold (quoted in de Grazia, 1964:482), to the question "What would auto workers do, had they more leisure time?" the answers ranked as follows: (1) work around the house, 96.8%, and (2) spend more time with the family, 76.8%. In other words, de Grazia concludes, "they mention such unfree things because they assume 'free' means off-the-job."

Americans, then, have not even been able to translate time off the job into free time. Such time is often taken up by busy work or second jobs. As de Grazia shows, due to advertising and other capitalistic "shapers of choice," our strongest drive is to *consume* and to *own* whatever industry produces, advertises, and sells. We call this "having a good time," and this is what the ideal of leisure has been perverted into. "Poverty brings one kind of corruption, prosperity another" (1964:4).

There is, of course, some free time left over. But is this truly free? Here a third argument can be made to show that machines are not conducive to freedom. As de Grazia indicates in his film paralleling *Of Time, Work and Leisure* (same title), "technology is no friend of leisure," because it "industrializes time" and brings forth the "tyranny of the clock" both on and off the job. Whatever saving of time there might be is inevitably fragmented, and timing is imposed upon the population due to the schedule of industrial society. And Seligman adds, "as the mode of work was increasingly directed and specified by advancing technology, it

became less flexible, offering less freedom and maneuverability to the individual" (1965:339). Thus automation, by subjecting man to mechanization, dehumanization, the impersonal movement of the clock, monotony, and conformity, makes both work and leisure enslaving. While man is by instinct a *homo faber* (Veblen, 1914; Seligman, 1965), technology has made him an *animal laborans*, replacing community by the collective, alienating the individual from his fellowmen, and at the same time causing the loss of individual self-identity (1965:351ff). For free time to be truly free, it must be available at one's whim, and this means that work, too, would have to be optional and deautomated. Thus industrial technology imposes rigidity and fragmentation on *all* time allocation, work as well as nonwork. As Huizinga noted, if leisure were genuinely free activity, it would generate seriousness, just as the play of children is serious. Thus leisure ought to be a serious activity, but instead, it has been corrupted by the technology of industrialism and thereby converted into unfree engagements of time (Seligman, 1965:356).

Furthermore, "the more timesaving machinery there is, the more pressed a person is for time." Think of electric home appliances. To purchase and repair them costs money and therefore extra work. To use them necessitates rigorous scheduling of activities. "To save time through machines, then, is not easy" (de Grazia, 1964:315).

The most crucial argument, however, is a fourth one made by de Grazia and his followers. "Machines give us free time, perhaps, but not leisure. We must create leisure ourselves. Leisure requires a sacrifice. Anybody can have free time. Not everybody can have leisure. Free time is a realizable idea of democracy. Leisure is not fully realizable, and hence an ideal, not alone an idea. . . . Leisure refers to a state of being, a condition of man, which few desire and fewer achieve" (1964:5). Seligman indicates that just as work, which is meaningful, must be distinguished from labor, which is meaningless, so leisure, too, must be distinguished from meaningless pastime. "Meaningful leisure shares with work the function of transmitting the values of a culture" (1965:354).

Thus in the end, value judgments must be made. No student of leisure and recreation can avoid them. George Soule (1957) recognizes this when he asks what we mean by a "rewarding experience." What do we mean when we say that activity X is more rewarding than activity Y? Could we make statements such as that two hours of leisure activity X are worth more than two hours of leisure activity Y? In short, we must address ourselves to the problem of the *worth* of various ways of spending time. With this question, we have come full circle, back to the central question raised in the previous chapter: Are Americans utilizing whatever increased free time they have in a rewarding fashion? Are not mass recreation, passive spectatoritis, and the mass culture conveyed by the mass media signs of serious flaws in our society's time use, flaws perhaps to be remedied along lines suggested by de Grazia?

For free time to be translated into leisure, our entire social system would have to change. For example, democracy as conceived today—laissez-faire market forces determining mass leisure—would have to be replaced by an enlightened despotism that would teach the masses true leisure.

Also, the machine's supremacy would have to come to an end. This could come about, de Grazia suggests, if economic failure (for example, overproduction followed by recession) or military failure undermined sufficiently our faith in technology. Had the author written a decade later, he would no doubt have identified the ecology movement as a further con-

tributor to the growing disenchantment with technology.

In conclusion, while technology logically held the promise of leisure, it has led, instead, to hard labor, consumerism, the tyranny of the clock, the fragmentation of time even off the job, and, finally, to passive and unfree recreation, not leisure. It is modern technology, Seligman argues, which has created the problem of the complete fission of work and leisure. Leisure has been converted into a mirror image of modern work. It is equally meaningless and equally incapable of carrying the burden of culture.

The major thesis of this book, in line with de Grazia, McLuhan, Ogburn, Seligman, Toffler, and a majority of the other sources I base my arguments on, is that if leisure is a contemporary social problem, it is essentially a problem in cultural lag. While political, technological, economic, and social-structural changes may all to some extent be advanced as partial solutions to America's *malaise,* if it is indeed granted that there is a malaise, the basic root of this condition must be located in the value system. In the next discussion, we begin to examine this problem.

THE ROLE OF VALUES

If we have failed, thus far, to establish true civilization and the good life, despite the greatest abundance the world has ever seen, it must obviously be because we are, in our inner selves, still incapable of reorienting ourselves to a world view that would be more attuned to the conditions created by the new technology.

It is voguish to depict our society as constantly and rapidly changing, possibly at an accelerated pace (Toffler, 1970). We are said to be living in a dynamic and progressive society on the move, where the pace of life is rapid, where growth and change are the only constants, to the point of inflicting painful "future shock" on some of us. All this presumably distinguishes us from those societies that are tribal, feudal, or in some other way more traditional and hence more static. However, this self-congratulation may be delusory (and such statements are indeed generally self-congratulatory, for despite all that may be said to be wrong with rapid change, the connotation inevitably equates change with progress and assigns to *us* a near monopoly over both). Closer scrutiny reveals that, insofar as overall social systems go, our society's character has changed perhaps less drastically than that of, say, Soviet society, Japan, Africa, India, perhaps even Western Europe. Let us admit this: while technologically, economically, demographically, and ecologically America rose in less than 200 years fron nonexistence to world supremacy, culturally and politically it has covered perhaps less ground than most other parts of the world.

Let us put it another way. If it were possible to return to our midst, in Rip van Winkle fashion, an early American, this man would probably have less difficulty adjusting than someone bridging the same time span in Japan, China, or Africa. Socially our society has been relatively stable; politically it is among the ten or twelve most conservative nations in the world; culturally it has changed relatively slowly. We have the oldest written constitution in the world and the oldest unbroken political regime. While we were indeed the first new nation (Lipset, 1963), our cultural and political history has, after that, been less revolutionary and more continuous than that of a majority of nations. In sum, while we have extended the boundaries of the technological infrastructure further than that of any other society, our cultural superstructure has been surprisingly static.

To view quantitative technological growth for qualitative cultural change, as done, for example, by Toffler, is an error. What is truly surprising is not that Americans have walked on the moon but that they often still feel and reason as their forefathers did. It is this observation which led Marshall McLuhan to generalize that each age draws its idealized values from the preceding era. Thus our mass culture's hero is the chivalrous cowboy, just as the medieval knight was Europe's romantic flight from the harsh reality of the Industrial Revolution. American mass culture is characterized by "Bonanza"-land romanticism, while the typical relationship is actually the bureaucratic one; we continue to identify the good life with the outdoors and the farm, while nearly all of us live in cities; we insist on the individualism of private cars, private homes, and the sanctity of private property in all areas of life, while conditions increasingly demand collective action and public solutions. What is truly amazing is not the rapidity of technological change, but the slowness with which technological, social, and political possibilities are accepted. What, for example, are the barriers to large-scale conversion to diesel or electric engines, as well as to mass transit? They are not technological, but political and cultural. Our social problems are not the fault of technology; they are the fault of our stubborn unwillingness to use available solutions, *including technological ones.*

The cultural lag that is most relevant for our topic is, of course, Americans' recalcitrant economic attitudes. In the next few pages, I discuss some of these attitudes, their history, and their distribution over the social strata.

The Protestant ethic, inner-direction, and consciousness I

In Chapter 1 we traced the work ethic in Western society, emphasizing, as Weber (1958) did, the role of Calvinism in fostering the capitalist mentality. It was pointed out that the typical early American not only valued hard work but is also alleged to have been an individualist. While the accuracy of the stereotype cannot be totally demonstrated, the fact that early Americans are repeatedly described in these terms—from Riesman's (1950) inner-direction to Reich's (1970) consciousness I—leads credence to such a description.

Elsewhere in this book I also trace America's changing national character and the emergence of the consumption ethic. Here, the point to remember is that work remains at the core of personal identity and as a source of meaning and mental health. Whatever else may have changed in our value system, the meaning of work has not, at least not significantly. Disregarding for a moment social class (work is, of course, less meaningful to the unskilled working class than to the middle-class professional or businessman, but so was alienation from work widespread among the proletariat even at the height of consciousness I), it can be said that work continues to function, for most, as a foundation of psychological stability and motivation.

The vocabulary justifying work may have changed from an ethicoreligious one to a psychological one. In an earlier era, work was seen as God's will, as virtue itself; laziness, for example, an afternoon spent in idleness, was a sin worthy of a formal church confession the following Sunday as recently as during our own childhood. The Freudian vocabulary seems already somewhat less old-fashioned. One works, according to Freud, not to satisfy God but one's superego. In fact, the ability to work was an integral part of Freud's conception of mental health. As dogmatic Freudianism has gradually been discarded for a more general psychotherapeutic vocabulary, the "health" functions of work have nevertheless been retained. As we are told by

contemporary psychiatrists, work is therapeutic, therapy for pain, loneliness, rejection, the death of a loved one, failure in love. And most recently, we have the new existential psychology which, while avoiding the value-laden concept of mental health and refraining from directing us to any specific activity, emphasizes the need for meaning (Frankl, 1963) and self-actualization in man's life, recognizing nevertheless that for both of these, work remains the single most common base.

Thus whatever form the ideology of work takes in successive eras, its psychological functions seem to remain unaltered. Absence of work produces anxiety, meaninglessness, the great inner void. As sociologists have shown (Jahoda-Lazarsfeld and Zeisl, 1932), unemployment is traumatic. It may produce mental illness, violence, alcholism, even suicide. Economic recessions are accompanied by rises in such social pathologies, as well as increases in violent collective behavior. Retirement is all too often seen by the aging employee as an approaching nightmare, the last step before death. And indeed, the self-fulfilling prophecy takes place when, so frequently, retirement signals the onset of psychological and physical decay, a decay that might be postponed were the individual given the cherished right to continue to work and enjoy work's motivational impact.

Gerontologists and recreation sociologists (e.g., Havighurst, 1957, 1960; Havighurst and Friedmann, 1954; Kaplan, 1960) attempt to fill the void in the lives of the retired, primarily by devising satisfactory recreational activities and facilities. We are told that some Scandinavian countries and other European social democracies have made greater headway toward alleviating the distress and enriching the lives of their senior citizens. Whatever the case may be, the fact that retirement and unemployment are psychologically so traumatic and socially so problematic is due to our prevailing value system. Retirement, as de Grazia argues in his motion picture, "should be a beginning, not an end." And while unemployment generally refers to the *forced* idleness suffered by those who can least afford it, there is another kind of unemployment which ought to be pursued, not avoided: leisure.

As with any widespread behavior pattern, there has been a tendency to lift work from the realm of *culture* and to reassign it to human *nature*. Nineteenth century industrial civilization produced such concepts as the *instinct of workmanship* and emphasized the concept of *homo faber*. It led Marx, Veblen, and others to the conclusion that only through work can man truly fulfill himself. Yet nature has produced not only man the worker, but also man the player —Huizinga's *homo ludens*. To justify the existing meaning of work on the grounds of human nature is to commit the common ethnocentric fallacy which raises existing values and institutions to absolutes and ignores the possibility of cultural change.

Work and social class

De Grazia correctly points out that the Protestant ethic identified by Max Weber only applied to a limited segment of the population. The work ethic did not make "every man a monk." The gospel of work did not absorb the working class, only the proprietors, the clerical classes, the professionals, and the self-employed. For the worker the division of labor and mass production meant that work increasingly came in pieces, causing alienation. Thus Weber and Marx, who have often been held up as antagonists, are incorporated by de Grazia, who indicates that both were correct, Weber's typification applying primarily to the upper groups and Marx's to the working class.

Today the situation remains similar.

Sociologists have repeatedly shown the industrial worker is essentially alienated from his work. Chinoy, in his classic study of automobile workers, notes that "features of work in mass-production industry alienate the worker from his labor and from himself" (1955:85). Dubin found that "the industrial workers' world is one in which work and the workplace are not central life interests for a vast majority" (1963:68). Professionals, on the other hand, as Orzack's (1963) study of registered professional nurses shows, view their work and their workplace as central life interests. Orzack's study is particularly significant in view of the fact that he uses Dubin's "central life interest" indicators, but with nurses. The author concludes that "work is obviously a highly valued, demanding and important feature of the many roles played in our society by professionals" (1963:82). Thus the work ethic is alive and well in the professional sector of our population. Whether its absence from among what is paradoxically called the "working class" brings us closer to the leisure society is doubtful, as will now be shown.

Not only does the distribution of work values differ by social class, but so does the *availability* of work. Wilensky argues that "while the affluent society may foster an underlying preference for leisure, the emerging structure of opportunity means that a growing minority works very long hours while increasing millions are reluctant victims of too much leisure" (1963:108). With a survey of six professional groups and a cross section of the middle mass in the Detroit area, the author shows that among those who work the longest hours are found many small proprietors (59% work fifty-five hours or more per week), solo lawyers (38% do likewise), and other self-employed. On the other hand, there is a growing group of reluctant victims of leisure consisting of the involuntarily retired, the intermittently unemployed, and the chronically unemployed. While variables such as education and religion complicate the picture (Jews tend to work longer than Roman Catholics and Protestants, whose propensity to work is virtually identical), Wilensky's conclusion is that socioeconomic status is generally positively correlated to length of work week: "High income . . . slightly but consistently boosts the 55-hour rates for (given) occupational groups" (1963:120). Thus, "estimates of annual and lifetime leisure suggest that the skilled urban worker may have gained the position of his thirteenth-century counterpart [but] upper strata have, in fact, lost out" (1963:136). Today, "marginal groups are concentrated in low-income, low-status jobs. The uneven distribution of non-work time among those working and the incidence of involuntary unemployment and retirement strongly suggest that men who have gained most leisure need and want more work. Here, the 'leisure stricken' are not replacing the 'poverty stricken'; the two are becoming one" (1963:137).

We have just related two variables to social class: work values and actual work. Both are apparently present in larger quantities in the upper strata than in the lower strata. This is incongruous, because a third variable—the need for work—is, of course, greater among the lower strata. As it is, neither the upper nor the lower strata approximate the character of a leisure class. However, we may be moving toward the realignment of these three variables, as unionism and the welfare state make for increasing income equalization and material security for all, thus reducing the need for work among those who neither wish to nor can. Future social stratification may consist of a hard working, achievement oriented and not excessively wealthy professional-managerial-technocratic class on the one hand, and an idle, hedonistic, and well-fed mass on the other. This welfare proletariat would, of course, be a mere perversion of the leisure class, unless it learned, in some distant utopia, to actively seek out meaning rather than expecting to be fed bread and circuses.

The consumption ethic, other-direction, and consciousness II

Although our cultural value orientation has not brought us closer to the leisure society, complex and important changes have nevertheless occurred in the national character since the Horatio Alger era. No longer does he—nor the equally mythical Benjamin Franklin—embody the ideal typical American. However, work orientation has not been massively replaced by its polar and logical opposite, a philosophy of leisure. Instead, the national character has moved in another direction. Furthermore, while the innumerable changes brought about in our culture and national character by industrialization, urbanization, bureaucratization, technology, and affluence may seem disparate, widely divergent sources concur that there is a fairly coherent pattern. At the most general level, our culture has remained firmly sensate (Sorokin, 1947), empirical, materialistic, and egotistical, exhibiting in these respects little change since the advent of the Industrial Revolution. Contemporary sociology, for example, is, through social engineering and scientific management, still largely in the process of carrying out Comte's program.

However, within the framework of our sensate civilization, certain important changes occurred, caused primarily by two fundamental economic developments: scarcity was replaced by affluence, and the vast increase in scale totally bureaucratized an economic structure formerly based on individual or small-group entrepreneurship. As a consequence, man's modus operandi has, of necessity, become more social, less individual. On this most social commentators agree. For example, Riesman (1950) describes the emergence of other-direction; Whyte (1956) notes the advent of the "organization man"; Wrong (1970) cautions against an "oversocialized conception of man"; Wheelis (1958) deplores the loss of individual identity. The literature abounds with other related statements, for example, Reich's concept of consciousness II, which summarizes much of what is here being discussed. It could be argued that the ultimate outgrowth of the total bureaucratization of relationships would be *sociopathy,* the self then becoming merely the sum total of one's roles and devoid of that irreducible inner core of individuality called the "I." More plausibly, it may be that twentieth century man's ego contours are merely somewhat softer than those of his predecessor. It is along such lines, then, that Americans are often said to have changed culturally and social-psychologically.

But what about work and leisure? Essentially, the work ethic was replaced by the consumption ethic. Although, as we saw earlier, work remains a central life interest for many professionals, it is also probably true that meaning is increasingly found in the consumptive sector of one's life, not in the productive part. The trend was first signaled by Veblen (1899), who described the conspicuous consumption of the upper strata. Many concur that the middle masses have, since then, followed in the footsteps of Veblen's leisure class, increasingly deriving status and other meanings out of consumption rather than work. While much of the literature dealing with this is argumentative rather than empirical (e.g., Packard, 1959), the thesis is widely accepted and highly plausible.

The economic doctrine of the consumption ethic is Keynesianism (cf. Heilbronner, 1953). That of the work ethic is classical economics. Classical economic theory took its point of departure in the principle of scarcity, arguing that a laissez-faire approach to supply and demand was the shortest route to prosperity. The prime emphasis was on savings, investment, and production. To prosper, classical economists argued with perfect logic, a society must above all save rather than spend, so as to maximize the investment of capital and the production of goods. Keynesianism, on the contrary, took its point of departure in the incongruous situation created by the Great Depression, when economic needs were profound, machines, materials, and labor for their satisfaction available, yet business was at a standstill. The prime emphasis now became the *spending* of money, not the saving of it. To become prosperous again, Keynes argued paradoxically, our society must go into deep debt, spending and investing sums that have actually not yet been earned, much less saved up. Governmental deficit spending was to remove unemployment and once again create a consumer market that would provide the incentive for renewed business activity. Thus the depression was attacked where it expected it the least. Money was not pumped into the business sector so as to promote production, but into the consumer sector so as to enhance consumption, and thus production only indirectly. Deficit, inflation, and national debt were small prices to pay for the revitalization of the capitalist system itself. As de Grazia points out, our era's motto was to become "buy your way to prosperity" (1964:214). Jobs were created and workers were paid in the hope that they would, god willing, not save all their earnings but spend much of it, eventually incurring additional debts, consuming in excess of their buying power, purchasing on installment plans. The consumer was called upon to save capitalism. And so it has been ever since. As Keynes predicted in 1937, "we shall be absolutely dependent for the maintenance of prosperity and civil peace on the politics of increasing consumption" (de Grazia, 1964:214).

Today, the economic system is so firmly rooted in consumerism that a return to the predepression era is inconceivable. This is the meaning of advertising and planned obsolescence, of course, whose funtion it is to sustain the high consumption level, enchaining us ever more deeply into financial debt and ecological plunder, but without which the economic system in which we are caught up would again collapse.

From production, then, the focus in our lives has shifted to consumption, not to leisure. This is the first meaning of the consumption ethic.

Second, consumption may be the model for other leisure activities as well. Toffler's (1964) description of the culture consumers, for example, deals exclusively with quantities of high culture and their monetary equivalents, not with the qualitative experience of it. One gets the feeling from such sources that the consumption of high culture, as the purchase of cars, houses, and motor boats, may have more to do with status seeking than with leisure. Certainly acquaintance with specific works of high culture has always been a source of prestige as much as genuine gratification. Today, much symphony and theater attendance may continue to be status behavior rather than leisure.

A third manifestation of the new prevailing ethic is the hedonism typical of the increasing segment of the middle class for which sexual, narcotic, and other sensate recreational experiences are becoming central life interests. To many Americans, marijuana, mate swapping (cf. Bartell, 1972; Denfeld and Gordon, 1972), encounters, sexual affairs (see Roebuck and Spray, 1972), and plain drinking or cocktail partying are highly important and meaningful activities. This is in line with Mills' characterization of our society as being sexual

and hedonistic (1970) and, again, Sorokin's view of the sensate civilization. Thus hedonistic recreation, in addition to our society's strong emphasis on material consumption and on high-culture consumption for extra-cultural reasons, can also be viewed as an expression of the prevailing ethic which, while replacing the older work ethic, at the same time extends core features of our civilization.

Toward the leisure society, autonomy, and consciousness III?

The previous discussion argued that the work ethic has been replaced by the consumption ethic rather than by leisure. For despite changes the culture remains essentially materialistic and sensate—materialistic both in the philosophical sense of locating ultimate reality and causality in matter, as does Western reductionist science, and in the everyday sense of greatly valuing money and material possessions, and sensate, also in the philosophical sense of viewing the only source of validity as being sensory and empirical (and not, for example, deductive or intuitive), as well as in the everyday sense of deriving pleasure from sensory stimulation.

The emergence of a true leisure society would necessitate a respiritualization of our culture, the rise of a fundamentally new civilization, for example, Sorokin's idealistic or ideational system. Autonomy, that elusive quality viewed to be so desirable by Riesman (1950) and contemporary humanistic psychologists, might be a characteristic of the members of such a society. While such an alternative is utopian and ill defined, some authors have already detected a trend in that direction. I refer again, of course, to Reich (1970), Roszak (1969; 1973), and others who see in the counterculture the seeds of a radically different value system. The third consciousness differs both from the work ethic and the consumption ethic; it differs from egotistical individualism as well as superficial role playing. What it might be, as it manifests itself in leisure, is the subject of the latter part of this book.

MORE FREE TIME?

Let us now examine some of the statistics that bear on our question. Let us, first, see to what extent technology has

reduced the length of the workweek; but let us also keep in mind that statistics can be misleading, as the lifestyle and composition of the contemporary labor force are in many ways not comparable to those earlier; let us, furthermore, examine the political and economic alternatives which manifest themselves as a consequence of automation; finally, let us

Table 4-1. Length of the average workweek in agriculture and nonagricultural industries, 1850 to 1972 *

Years	All industries	Agriculture	Nonagricultural industries
1850	69.7	72.0	65.7
1860	67.8	71.0	63.3
1870	65.3	70.0	60.0
1880	63.8	69.0	58.8
1890	61.7	68.0	57.1
1900	60.1	67.0	55.9
1910	54.9	65.0	50.3
1920	49.4	60.0	45.5
1930	45.7	55.0	43.2
1940	43.8	54.6	41.1
1950	39.9	47.2	38.8
1951	40.4	47.9	39.4
1952	40.5	47.4	39.6
1953	40.0	47.9	39.2
1954	38.9	47.0	37.9
1955	39.7	46.5	38.9
1956	39.5	44.9	38.8
1957	39.1	44.2	38.6
1958	38.6	43.7	38.1
1959	38.5	43.8	38.0
1960	38.5	44.0	38.0
1961	38.6	41.1	38.3
1962	38.8	42.0	38.5
1963	38.4	43.9	37.9
1964	38.7	42.5	38.5
1965	38.0	42.1	37.7
1966	38.7	42.3	38.5
1967	38.5	43.3	38.2
1968	37.1	43.1	36.7
1969	38.0	41.8	37.8
1970	37.7	42.1	37.4
1971	37.5	43.7	37.1
1972	37.6	42.8	37.4

*Sources: 1850-1960: Sebastian de Grazia. Of Time, Work, and Leisure. © 1962 by The Twentieth Century Fund, New York. First published in 1962. First Anchor Book paperback edition, 1964. p. 419. 1961-1972: Bureau of Labor Statistics (1961-1972). The averages published by the bureau were adjusted downward, as had been done by de Grazia up to 1960, to reflect zero hours of work for those "with a job but not at work." Also, we continued to use each year's May figures, as de Grazia, so as to avoid problems of seasonal fluctuation.

highlight a promising possibility as well as a dark side of free time today: the burgeoning four-day workweek, and the specter of spreading welfare and unemployment.

A shortening workweek?

Table 4-1 indicates that the length of the average workweek seems to have declined from 69.7 hours in 1850 to 37.6 hours in 1972—a gain of 32.1 hours of free time per week.

In addition to the 32.1 hours of gain reflected in Table 4-1, the fringe benefits of paid vacation, holidays, and sick leave are estimated by de Grazia to average out to an additional 2.5 hours per week (1964:60). Furthermore, retirement is now down to 60 or 65 years, and life expectancy is longer than in the nineteenth century; these two factors add an extra three years of free time to the average individual's life as compared to the turn of the century (1964:60). Also, children remain in school longer now, postponing their absorption into the labor force. Finally, there are additional factors such as military service, unemployment, and absenteeism, which all contribute to the overall decline of the proportion of time in a man's life spent participating in the labor force.

While retirement, school, military service, and unemployment are all nonwork, it would be unreasonable to equate these activities with free time and to attempt to translate them into an average weekly increment in free time. Therefore, let us follow de Grazia's argument and hold that we have gained 34.6 hours of free time since 1850 (32.1 plus 2.5 hours for fringe benefits).

If these 34.6 weekly hours were truly a gain of free time experienced by the average American worker, there would indeed be cause for joy. However, the figure is a statistical construct which does not do justice to the complex changes that have occurred in our lifestyle. In the

first place, the averages presented in Table 4-1 include part-time jobs. With the increasing number of youngsters and married women working part time, the aggregate averages create the false impression of a steadily declining workweek. Since the early statistics do not include part-time workers, and since these were then much less common, comparisons must be based on today's full-time workers only, those working thirty-five hours or more. Our statistics differentiating between full-time workers and all workers go back only to 1948. Even so, it can be seen that it makes quite a bit of difference whether the average workweek is computed for all employed, or merely for all who work full time. Table 4-2 gives these two sets of averages, along with those for persons who were actually at work.

While the decline shown in Table 4-2 is approximately the same for full-time workers and for all employed (about 8% since 1948), we may expect that the differences would have been greater prior to 1948, when full-time workers accounted for a larger proportion of the then much longer workweek. For example, between 1940 and 1956 the proportion of the nonagricultural work force working one to fourteen hours increased from 3.2% to 4.5%, while the proportion of full-time workers declined from 83% to 79% (Zeisel, 1958:150). This is to a large extent the result of women's increased participation in the labor force. Also, whatever part-time work did exist in earlier days generally failed to find its way into official statistics. As de Grazia (1964:62-63) notes: "the boy working part time peddling newspapers or jerking sodas in the ice-cream parlor was not considered a worker." In view of these changes, the more realistic estimate of today's average workweek is found in the last column of Table 4-2. When this is done, we see that the length of the workweek goes up by 6.2 hours. Following de

Table 4-2. Change in length of workweek (average weekly hours), 1948 to 1972*

Years	All employed	All at work†	At work 35 hours or more
All industries			
1948	40.8	43.4	47.7
1953	40.0	42.1	46.4
1958	38.6	41.0	46.6
1963	38.4	40.0	n.a.‡
1968	37.1	38.7	42.4
1969	38.0	39.6	43.8
1970	37.1	39.3	43.8
1971	37.5	39.1	43.5
1972	37.6	39.2	43.8
Agriculture			
1948	48.5	52.5	63.2
1953	47.9	50.0	62.5
1958	43.7	49.6	61.9
1963	43.9	47.1	n.a.
1968	43.1	46.3	54.8
1969	41.8	45.0	54.1
1970	42.1	45.3	55.4
1971	43.7	46.9	58.0
1972	42.8	46.0	56.1
Nonagricultural industries			
1948	39.6	41.9	45.6
1953	39.2	41.2	44.9
1958	38.1	40.0	45.1
1963	37.9	39.4	n.a.
1968	36.7	38.2	41.8
1969	37.8	39.3	43.3
1970	37.4	38.9	43.4
1971	37.1	38.6	42.9
1972	37.4	38.9	43.3

*Sources: 1948-1960: Sebastian de Grazia. Of Time, Work, and Leisure. © 1962 by The Twentieth Century Fund, New York. First published in 1962. First Anchor Book paperback edition, 1964. pp. 420-421. 1961-1972: Bureau of Labor Statistics (1961-1972). All figures are for the month of May.
†The "all at work" column differs from the "all employed" column in that it excludes those with a job but not at work because of vacation, illness, bad weather, etc.
‡n.a.: not available.

Grazia with our updated figures, we subtract this amount from the 34.6 hours of free time allegedly gained since 1850, leaving now only 28.4 hours in that category.

This is not all. De Grazia (1964:64-65) reminds us of additional factors that detract from the seemingly impressive gain in free time. Looking, for example, at moonlighting, we see that the number of persons with second jobs increased from 1.8 million, or 3% of the labor force in 1950, to 3 million, or 5%, a decade later. By 1960 the average second job took up about twelve hours per week. De Grazia's estimate that moonlighting, spread out as a statistical average over the entire labor force, takes another hour of free time away, can safely be doubled for today. We are now down to a gain of 26.4 hours of free time.

And what about the fact that in 1850,

85% of the population lived in towns of less than 2,500, whereas today this has declined to 26%? When comparing work habits at these two points in time, it is important to take into account the vastly increased amount of time spent commuting to and from work. Estimating the average speed of urban traffic at twenty miles per hour for private cars and thirteen miles per hour for public transit, de Grazia (1964:66-67) subtracts another 8.4 hours of free time: that is how much each of us spends on the freeway or in the subway commuting every week. This leaves us with a gain of eighteen hours of free time.

As a further factor, de Grazia estimates that we now spend five hours per week on miscellaneous do-it-yourself jobs, *excluding* hobbies and other activities that might qualify as leisure. The author argues that these five hours of extra work were not present in 1850. For example, groceries were often delivered, and do-it-yourself activities such as painting, carpentry, plumbing, and other home repairs and improvements were not as widespread because labor costs were lower and home ownership was less general. Indeed, governmental business statistics have documented the booming do-it-yourself market (U. S. Department of Commerce, 1958:274-281), attributing this primarily to the rise, since World War II, of home ownership as one of the fundamental features of the new American way of life. Thus we may reduce the gain in free time by another five hours, leaving now thirteen hours.

Finally, let us also note that the increased participation of (married) women in the labor force has the indirect effect of lengthening the workweek by compelling men to participate in household chores. With the equalization of sex roles comes increasing male participation in domestic work. When in 1850 men worked seventy hours per week, they did not generally shop, keep house, or cook.

Today, de Grazia (1964:74) estimates that they spend 2.3 hours per week on these and related activities. This leaves 10.7 hours of weekly free time gained since 1850.

Beyond these relatively measurable factors, there are many other changes which, when examined, indicate that even a gain of 10.7 hours is questionable. For example, today nearly one fourth of the population moves annually, and much of this is for new jobs, as in the case of company executives, professors, and military professionals. How is one to estimate the amount of *work-related* time such moves entail? Similarly, what about such work-related activities as expense account lunches, business trips, office parties, and professional conventions? Beyond that we may, with de Grazia, raise the facts of the contemporary pace of life, the nerve-racking nature of many contemporary jobs, and other similar *qualitative* changes since 1850, changes which may be difficult to quantify but which ought nevertheless not to be overlooked. Thus to grant that we have even ten more weekly hours of free time than our nineteenth century ancestors is generous. Actually, "the great and touted gains in free time since the 1850's . . . are largely a myth" (de Grazia, 1964:79). And, "taking all the years of a man's life together, . . . in 1900 for every two years of work [he] spent one year outside the labor force, and that same rough 2:1 ratio holds true today" (1964:61).

In contemporary America, de Grazia continues (1964:89-90), we spend on the average ten hours and forty minutes a day on work and work-related activities. Subsistence time (sleeping, eating) takes up an average of 10.5 hours. Deducting another twenty minutes for all other miscellaneous activities (fixing the car, praying, getting a haircut), we are left with 2.5 hours of daily free time.

The principal realization, when it

comes to estimating the alleged gains in leisure in modern times, is that *in long-term historical perspective no such gain can be detected.* It is only by comparing oneself with the era of darkest Manchesterism and the inhuman nineteenth century working conditions which prompted the moral outrage of Marx and Engels that we may tenuously sustain a feeling of privilege. As Wilensky (1963:109) points out, those were unusual circumstances, caused by the economic beginnings of the first industrial revolution in Western capitalist societies. Comparisons with earlier eras do not yield such a unilinear line of progress. "Among the citizens of antiquity, as well as among primitive agriculturalists, the number of days of leisure often approached half of every year." For example, "the Roman passion for holidays reached its climax in the middle of the 4th century when days off numbered 175" (1963:109). Assuming, pessimistically, a twelve-hour day, this would leave about 2,160 working hours per year for the average Roman citizen (1963:109). Compare this with Fourastié's (1960:171-173) estimate that French clerical and "intellectual" workers worked about 2,500 hours per year in 1800 as against 3,000 to 3,500 in 1950, and one detects a gradual long-term loss of leisure time throughout history for the upper strata. Similarly, upper civil servants in Britain worked approximately 1,655 hours in 1800, but 1,955 hours after World War II (Wilensky, 1963:138).

What about farmers and urban workers? Wilensky asks. Traditional European agriculture has, until the twentieth century, put in 3,500 to 4,000 hours per year (Fourastié, 1960:164). For urban workers, certain medieval craftsmen in Paris, for example, have been estimated to have worked 194 days per year for a total of 2,328 hours (Wilensky, 1963:110). From then to 1800 the trend in nonagricultural industries has been toward far longer hours. By 1850 the average workweek in French cities was seventy hours (Fourastié, 1960:38) (exactly, as we saw, the same figure as in America). The subsequent return of annual working hours to the 1,900 to 2,500 range merely means that current work schedules once again approximate those of medieval guildsmen (Wilensky, 1963:111). Thus comparing ourselves with most of the world's past societies, we seem to be working as hard as ever, and as the curves in Tables 4-1 and 4-2 indicate, the situation seems to be stabilizing into a permanent one, with little prospect of substantial gain in leisure time in the imminent future.

Some choices before us

Getting back to our independent variable—technology—we must begin to wonder what important benefits we have actually reaped as a result of industrialization, mechanization, and automation. The enormous gains in productivity brought about by these processes are an unquestionable good. The Bureau of Labor Statistics estimates that Americans would have had to work nearly twice as long in 1940 in order to produce all the commodities that were produced in 1960 (Henle, 1963:199). Assigning a value of 100 to 1967 productivity, this index of overall output per man-hour increased from 59.7 in 1950 to 104.6 in 1970 (U. S. Bureau of the Census, 1971:224). Thus one could, in our society, maintain the same level of material production and consumption, that is, the same standard of living, and yet reduce one's average workload by nearly one half over two decades. Or let us put it this way: today the average American at work produces as much per time unit as forty of his predecessors did in 1850. If we were to work a mere 1.5 hours per week, this would, theoretically, be sufficient to sustain the same standard of living as enjoyed a century ago. Yet our work habits seem to indicate that our needs have, along with our productivity, also increased fortyfold. Our inability to translate productivity into leisure is well documented by Henle (1963:199) when he points out that only 11% of the hours that have been made available by the nation's increased productivity since 1940 are accounted for in terms of reduced hours of work, increased vacations, and paid holidays. This inability results from the fact that a choice must be made from among the benefits accruing from increased productivity.

As outlined by Faunce (1963), there are essentially three possible types of uses for our increasing productivity and affluence. Our society may enjoy an increasing amount of leisure time, or it may use the extra time to increase its personal income, or it may, finally, decide to provide services and devote its extra energy to improve the quality of life. Where the emphasis will be is a matter of politics and values. Thus far we have seen an overwhelming emphasis on the second possibility—consumerism. The statistical information in the preceding pages documents our social system's inability to convert rising productivity into leisure. As Henle (1963:200) writes, "although the average employee has more leisure time today than in 1940, many individuals continue to prefer more work to more leisure in order to maximize their income." This author phrases the issue before us succinctly when he speaks of the conflicting demands for more leisure time on the one hand and for greater income to be spent on leisure time *activities* on the other. The first possibility, then, has not been realized very well in our society, and the preceding discussion has indicated that our value system is at the root of this condition.

The third possibility perceived by Faunce is to use "the increased national product resulting from a continuation of the present pattern of working hours

plus increased productivity from automation . . . to provide funds for hospitals, schools, and other service agencies [and] for research in the social, physical, and life sciences" (1963:95). And, "the conflicting values inherent in the possibility of alternative cultural orientations toward leisure or service require the careful consideration of decision-makers in American society." This issue, then, is a political one.

Postwar developments make one thing amply clear: among the alternatives of increasing free time, increased income, and improved services, the second possibility has prevailed far more frequently than the other two. Henle (1963:199) points out, for example, that much of the *paid* leisure time gained since 1940 (holidays and vacations) actually represents payment for time which in 1940 was spent away from the plant without compensation. "A review of the changes in paid leisure between 1940 and 1960 shows that there was no major shift in the standard workweek. Perhaps the most significant development was that more than half the total gain in paid leisure resulted from increased vacation and holiday time, rather than from a reduction in working hours." The passage of the Fair Labor Standards Act in 1938 established the forty-hour workweek. However, this merely formalized the de facto situation which had already been created by the depression. Since then, while many unions have been successful in obtaining additional fringe benefits, there has been no significant further reduction of the workweek. Furthermore, while there have been noticeable gains in free time in agriculture, for such industries as printing, women's apparel, and trucking, and in many white-collar fields, it should be noted that a growing sector of the labor force works increasingly *long* hours. This includes many self-employed, much of the construction industry (which was at a standstill in the

1930s), and some public employees. For federal employees, for example, the 1951 *Annual Sick Leave Act* reduced the annual paid leave from a uniform twenty-six days to a seniority-based scale ranging from thirteen days to twenty-six days. And as the current attitude of the courts toward public employees' collective bargaining rights suggests, this growing but ununionized segment of the labor force cannot be expected to soon negotiate substantial improvements in its working conditions. Putting aside the relative gains of unionized and nonunionized sectors of the labor force, I conclude with Henle (1963:199) that indeed insofar as gains have occurred since the 1930s, they have been in income rather than leisure.

The four-day workweek [1]

In recent years, an increasing number of private companies and public agencies have begun to experiment with the four-day workweek. This trend has received widespread publicity, and the general tendency has been to view it as one more step toward the leisure society. However, it must be stated at the outset of our appraisal that this remains a *forty-hour* workweek. Let us be clear about the fact that the current push toward a four-day workweek has nothing to do with a reduction in working hours. (The same can be said for glide time, a system for giving employees the flexibility of setting their own working hours.) It concerns merely the rescheduling of the workload. This rescheduling may benefit both the employer and the employee, it may benefit one but not the other, or it may benefit neither, and these are the questions to which we shall address ourselves in this section. But the current four-day workweek concept fails to even touch upon the more important issue of the desirability of a reduction in the overall length of the workweek.

Of the three variations to four-day scheduling, the most popular is known as the 4/10/40. Here the employee works four days a week for ten hours each day. A second concept is the 4-5/9/40. In this case an individual works nine hours per day alternating weeks of four and five days. In doing this he has worked eighty-one hours in two weeks. The last alternative is the 4-1/2/9/40. By following this schedule one would work four and a half days each week, full working days totaling nine hours.

The proliferation of the four-day, forty-hour workweek in recent years has been impressive. From "the modest inroads of a few years ago," it had, by 1971, been adopted "in some form or another, by well over 500 companies throughout the U. S. and that number was steadily increasing—by an estimated 60 a month" (*Newsweek:* 1971:63).

Among the widely publicized experiments with the four-day workweek belong those initiated in the Long Beach police department, the city of Atlanta, the Boston-based John Hancock Mutual Life Insurance Co., and New York's architectural firm of Haines, Lundberg and Waehler. In each instance, those administering as well as participating in the program have been overwhelmingly enthused about it. Among the Long Beach police, morale was reported much higher and "recruiting was way up" (*Newsweek,* 1971:63). Atlanta's Mayor felt that "the four-day week benefits the employer, the employee and the general public, at no extra cost" (1971:63). Elsewhere, too, the benefits were said to outweigh the costs. Employees at the New York architectural firm generally value the extra free day, and "most [employers] report that employee morale is up, absenteeism and sick leave are down, recruiting has gained, and, in some cases, productivity has increased" (1971:63).

[1] Elizabeth Dolezal's research, which served as basis for portions of this section, is hereby gratefully acknowledged.

Any sober appraisal of the 4/10/40 concept must begin with the understanding that many of the improvements suddenly manifesting themselves shortly after the rescheduling of the workload may be the result of the so-called Hawthorne effect. As Elton Mayo and his followers of the human-relations school of industrial sociology showed several decades ago (Mayo, 1945; Roethlisberger and Dickson, 1939), sometimes increases in productivity and workers' satisfaction may be erroneously attributed to changed working conditions, when they are actually the result of the manipulation itself and the extra attention enjoyed by workers participating in an experimental project.

The proponents of the 4/10/40 concept have argued for the following eight actual or potential benefits of such a schedule: the number of qualified applicants may rise, rendering active recruitment by the company unnecessary; the turnover rate may decline; use of sick leave and absenteeism may also diminish; productivity may rise permanently, especially when one considers the use of "quiet hours," the period of time during the morning before other companies have begun business and in the afternoon when other organizations are closed. In this period of time employees would be undisturbed by customers or phone calls and they could complete individual tasks more effectively. A fifth potential advantage might be the more efficient use of equipment and facilities, as these could be used on a twenty-four-hour basis, utilizing two shifts rather than three (since each shift would work longer hours). The general increase in the employees' job satisfaction is a sixth gain. Related to this is a seventh benefit, the extra long weekends making travel and other extended leisure activities possible. Finally, the 4/10/40 program would reduce commuting by 20%, and this benefit alone might make, in our age of pol-

lution and gas shortage, the four-day workweek a blessing.

However, many of these advantages have yet to be demonstrated, and the four-day workweek may also engender some distinct problems. In the first place, management is faced with scheduling difficulties. In order to continue serving the public five days a week, rotating shifts must be devised, scheduling different workers for different days. Second, workers may experience disruption of such activities as car pools and family routines. Meal planning might become a problem (breakfast having to be eaten earlier and dinner later), and family life might be disrupted in other ways as well. A fourth problem is the fatigue factor. The physiological impact of a ten-hour working day with the added time of commuting has yet to be determined. A fifth problem might be the fact that productivity, rather than increasing, might actually decline. We already argued that the increased productivity heralded by the advocates of the four-day workweek (e.g., Poor, 1970) may be temporary, and that there is a need for longitudinal studies of this problem. We should add that use of the "quiet hours" may just as easily lead to extra loafing as to greater efficiency. In fact, my own unsystematic questioning of some employees on such a schedule revealed that one perceived advantage was indeed the ability to "rap and drink coffee for an extra hour." Finally there is the matter of moonlighting, and again, proponents and opponents of the four-day workweek come to diametrically opposite conclusions. Those who favor the 4/10/40 concept argue that it will tend to diminish the amount of overtime an individual wishes to put in because of the nature of that type of a schedule, but it is quite conceivable that the free Monday or Friday will be devoted to overtime or to a side job.

In the overall appraisal of the four-day forty-hour week, only a few pros and cons are unequivocal. The 20% reduction in commuting which it would entail is, of course, an unquestionable good. An undeniable problem is the fact that Americans are still uneasy with leisure —the central theme of this book. James Rue, quoted by Vils (1971), voiced many persons' fears when he stated that "too many families are ill-equipped and ill-prepared to cope with that much leisure time. . . . Thousands can't get along on two days off. Of all the adjustments in marriage, recreation and use of leisure time are among the most difficult. For families who enjoy things together— camping, the desert, the beach, active sports—the four-day workweek is fine. But we are a nation of spectators— movies, TV, spectator sports—and I'm afraid we'd just be watching more TV. I'm fully convinced the four-day work-week is coming—and that it could be a disaster unless we are fully prepared for it."

Thus the transition to a four-day week would not work unless other radical adjustments and education toward constructive leisure took place simultaneously. Furthermore, the crucial question is as to *whom* the four-day work-week ultimately benefits. From the standpoint of management, it signifies a highly desirable reduction in labor costs and a more efficient use of capital. The point of view of labor, on the other hand, was well phrased by Steelworkers President I. W. Abel who declared that "the four-day, forty-hour week 'was a step backward' and that 'labor's aim is a shorter workweek, not a return to a ten-hour day'" (*Newsweek,* 1971:63). Understandably, labor's leadership, all the way down from George Meany himself, opposes the 4/10/40 concept.

In sum, it is not clear whether the benefits of a four-day, forty-hour week would outweigh its disadvantages or not. What is mostly needed at this time is research, particularly longitudinal panel studies, measuring quantitative changes over time in the variables just discussed.

The four-day workweek only becomes a radical departure when it consists of four, eight-hour days, reducing the workweek to thirty-two hours. This, of course, should be the real issue, whereas the 4/10/40 concept is a pseudoinnovation. The overall reduction of the workload, its desirability and feasibility, these are the subjects of this book, not the juggling of forty hours of work per week one way or another.

Welfare and the uneven distribution of leisure

Thus far we have examined our society in toto and viewed leisure as an unquestioned good, hopefully to be enjoyed in increasing amounts of time by all. Now we must look at the various subgroups of society, show the increasingly uneven distribution of leisure, and realize nonwork's darker side. When economic and technological change provide man with a voluntary choice between extra income and added leisure, he may enjoy leisure. But when those forces *impose* leisure upon him in the form of unemployment, forced retirement, and educational and occupational obsolescence, he is no longer the beneficiary of leisure, because leisure, by definition, remains leisure only so long as it is free. Thus leisure may be a benefit to be enjoyed or, in its perverted form, an affliction to be suffered. And in America, as Wilensky argues:

While the affluent society may foster an underlying preference for leisure, the emerging structure of opportunity means that a growing minority works very long hours while increasing millions are reluctant victims of too much leisure. [1963:108]

Most of the real gain in leisure in the U.S. has come to private nonagricultural industries—especially since 1850—and most markedly in manufacturing and mining, and to agriculture in the last 50 years, especially since 1940. Professionals, executives, officials and other civil servants, and the self-employed have benefited little, and in some occupations have lost out. In such industries as all-year hotels, buslines and local railways, and telegraphic communications, the workweek did not drop below 44 hours until the 1950s. . . .[In general] low-status jobs held by a majority of the labor force have shown the fastest drop in the workweek. [1963:111-112]

As far as the workers' lifecycle is concerned, Wilensky points out that whereas certain blue-collar jobs bring early retirement, "many professionals never stop working—they fade away, like old soldiers, pencils in hand. For reasons of both motive and opportunity, . . . the truck driver or the man on the assembly line . . . will sever his work ties earlier and more completely than the professor or physician" (1963:112-113). Thus, "men today work more years over the lifecycle than they did in 1900," and there is a minority of professionals who seem to put in increasingly many years. In sum, the author concludes, "with economic growth the upper strata have probably lost leisure. Professionals, executives, officials and proprietors have long workweeks, year-round employment" (1963:113).

What Wilensky demonstrates is that modern work schedules affect different occupational and demographic categories differentially. The author rejects the new romanticism of men like David Riesman who argue that work and play are in increasing interpenetration. Far from making work more leisurely or playful, modern technology has made it increasingly regimented, ordering the sequence and timing of tasks in more disciplined fashion, and causing more fragmentation and inflexibility of daily and weekly work schedules (1963:130). With modernization, an increasing portion of the working population becomes subject to unprecedented disciplinary constraints— a veritable straightjacket. This affects mostly those fully employed, particularly those in the massive new tertiary sector. As a consequence a second important

feature emerges: the bunching of leisure. Increases in free time have and will perhaps continue to lead to longer weekends and vacations, but not to shorter days. The consequences of such leisure bunching—a labor-saving device beneficial only to management—can be gauged from overcrowded weekends in Yosemite or from the bumper-to-bumper lines of campers crawling home on the Golden State freeway on Sunday evening. A third development of dubious value is the increasing female participation in the labor force. Wilensky sees this as the manifestation of a Parkinson's law for women (1963:133), whereby work expands so as to fill the free time created by labor-saving household appliances and declining family size, and also so as to counterbalance the drop in male participation in the labor force. The author concludes that the "female workweek is surely as long as it was a century ago. *Plus ça change, plus c'est la même chose"* (1963:134).

The major point, throughout Wilensky's discussion, is that there is a growing segment of the labor force that works increasingly hard. These are the long-hours men, primarily to be found among professionals and executives. The author's analysis (1963:113-123) rests on a survey of six professional groups and a cross section of the "middle mass." The professionals are lawyers, professors, and engineers, while the middle mass comprises clerks, salesmen, craftsmen, foremen, small proprietors, semiprofessionals, technicians, managers, and operatives with high income. The findings are striking: half the sample puts in over forty-five hours per week, and a sizeable minority works at least sixty hours. The variables that correlate most clearly with long hours include (1) high income, (2) self-employment, (3) religion (Jews work harder than Protestants or Catholics), (4) control over one's own schedule and, most significantly, (5) type of occupation (for example, solo lawyers work much harder than engineers). Correlates 2 and 4 indicate a tendency to choose, when such a choice is available, extra income over leisure. Correlate 5 indicates that hard work is not so much determined by occupational stratum or social class, as by the structural position in which one finds oneself in our changing economy. The long-hours groups are growing today because they often represent vanguard occupations, the new occupations increasingly crucial to our social system. For example, with the growing demand for education, health, recreation, welfare, and other services, those who specialize in these areas, as physicians in the past, can no longer afford not to work long hours. Systemic demands upon these specialists are such that leisure becomes an increasingly costly alternative (Wilensky, 1963:131).

It is of crucial importance to realize the *sociological* causes of man's work habits. There are many familiar psychologistic explanations for why some work harder than others: N-ach (achievement need), middle-class values fostering a deferred gratification pattern, Protestant ethic. Most such explanations are, in effect, fancy ways to say that because of socialization some men are lazier than others. However, the findings discussed here clearly point to *structural* rather than psychological determinants of work habits. An individual's schedule depends greatly upon his position in the social structure. For example, the average upper-echelon business executive has been shown to spend upward from sixty-three hours per week on work and work-related activities (Sheehan, 1958:120-121). As one moves up the social structure, duties, responsibilities, and functions increase. Another area is the academic community, where a professor may gradually acquire seniority, then tenure, be elected departmental chairman, then go on to become dean and

beyond; along that road, his involvement in committees and other administrative work greatly increases, and so do a variety of other functions.

Until recently, sociologists and other liberal environmentalists were confident that an age-old controversy had been settled in their favor. We knew, or so it seemed, that the poor, the unemployed, and the underprivileged were the victims of an unfair social system. However, the war on poverty's mixed results have been followed by a backlash and a revival of old issues. It is once again fashionable to locate the cause of an individual's predicament within that individual himself. I refer at this point not to the grossest manifestations of this tendency, the neoracism which men like Shockley and Jensen (1969) cloak in pseudoscientific respectability, but rather to contributions such as Banfield's *Unheavenly City* (1968), whose thesis it is that individuals who have internalized the values of the subculture of poverty and nonwork—the lower class—can probably not be made to become productive members of society, regardless of how much public money is spent trying to improve opportunity structures. The findings and arguments presented here go thoroughly against this notion. Sociological research such as Wilensky's demonstrates that hard work is a function of the economic, organizational, and structural roles and positions one occupies. While motivational factors (ambition, laziness) certainly play a role, these can themselves be the *effect* rather than the cause of an individual's occupational position. Give any man a challenging supervisory or professional role allowing for freedom, decision making, and the like, and a sixty-five-hour work schedule is suddenly more appealing than the same amount of time spent on the assembly line or collecting garbage. With economic growth and the advent of the technocracy, there is an increasing minority that works increasingly hard.

David Spilver

These are the incumbents of the technical, white-collar, supervisory, professional, and business positions which Wilensky calls the vanguard jobs.

At the same time, Wilensky continues, there are growing numbers of men condemned to leisure. "Those who have most leisure are typically reluctant victims: (1) the involuntarily retired, (2) the intermittently unemployed, (3) the chronically unemployed" (1963:126).

The main reason for the withdrawal from work among the aged is not "increases in real income, extension of pensions and social security, physical deterioration (compared with elderly men in earlier periods), or changes in self-employment, the pace of industry, or the level of employment" (Long, 1958:23, 13), but simply declining opportunity. Old men today suffer from (1) educational and occupational obsolescence, (2) compulsory retirement and age discrimination, and (3) a decline of such old men's jobs as watchmen, tailors, guards, locomotive engineers. (Wilensky, 1963: 126). Unemployment, both partial and chronic, "is concentrated among low-status service workers, and unskilled and semi-skilled manual workers in con-

struction, manufacturing and trade (they are disproportionately very young, elderly, non-white or foreign-born" (1963:127).

In terms of the overall national unemployment rate, 1973 was a relatively good year. After having soared to 6.1% in 1971, the rate declined to 4.8% in June of 1973. Still, this meant 4,320,000 unemployed Americans, using the fairly misleading official indicator. This indicator is based on a monthly sample of personal interviews which focus on the employment status of the households sampled during the week of the twelfth day of the month (known as the survey week). To be classified as unemployed, a person must have been looking for work during the past four weeks, citing steps that were taken to secure employment, and also must have been available for work at the time of the survey. These criteria exclude persons who performed a minimum of one hour work for pay or profit during the survey period; those temporarily absent from a job for reasons of illness, vacation, or strike; all persons on layoffs or who are expected to return to work within thirty days. Thus the unemployment statistics are not always the most meaningful measure of the situation, particularly in a time of economic distress when many have become too discouraged to look for work. In 1973, while the official figure was below 4.5 million, the actual number of people who experienced some unemployment may actually have been three times as high. Furthermore, many economists feared that within a year the boom would be replaced by a recession and that the unemployment rate would rise again by 1974, and indeed it did.

Wilensky, then, concludes that historically those who have gained most leisure are those who have the least resources to enjoy it, and who actually need work the most (1963:136-137). It is indeed an ironic commentary on our affluent technocracy that the upper strata have, compared for example to the thirteenth century, lost free time and that there is a growing minority that works fifty five hours per week or more, while "the leisure class today is not a class at all but a collection of occupational groups and age categories whose members (1) have motivation and opportunity to choose leisure over income or (2) are marginal to the economy and are therefore forced into leisure."

Unemployment and involuntary retirement, then, are leisure's perverted forms. And as such, they affect different groups differentially, being far from evenly distributed over the total population. This is the crucial point. It may seem good news that unemployment is, in a given year, at about 5%, but this misses the essential issue of *distribution*. In 1971, for example, unemployment for whites was at 5.2%, but for blacks it was 9.3%; it was 3.3% for white-collar workers, but 7.6% for blue collar; 4.8% for white males, but 5.9% for white females; persons between ages of 15 and 24 accounted for fully 44% off all registered unemployed, while making up only 17.4% of the population.

Doeringer and Piore recently (1971) coined the concept of the *dual labor market*. According to these authors, jobs may be separated into two categories, "primary" and "secondary." Jobs in the primary market possess such characteristics as high wages, good working conditions, employment stability, chances of advancement, equity, and due process in the administration of work rules. Jobs in the secondary market tend to have low wages and fringe benefits, poor working conditions, high labor turnover, little chance of advancement, and often arbitrary supervision.

Doeringer and Piore theorize that the secondary market acts as a permanent and involuntary confinement to those workers with major family responsibilities. It is also characteristic of the "working poor"—those workers who hold full- or part-time jobs, yet whose earnings are still below the poverty level. Piore also equates these workers with families caught in a cycle of poverty. There is also a great deal of discrimination by the employers and workers in the primary job market. Clearly, if discrimination can enlarge the secondary labor force, thereby lowering the wages that secondary employers must pay to fill their jobs, these employers have a very direct economic stake in the preservation of discriminatory practices. It is becoming increasingly clear that the population most often relegated to the secondary job market is the same population which is burdened by forced leisure, while Wilensky's "eager beavers" are found in the vanguard jobs of the primary labor market. The existence of a labor pool consisting disproportionately of women, poor, ethnics, foreign-born, young, blue-collar, unskilled, and elderly is a product of our economic structure.

Although there may not be a way nor a justification to increase the overall amount of work to be done, the system's discriminatory nature ought and can be remedied. Public welfare, which is society's prime tool in dealing with this problem, is not inherently bad; it is merely insufficient, inadequate in its current form, and misinterpreted as to its functions. In 1971, welfare included assistance to 2 million elderly, 80,000 blind, 900,000 disabled, and 9.1 million cases of aid to families with dependent children. Thus seven out of ten welfare recipients were AFDC cases. Roughly 16% of these families received aid because of an unemployed father; most of the other are fatherless because of death, divorce, desertion, or illegitimacy. It took 85,000 welfare case workers to administer the entire program. Welfare's discriminatory nature is well expressed by the simple fact that nearly half of the AFDC families were nonwhite (*Newsweek,* 1971:23).

What is being done about this vexing social problem? The programs that our society has implemented to deal with the dual problem of poverty-unemployment since their initiation as part of the New Deal are well known and varied. Today, they range from food stamps to such local efforts as California's WIN (Work Incentive Program), which enables a parent to obtain a skill while being counseled in employment preparation, or to receive on-the-job training while still receiving a public assistance grant and free medical care.

What is so indicative of the American mind is that proposed remedies are inevitably based on the presupposition that unearned public handouts are bad and that welfare recipients must somehow be made to earn, to work for what they get. On this, current reform programs all seem to agree: idleness must be opposed; welfare must be punitive. In the fall of 1968 the Office of Economic Opportunity sponsored the so-called "Smith experiment," which was designed to determine the effects on economic responsibility of providing families with a guaranteed financial base. The study included 1,359 households selected to either receive subsidies or to act as unsubsidized control families. The heads of 8% of the households were unemployed; 66% were employed full time. All the families had less than $5,000 annual income for a family of four. A graduated schedule of payments was established, whereby some families received the maximum guarantee of $4,352 for a family of four; others a minimum of $1,741. The control group was given $10 twice a month for filing a financial statement of income and expenditures during two-week periods. The results indicated that the working families that were paid on several different "incentive" scales have a better record of earnings than the similarly measured control group denied the extra cash:

earnings increased for 53% of the families getting assistance and for only 43% not getting it; earnings declined for 29% of the families getting aid for 31% of those not getting it (Cook, 1970).

The Smith experiment has been interpreted as a demonstration of the vigor of the Protestant ethic among even the lower strata of the population. It lends support to a redefinition of the meaning and function of public welfare, a redefinition advocated by conservative administrations. According to the conservative view, welfare must not be public assistance that would enable the poor to enjoy more leisurely lives, but an *incentive* to get them to work. Hence such catchy Nixonian slogans as getting "people off the welfare rolls and on to the payrolls," or replacing welfare by "workfare."

The current administration's ideas regarding welfare reform have been embodied in President Nixon's Family Assistance Plan (FAP), designed by Daniel Moynihan and first proposed by the president in the fall of 1969. It establishes the principle of a guaranteed minimum-cash income—$1600 for a family of four, which comes to about $2460 when including the value of food stamps that may be bought. As Moynihan sees it, the $1600 is merely the base grant you work out of as your income goes up. The main thing is to get the "sudden death situations out of welfare, to make sure anybody who gets a job and earns some money keeps more than he loses. All the incentives built into FAP tell you to better yourself, be more of your own person, have fewer people asking you what you are doing." FAP remedies the present system's rigid rules, whereby "you earn an extra dollar and you are out of public housing, earn an extra dollar and you are out of Medicaid, earn an extra dollar and you are out of food stamps" (*Newsweek,* 1971:26).

There are those who feel that FAP is far too progressive already. They point out, for example, that inclusion of the working poor under its provision could nearly double the number of those on welfare. The truth of the matter is that FAP and its various amended forms now under consideration fall pathetically short of providing adequate relief for the poor. Even as a baseline, $1600 per year for a family of four is extremely low. It is embarrassing for the government of the richest nation to even propose the figure as a standard. Over a decade ago the poverty line had, thanks, for example, to Michael Harrington (1962), already been set at nearly twice that amount. In 1970, only eight states—the Old South—had a policy of not paying more in public assistance than the FAP minimum. Most states' welfare programs were already more generous than the Nixon proposal. Furthermore, as *Newsweek* (1971:29) reports, "the federal booster drops off when the family's own income goes above $3920, *safely above the poverty line*"! The National Welfare Rights Organization, which represents the interests of the poor, advocated in 1971 a guaranteed minimum income of $5500.

FAP would also require all able-bodied adults, except mothers of preschool children, to sign up for job training, and the program would provide 150,000 new job-training slots and a network of day-care centers for half a million children, so that mothers—the majority of nonworking adults now on welfare—would be massively channeled into the job market. Most of the working poor would end up working at substandard wages of $1.20 an hour. Perhaps understandably, FAP has been accused of being a program not so much for workfare as for slavefare.

To remedy some of FAP's stinginess, Congress (Senator Ribicoff) and the administration (Secretary Richardson) agreed in 1972 to raise the cash baseline to $2600, but that election year saw no progress in welfare reform. By 1973 FAP and related bills were still languishing in congressional committees and presidential desks. Whatever the details of the ultimate compromise would be, any new welfare arrangement would continue to include those discretionary areas so demeaning to the poor. Local authorities would continue to determine what kinds of irregular income to ignore, how often checks are to be disbursed, and what property the family may have and still be eligible for aid. Typical perhaps of public and official attitudes toward welfare is a February 28, 1972, resolution of the Sacramento County Board of Supervisors summarized in the following covering memo:

It is recommended that (the) Board adopt the attached resolution prepared by County Counsel to designate welfare fraud investigators employed by the Sacramento County Welfare Department as peace officers.

MORE LEISURE?

In the previous discussion we examined the alleged increase in free time created by technology during the past century. Granting that there has been such progress if we compare today to the middle of the nineteenth century, we saw that it was nevertheless far more mediocre than is customarily assumed, particularly when realizing the differential impact of economic modernization upon the various segments of the population. Clearly, the many optimistic statements one encounters about a rapidly declining work load and a boom in free time and recreation are more voguish than factual.

Now, I must ask a follow-up question: if we assume that Americans have, in 1973, a certain amount of free time, can this be equated with leisure? In this discussion I attempt to show that free time and leisure are not necessarily identical. While people may have more free time, they may not necessarily have more leisure. To answer the question, one must define leisure. While it is difficult and probably undesirable to arrive at a concise definition of leisure,[2] it is nevertheless possible to zero in on the meaning of the term. We know from de Grazia's works that leisure does not derive its meaning from time or from work; it is therefore not the same thing as free time or nonwork. Leisure is a quality rather than a behavior; it is not *what* one does, but *how* one does it. Leisure is freedom; it is that which people choose to engage in. What is work to some may be leisure to others. A fundamental fact about leisure, then, is its multivariate character.

Types of leisure

The meaning of activity, as that of all phenomena, is that which is given to it by man himself acting, or observing; it is not inherent in the thing itself. It is the meaning given to an activity that determines whether it is leisure or not, rather than its intrinsic nature. The sociology of leisure deals with certain types of meanings that activity may have, rather than a specific category of activities. If we are to examine leisure patterns, and changes therein, we must first determine the types of meanings with which we are dealing. To say that leisure means freedom is merely a beginning. Beyond that, we must distinguish a variety of social-psychological meanings which activity takes on when it is said to be leisure. Leisure may mean relaxation from work or, to the contrary, a search for excitement; it may mean creative activity, or passivity.

The various meanings which leisure activities may have for the individual are frequently polar. This was perceived by Havighurst (1957), who arrived at nineteen dimensions along which leisure activities may vary. Examples of such polarities would be autonomy (as in a solitary mountain hike) versus other-di-

rection (a cocktail party), or competition (a game of tennis) versus cooperation (love making). Others (e.g., Faunce, 1963; Kando and Summers, 1971) have also realized the variable meanings along which leisure activities can range. A list of such "significance variables" (Havighurst, 1957) could include the following items:

autonomy	vs.	other-direction
participation	vs.	spectatorship
relief from boredom	vs.	escape from involvement
activity	vs.	passivity
search for excitement	vs.	recuperation from demanding job
creativity	vs.	noncreativity
time-killer	vs.	enjoyment
self-expression	vs.	instrumentality
competition	vs.	cooperation
solitude	vs.	gregariousness
ego-integration	vs.	role-diffusion

Leisure activities can be more or less competitive, more or less autonomous, more or less creative. In fact, such characteristics may be scaled, and relationships may then be examined quantitatively. For example, a given group may receive a high competition score for its leisure activities, and this may be correlated with that group's social class or occupation. Or, individuals may score low on autonomy in leisure, and this may be related to the nature of their job or their political preferences. Much interesting research could use such a format, testing a whole variety of hypotheses in which leisure activities could be either the dependent or the independent variable.

Among the many possible significance variables along which leisure activities may vary, one factor seems to be more essential than all others, probably because it underlies many of the polar characteristics that leisure is said to assume. Whether this be referred to as creativity, activity, participation, or some other attribute, most authors seem to distinguish *on some such basis* essential-

---

[2]See Chapter 2 for a definitional discussion of the concept.

ly two types of leisure. Often the distinction implies that one of these two types (the creative, active, challenging type of leisure) is superior to the other kind (passive, spectator-like, apathetic). Whether the value judgment be implicit or not, there runs through the literature a notion that leisure activities range, somehow, at bottom, from a positive high-energy pole to its opposite.

In our culture, leisure is rarely discussed independently from work. It is assumed that the nature of man's leisure activities is influenced by that of his work. Our culture's tendency to equate leisure with re-creation (recuperation from work)[3] means that it assigns to leisure, as its primary function, the *making up for the costs of work*. Common to laymen and sociologists alike is the view that "deprivations experienced in work are made up or compensated for in nonwork activities" (Kando and Summers, 1971:314). Such compensation may be supplemental, or reactive. In supplemental compensation, desirable features (autonomy, self-expression, creativity) insufficiently present at work are pursued in the nonwork context. In reactive compensation, undesirable work experiences (fatigue, tension) are redressed in a nonwork setting. Thus one begins to see how the nature of one's work can lead to two different types of focuses in one's leisure activities—a positive goal-seeking focus, or a passive, recuperative one.

My question, here, is whether leisure is increasing, a customary assertion these days. Rather than attempting to answer the question categorically, I felt that a more meaningful effort would be to distinguish various kinds of leisure. Thus the discussion shifts from a simple quantitative approach to hypotheses about the *changing nature* of leisure. Faunce (1963:90-91) provides us with in-

teresting propositions in this regard, propositions that relate leisure to work in the customary compensatory fashion: Since automation increases the amount of leisure time *and* changes the nature of work itself, this "combination of decreased physical effort . . . and decreased working hours would make possible a decrease in the properties of time spent in recuperation from work and permit more active involvement in leisure pursuits. Since recuperative time is likely to be non-creative there would be at least the possibility for more creative use of leisure." Furthermore, "passive recuperative time being primarily self-oriented, there would also be the possibility of an increase in service-oriented activities given more liesure time." Modern automated jobs are often characterized by social isolation, the author argues, and this "may result in a larger proportion of leisure time being spent in activities involving others." Thus Faunce predicts that as a result of automation, the leisure patterns of the workers will be increasingly (1) active and creative, (2) social, (3) participatory rather than passive, and (4) a relief from boredom rather than escape from involvement. The author summarizes his argument with the statement that "for any occupational group in which work is seen as a means rather than an end in itself, leisure is less likely to represent freedom from involvement than it is freedom to become involved" (1963:91).

Faunce's prediction may be interpreted as an optimistic expectation that the quality of mass leisure will improve. However, his hypotheses are all compensatory. And as Wilensky (1960) indicates, an alternative and equally sensible view is that a man's leisure activities, far from being compensatory and therefore somewhat the opposite of his work, are often a *spillover* of the same type of activities as those required on the job. For example, jobs requiring

---

[3]See Chapter 2 for discussions of both concepts.

discipline and concentration may lead workers to compulsive leisure activities of being "busy-occupied" and "passing time" since "attitudes acquired during work become so deeply ingrained that they are often carried into the life off the job" (Blum, 1953:101). Along similar lines, Katz (1965:295) noted that "work habits and interests of the white-collar worker spill over into his family and community life," and David Riesman, too, often feels that "those who work hard also play hard."

The point to which we are leading is that the impact of mechanization and automation upon leisure can be interpreted in a fashion diametrically opposed to that given by Faunce. In fact, this—pessimistic—interpretation lies at the core of the entire critical school's indictment of technocracy's impact upon the quality of life. A theme which commonly runs through de Grazia (1964), Ellul (1964), Howe (1948), Marcuse (1964), Roszak (1969; 1973), Zijderveld (1971), and other contemporary culture critics is that the mechanization, automation, and technification which were initially the hallmark of the economy are now penetrating into all other areas of life as well, including leisure. For example, camping, sports, and outdooor activities such as rock climbing and skiing are said to be increasingly matters of technical expertise, rational utilization of learned skills, and sophisticated equipment, with little emphasis on the free and spontaneous enjoyment of the experience itself. It is, in sum, good to keep in mind that the changing nature of work causes changes in the nature of our leisure activities as well, but that the direction of these changes may not be as positive as some would have it. Just as we saw that overall gains in free time are less impressive than is frequently averred, so the *quality* of our leisure may not be a matter of unequivocal improvement either. Let us now briefly examine what

people indeed do with their leisure time.

What to do with free time?

According to de Grazia's earlier calculations (1964:89, 422), work time takes up an average of ten hours and forty minutes a day (job about eight hours, commuting, do-it-yourself, moonlighting, another two hours and forty minutes). Adding this to a daily average of 10.5 hours of subsistence time (sleeping, eating, dressing), plus twenty minutes a day for such miscellaneous activities as praying and getting a haircut, we are left with an average of 2.5 hours of free time per day. The question is, what happens during these 2.5 hours?

De Grazia finds a partial answer to this question in an earlier study of free time allocation, which he summarizes (1964:97-98, 441-445): A national probability sample of over five thousand Americans over 15 years of age was asked what leisure activities they had engaged in "yesterday," that is, the day prior to the interview. Answers were as follows:

57%	watched television
38%	visited friends or relatives
33%	worked around the yard and garden
27%	read newspapers
18%	read books
17%	drove for pleasure
14%	listened to records
11%	went to meetings
10%	engaged in special hobbies
8%	went out to dinner

In addition to these top ten (obviously, the percentages add up to more than 100 because individuals engaged in more than just one leisure activity), less popular activities included sports, playing cards, singing or playing music, movies, dances, plays, and concerts.

These findings indicate that the activities one most frequently finds discussed under leisure and recreation—sports, music, high culture—are not at all the most important ones. They are not even to be found among the top ten. The typical American leisure pattern has been well established. Studies repeatedly indicate a familiar picture. Television inevitably reigns supreme, with an average of thirty five or more hours per week per household, and the top ten activities generally include such items as visiting, gardening, reading the paper, and various hobbies.[4] While there are important subcultural, socioeconomic, and regional differences,[5] it is the essential unity of American culture which strikes us at this point. For example, gardening seems to be among the top ten American pastimes because the ownership of a single-family dwelling has been a hallmark of the way of life of the great American middle class. And television, of course, transcends social class as the prime national pastime. Thus a recent study of recreation problems in California's "urban impacted areas" (Emrie, 1970) showed that recreational priorities among these urban poor are remarkably similar to the national pattern shown above. Among low-income Californians,

the twelve most popular leisure activities ranked as indicated below.

53 % watching television
27.5% reading
17 % sewing
15 % visiting friends or relatives
13.5% going to local park
13 % going to movies
12.5% swimming[6]
11 % driving or traveling
11 % attending churches or clubs
9.5% going to beach, lake, or mountains
9.5% fishing or hunting
9 % gardening

Unlike the earlier study quoted in de Grazia, Emrie asked, more generally, "what kinds of things do you do in your spare time," thereby discoving the *popularity* of certain activites rather than their actual frequencies. This leads us to the next consideration: how do people actually feel about their spare time? What do they *prefer* to do when faced with large amounts of it? We saw earlier that the much heralded shortening of the workweek is myth rather than reality. Now we should begin to understand what lies behind this myth. Workers—blue-collar as well as white-collar—simply do not and cannot opt for leisure. Despite the lip service paid to leisure by unions and management, the truth of the matter is that our lives and our attitudes are not geared to it, and cannot be geared to it until some fundamental social change occurs. We saw earlier that productivity has been increasing at least three times as rapidly as free time. This is actually a rather generous estimate of free time gains. But granting for a moment that one third of productivity increase has gone into free time, we then seem to be accumulating cash twice as heavily as free time. Two thirds of the free time we might enjoy is plowed back into work. Moonlighting and overtime are of course cases in point. The average weekly over-

---

[4]Sources of quantitative information about leisure and recreation are practically innumerable. Several older sources may be found in the de Grazia (1964) Appendix. See, for example, table 3 (the J. A. Ward Study), tables 6 and 6a (the life study), tables 7 and 7a, tables 8 and 14 (ORC Studies). See also the Editors of Fortune (1958), the classic 1934 Lundberg et al. (1958) study, and the massive twenty four-volume study of the Outdoor Recreation Resources Review Commission (1962). More up-to-date sources are used by Kraus (1971:316-330) and, for example, several cover stories in *U. S. News & World Report* (1969; 1972).

[5]The literature dealing with the leisure activities of particular demographic subgroups is vast. Kraus (1971) treats the various demographic correlates of recreation. Toffler (1964) does likewise for high culture. Studies of the black population include Frazier (1958) and Kraus (1968). Social class is the variable in Anderson and Gordon (1964), Emrie (1970), Veblen (1899), of course, and White (1958). Occupational status is the correlate dealt with in studies such as Clarke (1958) and Gerstl (1963). Goldstein and Eichorn (1961) examine rural-urban differences. Havighurst (1957) looks at old age, and Bradshaw (1971) at education.

[6]Obviously, swimming had to loom large in a California summer survey.

time hours of production workers on manufacturing payrolls increased from 2.8 hours in 1956 to 3.4 hours in 1967 (U. S. Department of Labor, 1967). The overtime hog becomes a pervasive figure. De Grazia (1964:131) estimates that overtime averages out to an extra half hour a day for every industrial worker.

Indeed, future declines in the length of the workweek would, in all likelihood, continue to be welcomed primarily as an opportunity to perform extra work, duties and chores which time at present precludes. This, people generally feel, would be the prime benefit of more free time. Faunce (1959) asked a group of automobile workers how they might use increased leisure if it became available. Their answers are as follows:

96.8%	would work around the house
76.8%	would spend more time with the family
53.6%	would travel
48.8%	would go to ballgames, fights, hockey games
42.4%	would fish and hunt
25.6%	would engage in other hobbies
24.8%	would engage in some form of athletics
24.8%	would read more
19.2%	would go back to school or learn a trade
17.6%	would be more active in school boards, P.T.A.
16.8%	would get another part-time job
15.2%	would join more social clubs
12.8%	would engage in more political action work
11.2%	would rest, relax, loaf
4.8%	would swim, boat
2.4%	would work on car
1.6%	would engage in church activities

A Roper poll quoted in de Grazia (1964:132) asked respondents what effect a four-day, or even three-day workweek might have on people. The answers were as follows:

1. People would get soft and lazy with all that leisure time (20%).
2. People would simply get bored having too little to do (20%).
3. People would find things to do so that they would be just as busy as they are now (32%).
4. People would enjoy the extra time, relax more, and be happier (24%).

If, as the usual expression goes, "American labor has taken gains in productivity in the rough proportion of one-third more free time to two-thirds more pay" (de Grazia, 1964:480), then much of what passes for leisure is really increased buying power. The so-called leisure explosion, then, is actually a boom in consumption. Because some of this added discretionary spending is for such items as recreational vehicles, second homes, and vacation lots, the customary view is that leisure is booming.

Before dealing with this new consumption, let us note that the assumptions leading to the conclusion of a leisure boom are themselves rather tenuous; as we argued earlier, it is overly optimistic to claim that one-third of the fruits of productivity has gone into increased free time. Longitudinal comparisons must be not of average workweeks, but of amounts of *work time,* which includes commuting, moonlighting, and so on. It then appears that gains in productivity have produced much less free time than is generally assumed. Furthermore, has leisure spending really increased as a share of total personal income? According to the economist, leisure spending should reverse the pattern of food spending; as total income goes up, the share spent on food should go down and that on leisure up. Yet, as the editors of *Fortune* magazine noted nearly two decades ago (1958:162), "the leisure market is a perverse thing . . . [its] share of disposable consumer income actually declined from 14% in 1947 to about 12% in 1953, despite the phenomenal rise in income." More recently, leisure's share may have increased slightly. Using a somewhat more restricted definition of the leisure market (excluding, for example, the vast expenditures for alcohol which the *Fortune* editors counted in), *U. S. News & World Report* (1972:42-46) provides figures which suggest that the share of gross national product spent on leisure increased from 8.5% in 1965 to 8.9% in 1969. However, the staggering inflation of the 1970s reversed this trend. The Department of Agriculture stated that food allocation of 22% of disposable income was an acceptable norm, despite the fact that the share had been, only recently, below 20%. The affluent society seemed no longer so affluent. The leisure boom and the recreation explosion were replaced by commodity scarcity and energy shortage as topics of central economic concern. Not only had industrial technology failed to provide massive free time; it did not even free us from material want.

Meanwhile there is, of course, an impressive consumption market of such items as recreational vehicles and outdoor activities. What, specifically, does the so-called leisure market entail? The $105 billion that were spent on leisure in 1972 (*U. S. News & World Report,* 1972) cover the following five areas, ranked in order of magnitude: (1) recreation-sports equipment and activities, (2) vacations and recreation trips in the United States, (3) travel abroad, (4) vacation land and lots, and (5) second homes. The chart below indicates the amounts spent in these areas based on estimates for 1972.

How many Americans participate in various leisure activities? Following is a ranked list* of some major forms of recreation in the United States, indicating the approximate number of participants in each.

picnicking	82.1 million participants
swimming	77.3
attending sports events	59.4
walking for pleasure	50.3
fishing	49.4

*Sources: *U. S. News & World Report* (1969, 1972) and Kraus (1971).

NOW: 105 BILLION DOLLARS A YEAR FOR LEISURE—
AND WHERE THE MONEY GOES
BASED ON ESTIMATES FOR 1972

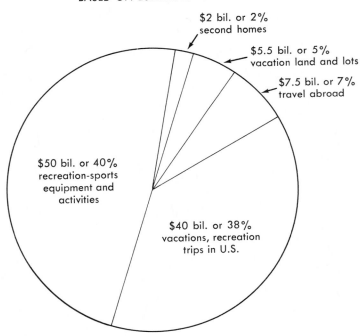

boating	41.1
visiting national parks	40
bicycling	37.1
camping	35.2
nature walks	30.5
hunting	20.9
horseback riding	16.1
waterskiing	11
golf	12
tennis	10
bird watching	7.5
travel to foreign countries	6
wildlife photography	4.9
snow skiing	4.5
surfing	1.5
skindiving	1
flying	1

Sport activities alone add up to 7 or 8 billion annual sporting occasions, that is, single participations in any sport by one person. There are in America 5 million camping vehicles, 2 million vacation homes, 500,000 swimming pools, 10,000 golf courses, and 5,500 marinas.

SUMMARY AND CONCLUSION

This chapter has probed in depth and offered facts pertinent to the issue raised previously, namely whether a leisure society may be developing. The greatest disagreement centers not on the nature and potential of modern industrial technology, but on whether that potential is being fulfilled. One finds, on the one hand, various dollars-and-cents descriptions of an allegedly booming leisure market enjoyed by more and more people who have more and more free time. On the other hand, a more exacting examination of the facts sobers one's optimism.

The first section of this chapter summarized the development of modern industrial technology, explained some of its negative consequences as perceived by the critical school and neoromanticists and, following primarily de Grazia, questioned whether the machine had brought freedom and leisure.

The second section discussed the changing yet in some fundamental ways remarkably persistent core value orientation of our civilization, suggesting that it may be the chief obstacle to the fulfillment of the leisure ideal. While attitudes toward work, amounts and intensity of work, and availability and need for work vary by social class, it was concluded that our civilization remains firmly materialistic, becomes perhaps more sensate, and is devoid of the spiritual focus found in leisure cultures.

The third section provided empirical data bearing on the issues. It was shown that Americans work today as hard as ever, and that the much heralded shortening of the work week is partly myth, partly reality. Two important contemporary work-related phenomena were discussed: the four-day work week and welfare. It was shown that the forced leisure of unemployment and retirement are vexing problems in our civilization, primarily because those who are burdened by it are those who need it the least and because nonwork signifies not only inactivity but also and most importantly psychological and social worthlessness.

In the final section, the question was asked whether our society has been able to translate technological gains into true leisure. At this time, it is clear that Americans are more affluent than their forefathers, both in time and in money. However, their difficulty has been in wisely applying these resources. It was shown in this final section that the nature of man's dominant leisure patterns, unlike that of work, is of his own choosing. Several studies tell us both what Americans would do had they more spare time, and what they in fact do with recent gains in spare time and money. It turns out that the development of our economy into a trillion dollar colossus has not produced a leisured nation. Even when using the dollar as our indicator (an inadequate index of leisure at best), we discover a sad and incongruous tendency. As men become more affluent, they should be expected to spend proportionally less in the primary sector of food and shelter and more in the discretionary areas of leisure and recreation. Yet this is not happening. We seem to be returning to a situation in which food's share of total spending will be somewhat greater than it has been in the recent past. As indicated earlier, authorities openly accept the fact that food's proportion might have to rise again to 22% of disposable income, and beyond. Such an average does not, of course, grasp the cruelty to the poor. Conversely, leisure's share has, in recent years, not quite been able to keep up with the growth of paper money: the very figures of those who argue "leisure boom" (*U. S. News & World Report,* 1969; 1972) show that during the past five years total personal income increased by about 50%, whereas the booming leisure market as defined and described in this magazine only rose by 48%. Back in 1953 the editors of *Fortune* (1958) had already noted leisure's declining share of the pie. Their explanation, at that time, was that income in modern America was more equitably redistributed (through taxes), resulting in wider mass participation in leisure but also in the decline of a lavish leisure class, thus creating *in the aggregate* the impression of less leisure. In the long run, the editors predicted, the leisure market promises to become the most dynamic component of the entire American economy.

It is the failure of this prediction and the causes of that failure that have been the focus of this chapter. Our civilization's inability to translate gains in free time and money into leisure and the causes of this failure are ultimately rooted in the very fiber of our social system. As de Grazia (1964:57) phrases it, "Along the line of history and technology's growth, leisure disappeared under the avalanche of work. When it raised its head again, it had changed form. It was now a matter of time free from work. The quest for leisure had been transformed into the drive for free time." Margaret Mead (1955:70-72) observed, we *spend, save,* and *waste* time; the Greek villager, even today, *passes* time. Here is the difference. Our very language makes us prisoners of our civilization. The dilemma is this: the same elements which were instrumental in creating the prerequisites for leisure—a materialistic and aggressive civilization able to develop technology and willing to use it—are now the obstacles to reaping the logical and beneficial outcome of these conditions. It may be that a civilization capable of creating the conditions necessary for true leisure, an affluent material base, has no use for leisure itself; and conversely, a culture whose ideology is supportive of leisure may not be able to erect leisure's material foundation. We see, consequently, that our vast affluence and the enormous energy that has been freed over the past decades are diverted into dead-end streets and blind alleys, requiring continued energy expenditure but no imagination. As we take it upon ourselves to police the world, colonize the moon, and remain first at every and all international competitive endeavors, expanding earlier societal models quantitatively but failing to innovate qualitatively, we tax ourselves and our resources to the utmost while maintaining intellectual torpor, safely steering clear from the fundamental existential and philosophical questions which would have to be faced if true cultural change were contemplated. By choosing comfort over anxiety, we also opt for decay rather than growth.

STUDY QUESTIONS

1. The title of this chapter asks "are we moving toward the leisure society?" What has been the role of the Industrial Revolution in this regard? Do you think that the consecutive industrial revolutions (How many? What were they?

When did they take place, and Where?) have had different consequences in terms of leisure? How? Technology can (1) increase the material wealth, (2) shorten the workweek, and (3) produce leisure. Give facts and figures concerning the first two (e.g., Faunce's) and speculate about the third.

2. Discuss what this book calls the neoromantic movement. Who are, among authors, social critics, and philosophers, some of this movement's major spokesmen? Why are hippies also part of this movement? The concept of technocracy sums up the major tendencies opposed by the new romanticism. What are these tendencies? For example, what are the three "techniques" discussed by Ellul? Show that Ellul's critique was anticipated by men like Riesman, Mills, and Whyte, and subsequently echoed by Reich, Roszak, and others.

3. The neoromanticists, unlike Rousseau, Thoreau, Tönnies, Jung, and other predecessors, have no place to go. Why is this? Show how today's technocracy is truly global (What four types of technocracies does Roszak distinguish?), and how the ecology movement is, therefore, the necessary and *innerworldly* romantic response to the technocracy. Finally, what does the neoromanticist have to say about the scientific ethos? What alternative truths does he embrace? (Make sure you clearly conceptualize science before embarking on a discussion of its alternatives.)

4. The logical promise held for us by technology was leisure. Instead, de Grazia and Seligman argue, it has led to labor, consumerism, alienation, and the fragmentation of time. Go over the various arguments presented in this chapter and show that technology has failed to free man for true leisure. In the first place, has technology led to a shortening of the workweek? By how much? Compared to when? Second, what do most people end up doing during most of that gained discretionary time? Third, how does industrial technology affect whatever spare time we might have? Finally, why may free time not be equated with leisure.

5. It is voguish these days to speak of "future shock" (Toffler) and of the allegedly ever more rapid (geometric) rate of change in our society. Actually, this book argues otherwise. What are some of my arguments to show that we need *more* change, not less of it? In what realms is change particularly urgent? Show that our failure to translate technological abundance into leisure can be viewed as a problem in culture lag.

6. Karl Marx's discussion of work in industrial society emphasized the aspects of boredom and alienation. Max Weber, on the other hand, focused on the Protestant work ethic as a major motivator under capitalism. How can we reconcile or simultaneously recognize these two seemingly contradictory features of work?

7. Define, describe, and explain the three value orientations or "consciousnesses" discussed in this chapter. Why are the Protestant work ethic and individualism integral aspects of consciousness I? Why are consumption, conformity and materialism typical parts of consciousness II? And what does leisure have to do with consciousness III? At what specific points in the history of America, and among which segments of the population was/is each of these three orientations dominant?

8. Much, since World War II, has been made of the so-called leisure boom. We are, allegedly, blessed with a far greater amount of leisure than were our forefathers. Using the data presented in this chapter and following the format of argument used by de Grazia, compare the current workweek with the average workweek in 1850, and the current amount of free time with that enjoyed at that time. What are the major factors to be listed in the gains column, and which factors belong in the loss column? By that method, have we lost or gained leisure since 1850? How much? And how do we compare with most other periods of human history, for example, antiquity, the Middle Ages, nineteenth century Europe?

9. Discuss the four-day workweek concept, with specific reference to the different formulas now in operation, the alleged advantages of such new arrangements and some of the problems they may cause. Who is probably the prime beneficiary of the four-day workweek? Why do the unions oppose it? What is the position taken in this book?

10. Leisure can be a benefit to be enjoyed, or an affliction to be suffered—in the form of unemployment. Using Wilensky's studies, show how those who need leisure the least have it the most, while those who could afford it the most work the hardest. Who, then, are the long-hours men, that growing minority of hard workers found mostly in the "vanguard jobs"? And who does "forced leisure" affect the most? How does this relate to the concept of the dual labor market? Finally, to deal with the problem of unemployment, the government has been considering the so-called Family Assistance Plan. What are the plan's major points? How does it propose to reform the welfare system? What are its major assumptions?

11. It is argued in this chapter that whether a person is engaging in leisure depends on the *subjective meaning* he attaches to his activity, rather than the activity itself. Thus any given

activity can be work or leisure, depending on how it is experienced. What kind of sociology of (work and) leisure has such a conception of leisure spawned? Discuss, for example, the contributions of Havighurst, and Kando and Summers and show what these sociologists try to study. Finally, discuss some of the *types* of leisure that were noted in this chapter, for example, compensatory versus spillover activities, active versus passive, individual versus gregarious. Is the *nature* of leisure and of the work-leisure relationship changing at this time? How? In which direction?

12. The final pages of this chapter deal, again, with values. Quote some of the studies discussed to show what people's priorities are when it comes to budgeting their time. What, then, is the major obstacle to the advent of the leisure society? What have we tended to do with our newly won productivity and affluence? Explain how, at this point in our history, our very strength, like that of the dinosaur, may be our main weakness from the standpoint of achieving the radical social innovations advocated by some leisure sociologists.

REFERENCES

Anderson, Charles and Milton Gordon
1964   "The blue-collar worker at leisure." Pp. 407-416 in Arthur B. Shostak and William Gomberg (eds.), Blue-collar World: Studies of the American Worker. New York: Prentice Hall, Inc.

Banfield, Edward C.
1968   The Unheavenly City. Boston: Little, Brown and Company.

Bartell, Gilbert D.
1972   "Group sex among the mid-americans." Pp. 292-303 in Joann S. DeLora and Jack R. DeLora (eds.), Intimate Lifestyles—Marriage and its Alternatives. Pacific Palisades, Calif.: Goodyear Publishing Co., Inc.

Blum, Fred H.
1953   Toward a Democratic Work Process. New York: Harper & Row, Publishers.

Bradshaw, Ted K.
1971   "Culture through education: the effect of educational experiences on cultural leisure patterns." Paper read at the 1971 Meeting of the Pacific Sociological Association, Honolulu, Hawaii.

Chinoy, E.
1955   Automobile Workers and the American Dream. Garden City, N. Y.: Doubleday & Company, Inc.

Clarke, Alfred C.
1958   "Leisure and occupational prestige." Pp. 205-214 in Eric Larrabee and Rolf Meyersohn (eds.), Mass Leisure. Glencoe, Ill.: The Free Press.

Cook, Fred J.
1970   "When you just give money to the poor." The New York Times Magazine (May 3).

de Grazia, Sebastian
1964   Of Time, Work and Leisure. New York: Anchor Books.

Denfeld, Duane and Michael Gordon
1972   "The sociology of mate swapping: or the family that swings together clings together." Pp. 304-315 in Joann S. DeLora and Jack R. DeLora (eds.), Intimate Lifestyles—Marriage and Its Alternatives. Pacific Palisades, Calif.: Goodyear Publishing Co., Inc.

Doeringer, Peter B. and Michael J. Piore
1971   International Labor Markets and Manpower Analysis, Lexington, Mass.: Heath Lexington Books.

Dolezal, Elizabeth
1972   "The four-day work week experience." Unpublished paper, California State University, Sacramento (Spring).

Dubin, Robert
1963   "Industrial workers' worlds: a study of the central life interests of industrial workers." Pp. 53-72 in Erwin O. Smigel (ed.), Work and Leisure—a Contemporary Social Problem. New Haven, Conn.: College and University Press.

Ellul, Jacques
1964   The Technological Society. New York: Alfred A. Knopf, Inc.

Emrie, William J.
1970   Recreation Problems in the Urban Impacted Areas of California. Sacramento, Calif.: State of California Department of Parks and Recreation.

Faunce, William A.
1959   "Automation and leisure." In H. J. Jacobson and J. S. Roucek (eds.), Automation and Society. New York: Philosophical Library.
1963   "Automation and leisure." Pp. 85-96 in Erwin O. Smigel (ed.), Work and Leisure —A Contemporary Social Problem. New Haven, Conn.: College and University Press.

Fortune, the Editors
1958   "$30 billion for fun." Pp. 161-172 in Eric Larrabee and Rolf Meyersohn (eds.), Mass Leisure. Glencoe, Ill.: The Free Press.

Fourastié, J.
1960   The Causes of Wealth. Glencoe, Ill.: The Free Press.

Frankl, Viktor E.
1963   Man's Search for Meaning. New York: Beacon Press.

Frazier, E. Franklin
1958   "Society: status without substance." Pp. 228-237 Eric Larrabee and Rolf Meyersohn (eds.), Mass Leisure. Glencoe, Ill.: The Free Press.

Gerstl, Joel E.
1963   "Leisure, taste and occupational milieu." Pp. 146-167 in Erwin O. Smigel (ed.), Work and Leisure—A Contemporary Social Problem. New Haven, Conn.: College and University Press.

Goldstein, Bernice and Robert L. Eichhorn
1961   "The changing Protestant ethic: rural patterns in health, work and leisure." American Sociological Review 26:557-565.

Goodman, Paul
1960   Growing up Absurd. New York: Random House, Inc.

Goodman, Paul and Percival Goodman
1947   Communities: Means of Livelihood and Ways of Life. New York: Random House, Inc.

Harrington, Michael
1963   The Other America—Poverty in the United States. Baltimore: Penguin Books Inc.

Havighurst, Robert J.
1957   "The leisure activities of the middle-aged." American Journal of Sociology 63 (September):152-162.
1960   "Life beyond family and work." Pp. 299-353 E. W. Burgess (ed.), Aging in Western Societies. Chicago: University of Chicago Press.

Havighurst, Robert J. and Eugene A. Friedmann
1954   The Meaning of Work and Retirement. Chicago: University of Chicago Press.

Heilbroner, Robert L.
1953   The Worldly Philosophers. New York: Simon & Schuster, Inc.

Henle, Peter
1963   "Recent growth of paid leisure for U. S. workers." Pp. 182-203 in Erwin O. Smigel (ed.), Work and Leisure—A Contemporary Social Problem. New Haven, Conn.: College and University Press.

Howe, Irving
1957   "Notes on mass culture." Pp. 496-503 in Bernard Rosenberg and David Manning White (eds.), Mass Culture—The Popular Arts in America. New York: The Free Press.

Jahoda-Lazarsfeld, M. and H. Zeisl
1932   Die Arbeitslosen von Marienthal, Leipzig: Hirzel.

Jensen, Arthur
1969   "How much can we boost I.Q. and scholastic achievement?" Harvard Educational Review 39:1-123.

Kando, Thomas and Worth C. Summers
1971   "The impact of work on leisure: toward a paradigm and research strategy." Pacific Sociological Review (special summer issue): 310-327.

Kaplan, Max
1960   "The uses of leisure." Pp. 407-443 in Tibbits, C. (ed.), Handbook of Social Gerontology: Societal Aspects of Aging. Chicago: University of Chicago Press.

Katz, Fred E.
1965   "Explaining informal work groups in complex organizations: the case for autonomy in structure." Administrative Science Quarterly 10 (September):204-223.

Kraus, Richard
1968   Public Recreation and the Negro. New York: Center for Urban Education.
1971   Recreation and Leisure in Modern Society. New York: Appleton-Century-Crofts.

Lipset, Seymour M.
1963   The First New Nation. The United States in Historical and Comparative Perspective. New York: Basic Books, Inc., Publishers.

Long, C. D.
1958   The Labor Force Under Changing Income and Employment. Princeton, N. J.: Princeton University Press.

Lundberg, George A., Mirra Komarovsky and Mary Alice McInerny
1958   "The amounts and uses of leisure." Pp. 173-198 in Eric Larrabee and Rolf Meyersohn (eds.), Mass Leisure. Glencoe, Ill.: The Free Press.

Marcuse, Herbert
1962   Eros and Civilization. New York: Vintage Books.
1964   One-Dimensional Man: Studies in the Ideology of Advanced Industrial Society. Boston: Beacon Press.

Mayo, Elton
1945   The Social Problems of an Industrial Civilization. Boston: Graduate School of Business Administration, Harvard University Press.

McLuhan, Marshall
1964   Understanding Media: The Extensions of Man. New York: McGraw-Hill Book Co.

Mead, Margaret
1955   Cultural Patterns and Technical Change. New York: The New American Library Inc.

Mills, C. Wright
 1951   White Collar—The American Middle Classes. New York: Oxford University Press.
Newsweek
 1971   "Welfare—the shame of a nation." (February 8):22-30.
 1972   "The welfare mess." (June 26):29.
 1973   "Careening toward phase four." (July 16):63-64.
Ogburn, William Fielding
 1922   Social Change with Respect to Culture and Original Nature. New York: B. W. Huebsch.
Orzack, Louis H.
 1963   "Work as a 'central life interest' of professionals." Pp. 73-84 in Erwin O. Smigel (ed.), Work and Leisure—A Contemporary Social Problem. New Haven, Conn.: College and University Press.
Outdoor Recreation Resources Review Commission
 1962   Commission's report in 27 volumes, Washington, D. C.: U. S. Government Printing Office.
Packard, Vance
 1959   The Status Seekers. New York: David McKay Co., Inc.
Poor, Riva
 1970   Four Days, Forty Hours: Reporting a Revolution in Work and Leisure. Cambridge, Mass.: Bursk and Poor.
Reich, Charles A.
 1970   The Greening of America. New York: Random House, Inc. and Bantam Books, Inc.
Riesman, David, Nathan Glazer and Denney Reuel
 1950   The Lonely Crowd, New Haven, Conn.: Yale University Press.
Roebuck, Julian and S. Lee Spray
 1972   "The cocktail lounge: a study of heterosexual relations in a public organization." Pp. 67-76 in Joann S. DeLora and Jack R. DeLora (eds.), Intimate Lifestyles—Marriage and its Alternatives. Pacific Palisades, Calif.: Goodyear Publishing Co., Inc.
Roethlisberger, F. J. and William J. Dickson
 1939   Management and the Worker. Cambridge, Mass.: Harvard University Press.
Rose, Arnold M. and Caroline B. Rose
 1969   Sociology—The Study of Human Relations (third revised edition). New York: Alfred A. Knopf, Inc.
Roszak, Theodore
 1969   The Making of a Counterculture. Garden City, N. Y.: Doubleday & Company, Inc.
 1973   Politics and Transcendence in Postindustrial Society. New York: Anchor Books.

Seligman, B. B.
 1965   "On work, alienation and leisure." American Journal of Economics and Sociology 24 (October):337-360.
Sheehan, R.
 1958   "The Executive Lunch." Fortune (January):120-124.
Skinner, B. F.
 1970   Beyond Freedom and Dignity, New York: Alfred A. Knopf, Inc.
Sorokin, Pitrim
 1947   Society, Culture and Personality. New York: Harper & Row, Publishers.
Toffler, Alvin
 1964   The Culture Consumers. Baltimore: Penguin Books.
 1970   Future Shock. New York: Bantam Books, Inc.
U. S. Bureau of the Census
 1971   Statistical Abstract of the United States, 1971. Washington, D. C.: U. S. Government Printing Office.
U. S. Department of Commerce
 1958   "The do-it-yourself market." Pp. 274-281 in Eric Larrabee and Rolf Meyersohn (eds.), Mass Leisure. Glencoe, Ill.: The Free Press.
U. S. Department of Labor, Bureau of Labor Statistics
 1961-1972   Employment and Earnings, monthly report.
 1967   Bulletin No. 1600 (table 65).
U. S. News & World Report
 1969   "83 billion dollars for leisure—now the fastest growing business in America." (Sept. 15):58-61.
 1972   "Leisure boom—biggest ever and still growing." (April 17):42-45.
Veblen, Thorstein
 1899   The Theory of the Leisure Class. New York: The Macmillan Company.
 1914   The Instinct of Workmanship. New York: The Macmillan Company.
Vils, Ursula
 1971   "Four-day work week—boon or bust?" Los Angeles Times (June...):18.
Weber, Max
 1958   The Protestant Ethic and the Spirit of Capitalism. New York: Charles Scribner's Sons.
Wheelis, Allen
 1958   The Quest for Identity. New York: W. W. Norton & Company, Inc.
White, R. Clyde
 1958   "Social class differences in the uses of leisure." Pp. 198-205 in Eric Larrabee and Rolf Meyersohn (eds.), Mass Leisure. Glencoe, Ill.: The Free Press.

Whyte, William H., Jr.
1956 The Organization Man. Garden City,
N. Y.: Anchor Books.
Wilensky, H. L.
1960 "Work, careers and social integration."
International Social Science Journal 12
(Fall):543-560.
1963 "The uneven distribution of leisure: the
impact of economic growth on 'free time'."
Pp. 107-145 in Erwin O. Smigel (ed.),
Work and Leisure—A Contemporary Social Problem. New Haven, Conn.: College
and University Press.
Wrong, Dennis H.
1970 "The oversocialized conception of man in
modern sociology." Pp. 29-39 in Gregory
P. Stone and Harvey A. Farberman (eds.),
Social Psychology through Symbolic
Interaction. Waltham, Mass.: Ginn-Blais-
dell.
Zeisel, Joseph S.
1958 "The workweek in American industry
1850-1956." Pp. 145-153 in Eric Larabee
and Rolf Meyersohn (eds.), Mass Leisure.
Glencoe, Ill.: The Free Press.
Zijderveld, Anton C.
1971 The Abstract Society—A Cultural Analysis of our Time. New York: Anchor
Books.

chapter 5

High culture

The general area with which this book deals is *culture* meaning certain recreational and artistic activities, not culture in its standard sociological sense. This entire area is often referred to as *popular culture,* a term which covers the mass media, mass recreation, as well as the performing arts and the fine arts. Often a triadic distinction is made between highbrow, lowbrow, and middlebrow, the three levels of a society's cultural activities (e.g., Glazer, 1964:61). It is more practical, however, to make a dichotomy between "high" and "mass." As Jacobs (1964:xi) writes, "a distinction between . . . two levels is crucial. For in a nutshell one can say that everyone is concerned with two main problems: what happens to highbrow culture in mass society? And what does the great increase in middlebrow culture do to people?" Therefore, we begin by distinguishing between *high culture* and *mass culture.*

The high culture–mass culture polarity covers at least four dimensions that may be related historically but not logically. First, mass culture simply refers to those cultural and recreational activities in which many people engage, while high culture consists of activities in which only a few participate. Thus, a first distinction is simply quantitative.

Second, high culture is used to denote the cultural predilections of the urban, aristocratic, wealthy, ruling elite, while mass culture is the culture of the masses. This is a sociological distinction in terms of stratification.

The third distinction between high culture and mass culture is qualitative, controversial, and only subscribed to by conservative intellectuals, middle-class sociologists, snobs, and Europeans. It boils down to equating high culture with good culture and mass culture with bad culture. Now this distinction is obviously rooted in the second distinction. It can be explained by the fact that those who pass judgment on the quality of culture in such a fashion, who deplore mass culture (football and rock music) and extol high culture (ballet and Brahms), themselves belong to and are spokesmen for the elitist tradition. Just as upper-class scholars earlier in Europe "demonstrated" that the masses were inferior to the elite—either genetically or environmentally—so today's elitists view mass culture as *necessarily* inferior to high culture. Quantity and quality are incompatible. We are often reminded that the same cultural products, say Dostoevski's novels, that are appreciated in their superior purity by the cultured classes may be excerpted, produced in Cinemascope, or otherwise vulgarized for mass consumption.

The fourth distinction between high culture and mass culture simply states that the two areas consist of different activities and different products, *with no necessary value judgment implied.* Thus, ballet, for example, would fall under the heading of high culture, while most spectator sports are part of mass culture. Also, within a given cultural area we have activities that are part of high cul-

ture as opposed to activities that belong to mass culture. Thus in cinema, Hollywood stands for mass culture, while high culture is represented by art pictures such as those made by Ingmar Bergman abroad and the New American Cinema in the United States. In music, popular music is part of mass culture, while classical music belongs to high culture. In literature, Ian Fleming and Jacqueline Susann belong to mass culture, while the classics and such contemporary writers as Faulkner, Malamud, and Baldwin form a part of high culture. The fact that ballet, art movies, classical music, and classical literature belong to high culture, while spectator sports, most Hollywood films, popular music, and mass literature are part of mass culture is related to the other distinctions made, particularly to the quantitative distinction. Traditionally, more people watch football games than ballet. However, we are dealing here with a distinction that is more than quantitative, as is illustrated by the fact that far fewer Americans practice, say, soccer (mass culture) than classical music (high culture).

Here, I shall mostly use the fourth distinction between high culture and mass culture. As defined in Chapter 3 (see p. 42), by high culture, I mean the recreational and artistic activities which have traditionally been separated from mass culture, such as ballet, classical music, art movies. Such activities may or may not be engaged in by many people. They may or may not be the domain of the upper strata. They may or may not be high quality. *Whether* specific high cultural activities are popular, and what their class correlates are, will be precisely among the empirical questions which we shall try to answer.

ARE AMERICANS "CULTURED"?

For many years a major debate has raged concerning the quality of American culture. Mostly, the question has been, Does high culture flourish in America? There are three possible positions on this issue—two extreme and argumentative positions that claim that America is and is not cultured, respectively, and a third more empirical middle position.

First, then, there are those who consider and have always considered America to be a cultural wasteland. This opinion has been held by numerous European critics, by elitists in general, and by upper-strata American "renegades." It is, in fact, the elitist conception of culture discussed earlier and applied to the American scene. William Waldorf Astor, for example, reputedly said: "America is good enough for any man who has to make a livelihood, though why traveled people of independent means should remain there more than a week is not readily to be comprehended" (quoted in Toffler, 1964:9).

Along similar lines, Mencken still complained well into the twentieth century that "the leading American musical director, if he went to Leipzig, would be put to polishing trombones and copying drum parts" (Toffler, 1964:23).

Such opinions may have been European or American in origin and they may have been motivated by feelings of inferiority, guilt, or snobbish elitism, but historically speaking they were correct. As Veblen (1899) showed, the leisure activities comprised under high culture have traditionally been the domain of more or less aristocratic elites. However, America's very emergence signified the replacement of aristocracy by democracy, of elitism by equality, of rigid social stratification by rapid social mobility. Thus, high culture thrived in Europe because there it was sponsored by significant elites, whereas mass culture became a possibility in America because here it acquired the support of a broad mass. Thus in American history, economic growth, technological progress, and so-

cial equalization produced the typical culture. This being essentially a mass culture, it was abundantly accused of being primitive and impoverished, at least by European standards. The only segment of North America where high culure blossomed early was the antebellum South, whose feudal social structure was as polarized as European society had been. There, theater, for example, developed early, both because of the absence of New England's Puritanism and because of an aristocratic clientele to sponsor it. In the North, theater long remained outlawed. Thus, what was said in the first chapter about America's hostility to all aspects of leisure applies to high culture *a fortiori*. The country's antileisure attitude was caused by cultural factors (the Protestant ethic) and economic conditions (the Frontier). Its animosity or indifference toward high culture in particular was the result, in addition, of mass democracy. Those who view America as a cultural wasteland look back and emphasize such historical facts.

A second category of opinions asserts more or less the opposite. Not arguing with the culture critics about America's early history, many contemporary authors nevertheless argue that we are now, finally, experiencing a cultural explosion. White, in an article entitled "Mass Culture in America: Another Point of View" (1957), concludes: "There has been such a rehearsal of all that is ugly and bathetic in our popular arts by critics . . . that it is time that the other side of the coin be examined" and he presents a "hopeful picture of our future as we go into the era of extended leisure." White's optimism is shared by others, for example, Toffler (1964). Representatives of this school of thought inevitably bombard us with statistics that allegedly show great increases in spending for all areas of high culture by Americans, thereby implying that Americans are rapidly becoming cultured, for example, White (1957): "Since 1920 more than twenty million recordings of Arturo Toscanini alone have been sold. . . . The 1955 attendance at serious music events is about double that of 1940." and Toffler (1964): "The number of volumes in public libraries has shot up from 143,000,000 in 1950 to 210,000,000 in 1960 . . . the number of art galleries in New York doubled between 1950 and 1960."

A sober appraisal of current factual developments leads to a third position. It reveals that neither the pessimists nor the optimists are entirely correct. In the next few pages I hope to show that American cultural life is rich and growing in many areas, most of all in terms of amateur participation, but that it is nevertheless difficult to speak of a cultural explosion, least of all in terms of professional developments.

Bernard Berelson is a lifelong student of mass media who has devised ingenious methods for the "quantification of quality." Particularly helpful for our purpose is a study (1964) in which he made an attempt at separating high culture from mass culture, quantifying the proportion occupied by high culture in the production and consumption of such products and media as books, magazines, motion pictures, and television programs among adult Americans. Thus, Berelson's study

boils down to estimating the extent of "culturedness" of Americans. He found, for example, that 15% of all adult book reading in America was "cultural," that is, involving such works as Twain's, Dickens', Tolstoy's and other classics. For newspapers, 1% of the total time spent with newspapers was considered "cultural." This included reading such features as literary criticism, music reviews, and Walter Lippmann's columns. In Table 5-1, I have rearranged and summarized Berelson's estimates based on thirteen cultural activities.

The results in Table 5-1 are somewhat ambiguous. Some of the estimates refer to percentages of products (movies, theater), while other figures represent the percentage of consumption. Most questionable, of course, are Berelson's subjective criteria for including certain products in high culture, while excluding other ones. Thus, commercial television programs that qualified as "cultural" included all early morning educational programs. Motion pictures qualifying as cultural included *West Side Story* and Tennessee Williams' *Sweet Bird of Youth*, but not, for example, Nabokov's *Lolita*. Rock music was excluded from the category of high culture. Nevertheless, the attempt to quantify and sift out the amount of high culture from the total

---

Table 5-1. *Percentage of various media and other products qualifying as high culture*

Concerts, operas, and ballet	100
Theater productions	25
Motion pictures	10
Commercial television viewing	n.a.*
Educational television viewing	35
Radio listening	1
Records	n.a.
Amateur Music	20
Museums	n.a.
Book Reading	15
Magazines	n.a.
Newspaper reading	1
Adult education	15

In sum, the average adult American spends 4.5% of his leisure time (figured at three hours a day) "in the presence of (high) culture."

*n.a.: not available.

body of mass culture is worthwhile. It begins to tell us something about how "cultured" Americans are.

In the following pages I document trends and developments in America in the following major cultural areas: classical music, ballet and professional dancing, theater, art movies, art, and literature.

TRENDS IN SPECIFIC AREAS OF HIGH CULTURE[1]
Classical music

In this section we deal with classical music in the following media: symphony concerts, opera, electronic media (records and radio), and amateur music.

Orchestras are by far the nations' longest-lived performing organizations. The first major American orchestra, the New York Philharmonic, was founded in 1842. It has an illustrious history, having been led by such men as Mahler (1907) and Toscanini (1928–1933). By 1939 there were approximately 600 orchestras in the United States. This increased to 1,441 by 1970—a 140% rise in thirty years, to the present point where the country has more than one half of the world's orchestras. However, the vast majority of these organizations (over one thousand) are community orchestras consisting of amateur musicians. We now have approximately thirty-three metropolitan orchestras and twenty-eight major orchestras. Some among these, for example, the Philadelphia and the Cleveland Symphonies, are among the world's best.

It is said that the audience for classical concerts is growing rapidly. For example, annual attendance at the Detroit Symphony increased from 300,000 in 1950 to 700,000 in 1960. Supposedly, twice as

many people attend concerts and recitals as major league ball games. Indeed, money spent to operate the nation's twenty-eight major orchestras increased from $13,838,000 in 1955 to $58,753,000 in 1970—an increase of 274% in fourteen years. Yet from 1947 to 1964, paid attendance for twenty-five major orchestras increased annually by a mere 1.1%. Since the population grew more rapidly than that, there has, over the period of time, been *no per capita increase in paid attendance for the typical major orchestra.*

The first recorded opera performance in America took place in 1735 (Charleston, S.C.). This art form remained rare in the United States. It has been said that the musical represents the American equivalent of the European opera. Also, operas are extremely expensive to produce professionally. Thus, due perhaps to cultural and economic reasons, by 1941 there were only seventy-seven opera-producing companies in the country, most of them amateur groups. According to the Census Bureau the number of opera-producing companies then grew to 918 by 1967. Of course this phenomenal 1,200% increase over twenty-eight years represents almost exclusively a growth in amateur opera. For in 1964, America only had seven major opera companies, plus forty professional opera-producing groups. The annual increase in the number of professional opera performances was 4.2% (between 1952 and 1964), and *annual per capita increase in paid attendance was 2.7%.*

Trends in the electronic consumption of classical music are equally ambiguous. Those who contend that we have been undergoing a cultural boom point to such facts as America's four hundred FM stations that play exclusively classical music and our annual expenditure of $90 million for 17.5 million classical records. However, the early 1960s actually witnessed a slight *drop* in the dollar volume

---

[1] Facts and figures presented in this section were drawn from Baumol and Bowen (1966), Berelson (1964), Dulles (1965), Kraus (1971), Statistical Abstracts of the United States (1971), and Toffler (1964).

of classical record sales, and this at a time when overall spending on radios, television sets, records, and instruments grew by 7% annually!

We have the same problem interpreting data on amateur music. The cultural explosion supporters write that there are "more piano players than fishermen (or at least, that pay for fishing licenses)." Indeed, the number of amateur musicians grew from 19 million in 1950 to twice that many by the late sixties, at which time $600 million were spent annually for musical instruments. However, whether these data are accurate indicators of a cultural boom depends on one's conception of culture. Berelson, for one, estimates that only 20% of amateur music has anything to do with culture. This, of course, is based on an implicit value judgment which tends to equate culture with classical, and which I do not necessarily share. However, one should indeed temper one's optimism regarding these figures when it is realized that they indicate, at best, flourishing amateurism and, at worst, mass consumerism.

Ballet and professional dancing

Ballet was introduced in the United States from France in the 1820s, but it only began to acquire popularity with Americans recently. Today, classical and modern ballet are said to be the fastest growing art form in America. According to *Dance Magazine,* the number of professional American dance groups increased from 78 in 1959 to 116 in 1964— an increase of nearly 50% in five years. Of course, these are not all high-caliber groups. There are actually only three renowned companies (the New York City Ballet, the American Ballet Theater, and the San Francisco Ballet) that specialize in classical ballet and that equal such famous foreign troupes as the Bolshoi or the Royal Ballet, plus perhaps a dozen other leading dance groups, either mod-

ern or classical. Also, the category "professional dancing" is difficult to interpret, particularly as our discussion is in the context of high culture.

With these caveats, data nevertheless indicate substantial growth. In New York the number of professional dance performances has been increasing at the annual rate of 4.2%, or 2.7% per capita (from 110 performances in 1952 to 340 in 1965). Furthermore, touring activity around the country has expanded even more rapidly—from 46 touring performances in 1952 to 199 in 1967. This was, above all, made possible by the development of the college and university circuit.

Here, then, is a performing art that is unquestionably expanding the size of its audience, most rapidly outside the major cities.

Theater

At the first recorded theatrical performance in North America (1665, Virginia), the performers were arrested. For a long time thereafter theater did not fare much better, especially in the Puritan North. New York's first permanent theater, the John Street, did not open until 1767. Then, the nineteenth century gradually saw theater become the nation's foremost mass cultural activity. In Dulles's words, "the theater was a democratic institution, playing a role which in later years it largely surrendered, first to the vaudeville stage and then to the moving picture" (1965:100). Halls were huge, as, for example, New York's Broadway with its four thousand seats. This was theater's golden age. Still, most actors had to be imported from Britain and so were a large number of plays, Shakespeare remaining staple throughout the nineteenth century.

Today, movies, and television of course, alter the very nature and functions of the theater. The question as to whether we are experiencing a cultural boom must, again, receive a qualified answer. It is pointed out by the cultural explosion advocates that there are more theater-goers today in America than boaters, skiers, golfers, and skindivers combined. By the mid-sixties, each year over 100 million people attended approximately 500,000 theater performances, produced by over twenty-five thousand groups. What are we to make of these figures?

In the first place, one must of course distinguish between professional and amateur theater, realizing that the figures refer, to an overwhelming extent, to amateur activities. We now have roughly five thousand nonprofit theater groups, five thousand college-affiliated groups, and another fifteen thousand groups related to clubs, churches, and schools. Thus, as an amateur enterprise, theater is indeed a massive phenomenon.

Second, once commercial theater has been isolated, distinctions must be made between a number of internal areas. Until recently, Broadway constituted the bulk of professional theater. However, a number of recent developments have changed this. There is now a vigorous commercial summer theater, regional theater, and off-broadway theater. Now these three areas are currently rapidly expanding, and this is what the cultural explosion proponents focus upon. Broadway itself, however, is steadily declining.

On Broadway, the annual number of new productions declined from 264 to 62 over a forty-three-year period (1927 to 1970). The number of theater buildings declined from eighty to thirty six (1929 to 1964). Although there has been a very slight increase in the annual number of admissions due to longer-running plays, *the number of productions has gone down by a 3.15% annual average* (1947 to 1964).

Now for the growth areas. The commercial summer theater, comprising over 160 groups in 1962, had, by then, doubled since the war. Off-Broadway plays, produced since the early fifties, numbered 118 new productions per year by 1969 (nearly twice as many as annual new Broadway productions). On the average, the number of new off-Broadway shows increased each year by 13% and the number of performances by 18%. Finally, the regional theater, not in existence until the 1930s, counted by 1964 at least thirty professional full-time companies. This area did experience a boom indeed.

In sum, America may have roughly fifty to sixty permanent professional theater companies. Off-Broadway, summer stock, and regional theaters are successfully expanding their audiences, while Broadway is not. Many millions of Americans participate in amateur theater.

Art movies

The cultural explosion advocates point to the increasing number and popularity of art theaters and art movies. On the other hand, Hollywood's long-term decline is also a fact. How are we to interpret the various trends in the motion picture field?

In terms of attendance, the motion picture industry peaked in 1929, when an estimated 110 million people, or four fifths of the entire population went to *see a show once a week throughout the entire year.* Although there were some good years after that (weekly attendance of over 100 million in the late thirties, and again a resurgence during the first postwar years), the movie audience has steadily declined, reaching a weekly attendance figure of less than 20 million in the late sixties. Receipt figures tell the same story. In 1929 receipts amounted to over a billion dollars. This increased to $1,692 million in 1946 but declined, by 1962, to $1,275 million. In other terms, in 1946 Americans spent $1.05 per $100.00 of disposable income on movies, but in 1962 only $0.32. The number of movie theaters declined from nineteen thousand in 1950 to fourteen thousand in 1970. A detailed discussion of trends in the motion picture industry is given in Chapter 7. Here, the point is simply to note the industry's overall decline.

The decline of Hollywood was obviously caused to a great extent by television. This means that insofar as cinema survives, its *functions* change. Just as theater, once having relinquished its mass-cultural role to movies, became once again a more specialized art form, so with movies, once their mass-cultural functions were taken over by television. Hence, the seeming paradox of Hollywood's sudden excellence at a time of financial decline. Typical of Hollywood in the sixties and seventies are not the extravaganzas *(Cleopatra, Ben-Hur)* and the sex films, which constitute a pathetic last ditch effort to compete with commercial television for the mass audiences. Rather, Hollywood now becomes an outlet for such relatively inexpensive quality work as Fonda's *Easy Rider,* Kubrick's *2001: A Space Odyssey* and *A Clockwork Orange,* Newman's *Rachel, Rachel* and *Sometimes a Great Notion,* Nichols' *The Graduate, Who's Afraid of Virginia Woolf,* and *Carnal Knowledge,* and Nicholson's *Five Easy Pieces.*

Finally, we have a proliferation of art theaters around the country—houses that show mostly foreign or underground movies. In 1950, there may have been a dozen such theaters, most of them in New York. By 1964, Toffler estimates their number at five-hundred, grossing $125 million annually.

A cultural explosion in the movie industry? Again, no clear-cut answer can be provided. While it is true that more good films are being produced and more theaters show exclusively art movies (foreign or underground), this may be the result of the redefinition of the task and functions of movies per se, which has been taking place under the impact of television. As a major consumer and entertainment industry, movies are declining. They may be in the process of redefining themselves more clearly as an art form, which would be, ironically, one of commercial television's few sanitary latent functions.

Art

A typical "cultural boom" statement is made in the 1962 recreational study conducted by the Stanford Research Institute. It says that there are now "as many painters as hunters." Along similar lines Toffler argues that "Americans have become a nation of museum-goers . . . museums are making room for unaccustomed crowds." To sort out the facts, we must distinguish between professional and amateur art, between doing art and consuming art, and between art and nonart.

To begin with, Toffler reports that the number of amateur painters grew from about 30 million in 1950 to 40 million in 1960. At that time, approximately 1 million were taking lessons, and the sum of $200 million was spent on paintings, prints, and art material.

Professional art was exhibited in about three hundred galleries in 1950 (half of them in New York), but by 1964 New York alone had over three hundred, and several hundred more had mushroomed around the country. While the art market may have boomed during the early sixties, it certainly dried up by the end of that decade. Whether this was a temporary setback caused by the economy-wide recession remained to be seen.

The consumption of art, finally, can be gauged from a Department of Health, Education and Welfare survey of the nation's 4,950 museums in 1966. The median annual expenditure per museum was $7,000, the median number of visits twelve thousand. Since no comparable figures are available for earlier dates, their meaning is difficult to apprehend.

Nevertheless, some sense can be made here. First it should be realized that only 14.5% of the museums surveyed were entirely devoted to art, only 29.5% exhibited any art at all. Second, consider the following comparison: in 1960 the nation spent $300 million to operate 620 art museums, while spending $1.3 billion in its sixteen thousand movie houses. The perspective of mass leisure dwarfs the significance of art.

Literature

Toffler, attempting also to demonstrate a cultural explosion in this area, argues that book sales and library circulation have soared three times more rapidly than the population. The number of volumes in public libraries increased from 143 million in 1950 to 210 million in 1960, and the number of borrowers increased by about 50%. By 1960, 800 million books were being checked out annually, and the country spent $300 million to run its public libraries. Data on book sales show these trends to continue. Annual book and map expenditures ran $674 million in 1950, $1,304 million in 1960, and $3,226 million in 1969. In terms of the dollar volume of book sales, the industry has been expanding at an accelerated pace. Sales did not quite double during the decade of the fifties, but *did amply so during the next nine years.* Yet it is not quite clear to what extent this trend represents *cultural* growth. Berelson estimated in 1964 that only 15% of book reading qualified as high culture (see Table 5-1). Whether this segment of the book market has or has not been expanding, and at what rate, is not clear.

The overall picture

There is, then, according to the optimists, a booming high culture market. The 1962 Stanford Research Institute study reports that "consumer spending on the arts rose by 130% (1953-1960), or considerably more than twice as fast as

spending on all recreation, and better than six times as fast as outlays for spectator sports or admission to movies" (quoted in Baumol and Bowen, 1966:37). According to Toffler, by 1963 Americans spent or donated at least $3 billion for high culture. This figure was up 70% from a decade earlier, that is, growing four times as rapidly as the population. It was estimated that the high culture market would reach $7 billion by 1970.

As we saw, statements such as Toffler's and the Stanford Research Institute obscure the issue. If there is such a thing as a high culture market, it consists of a variety of areas, some of which are expanding, some not, some of which overlap with other areas and have not been isolated from such mass consumption sectors as movies and mass literature. Where, then, do we find growth and where must we deny a cultural explosion?

Our information on symphony orchestras indicates that this is a thriving *amateur* activity, but with little or no professional expansion. For opera, the story is essentially similar. That music is a thriving amateur activity was also evidenced by soaring sales of instruments (although classical records are not doing well). When it comes to art, the story repeats itself, many do-it-yourself amateurs, but trouble for the profession. Theater, again, is a massive amateur activity nationwide; professionally it thrives in its newer forms (off-Broadway, summer stock, regional theater) while declining on Broadway. *Ballet is the only exception among the performing arts and the fine arts, to the general situation of relative professional stagnation.* Even here, we are cautioned not to misinterpret improved record keeping for actual growth. (See Baumol and Bowen, 1966:53.)

We have not yet summarized all pertinent areas. In one respect, there does seem to be heavy investment in the arts. There is a recent proliferation of cultural centers across the land, from New York's

Lincoln Center to the Los Angeles Music Center. In 1964, Baumol and Bowen found that among major American cities, twenty-four had cultural centers built before World War II, twenty-six completed since 1950, and forty expecting completion by 1970. Here, then, is major cultural expansion. When it came to movies, we saw that art movies were becoming more popular and art theaters more numerous, while the overall motion picture industry is, of course, declining. Literature, finally, can only be said to be booming when considering total book sales and library circulation. Whether good reading is on the increase, as cultural explosion advocates imply when quoting overall book sales, is not at all clear.

So, are Americans "cultured"? Are they becoming more cultured?

Some say yes, estimating the number of culture consumers at 40 million. (This is Toffler's optimum estimate.) Others (e.g., Baumol and Bowen, 1966, who explicitly attempt to refute Toffler) are skeptical, qualifying only one tenth of that figure into some category of cultured audience.[2] What makes, in fact, a high-culture consumer will be dealt with in the following discussion. Here, we must note that Americans spend large sums of money on cultural centers, that they are playing music, acting, and singing in vast numbers as amateurs, and that ballet, the new theater, and new cinema are promising professional activities. Otherwise, claims concerning a cultural explosion are often based on confusion, confusing, for example, mass literature, sales of electronic equipment, and other forms of consumer activities with high culture. As far as the performing arts are concerned, Baumol and Bowen demonstrate that in

1963, Americans over 13 years of age spent $3.23 per capita in this sector, compared with $9.51 spent for various electronic equipment, $2.25 for spectator sports, $13.00 for books and maps. These authors conclude that there may have been a modest expansion in the performing arts, but by no means an explosion. Insofar as there has been growth, this has been mostly in the high-culture areas—New York, California—having little impact on the rest of the country (geographical dispersion is dealt with in the next discussion). Furthermore, with controls for inflation and population growth, the per capita increase in expenditure for the performing arts has only been 8% for the entire 1932 to 1963 period. And when taking into account the general increase in affluence, Baumol and Bowen arrive at the startling conclusion that the amount spent on the arts has actually fallen off by about one fourth since 1929, namely from fifteen cents of each $100 of disposable income to only eleven cents! Finally, while during most of this period the annual increase in the total amount of money spent for high culture just about matched increases in the gross national product, since 1961 high culture has no longer kept pace with the overall economic growth. This points to one deplorable fact: by whatever statistical indicator, it can be shown that as America becomes wealthier, it devotes less and less of its wealth to the very items which one would expect to *then* assume precedence.

Psychologists from Freud on, followed by Maslow, have postulated that individuals and societies operate according to certain priorities, or hierarchies of needs. They have explained to us that, as primary needs begin to be satisfied by way of rising standards of living, one may expect increasing devotion to the hitherto neglected areas—the realm of the spiritual and the cultural. In Toffler's words, "there is a certain income point . . . beyond which a family need no longer

---

[2] Of course, 40 million, 4 million, or any other figure is in and of itself meaningless. How the various sources arrive at their respective estimates is dealt with in the following discussion, where we go into the demographic and socioeconomic characteristics of the high-culture consumers.

concern itself solely about basics. . . . It begins to care about the better things of life—meaning, very often, non-material things" (1964:40). We may expect that, as income rises, the share spent on leisure and high culture should go up. *Yet this is not happening.* The editors of *Fortune* magazine (1958), observing this fact, as early as 1955 (pointing out that leisure's share of disposable income has declined from 14% in 1947 to 12% in 1953), could do no better than to label the leisure market a "perverse thing" and to say that it nevertheless includes a core area which is expected to grow vigorously in the future. This fails to get at the issue. The point I wish to make is that there is no necessary law of economics or human nature which says that men will devote themselves increasingly to high culture once their primary needs have been taken care of. There is no hierarchy of needs inherent in the nature of things. Men and societies *decide,* politically, upon priorities. If our society refuses to relinquish the work ethic even when full employment is no longer imperative, if our economic system remains guided by the profit motive, thus compelled to produce goods far in excess of needs, if our society opts for war ahead of well-being, then we may never devote our resources to high culture, regardless of their magnitude.

Are Americans "cultured"? Our social system seems to feel that they are sufficiently so for the time being and that we have more urgent priorities than high culture. The ironic thing is, of course, that back when we did not have a trillion dollar gross national product we could afford relatively more high culture. Of course, we did not have the burden of empire at that time.

SOME CORRELATES OF HIGH CULTURE

Almost by definition, high culture is the culture of and for the elite. This means, common-sensically, that the producers and consumers of high culture are more likely to be among the upper social strata, being better educated, wealthier, more influential, and more prestigious than the other strata. Do we have more precise information as to who the high culture producers and consumers are? What is generally their social status, their age, their occupational position, their religion? What are some of their values? Are they more often men? Or women? Where, geographically, do they tend to cluster? To answer these and related questions, I shall first briefly deal with the production of high culture and then with its consumption. The following nine correlates of high culture will be examined: sex, age, race and ethnic descent, geography, religion, values and tastes, education, occupation, and social class and mobility.

The production of high culture

Little systematic information exists about the social position and background of artists, intellectuals, and scientists as a sociological category. The sociology of knowledge and the sociology of art relate certain cultural productions to the social background of their producers, but mostly on an individual basis. Nevertheless, some generalizations can be made, both historically and for contemporary America.

First, we have the oft-discussed alienation of the modern artist and intellectual. This phenomenon is relatively new, dating from the age of romanticism. Bach was still a well-settled burgher earning a decent living as composer-kapellmeister; subsequent generations of composers—Beethoven, Schumann, Mahler—began to feel a weltschmerz well expressed in their works. Similarly in other fields, Rimbaud, Baudelaire, Thoreau, van Gogh, and Dostoevski were all equally unhappy, pathological, and alienated, epitomizing the modern (but only the modern) creative genius. We thus arrive at the contemporary view that artists and intellectuals ought to be non-committed by definition. Schumpeter (1949), for example, points out that the status of intellectuals has been incompatible with political commitment. This, of course, ties in with the notion that acceptance of institutional positions, monetary rewards, or any kind of power constitutes a cop-out because it must be repaid at the cost of freedom and integrity.

Whether we like it or not, the American culture-producing elite indeed fits our postromantic conception of it. It is alienated from the mainstream of American life and from the centers of power. As Shils observed some time ago, it has "not felt bound by any invisible affiliation with the political, economic, ecclesiastical, military, and technological elites" (1964:26). It is not only alienated, it is also insulated in the only institutional base of operation it has—the university. And how bad its relations with the outside world are became clearer yet during the late sixties, when the resumption of town-gown hostilities (going back to America's traditional anti-intellectualism) expressed itself in budget cuts, firings, military occupation of campuses, and other manifestations of the public's animosity toward the intellectuals.

What about social class? Having said that being an artist or an intellectual means being alienated would seem to contradict the notion that the producers of high culture logically belong to the elite. Remember, however, that the alienation and powerlessness of the intelligentsia is relatively recent. Historically, the production and preservation of high culture was indeed in the hands of the political elite, as Veblen (1899) showed. Literacy was a rare privilege, and so was the prerogative to "do culture" rather than to toil. Think, for example, of the Indian Brahmans or the Chinese mandarins, who were not only the intelligentsia but also the potentates. Today

in the West the producers of high culture may still descend mostly from upper strata (where funds for a liberal arts education and for training in artistic skills are available, and where a cultural tradition is transmitted), but there is very often no identification with the centers of established power. To that extent, the high-culture producers do not belong to the elite. Furthermore, the oft-observed lack of community, solidarity, and consciousness of kind among modern artists and intellectuals is a direct consequence of this. Members of the intelligentsia are first and foremost individualists whose primary aim is to innovate rather than to consolidate, to dissent rather than to belong. Among artists and intellectuals, social class is a relatively irrelevant variable.

Related to this is a third characteristic of the high-culture producers. Whatever their social background (which, as said, is still mostly upper class, as it has been in the past), their ideology and social function have, ever since romanticism, become increasingly subversive and revolutionary. Thus it is anachronistic to view high culture mostly as the embodiment of the collective heritage and to view the task of the intelligentsia as a task of conservation, as do conservative sociologists, for example, Shils (1964). Marx was among the first to alert us to the middle-class intellectual's revolutionary functions. Thus in the realm of politics we have Marx, Engels, Lenin, Mao Tse-tung, Fidel Castro, and others who, while speaking for the proletarian revolution, themselves all come from the upper strata. Similarly in the arts, while the producers of high culture may come from the upper strata, their artistic contributions are more often revolutionary than conserving. The most blatant example of this is the rich counterculture of the late sixties—mostly middle-class youngsters who produced a vast amount of revolutionary music and poetry.

In sum, while historically the high-culture producers may have been members of the elite and essentially conservative, romanticism ushered an era in which many of them have become alienated, powerless, revolutionary either politically or culturally, and affiliated at best with academic institutions.

The consumption of high culture

When it comes to the high-culture consumers, there is very little agreement as to who these people are. Estimates as to their number in America range from Toffler's optimistic 40 million to Baumol and Bowen's 4 million, or from 30% to 3% of adult Americans. Again, one figure obviously implies that we have a cultural explosion on our hands; the other does not. The conflicting claims apparently result from the use of different criteria and from different conceptions of the high-culture consumer. Let us look at some of his demographic characteristics.

Sex. Our traditional value system has relegated high culture to women and to sissies. Men were too busy for "culture." Now one of the manifestations of the cultural explosion, we are told, is increasing male participation in high culture. According to Toffler there is a shift toward equal sex ratios among amateur painters, concert-goers, theater-goers. Yet Bradshaw (1971) found that among college students women are more frequently culture oriented than men. On a composite scale measuring concert attendance, theater attendance, listening to classical music, reading poetry, attending art museums, and reading non-course-related books, 15% of the women scored very high, against only 10% of the men. Baumol and Bowen, too, feel that the audience for the performing arts is more heavily female than male, particularly in the areas of symphony concerts, dance, and Broadway shows. Most revealing is a *Playbill* survey of the Broadway audience which shows *little change in the sex-*ual composition of the audience* during the decade surveyed (1955–1965).

Age. Here, too, tradition has dictated certain limitations. High culture has been associated more with old people than with the young. Of course, the fault may be with the old themselves, for as recently as 1959 a reputable sociologist had the narrowmindedness to assert that "the eagerness of youth for the mediocre and brutal culture, . . . and [its] own creative poverty are a universal phenomenon"! (Shils, 1964:12). In any event, the cultural explosion thesis has also been applied to age; high culture is now allegedly expanding its appeal to the young. Toffler, for example, claims that the average age of the high-culture consumer is dropping.

Baumol and Bowen found that the median age for the performing arts audience is 38, against 30.3 for the general urban population. To be sure, when children are excluded from this comparison, the high-culture consumers are younger than the general population. The only relatively old culture audience is that for symphony concerts. Baumol and Bowen did their own independent survey (1966) of the British audience for the performing arts and found it to be considerably younger than ours. The proportion of the American audience aged 10 to 24 was twice as high as that in the general population, but in England this was three and a half times as high. Finally, and most importantly, the *Playbill* study shows that the American *audience has not been getting younger,* at least on Broadway, between 1955 and 1965. Thus, the twofold thesis that high culture has traditionally been for the old and that this is now changing may have to be revised.

Race and ethnicity. No exact data were available to analyze the ethnic composition of the high-culture-consuming public. However, a few generalizations can be made. Many of Baumol and Bowen's respondents concurred that classical music and opera were most heavily attended by Americans of German, Italian, and Jewish background. All sources concur about two facts. In the audience for high culture, Jews are heavily over-represented and Negroes conspicuously lacking.

The Negro absence from among the high culture audience is the result of a number of factors. In the first place it is to some extent of course a class phenomenon rather than a purely race phenomenon. Several studies (Emrie, 1970; Kraus, 1968; Outdoor Recreation Resources Review Commission, 1962) have documented the Negroes' general inability to fully participate in society's recreational life due to economic deprivation and segregation of facilities. Their lack of participation in high culture, then, is partly just one facet of this general condition, and it can be expected to be remedied as the overall position of Negroes improves.

There are, however, more fundamental sociological and cultural reasons for the Negro's nonparticipation in high culture. Frazier's description of the *Black bourgeoisie's* leisure life shows that even affluent blacks feel little affinity for high culture. "This class as a whole," writes Frazier, "has no real appreciation of art, literature or music. . . . Expensive editions of books are bought for decoration and left unread [and] education from the standpoint of culture has completely lost its significance" (1958). What Frazier describes is the typical nouveau-riche syndrome: a class of individuals to whom income, conspicuous consumption, and social functions are everything. The question is whether the black bourgeoisie will, in time, come around to greater cultural and intellectual appreciation. It is possible that this will indeed happen and that it is currently being signaled by the great influx of blacks into the colleges. Yet those who expect blacks to soon emulate whites, in this respect, may turn out to be wrong. Frazier himself pointed out that high culture received perhaps more

attention from blacks at an earlier time than now. We have had the likes of W. E. B. Du Bois throughout American history, and there may not be a trend toward more cultural appreciation among blacks. For what is high culture, after all, if not part of the highly culture-bound European tradition which has biased American cultural standards so unfavorably toward blacks? To the extent that high culture is a European affair, it may be irrelevant to blacks, who have long ago shown their ability to develop their own art forms and their own standards of cultural excellence. Statistics may show that few blacks attend Beethoven concerts, but then, how many whites attended John Coltrane's performances? As Kraus (1968) showed in a survey taken in the New York area, Negroes have very high rates of amateur participation in choral music, drama, and dance. This suggests that Negro cultural activity is not only determined by cost and availability, but also by the subculture of the American Negro, as is emphasized by Kaplan (1960). The point is that it is wrong to equate black cultural progress with black participation in high culture. Realizing the rich Afro-American cultural heritage is of course what the whole black culture movement of the sixties and seventies has been about. Of course, the development of a distinct black cultural identity does not necessarily preclude the integration of African and classical European elements at the highest possible level of excellence, as illustrated by John Lewis's Modern Jazz Quartet.

Geography. Two factors will be examined here. First a brief comment on the urban-rural correlate of high culture, and then a report on Baumol and Bowen's findings on the regional distribution of high culture.

The rural population is clearly much lower on cultural participation than any segment of the urban population. This holds even in America, where media pen-

Table 5-2. *Percentage distribution of performing arts establishments per capita, by region, 1963**

Region	Symphony orchestras, operas, ballets	Other classical music groups	Theatrical presentations
New England	10.6	14.6	9.8
Middle Atlantic	13.2	18.1	31.7
East N. Central	8.2	11.8	9.0
West N. Central	8.3	9.1	7.9
South Atlantic	9.3	3.0	6.0
East S. Central	8.2	7.9	3.0
West S. Central	8.8	7.0	4.1
Mountain	13.4	11.2	8.6
Pacific	20.2	17.4	20.1
United States	100.0	100.0	100.0

*From William J. Baumol and William G. Bowen, Performing Arts: The Economic Dilemma. © 1966 by The Twentieth Century Fund, New York. P. 442.

etration is nationwide and where even the farmer is becoming leisure oriented (Goldstein, 1961). Wilensky (1964), for example, found that farm isolation was a good predictor of the extent to which an individual is exposed to poor quality culture (through television).

As far as the regional dispersion of high culture is concerned, Baumol and Bowen have some good data. With population density control, the percentage distribution of performing arts establishments in 1963 ranges from a high of 31.7% for the Middle Atlantic region (mostly New York) to lows of 3.0% for parts of the Deep South. Table 5-2 reproduces these authors' findings.

Table 5-2 reveals that even with population density control, New York, California, and the states adjacent to these two states account for one third of all musical establishments and one half of the theatrical groups. In terms of total receipts (a better indicator than the number of enterprises), New York's preponderance is overwhelming: in 1963, 39% of all receipts from classical music, and 56% of all theater receipts! Per capita, New Yorkers spent $1.42 on concert tickets and $17.94 on theater tickets, against 0.29¢ and $1.88, respectively, nationwide. Furthermore, a comparison of 1958 with 1963 showed that performing arts activity was not growing fastest in the states where such activity was initially lowest—in other words, no evidence of geographical spread. In fact, nineteen states showed a decline in classical music activity or theater activity or both.

Religion. Wilensky (1964) found that religion, when combined with the "generation-American" variable, was a very good predictor of whether a person was exposed to much highbrow culture through the media. His findings indicate that, in terms of highbrow cultural exposure, religious categories rank as follows:
1. No religious preference
2. Jewish
3. Established Catholic (with four grandparents born in the United States)
4. Protestant
5. Recently immigrated Catholic

The "media purist," Wilensky concludes, is often Jewish, or inactive Protestant, or he has no religious preference, and he has often intermarried with a person of another faith.

Bradshaw's recent study of students' cultural orientation confirms part of this. Among respondents who said they believe in God, only 9.5% rated very high on culture, against 25% among those who did not believe in God.

Values and tastes. Three broad areas

will briefly be dealt with under this heading: political orientation, social orientation, and consumer style.

Politically, the high-culture consumer is liberal, generally left of center. Wilensky's "media purists" were mostly liberal Democratic professors and a few moderate Republican lawyers. Bradshaw's cultured students often favored such radical reform as the legalization of marijuana.

While politically critical of the major centers of power, the high-culture consumer nevertheless takes an above average part in community politics and activities. He belongs to and participates in more than his share of organizations. Furthermore, a survey by *Harper's Magazine* and the *Atlantic Monthly* showed that high-culture consumers tend to belong to *civic* organizations (parent-teacher associations, Red Cross), while their neighbors—socioeconomically their equals, presumably—are more involved with *church*-related organizations (Toffler, 1964:50). There is something subcultural about high-culture consumers. They come from families in which high culture has been a way of life for generations, and they frequent one another. For example, students who frequent professors, Bradshaw found, are twice as likely to score high on culture than the average. And Wilensky suggests that it may take close "supervision over more than a generation to inculcate a taste for high culture" (1964:194).

The high-culture consumer leads a relatively ascetic lifestyle. Wilensky's media purist spends little money on luxury, cars, vacation, or house. He is more likely than average to be an apartment dweller. The *Harper's Atlantic* study showed that the high-culture consumer's outdoor recreational activities consist mostly of tennis, skiing, and boating, while others of comparable socioeconomic status prefer to hunt, bowl, take photographs, cook outdoors, and do woodwork. Regardless of income, Toffler maintains, high-culture consumers prefer to travel to Europe, while others' first choice would be Hawaii. Domestically, they prefer to fly, where others would drive. They are the most likely to own stereos and hi-fi's and to listen to FM radio. If anyone, it is the high-culture consumer who does not own a television.

Education. The single best predictor of what Wilensky calls "leisure competence" is, as expected, education. In other words it is along this variable that high-culture consumers are most clearly distinguishable.

Since there is an obvious relationship between educational level and high-culture consumption, this has led those who talk cultural explosion to believe that the rapid expansion of the college population automatically leads to a cultural boom. Thus, Toffler optimistically quotes data showing that 80% to 83% of the Minneapolis Guthrie theater audience has attended college, and so has 66% of the Broadway audience (Toffler, 1964:41-42).

That education and high-culture consumption are strongly related is best shown in Baumol and Bowen's data, reproduced in part in Table 5-3.

Table 5-3 shows, among other things, that less than 3% of the performing arts audience had failed to complete high school, against over 50% of the urban population at large (1960). Yet a simple reference to amount of education does not tell us enough about the high-culture consumer. As Wilensky cautions us, "educated strata—even products of graduate and professional schools—are becoming full participants in mass culture; they spend a reduced fraction of time in exposure to quality print and film. This trend extends to the professors, writers, artists, scientists—the keepers of high culture themselves—and the chief culprit is TV" (1964:190). In fact, Wilensky found that from zero education to "some college," sheer amount of education

Table 5-3. *Educational profile of the United States' performing arts audience (25 years and over), compared with the total urban population**

	Males		Females	
	Performing arts audience	*Urban population*	*Performing arts audience*	*Urban population*
Less than 4 years high school	2.2%	56.6%	2.8%	55.1%
4 years high school	6.5%	22.1%	15.3%	28.9%
1–3 years college	12.8%	9.8%	23.6%	9.5%
4 years college	23.1%	6.2%	26.7%	4.5%
Graduate school	55.4%	5.3%	31.6%	2.0%
Median category	Graduate work	2 years high school	4 years college	3 years high school

*From William J. Baumol and William G. Bowen, Performing Arts: The Economic Dilemma. © 1966 by The Twentieth Century Fund, New York. p. 76.

makes little difference (in a person's culture competence).

Apparently for education to be a strong correlate of culture competence, we must look not only at its (1) *quantity,* but also at its (2) *quality,* and its (3) *type.* Now as far as quantity is concerned, reliable sources concur that it is *beyond* college that this variable begins to make a substantial difference. Baumol and Bowen show that a plurality of high-culture consumers not only attended college, but also graduate school! Of the men, 55% had done so, against 5% of the male urban population at large, and 33% of the women (against 2% of the female urban population at large). Thus, high-culture consumers tend to be a highly select category of individuals who oftentimes studied beyond the baccalaureate. This is most so in the case of chamber music and regional theater audiences, while Broadway audiences are of a relatively lower educational level.

The *quality* of the high-culture consumer's education distinguishes him more sharply from the general public. All but two of Wilensky's media purists were educated in high-quality liberal arts colleges and graduate schools (meaning mostly Ivy League institutions), or abroad. Bradshaw (1971) confirms this. Among students attending high-quality private liberal arts colleges, 33% scored high on cultural participation; at high-quality universities this was 21%; at low-quality universities 17%; and at junior colleges only 11%.

Finally, high-culture consumers also distinguish themselves through the type of education they receive—mostly a humanistic liberal arts education. Bradshaw found that among humanities majors, 25% scored high on culture; for social science majors this was 14%; for physical science and education majors 8%; for engineering majors 5%, and for business majors only 2%.

Occupation. There is probably more research on the relationship between occupation and leisure than on any other correlate of leisure. This is no doubt because work-leisure, or "work-vs.-leisure," has been the central axis in the sociology of leisure. In other words, the first logical thing for a sociologist, when doing research in leisure behavior, is to somehow relate and contrast it to work. This, after all, is one of the central polarities in Western man's life.

There are, when relating work and leisure, at least two possible approaches. One may look at a variety of substantive occupations and attempt to establish correlations between them and specific forms of leisure, or one may focus on the meaning and functions of work activities and leisure activities and relate work and leisure to one another in these terms. The bulk of past research has followed the former approach, relating substantive work *forms* (occupations) to specific forms of leisure (for example, Anderson and Gordon, 1964; Bradshaw, 1971; Clarke, 1956; Gerstl, 1963). Some sociologists (Havighurst, 1957; Wilensky, 1964) have begun work along the latter line, relating the *meaning* of various types of work to nonwork. In a recent article (Kando and Summers, 1971), we proposed a framework within which systematic research could be done on the relation between the meaning of work and leisure as experienced by individuals subjectively. For example, a person's leisure activities may provide *compensations* for what work fails to offer, or they may have characteristics that are a *spillover* of some of the features of his work. Both possibilities exist, regardless of what a person's specific occupation may be. That the meaning of one's work (the way one experiences it, e.g., whether it is depriving, stimulating, dull, tiring, rewarding) is important in determining leisure activities may be illustrated by the fact that two individuals with the same job, say college professors, may prefer different leisure activities. One may feel physical deprivation and therefore engage in athletics (compensation), while the other, feeling no such deprivation, spends more of his leisure time reading and writing (spillover).

Because no research has been done on the relationship between the meaning of work and nonwork, I shall report mostly on the relationship between specific occupations, or occupational categories, and leisure activities.

Because occupation and social class are almost inextricably linked, it seems at first difficult to separate the two and find out whether, and to what extent, the relationship between occupation and leisure is spurious. Yet gradually there is more and more research in which social class is successfully controlled (for example, Gerstl, 1963) and which demonstrates occupation's independent influence upon leisure. This shows that researchers are becoming aware of the need to relate not just specific occupations to leisure activities, but, as we argued, to go deeper and to relate the context, functions, and meaning which people's jobs have for them, to the leisure activities in which they engage. Thus we shall examine existing research as it develops from an early focus on specific occupational categories, to a recently growing emphasis on the nature of the individual's job.

The cultural explosion argument is essentially the same in all its facets. It says that high culture is becoming democratized, whether with respect to sex, age, race, social class, or occupation. Thus, to quote Toffler again, whereas at the turn of the century high culture was mostly for the wealthy and for the alienated artists and intellectuals, today things are allegedly different. Not so, according to Shils (1964), who points out that intellectuals still loom large among the high-culture consumers. Occupationally, according to this author, the high-culture audience consists mostly of professors, teachers, research scientists, students, journalists, and artists. High-culture has few friends among the plutocracy, politicians, engineers, and various other occupations that are, in terms of social class, at least equivalent to the more intellectual professions.

What light does empirical research

shed on this question? Alfred C. Clarke did an early study of the relationship between leisure and occupational status. He established five prestige levels, each representing mostly certain occupational groupings. Level I included primarily professionals, level II managers, officials, and proprietors, level III sales and clerical workers and white collar employees, level IV skilled craftsmen and kindred workers, and level V service workers and semiskilled and unskilled laborers. Clarke's findings establish a clear relationship between leisure activities and occupational prestige levels, as can be seen from Table 5-4.

As can be seen from Table 5-4, occupational prestige level I is most active in high culture. There is, all the way down the line, a relationship between the high culture—mass culture variable and prestige levels. The lower the prestige level, the more typical of mass culture its favored leisure activities seem to be. While this grossly simplifies the issue as well as Clarke's findings, it nevertheless has usefulness.

Baumol and Bowen provide data that are more recent and more detailed than Clarke's, but supportive of his findings. The occupational distribution of the performing arts audience observed by these authors is reproduced in Table 5-5.

Table 5-5 indicates that the performing arts audience is almost entirely white-collar, hardly blue-collar at all, heavily professional, and heavily academic (teachers and students). More detailed analysis revealed differences among the various arts. For example,

Table 5-4. Selected leisure activities by prestige level participating most frequently

Activity	Prestige level participating most frequently				
	I	II	III	IV	V
Attending theatrical plays	X				
Attending concerts	X				
Attending special lectures	X				
Visiting a museum or art gallery	X				
Reading for pleasure	X				
Attending parties		X			
Playing golf			X		
Working on automobile				X	
Watching TV					X
Attending baseball games					X

From Alfred C. Clarke, 1956. "Leisure and occupational prestige." American Sociological Review 21 (June):301-307.

Table 5-5. Occupational profile of the United States' performing arts audience, compared with the total urban population*

	Males		Females	
	Performing arts audience	Urban population	Performing arts audience	Urban population
Professional	63%	12.7%	63.2%	14%
(teachers)	10.3%	1.1%	25.4%	5.6%
Managerial	21.4%	12.6%	7.2%	3.9%
Clerical and sales	13%	17.2%	(Clerical) 24.9%	34.3%
			(Sales) 2.8%	8.5%
Blue-collar	2.6%	57.5%	1.9%	39.3%
Students	13.9%		15.1%	
Housewives			35.2%	

*From William J. Baumol and William G. Bowen, Performing Arts: The Economic Dilemma. © 1966 by The Twentieth Century Fund, New York. p. 75.

chamber music is even more heavily attended by professionals, teachers, and
students than the average performing
art, while Broadway shows attract fewer
professionals and more businessmen.

The Minneapolis Guthrie Theater
study findings quoted in Toffler (1964:42)
generally corroborate Baumol and
Bowen's findings: 32% to 35% of the
Guthrie audience were professionals or
"technicians" (as against 12.8% of the
labor force). The next largest occupational category in this audience was that of
the business executives. Only 3.1% of the
audience consisted of blue-collar
workers. Toffler noted, when discussing
these findings, that the groups most conspicuously absent from among the high-
culture consumers are the farmers, service employees, and blue-collar workers.

Anderson and Gordon (1964) did a
study of the blue-collar worker's leisure
life. "Is the worker," they asked, "with
his increased income and leisure time,
using these to improve himself intellectually, civically, esthetically, or is he
not?" The authors found that he is not.
For the working class, "leisure has a
stamp of constancy and fixedness." Even
though he may not watch as much television as the stereotype has it, the blue-
collar worker does not consume much
high culture either. Mostly, he engages
in handy work, automobile rides, and
outdoor activities. The authors concluded
that the most important factor prevent-
ing widespread high-culture consumption among the working class is its subcultural orientation.

In addition to the individual's occupation, it is useful to examine his family's
occupational ranking. Bradshaw found
the following amounts of cultural participation among students with parents in
specified occupational categories:

Among students whose parents were
professionals, artists, architects, or
designers, 24% scored high on the
author's culture scale.

Among students whose parents were in
semiprofessional, scientific, or technical occupations, 16% scored high
on the culture scale.

Among students whose parents were in
business or in teaching, 12% scored
high on the culture scale.

Among students whose parents were in
sales, clerical work, or blue-collar
work, 9.5% scored high on the culture scale.

Third, we may also wish to look at the
relationship between culturedness and
future occupational choice. We shall thus
have examined the occupational variable
from the angles of past (parent's occupation), present (individual's own occupation) and future (occupational choice).
Bradshaw found distinct differences
among the students' cultural orientations, depending on their occupational
choice. Four occupational choice categories ranked as follows:

Engineer, scientist, and business: 6%
scored high on the culture scale.

Teaching: 9% scored high on the culture scale.

Professionals and semiprofessionals:
15% scored high on the culture scale.

Artist, architect, designer: highest percentage on the culture scale (no figure given).

Thus far we have dealt with research
on the leisure and cultural predilections
of certain occupational strata. Now we
arrive at research that examines the leisure and cultural preferences of different
occupations that *belong to the same stratum, but entail different kinds of activities.* There is here an important underlying assumption which was absent in previous research: that an individual's leisure and cultural preferences will in part
be determined by the nature of his work
experience. The best example of a study
along these lines is Gerstl's (1963) "Leisure, Taste and Occupational Milieu." In
this study, the author's explicit aim is to
hold social class constant while relating

occupation to leisure. To this end, Gerstl compares three upper-middle-class occupations, each entailing a different work situation. The dentist is chosen to represent the typical independent practitioner; the advertising man is taken as representing the organization man in business; and college professors represent the salaried intellectuals. Gerstl's findings show that the professors' leisure activities are generally more cultural than those of the dentists and the admen. For example, while dentists and admen tended to watch between five and ten hours of television per week, one half of the professors did not even own a television, and two thirds of those who did, watched it less than four hours per week. Asking the subjects what magazines, books, plays, and music they enjoyed most frequently, Gerstl then dichotomized the responses into upper and lower brow. The tastes of the three occupational categories are compared, in these terms, in Table 5-6.

Gerstl's findings make two important points. They show that some occupations (namely college professors) indulge more in the "higher things of life" than other ones. This corroborates the previous findings discussed. In addition, they also show that the *type* of leisure and cultural activity in which respondents engage has something to do with the nature of their

work. For example, dentists were highest on such manual activities as woodwork, gardening, and other do-it-yourself activities. Admen, insofar as they engaged in high culture, differed from professors. The latter were most active in music (listening as well as amateur playing), while admen were more active in amateur painting and reading. Thus, we begin to see that leisure and high culture are not merely related to occupational stratum, but also to the nature of a man's work.

Wilensky (1964) did a study that elaborates this approach. A comparison of a number of occupational categories revealed distinct differences in leisure patterns. Some of Wilensky's findings are reproduced in Table 5-7.

Table 5-7 shows that leisure and cultural activities differ not only between occupations, but also depending upon the work *context*. Thus, Wilensky shows, it is important to distinguish between solo lawyers and firm lawyers; between professors affiliated with an urban university and professors at a denominational institution; engineers employed by different types of companies. For comparative purposes, Wilensky's data on the leisure and cultural activities of a sample of the "middle mass" and a sample of severely deprived individuals are also reproduced in Table 5-7.

Wilensky's study, then, makes two points. First, cultural activities are clearly related to (occupational) stratum, as may be seen, for example, from the fact that only 1% of the middle mass reads at least one quality newspaper, as against 40% of the professors, 33% of the lawyers, and 10% of the engineers. Also, the nineteen "media purists" identified by the author (those who cultivate only the very best in the media) turn out to be sixteen professors and three lawyers. The second point of Wilensky's study is what we are driving at throughout this section—that work context and work ex-

Table 5-6. *Percentage of upper-brow responses by occupation**

	Admen	Dentists	Professors
Theater	68	32	96
Concert	44	28	100
Musical taste	16	24	96
Hours reading	52	20	60
Number of books	56	16	80
Magazine type	0	0	68
Mean score	40	20	83

*From Joel E. Gerstl. 1961. Leisure taste and occupational milieu." Social Problems 9 (summer) 1961. Copyright © by The Society for the Study of Social Problems.

Table 5-7. *Efforts to be discriminating in media exposure, by occupational group and stratum, in percentages**

	Lawyers			Professors			Engineers				
	Solo	Firm	Total	Church	Urban	Total	Diver-sico	Unico	Total	Middle mass	Under-dogs
Daily newspaper† Reads at least one quality paper	22	50	36	26	50	42	10	12	11	1	0
Does not read a quality paper	78	50	64	74	50	58	90	88	89	99	100
No. of quality magazines read regularly‡											
Three or more	5	13	9	67	64	64	8	2	6	0	0
One or two	31	34	33	25	13	17	51	60	56	3	0
None	64	52	58	3	1	2	39	37	38	96	100
Missing data	0	0	0	3	22	16	2	0	1	0	0
Cultural, "educational," selected "special" TV shows											
No favorite	72	58	65	42	51	49	66	70	68	80	94
One favorite	10	22	16	16	16	16	18	19	18	11	4
Two or more	18	21	19	42	32	35	16	11	14	9	2
Clear theme of cultural criticism appears in the interview											
Clear cultural criticism	38	50	44	74	76	76	32	32	32	13	3
No clear cultural criticism	62	50	56	26	24	24	68	68	68	87	97

*From Harold Wilensky, 1964. "Mass society and mass culture: interdependence or independence?" American Sociological Review 29 (April):173-197.
†*New York Times, Herald Tribune, Washington Post, Christian Science Monitor, Manchester Guardian, St. Louis Post-Dispatch, Wall Street Journal.*
‡Includes forty-one nonprofessional periodicals, plus major law reviews, professional journals of engineering societies, and, for professors, all learned and professional journals.

perience are crucial determinants of leisure and cultural activities. The study shows that the size of a man's work place and the length of his workweek, among other factors, are excellent predictors of his leisure competence (i.e., whether his media consumption is refined or not). The self-employed are quite low on leisure competence, while salaried employees in larger work places of up to five hundred rank increasingly higher on it.

Similarly, the longer one's workweek, the higher one's leisure competence. Among long-hours men only 17% scored low on leisure competence, as against 65% among short-hours men, and 61% among the unemployed.

These last findings get at the central problem in the work-leisure relationship. Wilensky explained his findings by hypothesizing that "demanding work makes a wider (cultural) universe available" and that "those who have the most leisure have the least resources for its creative use." Riesman (1958) phrased the same notion succinctly: "Those who work hard play hard." Such statements may be summarized under the labels of "spillover" or "fusion." Riesman and Bloomberg (1957) asked, "Work and Leisure: Fusion or Polarity?" and so far this section has presented material that seems to say "fusion"; *the same features that typify an individual's work are also present in his leisure activities.* However, in addition to spillover, the opposite possibility of compensation exists. An individual's leisure activities may be the opposite, in nature, of his work. Havighurst (1957) developed a scale consisting of nineteen "significance variables," (e.g., autonomy vs. other-directedness, enjoyment vs. time-killer, creativity vs. physical energy output), which would make it possible to test the compensatory hypothesis by scoring both work and nonwork along such a common scale. To date, no further research along these lines has been undertaken, and we are therefore unable to distinguish between compensation and spillover. That both occur is clear, but we do not know when and under what conditions. This was the main problem we addressed ourselves to in a recent article (Kando and Summers, 1971). Above all, it was suggested, it is not sufficient to relate specific occupations to leisure and cultural activities, but one must get at the work *experience* and see whether, in those terms, work and leisure compensate for one another.

Social class. A number of sociologists (Anderson, 1961; Kaplan, 1960) have tended to minimize the importance of social class as a determinant of leisure and culture. The theory behind this is generally that with the advent of mass society, cultural uniformity grows (Wilensky, 1964) and tastes become more and more homogenized (Kraus, 1971). Furthermore, the cultural explosion thesis is merely a disguised variant of this theory.

What Toffler and others who talk cultural boom say, essentially, is that mass democracy is bringing the higher things to all the people. As we shall see shortly, the existence of such a trend has not been documented. Furthermore, the view that all tastes are becoming homogenized is poorly founded. David Riesman suggested that we may be moving toward marginal differentiation, that status lines may be determined by symbols and attributes of increasingly subtle distinction. Simply, when all people own cars, the kind of car one owns becomes important. So, while to us future society may look highly homogeneous and uniform, to its own members it will seem as varied and stratified as ever. In any event, Kraus is correct when writing that "it would be sheer nonsense to suggest that basically the pastimes of all levels of society are the same and that it is only a matter of where we sit at the opera" (1971:295).

Those who talk cultural explosion, then, argue that there is a boom and that this is because of the growth of a "comfort" class. Toffler maintains that, whereas in 1900 only the upper class, the Europe-oriented rich, consumed high culture, we now have a large comfort class earning upward from $10,000, and therefore able to enjoy the higher things. For example, in 1960, Toffler points out, the median income of the Broadway public was $10,032 or $10,419. *Saturday Review* subscribers earned an average of $13,090. These, supposedly, are the new masses of high-culture consumers. Many of these, Toffler adds, are highly mobile, both geographically and socially.

The truth of the matter is that the growth of the middle class, or middle masses, and the rising standard of living have not led to a cultural boom. As Shils points out, high-culture consumption remains primarily an upper-class affair. The middle class gets some through the media. The lower class, the blue-collar workers, and the farmers almost none.

Table 5-8. Rates of use of leisure per 100 persons of all ages, by social class*

	UM	LM	UL	LL
Parks and playgrounds	1.75	6.85	9.5	19.7
Community Chest Services	8.75	11.95	10.1	15.45
Church	51.5	71.1	73.65	79.45
Libraries	19.3	22.85	16.4	11.9
Lecture study	14.5	6.15	2.9	4.7

*From Clyde White. 1955. "Social class differences in the uses of leisure." American Journal of Sociology 61 (September):145-150. Copyright © University of Chicago.

The relationship between culture and social class was examined early by White (1955). This sociologist distinguished between four classes—upper middle, lower middle, upper lower and lower lower. He found a positive relationship between class and some cultural activities, and a negative relationship between class and some other forms of leisure activities. A selection of White's findings is reproduced in Table 5-8.

Table 5-8 shows that White found the leisure activities of the upper strata to be more cultural than those of the lower strata. This (evident) finding was also documented by Wilensky (1964), whose middle masses and underdogs in no way matched the rates of cultural participation among professors, lawyers, and engineers (see Table 5-7). Furthermore, Baumol and Bowen, contrasting the performing arts audience with the general population, found that the former—the high-culture consumers—are vastly more affluent than the latter. Some of these authors' findings are presented in Table 5-9.

Thus, Baumol and Bowen revealed that the culture audience's income is twice as high as that of the general population, that the number of people with an income of over $15,000 is six times as high among the high-culture audience as among the general population, that the number of people with an income in excess of $25,000 is almost twelve times as large in this group as in the general population. These authors also discovered a relationship between income and

Table 5-9. Income profile of United States' performing arts audience, compared with the total urban population*

	Performing arts audience	Urban population (1960 census)
Over $5,000	91.3%	64.8%
Over $15,000	39.5%	5.4%
Over $25,000	17.4%	1.5%
Median income	$12,804	$6,166

*From William J. Baumol and William G. Bowen, Performing Arts: The Economic Dilemma. © 1966 by The Twentieth Century Fund, New York. p. 75.

frequency of attendance at cultural activities, and between income and type of cultural activity (e.g., the theater audience is the most affluent of all).

There is no evidence linking social mobility to high-culture consumption. Wilensky's data show little difference between the "leisure competence" of those who have been upwardly mobile, downwardly mobile, fluctuating, or stable. In terms of intergenerational mobility (measured by comparing the respondent's own occupation, education, etc., with those of his father), Wilensky again showed little difference in the leisure competence of those who have lost, gained, or maintained their status. Contrary to Toffler's contention that the high-culture consumer is often a mobile person, there seems to be considerable intergenerational continuity of culture. Wilensky's media purist inherits his occupational and educational status from a father who often is already an established professional or executive. Similarly Bradshaw showed the following relationship between students' "culture scores" and their fathers' education:

Of those whose father only went to grammar school, 6% scored high on the author's culture scale.

Of those whose father went to high school, 11% scored high on culture.

Of those whose father went to college, 14% scored high on culture.

Of those whose father went to graduate school, 22% scored high on culture.

What, then, is the relationship between culture and social class? Clearly it is a strong positive association. What is more pertinent here, there is no evidence of a leveling trend whereby our increasingly middle-class society would, as the cultural explosion advocates maintain, be increasingly cultured. As we saw earlier in this chapter, the gross national product may be rising, but the proportion spent on leisure and high culture is not.

There is, of course, a development which Riesman noted in 1958 and which gained greater momentum in the 1960s. In the fifties, while the lower strata's zest for material consumption was growing, their affluence being relatively new, the upper strata were developing a malaise with materialism, a search for something more profound, as evidenced, for example, by the psychoanalytic vogue. The phenomena observed by Reisman are, of course, directly connected to the subsequent emergence of the counterculture, a largely middle-class phenomenon. Tom Wolfe's (1971) *Radical Chic and Mau-mauing the Flak Catchers,* the demography of the Peace Movement ever since Eugene McCarthy's presidential candidacy, and the entire counterculture in general show that we have a social movement whose main features are both youth and upper class. To the extent that this movement is growing, America's cultural awareness is indeed increasing, increasing at the expense of materialistic values. However, this is not what men like Toffler have in mind when they speak of a cultural explosion. Furthermore, the political and numerical importance of the counterculture has yet to be established. In a later chapter we shall present some analyses that view it as highly significant (Reich, 1970; Roszak, 1969) and some that do not (Berger, 1971; Nobile, 1971). Here, the point has been that social class remains a crucial determinant of cultural participation, still restricting high culture mostly to the upper strata.

SUMMARY AND CONCLUSION

This chapter has focused on high culture, on some of the problems and issues pertaining to that topic within the specific American context, and on the sociological characteristics of the high culture audience in America. First, we asked and tentatively answered the oft raised question "Are Americans 'cultured'?" From America's very inception, there have been those who have viewed the New Continent as a cultural wasteland, but also, their numbers increasing more recently, those who see in this country's wealth the basis of an unprecedented cultural efflorescence. Bernard Berelson, we saw, made a valiant effort at cutting this Gordian knot, quantifying "culturedness" and concluding that the average adult American spends perhaps 4.5% of his three daily leisure hours "in the presence of [high] culture."

We then added some relief to Berelson's findings by examining high culture longitudinally for quantitative trends over time. The following areas of high culture were covered: classical music, ballet and professional dancing, theater, art movies, art, and finally, literature. The following overall pattern emerged: the number of amateurs engaging in various high cultural activities, for example, playing classical music, theater, has increased significantly in recent decades, and so has the construction of multimillion dollar cultural centers. However, as far as the fine arts and performing arts *professions* are concerned, no expansion could be detected, except in the case of ballet. Thus high-culture patronage has, generally speaking, not kept pace with the growth in gross national product.

The final section of the chapter examined the sociological correlates of both high-culture producers and consumers. As far as the former group is concerned, it was noted that the contemporary artist and intellectual tend to be alienated from the power structure and from the dominant majority, sometimes to the point of taking a revolutionary subversive stance, but that this is a relatively recent historical phenomenon, going back no further than nineteenth century romanticism. Finally, the high-culture audience was examined in terms of sex, age, ethnicity, geography, religion, values, education, occupation, and social class. It was shown that women continue to dominate the high-culture audience; that this audience is somewhat younger than the general population; that Jews are overrepresented and Negroes underrepresented in this audience; that rural regions do not participate in high culture and that most cultural activity is concentrated in New York primarily and on the West Coast to some extent; that high-culture consumers are religiously frequently inactive, nonpracticing, or agnostics; that their political values are left of center, but they are politically and civically very active; that they lead materially relatively ascetic lives, even though they are far more affluent than the general population; that they have received more education than average, often at high-quality institutions, and that this education is more often humanistic than technological or vocational; that the high-culture audience is almost entirely white collar, most of all professionals and teachers; that leisure and culture are not only related to occupational level, but also to the form, content, and context of an individual's

work and to such variables as length of work week; and that social class remains a very important determinant of leisure and culture, the high-culture audience being a socioeconomic elite.

Two fictions, above all, must now be considered dispelled: that there is a rapid democratization of the high-culture audience, and that this is happening mostly in the United States. The *Playbill* study quoted earlier shows that, insofar as the theater is concerned, today's audience is similar to that of ten years ago in most demographic respects dealt with in this chapter, the only difference being that it may now be somewhat richer. This leads Baumol and Bowen to conclude that "if there were a cultural boom, a movement toward mass culture, there is little sign of it in the composition of the commercial theater." Trends in other fields of high culture, as we saw, are similarly unclear. There has been little change in the sexual, racial, and age composition of the high-culture audience, and cultural activities are not spreading out from their traditional geographical centers. Neither is there a downward spread of high culture into the middle and lower socioeconomic strata, as compared with a few decades ago. Furthermore, Baumol and Bowen's study of the British high-culture audience shows that in that country, at least, the high-culture-consuming population is slightly less affluent, counting more professionals and fewer intellectuals. In America, participation in high culture remains a rare and selective phenomenon.

STUDY QUESTIONS

1. A long-standing question has been whether Americans are "cultured." Try to answer that question, discussing specifically (1) some of the traditional views held by Europeans and Europe-oriented intellectuals in this regard, (2) the views of those, on the other hand, who fail to share such negativism (e.g., Toffler), and finally (3) the approach and findings taken by Berelson.
2. Discuss major trends in the following six areas of high culture: classical music, ballet and pro-

fessional dancing, theater, art movies, art, literature. What overall picture emerges out of the data? How has amateur participation fared, and how have the professional fine arts done?

3. Discuss some of the social and psychological traits of the typical contemporary culture producer. Is social class an important variable in this regard? How? How do we account for the alienation of the modern artist and intellectual? When, historically, does this emerge?

4. Discuss the following nine characteristics of the high-culture audience: sex, age, race and ethnicity, geography, religion, values and tastes, education, occupation, social class. Among which sexual, racial, demographic, regional, social, ed-

ucational, occupational, and religious groups do we find most of the high-culture consumers?

5. In the final analysis, are we to agree or disagree with those who claim that America has been experiencing a cultural explosion? Document your answer by referring, again, to specific trends in each of the six areas discussed in this chapter: classical music, ballet, theater, art movies, art, literature. Have the socioeconomic characteristics of the high-culture consumers changed in recent decades? Is there a downward diffusion of high culture taking place? Finally, how do we compare with some foreign countries, for example, Britain?

REFERENCES

Anderson, Charles and Milton Gordon
1964 "The blue-collar worker at leisure." Pp. 407-416 in Arthur B. Shostak and William Gomberg (eds.), Blue-collar World: Studies of the American Worker. New York: Prentice-Hall, Inc.

Anderson, Nels
1961 Work and Leisure. New York: The Free Press.

Baumol, William J. and William G. Bowen
1966 Performing Arts—The Economic Dilemma. New York: The Twentieth Century Fund.

Berelson, Bernard
1964 "In the presence of culture." Public Opinion Quarterly 28 (Spring):1-12.

Berger, Peter and Brigitte Berger
1971 "The blueing of America." The New Republic (April 3):20-23.

Bradshaw, Ted K.
1971 "Culture through education: the effect of educational experiences on cultural leisure patterns." Unpublished paper read at the 1971 meetings of the Pacific Sociological Association, Honolulu, Hawaii.

Clarke, Alfred C.
1956 "Leisure and occupational prestige." American Sociological Review 21 (June):301-307.

Dulles, Foster Rhea
1965 A History of Recreation: America Learns to Play. New York: Appleton-Century-Crofts.

Emrie, William J.
1970 Recreation problems in the urban impacted areas of California. Sacramento, Calif.: State of California Department of Parks and Recreation.

Fortune, the Editors
1958 "$30 billion for fun." Pp. 161-172 in Eric Larrabee and Rolf Meyersohn (eds.), Mass Leisure. Glencoe, Ill.: The Free Press.

Frazier, E. Franklin
1958 "Society status without substance." Pp. 228-237 in Eric Larrabee and Rolf Meyersohn (eds.), Mass Leisure. Glencoe, Ill.: The Free Press.

Gerstl, Joel E.
1963 "Leisure, taste and occupational milieu." Pp. 146-167 in Erwin O. Smigel (ed.), Work and Leisure. New Haven, Conn.: College and University Press.

Glazer, Nathan
1964 In panel discussion. Pp. 155-200 in Norman Jacobs (ed.), Culture for the Millions? Mass Media in Modern Society. Boston: Beacon Press.

Goldstein, Bernice and Robert L. Eichhorn
1961 "The changing Protestant ethic: rural patterns in health, work and leisure." American Sociological Review 26 (August):557-565.

Havighurst, Robert J.
1957 "The leisure activities of the middle-aged." American Journal of Sociology 63 (September):152-162

Jacobs, Norman (ed.)
1964 Culture for the Millions? Mass Media in Modern Society. Boston: Beacon Press.

Kando, Thomas and Worth C. Summers
1971 "The impact of work on leisure: toward a paradigm and research strategy." Pacific Sociological Review (special summer issue):310-326.

Kaplan, Max
1960 Leisure in America. New York: John Wiley & Sons, Inc.

Kraus, Richard
1968 Public Recreation and the Negro. A Study of Participation and Administrative Practices. New York: Center for Urban Education.

1971 Recreation and Leisure in Modern Society. New York: Appleton-Century-Crofts.

Larrabee, Eric and Rolf Meyersohn (eds.)
1958 Mass Leisure. Glencoe, Ill.: The Free Press.

Nobile, Philip
1971 The Con III Controversy: The Critics look at the Greening of America. New York: Pocket Books.
Outdoor Recreation Resources Review Commission
1962 Trends in American Living and Outdoor Recreation. ORRRC Study Report 22. Washington, D. C.: U. S. Government Printing Office.
Reich, Charles
1970 The Greeing of America. New York: Random House, Inc.
Riesman, David
1958 "Leisure and work in post-industrial society." Pp. 363-385 in Eric Larrabee and Rolf Meyersohn (eds.), Mass Leisure. Glencoe, Ill.: The Free Press.
Riesman, David and Warner Bloomberg, Jr.
1957 "Work and leisure: fusion or polarity?" Pp. 69-85 in C. M. Arendsberg et al. (eds.), Research in Industrial Human Relations: A Critical Appraisal. New York: Harper & Row, Publisher.
Rosenberg, Bernard and David Manning White (eds.)
1957 Mass Culture: The Popular Arts in America. New York: The Free Press.
Roszak, Theodore
1969 The Making of a Counterculture. Garden City, N. Y.: Doubleday & Company, Inc.
Schumpeter, Joseph
1949 Capitalism, Socialism, and Democracy, ed. 3. New York: Harper Brothers.
Shils, Edward
1964 "Mass society and its culture." Pp. 1-27 in Norman Jacobs (ed.), Culture for the Millions? Mass Media in Modern Society. Boston: Beacon Press.
Smigel, Erwin O. (ed.)
1963 Work and Leisure. New Haven, Conn.: College and University Press.
Statistical Abstracts of the United States
1971 Washington, D. C.: U. S. Government Printing Office.
Toffler, Alvin
1964 The Culture Consumers. Baltimore: Penguin Books Inc.
Veblen, Thorstein
1899 The Theory of the Leisure Class. New York: The Macmillan Company.
White, Clyde
1955 "Social class differences in the uses of leisure." American Journal of Sociology 61 (September): 145-150.
White, David Manning
1957 "Mass culture in America: another point of view. Pp. 13-21 in Bernard Rosenberg and David Manning White (eds.) Mass Culture: The Popular Arts in America. New York: The Free Press.
Wilensky, Harold
1964 "Mass society and mass culture: interdependence or independence?" American Sociological Review 29 (April):173-197.
Wolfe, Tom
1971 Radical Chic and Mau-mauing the Flak Catchers. New York: Bantam Books, Inc.

chapter 6

Mass culture: the printed media

This chapter attempts to provide an overview of the fields of mass culture and the printed media. This area is vast, large enough for the existence of entire academic departments, research institutes, and specialized journals.[1] Obviously, we can only deal with the major branches and the most salient issues in the field. The purpose of this chapter is essentially to introduce the reader to the study of mass culture and mass communication as major topics for the sociology of leisure and popular culture. Wher-

[1]Major universities, for example, Columbia, Missouri, and Northwestern, have not only departments but entire schools of journalism; there are also Centers for the Study of Popular Culture (Bowling Green State University) and Institutes for the Study of Sport and Society (Oberlin College). Some of the specialized journals in the area of mass media are the *Columbia Journalism Review*, *Gazette*, the *Hollywood Quarterly*, the *Journal of Advertising Research*, the *Journal of Broadcasting*, the *Journalism Quarterly*, *Marketing/Communications*, *Media-Scope*, the *Merrill-Palmer Quarterly*, the *Montana Journalism Review*, the *Public Opinion Quarterly*, the *Publishers Weekly*, *Studies in Public Communication* and the *Television Quarterly*.

Ken Lambert/Photoworld

ever possible, bibliographical footnotes are provided as an aid to further research in particular subareas.

Why do I devote a chapter to the simultaneous treatment of mass culture and mass media? In part, it is because I feel that the two are closely interrelated. Recall that I defined mass culture as *cultural elements traditionally not included in high culture, and transmitted by the printed press, the electronic media, or by other forms of mass communication* (Chapter 3). One need only glance at the contents of a famous reader in mass culture (Rosenberg and White, 1971) and a recent one in mass media (Wells, 1972) to note their similarity. Both deal with the printed media (newspapers, magazines, books), electronic media (radio, television), advertising, etc. Conceptually, we may distinguish mass media from mass culture by noting that the former constitute the *form,* whereas the latter is the message, or *content.* Thus the sociology of mass media must, properly speaking, address itself to the social problems centering around the various media *qua media,* while the sociology of mass culture deals with the stories, shows, plots, personalities, and character of particular papers, films, books, and television and radio programs. However, while McLuhan's claim that medium and message are one and the same may be an exaggeration, there is a kernel of truth in that thesis. Indeed, mass media cannot be studied independently from their content, and neither can there be a sociology of (mass) culture that does not examine communication technology. Our approach must be based on the realization that technology and culture (form and content, medium and message) are so mutually interrelated as to be inseparable. Mass culture and the mass media, then, must be dealt with jointly.

The following five areas of mass culture are treated in this chapter: newspapers, magazines, books, comics, and the underground press (including the countercultural comix). Cinema is handled separately in the following chapter.

Each area of mass culture is briefly treated in terms of its historical development. I then provide some information about the area's quantitative growth and current magnitude. I also examine its demographic correlates, dealing with sex, age, race and ethnicity, geography, religion, values and tastes, education, occupation and social class.

The major focus is on the most salient issues and problems that have been raised in the literature pertaining to each area of mass culture. Thus when discussing newspapers, we address ourselves to the oft asked questions about the nature and magnitude of monopolistic trends and the alleged erosion of neutrality in reporting. My treatment of magazines will focus on what has been said in the literature about their changing normative content, and how this may reflect the changing culture at large. When dealing with books we shall ask, following many other students of mass culture, questions about the quality of Americans' reading habits. Similarly, my discussion of comic strips and comic books must raise questions about the impact of their content upon the readers' minds and behavior, particularly the young.

Long before Johann Gutenberg allegedly invented movable type, block printing by woodcut had been in existence. When historians write about the invention of printing during the first part of the fifteenth century, they mean, of course, the introduction of separate and movable characters. Whether this invention should be credited to Gutenberg (as is generally done in his native Germany and in most other parts of the world), to Coster (as do that man's fellow Dutchmen), or to someone else is not important. In all probability, the movable print was an idea whose time had come and which therefore, as so many other inventions, blossomed independently and more or less simultaneously in different minds. This happened before 1450, and the first large book printed with movable type is said to be (What else?) the bible (Mainz, 1456).

Today, some 450,000 different books are published in the world annually. While this figure is merely the grossest estimate (exact figures fluctuate, depending on whether one includes picture books, university theses, government publications, advertising books, second and subsequent revised editions, etc.), it is nevertheless expressive. One feels pangs of anxiety at this information explosion, at the production of a quantity of print undigestable by even well-staffed libraries, let alone the would-be informed individual. As a nation, incidentally, we do not rank first in overall book production: the Soviet Union does, with 74,611 books published in 1969 (Statistical Abstracts of the U. S., 1971:802), as against 62,083 in the United States. Per capita, eastern European countries generally rank highest, along with some of Western Europe, for example, the Netherlands. And then there is Angola, which has published eight books.

Newspapers and magazines form, of course, the bulk of today's newsprint consumption. There are in the world approximately seven thousand daily newspapers, with a circulation of over 300 million (Statistical Abstracts; 1971:821). The United States account for the largest number, over eighteen hundred, with a circulation of 62 million (Statistical Abstracts, 1971: 491 and 821). In addition, we have in this country roughly ten thousand weekly, semiweekly, and other newspapers, plus another ten thousand periodical magazines and trade publications (Ayer and Son, 1971). Precise figures in such matters are difficult to obtain, as frequencies fluctuate from year to year, and because it is not clear how inclusive any given statistic is. For example, Ayer's estimate of the number of American periodicals does not include

the booming underground press, nor the narrowly specialized scientific, professional, and artistic publications with minor local audiences only. The main points, however, should be clear. The printed medium has reached, by the twentieth century, a magnitude calling for *measurements in tonnage rather than in numbers of publications!* Thus industry measures newspaper production and consumption in tons of newsprint, that is, in the amount of paper used by the printed press. In 1969, world production of newsprint amounted to 23 million short tons, roughly 9.5% of all paper produced (Statistical Abstracts, 1971:793). While worldwide the printed medium continues to grow, in advanced societies such as the United States it has reached a plateau. The partial but ongoing substitution of the printed medium by the more advanced electronic media in Western society is, of course, one of the central themes in the history and sociology of mass media. Marshall McLuhan is merely the most vociferous interpreter of an inescapable fact noted by many. In the United States, annual newsprint consumption now stagnates under 10 million tons. The number of daily newspapers has declined from its all-time high of 2,202 in 1910 to 1,818 in 1971. Other newspapers have also declined, and the number of periodicals has grown only in proportion to the population.

The only growth sectors in this area are the specialized periodicals that succeed because of their intensive exploitation of a narrow market component (e.g., *Playboy* and the ski magazines), and the book business. From 1950 to 1970, book publications increased nearly fourfold.[2] This, combined with the fact that the average price of a book has more than

---

[2]Sociology-economics, incidentally, has now become the largest single subject category, increasing over the last two decades by an incredible 1,100%, and now eclipsing all other classes of literature, including fiction, science, and juvenile literature.

doubled during the past decade, accounts for some of the misleading statistics we sometimes encounter. We learn that we now spend upward from $9 billion a year on the printed medium, as against $2 billion in 1950 *(U. S. News & World Report,* 1972) and are led to believe (1) that the printed media thrive and (2) that Americans read far more than ever before. The truth of the matter emerges when we separate books from the rest. The slow, historical eclipse of reading, writing, and literacy as generalized societal habits by other forms of communication becomes inescapable. Let us now examine the various printed media in detail.

NEWSPAPERS
Historical development and current quantities

On September 25, 1690, Benjamin Harris published *Publick Occurrences, Both Forreign and Domestick,* America's first newspaper (Boorstin, 1961:7). Since then, the history of the American press has been linked perhaps more closely than that of any other institution to the consecutive stages of development of the country itself. Raymond Nixon's fine trend study of American newspapers (1972) discerns five periods, each a distinct chapter in the history of both America and its press. In colonial days, the American press was identified with the fight for freedom. This was reflected in the form of the papers themselves. "The tiny papers of political journalists like Sam Adams and Tom Paine were little more than propaganda leaflets. They

did not have to be self-supporting" (1972:10). From the foundation of the New York *Weekly Journal* to the rudimentary papers financed by Benjamin Franklin, the spirit of the American press at this time is best symbolized, of course, by the First Amendment.

The period immediately following independence is characterized by Professor Nixon as a period of "political party leadership." Papers had yet to become financially self-sustaining enterprises. They were, rather, official party organs.

Only with the appearance of the first "penny papers," in 1833, do we see the first trend toward mass circulation. This is when capitalism in America begins, and the press's character inevitably changes to reflect this. The press becomes less of a political institution, more an economic one. Editors like Horace Greeley remain forever associated with this period.

The fourth chapter in the history of the American press—covering roughly the last two decades of the nineteenth century and the first two of the twentieth —is an extension of the previous era. As capitalism expands, so newspapers, too, now become truly big business. An important change is that advertising now becomes the major source of revenue, rather than circulation, as earlier. The press is now increasingly dominated by publishers (men like Pulitzer of the *New York World,* and the Ochs family of the *New York Times*) and financial interests, rather than editors.

Finally, it is Nixon's feeling that the

***Table 6*-1.** *American daily newspapers since 1880**

	1880	1909-1910	1920	1930	1940	1945	1950	1955
Number of dailies	850	2,202	2,042	1,942	1,878	1,744	1,772	1,760
Circulation (thousands)	3,093	22,426	27,791	39,589	41,132	45,955	53,829	56,147

*Source: Nixon (1972:11) and Statistical Abstracts of the United States (1971:490-491).

1930s ushered an era of renewed social responsibility and intermedia competition. According to this author, the advent of radio and television as independent sources of information has forced newspapers on their toes, so that the quality and objectivity of reporting are no longer subordinated to financial interests, as they were at the turn of the century. This contrasts, we should note, with the highly critical view of contemporary newspapers held by a man like Daniel Boorstin (1961), according to whom papers have degenerated into manufacturers of phony events, packaged news, sensationalism, myths, and illusions, as has all of our mass culture.

Our first concern, here, is with the daily press. Table 6-1 gives the facts about daily newspapers since 1880.

The steady decline of the daily press over the past sixty years is apparent. In terms of the number of papers published, the all-time peak was 1909-1910. And whereas overall circulation has continued to increase, *per household* consumption peaked in 1919 (Wells, 1972:7).

But what about the thousands of weekly, semiweekly, and other newspapers? We hear that the so-called community press is doing better than ever. Thanks to the advent of centralized printing, which now permits someone with relatively little capital to start a newspaper, it is said that "weeklies aren't weaklies anymore" (Bowers, 1972:21). "By 1964, there were 1,100 plants printing two or more daily or weekly newspapers, totaling 2,900 newspapers" (1972:19). Presumably, then, the crunch is not hitting all newspapers.

In Table 6-2, we provide figures on all newspapers, including weeklies and semiweeklies.

Whether the community press is faring well cannot be gauged from the aggregate statistics at our disposal. It is true that the number of semiweeklies and "other" newspapers has increased substantially since 1950, thereby contrasting with the general pattern. However, in recent years that growth, too, may have come to a stop. There was no further increase in the "other" category from 1969 through 1971 (Statistical Abstracts, 1971:491). No sector of the newspaper industry seems to be able to escape the general pattern of stagnation or slow decline.

Sociological correlates

Who reads newspapers? Or, more specifically, what are the newspaper reading habits of the various demographic, economic, cultural, and other subgroups of the population? Let us look, as we did in the previous chapter, at sex, age, race and ethnicity, geography, religion, values and tastes, education, occupation, and social class.

According to Leo Bogart (1964) it is difficult to make statements about the sociological correlates (e.g., social class) of American mass media. His thesis is that mass media in America tend to reach an *amalgamation* of people rather than particular subgroups (socioeconomic or otherwise) because (1) ours is an open society and (2) our advertisement-supported media must always maximize their audiences. Old myths die hard. One persistent myth has been the melting pot. Although W. Lloyd Warner's pioneering work led to the subsequent unequivocal demonstration that ours is *not* a classless society, men like Bogart continue to describe it as a uniquely "open" one. This merely rephrases the conventional ste-

1960	1965	1968	1969	1970
1,763	1,751	1,752	1,758	1,748
58,882	60,358	62,535	62,060	62,108

Table 6-2. American newspapers since 1950*

	1950	1955	1960	1965	1968	1969	1970
Dailies	1,772	1,760	1,763	1,751	1,752	1,758	1,748
Weeklies	9,794	9,126	8,979	8,989	8,858	8,855	8,903
Other	427	429	482	551	602	648	642
Total	11,993	11,315	11,224	11,291	11,212	11,261	11,293

*Source: Statistical Abstracts of the United States (1971:490-491).

reotype and perpetuates the mistaken belief that America, due to its unique history, lacks the subcultural demarcation lines found, for example, in Europe. The European situation was well captured in a book like Hoggart's *The Uses of Literacy* (1957), which shows the distinctiveness of the values, tastes, and media-consumption habits of the British working class. Such social-class and subcultural differentiation is all too smugly said to be absent in the United States (Bogart, 1964:418-419). The reasons for this remain unclear. The alleged homogeneity of American culture and media consumption is attributed to the virtually universal literacy rate, a capitalist economy to which advertising is central, and modern mass communication technology. But surely Great Britain does not differ significantly from us in these terms? Bogart's thesis, then, must be viewed as both erroneous and contradictory. It is erroneous because it is based on a defunct and refuted model of American society, and it is contradictory because the author himself subsequently shows significant sociological correlates of reading, viewing, and listening habits.

While different segments of the same newspapers and different papers may be read by the two sexes, statistics do not reveal overall differences between the amount of newspaper reading done by men and that done by women. Certain types or portions of newspapers are for women, for example, the household, leisure, and women's sections of Sunday editions. Other material, for example,

technical, editorial, financial, sports, and professional information, is mostly read by men. These matters follow, of course, conventional sex role ascriptions. In most statistical analyses the unit is the household, thus making it difficult to determine the comparative amount of newspaper reading done by the various members —male vs. female, young vs. old. The reading habits of the young, too, distinguish themselves first and foremost qualitatively. The very young read the comics, and the not so young read, in addition to the favorite sections of the family paper, perhaps a number of youth publications, including the activist community press, the underground papers, and the thousands of high school and college papers across the nation.

A study by Greenberg and Dervin (1972) compared the patterns of media consumption of low-income respondents with those of the general population, and also those of whites with those of blacks. While the newspaper usage of the two socioeconomic groups differed sharply, no significant racial differences were found. Fewer low-income respondents reported reading a newspaper every day, and fewer reported reading all of the newspaper. While the general population sample was likely to read the front page, the comics, and sports, the low-income group reported reading mostly headlines and classified ads. But as stated, black-white differences (within the low-income sample) were not significant. This leads the authors to conclude that (low-income) blacks are considerably like whites in terms of newspaper consumption. There were, of course, important differences in other forms of media consumption, and we shall pick these up in the following sections of this chapter.

A thorough analysis of newspaper consumption by race, ethnicity, and religion would be an extensive study in and of itself. While the hundred or so Negro newspapers in the country are included in the statistics presented earlier, the hundreds of foreign language papers are not. Each ethnic, national, cultural, and linguistic subgroup in America has its own newspapers. So do the religions and denominations, from such sectarian publications as the Jehovah's Witnesses' *Watchtower* to such prestigious national papers as the *Christian Science Monitor*. Regionally, the number of daily newspapers ranges from 126 in California to 3 in Connecticut, although circulation is highest in New York (7.5 million) and lowest in Alaska (71,000). Meaningful comparisons are, of course, per capita. For example, in proportion to population, Massachusetts consumes three times as much newspaper as does Mississippi. In the final analysis, the bulk of the variance in newspaper consumption by region, race, and ethnicity can be traced to occupation (farming vs. urban employment), social class, and education. We now therefore turn to these more fundamental variables.

Socioeconomic status, the most relevant variable for our discussion, is really a complex cluster that includes at least class, education, and occupation. Sociologists have distinguished between "print-oriented" and "broadcast-oriented" people, and they have found, inevitably, correlations with social class, education, occupation, and other components of socioeconomic status. The "readers" tend to be in higher occupational, educational, and socioeconomic brackets than the "watchers" and the "listeners." For example, a study by Foote, Cone and Belding reported by Bogart (1964:420) shows that of the women classified as readers, 54% had husbands in white-collar occupations, compared with 21% of those classified as viewers. Similarly, another study (see Bogart, 1964:421-422) showed that blue-collar households watch more television and read less than the national average.

A 1961 study (see Bogart, 1964:421) showed the role of education in media consumption. The question was asked, "Generally speaking, which do you feel closest to—the television channel you watch most often, the radio station you listen to most often, or the newspaper you read most often?" Table 6–3 gives the answers.

In line with these findings, Gary Steiner (1963) found that "at the very lowest educational bracket (less than grade-school education), television actually receives higher marks than newspapers as the most important and the most educational medium which presents things the most intelligently. Among the high school educated, newspapers and magazines assume far greater importance" (quoted in Bogart, 1964:421).

Zeroing in on newspapers, the 1961 study cited earlier (Bogart, 1964:424-

Table 6-3. *Dependence upon media according to education (percentages)**

	Grade school	High school	College
Television channel	34	39	18
Radio station	17	12	14
Newspaper	34	39	53
All the same, don't know	16	10	15

*From Leo Bogart, "The mass media and the blue-collar worker." In Arthur B. Shostak and William Gomberg (eds.), Blue-collar World: Studies of the American Worker, © 1964. By permission of Prentice-Hall, Inc., Englewood Cliffs, N. J.

Table 6-4. Average weekday newspaper reading, by occupation (percentages)*

Readers	All U. S.	Skilled manual workers	Machine operators, semiskilled workers, farmers	Unskilled workers
Subscribers and purchasers	72	76	72	61
Other readers	8	6	10	8
Total	80	83	82	69

*From Leo Bogart, "The mass media and the blue-collar worker." In Arthur B. Shostak and William Gomberg, (eds.),Blue-collar World: Studies of the American Worker, © 1964. By permission of Prentice-Hall, Inc., Englewood, Cliffs, N. J.

Table 6-5. Weekday newspaper reading habits, by education (percentages)*

	Grade school	High school	College
Read every day	53	65	77
Read less often	47	35	23
Read one paper	73	67	54
Read two or more papers	27	33	46

*From Leo Bogart, "The mass media and the blue-collar worker," In Arthur B. Shostak and William Gomberg (eds.), Blue-collar World: Studies of the American Worker, © 1964. By permission of Prentice-Hall, Inc., Englewood, Cliffs, N. J.

426) provides useful findings. Table 6-4 shows the relationship between readership and occupation.

Apparently, as one moves down the occupational ladder, not only does readership decline, but most strikingly so does the purchase of newspapers.

Regularity and amount of newspaper readership are directly related to education. Table 6-5, from the same study, indicates this.

Not only is there a direct relationship between amount of newspaper reading and education, but in addition, the lower the education, the more parochial the reading interests. The same study shows, for example, that the readers' interest in local affairs decreases and their interest in national and international affairs increases with education.

Furthermore, the higher the education, the more active the use of the newspaper. For example, clipping of newspaper items, writing letters to the editor, and placing classified ads all increase for readers with high education.

Finally, a study of W. R. Simmons (quoted in Bogart, 1964:426) gives an illustration of the differential appeal that major newspapers in a given metropolitan area can have. The seven newspapers in existence in New York City in 1962 were used in the study (see Table 6-6).

Familiarity with the contents and history of failures of some of the papers listed in Table 6-6 suggests that both the popularity and the viability of a newspaper depend upon its mass appeal, and that blue-collar weighs surprisingly heavily in this.

Major trends and issues

What are some of the major issues one comes across in the literature on newspapers? Many of these are problems shared

Table 6-6. Blue-collar* readers as percentage of total†

Mirror	58
News	56
Journal-American	40
Post	33
Times	24
World-Telegram and Sun	20
Herald Tribune	17
All adults	47%

*Craftsmen, foremen, operatives, service workers, and manual laborers.
†From Leo Bogart, "The mass media and the blue-collar worker." In Arthur B. Shostak and William Gomberg (eds.), Blue-collar World: Studies of the American worker, © 1964. By permission of Prentice-Hall, Inc., Englewood Cliffs, N. J.

by other media as well. The problems of modern mass media seem to be as numerous as the assessments that are made of them. Probably most of the critical discussions of the press address themselves to political matters, for example, matters of propaganda, freedom of the press, rampant monopolism, bias in news reporting, and responsibility to the public. Some authors, in addition, have been concerned with the cultural quality of newspapers. And then there are questions about the press's current magnitude and economic status.

The latter issue was partly dealt with in the previous pages, so I shall dispose of it first. The question, quite simply, is how well the newspaper business is doing. I provided data (see Tables 6-1 and 6-2) to show that whereas circulation has maintained a slow upward trend, the number of newspapers has not been able to expand. There may be some exceptions. Bowers (1972) and others detect great vigor in the community press, that is, in the local, often suburban, newspapers appearing on some other than daily basis. They attribute this to the emergence of centralized printing, that is, the joint use of printing plants by several small independent newspapers. While

some categories of newspapers, for example, the semiweeklies, have increased in recent years, the overall pattern remains one of stagnation or slow decline. Bowers may be overlooking the fact that community papers may be folding as often as they are mushrooming, leading short-lived existences at best.

The internal structure of the newspaper business will be examined in a moment. Here, let me sum up by characterizing the industry *as a whole* as the static old giant of the media market, comparable to coal in the energy market and railroads in transportation. Every sector of a modern dynamic economy is essentially of a dual nature, in the sense that it comprises advanced growth technologies on the one hand, and older means whose expansion has reached static maturity on the other. While the new grows at the expense of the old, as hydroelectric power makes inroads into coal, air travel overshadows sea fare, and the automobile eclipses the passenger railroad, one generally errs in predicting the total replacement of the old by the new. Historically, the more familiar pattern has been *cumulative* rather than *substitutive*. In the field of mass media, the printed press represents the old, electronic media the new. But to view their relationship as antithetical rather than coextensive, as do the McLuhanites, is a fallacy. Bogart (1963) correctly pointed out that the period of greatest newspaper decline occurred before the age of television. The daily press has successfully survived the electronic onslaught.

The bulk of the literature on newspapers deals with qualitative rather than quantitative issues. In the first place, let me quote again that flamboyant conservative, Daniel Boorstin: "There was a time when the reader of an unexciting newspaper would remark, 'how dull is the world today!' Nowadays he says 'what a dull newspaper!'" In other words, Boorstin argues, "the responsibility for making news was entirely God's—or the Devil's . . . [today] news is whatever a good editor chooses to print" (1961:7-8). As a result, newspapers now flood us with a constant stream of synthetic, contrived, fabricated news—the so-called pseudoevents (1961:9). Pseudoevents are things like presidential press conferences, Senate hearings, or celebrity scandals. These are devoid of inherent importance, yet fill up the bulk of contemporary newsprint. This contrasts with the original purpose of journalism, which was to report genuinely important phenomena, such as natural disasters, wars, and other spontaneous events. Boorstins' point, made over a decade ago, remains more than ever valid. Today, only the illustrations might have to be updated. Indeed, what better example of a pseudoevent can there be than Watergate?

Boorstin's indictment of newspapers—part of a more general attack on all mass media—is a conservative, romantic statement. At bottom, it says that the quality of newspapers has deteriorated. Recall that Raymond Nixon (1972) feels otherwise, arguing that the emergence of electronic media has created an intermedia competition which forces newspapers to greater responsibility and responsiveness to public needs, in sum better quality reporting.

Whether newspapers have deteriorated is a moot point. I can, however, offer a critical examination of what I feel to be the crucial determinants of the press's behavior, and an evaluation of its performance under those conditions.

The press[3] operates under the cross-pressures of at least three opposing forces. On the one hand it embodies, upholds, and does battle for all that is lofty and noble in the principles of the First Amendment. In this sense, to think of the press is to think of freedom and democracy. This is the ideal. On the other hand, the behavior of newspapers is first and foremost the outcome of fundamental economic and political exigencies; the press must sell itself and the goods which it advertises to the largest possible public, and it must also uphold the power structure to which it is integrally committed. Consequently it can neither abstain from disseminating sensational yet potentially false information, even when the welfare of possibly innocent parties would dictate it, nor can it afford to be overly critical of established power relationships, even in the face of gross injustice. This is reality. Given these parameters, the press must at all times be fundamentally conservative in its ideology and in its reporting, while having nevertheless to release a maximum amount of sensational and poorly verified information. The reality of the situation is an uneasy one, conflict between the two seats of power, press and government, never far around the corner.

While government and the press are allies at the most fundamental level—together, they represent and uphold our bourgeois society—they frequently clash at the surface because their internal needs are contradictory. The governmental bureaucracy's ultimate objective is to maximize order, but order is dull; the press's needs are diametrically contrary, as it thrives on chaos, violence, sex, adventure, romance, conflict, crime, in one word, news.

Watergate represents the culmination of perhaps the most severe clash between press and government, but friction between the two is endemic to our social system. Governmental efforts at controlling the press can be traced back as far as one chooses. While the Federal Communications Commission goes back to 1934, it was preceded by a Federal Radio Commission created in 1927[4] and federal

---

[3]It should be understood by now that "press" and "newspapers" are used interchangeably, except when specific differences are dealt with.

[4]Under Commerce Secretary Herbert Hoover.

legislation designed to regulate mass media goes back to at least 1912 (Nye, 1970:391).

In the seesaw battle between press and government, the liberal has generally sided with the government, arguing that it has failed to restrain an unfettered, monopolistic press. Enter Nixon, Agnew, and Mitchell. To these men even the orthodox press, which overwhelmingly endorsed Nixon in all three of his presidential campaigns, appeared too liberal. The law-and-order administration overshot its target, the hippie, and considered to do what no previous administration had contemplated: media regulation. This may have been Nixon's single fatal error. The point here is not that the media were being threatened with measures like discretionary relicensing of stations by a right-wing administration (radical intellectuals might not object to such manipulation if its thrust were in the opposite direction), but that the threat was made at all. The Nixon administration's attack on the press was aimed at forcing it into the same type of uncompromising law-and-order attitude toward political dissent and cultural innovation that was its own. This demanded not only more conservative reporting and editorializing but, most importantly, censoring oneself and not reporting all the news that's fit to print. In America, the press could not accede to this. This kind of conservative censorship would mean, among other things, the desensationalization, desexualization, and decriminalization of our essentially tabloid national press. It would reduce the *Times* to *Pravda,* and who would read, much less buy, a paper like that?

Watergate, the press's retaliation, has been a colorful episode. Yet we must remember that it is not altogether that momentous. The press makes the most of it, of course, dubbing it a constitutional crisis and referring, superlatively, to a couple of presidential firings as a "Satur-

day night massacre." However, what happened on Saturday, October 27, 1973, was no Saint Bartholomew.

My analysis of the press's behavior is based on a distinction between ideal and reality. Reality consists of the growing friction between the needs of a capitalist press and an increasingly smothering governmental bureaucracy. The ideal is total freedom of the press. It becomes the ideological justification of a press under governmental attack. It is no surprise that we hear so much these days about the Constitution of the United States, the Bill of Rights, and the First Amendment.

One arena in which the conflict between press and government has unfolded in recent years is the judiciary. The pressure by the courts upon the press to release confidential information has been mounting. Subpoenas, followed by contempt citations and indeterminate jail sentences, have increased. In June, 1972, the Supreme Court decided in the Caldwell case that "newsmen do not have the constitutional right to withhold information from grand juries." As Cohn (1972) explains, what reporters object to most vigorously is to submit "out takes" (the often confidential material not used publicly). Crucial also is the question as to whether information sources should be divulged. The danger is that the journalist may be intimidated into becoming a planted government agent and that potential sources of valuable information dry up as a consequence. At this time, congressional legislation safeguarding the reporters' right to protect his sources has yet to be acted on.

Carolyn Jaffe (1972) raises a related issue, the potential interference with justice of pretrial press publicity. Since sensational disclosures about violent crimes, even when unfounded, are the stuff that makes copy sell, we have the familiar "trials by the press." Unbiased jury trials are often hard to arrive at. Jaffe lists a number of possible remedies to combat this. Among those, contempt citations against papers giving undue and prejudicial pretrial publicity to criminal cases would seem to be the most promising. Its deterrent effect has been successfully demonstrated in Great Britain.

Pressure upon the American press, then, has most frequently come from the right, particularly in recent years. As Hedrick Smith (1972) shows once again, Nixon's press conferences and the entire Washington atmosphere have been unmitigated intimidation. The simple fact has been that critique of the administration by an honest young journalist was frequently followed by job loss. However, this is precisely an indication that the press, as a whole, has failed to live up to its responsibilities. Throughout the 1960s and the early 1970s, Knopf (1972) and Blumberg (1971) show, the press's treatment of racial, political, and antiwar disturbances has been biased and sensationalized. Destructive events received undue attention, and successful experiments in social change were overlooked. The violent crisis at San Francisco State made front-page coverage, but the peaceful settlement requiring no police or national guard at Brandeis was ignored. In one instance, a harmless groundhog hunter carrying a rifle was widely identified in the national press as a racial sniper (Knopf, 1972:351).

At the same time, when the establishment resorts to violence on a scale reminiscent of fascism itself, the press minimizes it, feigning a "neutral " position. For example, during the 1968 Democratic Convention in Chicago, Mayor Daley's police savagely manhandled yippie demonstrators, peaceful onlookers, and reporters alike. Yet the press, after a few days of courageous outrage elicited by police assaults on its own personnel, returned to the fold, cautious not to break its traditional ties with the establishment. Thus the *Chicago Tribune,* in one of the understatements of the century,

denounced "bad judgment by the police," quickly adding that "the press is not the enemy of the police force; it is the policeman's friend. Policemen so lacking in judgment that they needlessly beat up a representative of the press don't belong on the police force," (Blumberg, 1971:301). And James Reston merely deplored the impact of "the vicious clashes between demonstrators and police" on the Democratic Party. The Walker (1968) Report had apparently few supporters, even among the press.

Newspapers, then, are by their very nature as selective in their perception and presentation of facts as the newsmen, editors, and publishers responsible for their existence. In a nice empirical study, White (1972:191-198) documents the crucially selective role of one such individual—the newspaper wire editor. Of the 12,400 inches of press he receives from the wire services each week, he uses perhaps one-tenth. White's point is that this "gatekeeper" uses essentially subjective value judgments to sift the news. Pieces of wire copy are rejected with notations like "he's too red," or "B.S." or "don't care for suicides." In general, "Mr. Gates" rejects stories that are uninteresting and stories that are too radical. Thus we see again the parameters which serve as acceptance criteria to an average orthodox newspaper.[5]

No medium is a more important tool of propaganda and source of information than the newspaper. As Qualter (1972) points out, newspapers are still the major source of political information and opinion in literate societies. This is particularly so in the case of subscribers, as Brinton and McKown (1961) have shown. In America the reputation of newspapers has become that of "the traditional crusader for the liberties of the people against the tyranny of Government"

---

[5]Other studies dealing with the gatekeeper role include Carter (1958), Donohew (1967), Gieber (1956), Gieber and Johnson (1961), Judd (1961), and Rivers (1965).

(1961:282) but at the same time it is no longer possible to distinguish in their columns between fact and opinion. Different papers use different opinionated language and allocate different amounts of space to the same story, reporting details selectively, judiciously using certain types of headlines, reporting an event on the front page, back page, or not at all. The same problem, for example, off shore oil drilling, can be raised in different ways:

RESUMPTION OF OIL DRILLING THREATENS SAFETY OF COASTAL RESIDENTS

vs.

RENEWED OIL DRILLING TO ALLEVIATE ENERGY SHORTAGE

Or, to provide another example:

CITY COUNCIL BLOCKS CAMPUS ROCK CONCERT, CITES FIRE AND HEALTH HAZARD

vs.

CITY BREAKS WORD: ROCK CONCERT OFF

While a government-press coalition as in Nazi Germany has not taken place in the United States, students of mass media concur that our press is by no means free of propaganda. The orthodox media, Balk (1972) points out, are essentially conservative and increasingly monolithic. Free competition of ideas in the opinion industry is as much a myth as free enterprise in other sectors of the economy. As elsewhere, monopoly is the key to higher profits. As Raymond Nixon (1972) shows, concentration of newspaper ownership has been increasing for many years. As a consequence, the number of American cities with two or more competing dailies declined from 689 in 1910 to 45 in 1968. Today, 97% of our cities are one-daily or joint-operation cities. Furthermore, the trend is now toward the formation of ever larger national newspaper groups. Table 6-7 lists the top ten national daily newspaper groups as of 1968.

Table 6-7. *Top ten daily newspaper groups with seven-day circulation of 1 million or more**

Name of group	Number of dailies	Weekday circulation	Sunday papers	Sunday circulation	Seven-day circulation
1. Chicago Tribune Newspapers	7	3,627,916	5	4,959,453	26,337,375
2. Newhouse Newspapers	23	3,190,180	14	3,391,495	22,455,248
3. Scripps-Howard Newspapers	17	2,504,466	7	1,841,753	16,788,344
4. Hearst Newspapers	8	2,080,647	7	2,712,635	14,850,223
5. Knight Newspapers	7	1,390,117	6	1,508,523	9,847,865
6. Gannett Newspapers	29	1,290,710	8	611,558	8,289,612
7. Cowles Newspapers	11	1,108,637	7	1,342,057	7,993,868
8. Ridder Publications	16	1,143,847	10	1,128,047	7,941,820
9. Times Mirror Company	3	964,702	2	1,222,059	7,006,908
10. Ochs Estate Newspapers	3	914,576	2	1,559,383	6,890,803

*From Raymond B. Nixon. 1968. "Trends in U. S. newspaper ownership: concentration with competition." Gazette 14(3):181-193.

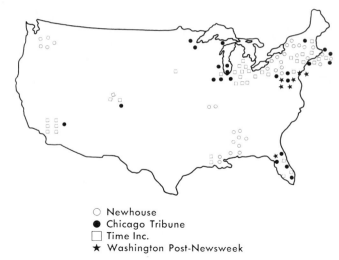

○ Newhouse
● Chicago Tribune
□ Time Inc.
★ Washington Post-Newsweek

Fig. 4. Selected "media baronies" in the United States. Adapted from "The American media baronies and atlas." Atlantic Monthly, *July, 1969.*

Finally, what are we to make of Nixon's argument that the increasing concentration of newspaper ownership is counterbalanced by vigorous intermedia competition, so that the press does not, after all, become a monopolistic propaganda tool? The unfortunate fact is that the concentration is taking place at the *multimedia* level, not merely among newspapers. Thus we have what the *Atlantic Monthly* (1972:103-111) aptly describes as the media baronies. One owner may, for example, dominate all of a city's media, as does Donald W. Reynolds, owner of Fort Smith, Arkansas' two newspapers and its only TV station; or as the Plym family, owner of Niles, Michigan's only daily newspaper, its only AM radio station, only FM station, where there is no local TV outlet (*Atlantic Monthly* Staff Writers, 1972:103).

Beyond this are the growing national communication conglomerates. I conclude this section with a somewhat altered illustration from the *Atlantic's* highly suggestive "Barony Atlas."

Each of the four empires shown in Fig. 4 owns, in addition to numerous broadcasting stations in various parts of the globe (a similar world map could be drawn), a variety of publications. Among the better known: *Time, Life, Fortune,* and *Sports Illustrated* are owned by Time, Inc. (Headquarters: New York). *Vogue, Glamour, Mademoiselle, House and Garden* plus the major dailies in Portland, Saint Louis, Syracuse, and Birmingham are owned by Newhouse (Hq.: Syracuse). The *New York Daily News, Chicago Today,* and, of course, the *Tribune* are owned by the Chicago Tribune (Hq.: Chicago). The *Washington Post,* the *Herald Tribune,* and *Newsweek* are owned by the Post Company (Hq.: New York).

MAGAZINES
Historical developments and current quantities

In colonial America, the most popular medium was the periodical almanac. The first colonial almanac appeared in New England in 1639 (Hofstadter et al., 1959, vol. 1:114) and by 1731 they were being read in all the colonies. Benjamin Franklin first published his *Poor Richard's Almanac* in 1732, soon selling ten thousand copies a year.

Poor Richard, 1747.

A N

Almanack

For the Year of Chrift

I 7 4 7,

It being the Third after
LEAP-YEAR,

And makes fince the Creation **Years**

By the Account of the Eaftern *Greeks*	7255
By the Latin Church, when ☉ ent. ♈	6946
By the Computation of *W. W.*	5756
By the *Roman* Chronology	5696
By the *Jewiſh* Rabbies	5508

Wherein is contained,

The Lunations, Eclipfes, Judgment of
the Weather, Spring Tides, Planets Motions &
mutual Afpects, Sun and Moon's Rifing and Setting, Length of Days, Time of High Water,
Fairs, Courts, and obfervable Days.

Fitted to the Latitude of Forty Degrees,
and a Meridian of Five Hours Weft from *London,*
but may without fenfible Error, ferve all the adjacent Places, even from *Newfoundland* to *South-
Carolina.*

By *RICHARD SAUNDERS,* Philom.

PHILADELPHIA:
Printed and fold by *B. FRANKLIN.*

The first large-scale magazine boom occurred in the middle decades of the nineteenth century. William T. Porter's
weekly *The Spirit of the Times* (1831–
1861) became one of the largest, providing entertaining sporting and theatrical
information to over forty thousand people (Hofstadter et al., 1959, vol 1:448).
Other established magazines during that
period included *The North American Review* (Boston), the *Knickerbocker Magazine* (New York), and the *Southern Literary Messenger* (Richmond). These periodicals, printing the words of men like Cooper, Poe, Hawthorne, and Longfellow,

Table 6-8. *Magazines with greatest circulation
in selected areas**

Area	Magazine	Circulation
Cars	*Hot Rod Magazine*	817,972
Crafts	*Mechanics Illustrated*	1,555,607
Dogs	*Dogs*	103,000
Dress	*Seventeen*	1,489,320
General education	*Time*	4,268,091
	Newsweek	2,611,184
	Cosmopolitan	1,231,094
Men	*Playboy*	5,290,027
	Esquire	1,178,965
Sports	*Sports Illustrated*	2,043,411
	Boys Life	2,542,786

*Source: 1971 Ayer Directory of Newspapers, Mag-
azines and Trade Publications.

had a national circulation. Ladies' magazines included *Godey's Lady's Book* and
The Ladies Magazine, which also
achieved a circulation of forty thousand
after their merger in 1836 (Hofstadter et
al., 1959, vol 1:454).

By 1971, there were 9,657 periodicals
being published in the United States
(Statistical Abstracts, 1971:491), an all-
time high. This included the weekly
magazines in newspapers and the
various professional, technical, and trade
journals. The *Reader's Digest* had, then,
the largest circulation (15 million), although that has since been surpassed by
Playboy's phenomenal success. According
to Hugh Hefner (January, 1974, *Playboy*
interview), the magazine's circulation
now exceeds 26 million. For 1971 the
leaders in selected subareas are listed in
Table 6-8.

I estimate that the combined magazine circulation per issue was, in 1971,
between 600 and 900 million. Of course,
far more people look at magazines than
purchase them. Family magazines like
Life, Look, and the *Saturday Evening
Post* have had perhaps four to five
readers for every subscriber; they were
picked up and read in innumerable dentist's and lawyer's waiting rooms. They

Table 6-9. American periodicals since 1950*

	1950	1955	1960	1965	1968	1969	1970	1971	1973
Weeklies	1,443	1,602	1,580	1,716	1,796	1,787	1,856	1,873	2,022
Monthlies	3,694	3,782	4,113	4,195	4,331	4,353	4,314	4,277	4,107
Other	1,823	2,164	2,729	3,079	3,273	3,294	3,303	3,507	3,501
All	6,960	7,648	8,422	8,990	9,400	9,434	9,573	9,657	9,630

*Source: Statistical Abstracts of the United States, 1971:491.

may have been read by ten times their circulation (cf. Wells, 1972:27). Table 6-9 presents the growth pattern of American periodicals since 1950.

From Table 6-9, periodicals would seem to have escaped the fate of general decline in the printed press. We shall return to this in a moment. First, let us turn to our demographic correlates of magazine reading

Sociological correlates

Different demographic groups evidently read different magazines. More than any other medium, the magazine is often targeted at a specific segment of the population. In no other area of media consumption tend the sexes, for example, to be such separate audiences. There are, in the first place, the magazines for men. These include two categories, the sports, trade, and technical periodicals (e.g., *Mechanics Illustrated, Sports Illustrated*) and the sex journals *(Playboy, Esquire)*. Second, there are women's magazines, and again two broad types can be distinguished, the fashion and household publications *(Vogue, Better Homes and Gardens)* and the primarily lower-class romance and confession magazines *(True Story, True Confessions).* Women's only middle-class sex magazine remotely equivalent to *Playboy* has been *Cosmopolitan.* Recently, of course, women's liberation has changed some of this, producing publications like *Playgirl* and *Ms.* As a third logical category, let us mention those magazines that are not sex based, for example, the now defunct *Life* and

Look and the political weeklies *Time* and *Newsweek.*

Age levels, too, often represent distinct magazine audiences. For example, *Seventeen* is a teenage fashion magazine, and *Mad* is popular with two categories of readers only—teenagers and sociologists.[6] The teenage magazine, Lewis (1972:224) points out, is a postwar invention, as is the teenager himself. After World War II, technological affluence created a new minority, the teenager. Totally disfranchised, his sole function was to consume. The teenage market was developed, and so were teenage magazines.

Can we, in addition, generalize about the overall magazine reading habits of various sex and age groups? A survey for the Motion Picture Association of America asked a national probability sample of 5,021 persons representing the total population of the United States what leisure activities they had engaged in yesterday. Table 6-10 shows the percentages of respondents among the sex and age categories reading magazines.

The variances in Table 6-10 show that men read magazines less than women, and the middle-aged read less than the old and the young, which means that

---

[6]Before the underground press, the comix, and other artifacts of contemporary youth culture, *Mad Magazine* stood as the prime symbol of teenage rebellion among printed media. Sociologists concerned with the youth culture of the 1950s inevitably attribute great significance to that periodical. See, for example, Daniels (1971), Lewis (1972:225-227 et passim), Manago (1962), Pekar (1972), Winick (1968).

Table 6-10. *Percentage of population reading magazine "yesterday," by sex and age**

Sex		
Men		25
Women		27
All		27
Age		
15-19		31
20-29		29
30-39		25
40-49		25
50-59		23
60+		27
All		27

*From "The public appraises movies," a survey for the Motion Picture Association of America, Inc., by Opinion Research Corporation, December, 1957.

those who work read less than those who don't. The same research also showed that only 26% of employed women read magazines, vs. 28% of those not employed.

Race, ethnicity, and religion are variables which, as with newspaper consumption, cause *qualitative* rather than *quantitative* differences in reading habits. Greenberg and Dervin (1972:265-272), for example, did not find significant differences in the overall amount of magazine reading of blacks and whites of *similar* socioeconomic status. Likewise, if Jews or Unitarians are found to spend more time reading magazines than Baptists or Catholics, this is not the result of religion as an independent variable, but social class and education. It may be true that the media purist, as Wilensky (1964) shows, is most likely to be Jewish or inactive Protestant—and this, then, is the man who reads both better and more magazines than others—but much of that relationship is spurious.

When Madison Avenue looks at ethnic markets, it is aware of their heterogeneity. The black audience, for example, is becoming appealing because of the growing black bourgeoisie. Magazines and supplements like *Ebony* and *Tuesday* are obviously not aimed at a ghetto audi-

ence.[7] When the editors of *Media-Scope* (in Lewis, 1972:186-191) suggest that these magazines reach "the Negro market," they mean, of course, the rich Negro. *Ebony* is an interesting mix of values. Its political articles inevitably deal with Negro issues. For example, in the November, 1973, issue, Carl Rowan writes about the West African famine and what American brothers can do to alleviate it; Carl Stokes tells the readers why he quit as mayor of Cleveland, and a special survey tells us what the ten best American cities for blacks are. Most of the remaining departments are devoted to individual success stories, for example, how the Cooper brothers made it big in business, a cover story about the top black Hollywood actresses, a story about millionaire singer Al Green, and a historical sketch about early black pioneer businessmen. Most stories deal with individual personalities, and they all carry the same moral: there is hope, opportunity, and progress for American Negroes. A rare exception to the Horatio Alger flavor might be, for instance, a story about Texas prison inmates. Here, at last, we are reminded of the other reality of Negro life in America. And coincidentally or not, one sees in all the magazine's ads and photographs only pale-faced near-whites, until one hits the deep black faces of the Texas inmates.

Specialized religious publications are as numerous as are denominations. In 1971 the United States had eighty-two religious bodies with a membership of fifty thousand or more, each with its own periodicals. These religions range from rigid fundamentalism to modern libertarianism. The Jehovah's Witnesses provide a good example of a body close to the fundamentalist end of the religious

[7]In 1967, *Ebony's* circulation was approximately 1 million. In addition, the Johnson Publishing House also issues a weekly Negro news magazine, *Jet* (350,000 circulation), and a monthly for Negro women, *Tan* (122,000) (Lyle, 1969).

continuum. The group's two semi-monthly organs, the *Watchtower* and *Awake!*, each claim a circulation of nearly 8 million, printed in twenty-nine languages. They document the group's world view. Some articles deal with and deplore the trend toward peaceful coexistence with communism (*Watchtower*, December 1, 1973); other stories dismiss all politics as corrupt; and many pages are devoted to the evils of drugs (*Awake*, December 8, 1973). Thus current social issues are raised, and the religious periodicals mix relevance with conservatism.

What about regional and ecological determinants of magazine consumption? For this, let us go back to the survey taken for the Motion Picture Association of America (quoted in de Grazia, 1964:441-445). Table 6-11, based on that study, presents magazine reading by region and according to urban-rural residence.

Tentative as Table 6-11's findings may be, they are revealing. Magazine reading is low in the South and Midwest, the rural parts of the country. Yet the second part of the table shows no positive relationship between reading and urbanism. It indicates that magazines are read the

Table 6-11. *Percentage of population reading magazine "yesterday," by region and urban-rural residence**

Region	
Northeast	30
North Central	24
South	23
West	34
All	27
Rural-urban	
Rural	27
Below 100,000	31
100,000-999,999	28
1 million+	22
All	27

*From "The public appraises movies," a survey for the Motion Picture Association of America, Inc., by Opinion Research Corporation, December, 1957.

most in small and middle-sized cities, the least in metropolises. All in all, we see once again that the ultimate predictors of culture consumption must be social class, education, and occupation, rather than the variables hitherto examined.

Turning to the socioeconomic status cluster, then, we first see a linear correlation between income and magazine consumption (Opinion Research Corporation, 1957, cited in de Grazia, 1964:443). This is echoed in findings cited by Bogart (1964:426-427): Blue-collar workers' exposure to magazines is less than average, and the difference between skilled and unskilled workers is even greater than that between skilled workers and the general public. A study of the readership of nine leading magazines (*Life, Look, Saturday Evening Post, Time, Better Homes and Gardens, Good Housekeeping, Ladies' Home Journal, McCall's* and the *Reader's Digest*) showed that all except *Good Housekeeping* were more likely to reach the general public than blue-collar workers. However, the three leading news magazines (*Newsweek, Time,* and *U. S. News & World Report*) were read more frequently by skilled blue-collar workers than the national average.

So far we have considered occupation (blue-collar) as an indicator of class (working class). However, occupation is also an independent variable in its own right, as Gerstl (1963) showed. Holding social class constant, this author compared the leisure activities of admen, dentists, and professors. While the socioeconomic status of these three groups is rather similar, their jobs differ sharply. Gerstl showed that the *kind* of job one has may influence one's taste and leisure activities.[8] Turning to magazine con-

[8]The relationship between the *nature* or *meaning* of one's work and one's leisure activities is focused on by several authors, including Havighurst (1957), Kando and Summers (1971), and Wilensky (1960). We have argued that the relationship may be compensatory, or a spillover, and that there are ways to determine which one it is in a given setting.

sumption, the author distinguishes be-tween lowbrow periodicals *(House and Garden, Life, Saturday Evening Post, Reader's Digest, Argosy)*, high-brow *(Harper's,* the *New Yorker, Saturday Review, Encounter)*, and crossbrow *(Time, Newsweek)*. The astounding finding is that only the professors read *any* of the magazines classified as highbrow. The admen spend a fair amount of time reading (52% read more than five hours per week vs. 60% of the professors), but most of this is lowbrow. The dentists simply don't read (20% put in more than five hours a week).

Wilensky's important study of mass culture (1964) shows similarly dismal tendencies. A comparison of lawyers, engineers, professors, a sample of the "middle mass" and of "underdogs" reveals that only the professors generally read quality magazines (defined as a specified list of forty-one nonprofessional periodicals plus major law reviews and professional journals). Whereas 91% of the professors read one or more such magazines regularly, only 33% of the lawyers, 0.5% of the middle mass, and none of the underdogs do so (1964:192).

The single most powerful predictor of culture consumption is education. No other factor accounts for as much of the variance observed in such variables as leisure, taste, and lifestyle. The same Wilensky study amply demonstrates this, as one of its central theses in fact is that level and quality of formal education are by far the most important predictors of the quality of a person's cultural exposure (1964:187). And the Motion Picture Association of America study referred to earlier shows that magazine reading varies more sharply by education than by other variables. Table 6-12 presents the study's portion that pertains to this.

Thus education, occupation, and social class determine both the quality and the quantity of magazine reading.

Table 6-12. *Percentage of population reading magazine "yesterday," by education**

Less than eighth grade	12
Eighth grade	19
High school, incomplete	24
High school, complete	29
College	40

*From "The public appraises movies," a survey for the Motion Picture Association of America, Inc., by Opinion Research Corporation, December, 1957.

There are two types of periodicals whose qualitative and class-bound character has fascinated sociologists and led to a substantial amount of research. One is *Playboy* and the other is the confession magazines. Both have been content-analyzed, and the researchers' main point has often been the documentation of the former's eminently middle-class and the latter's marked working-class character.[9]

While *Playboy*'s manifest objective is to provide vicarious sexual thrill to an essentially single, young, middle-class, urban, white-collar, male audience, its more important latent function, according to Gerson and Lund (1972), is the socialization of those men into a certain lifestyle. The *Playboy* philosophy, the *Playboy* forum, the goods, styles, and fashions that are advertised, the books, films, vacation spots, and celebrities that are appraised, all coalesce to provide a role model for a certain type of reader. And who is this reader? He, of course, changes as does the magazine itself, both adapting to a rapidly changing culture. Thus while only a few years ago the what-sort-of-man-reads-*Playboy* ads showed a short-haired, jocklike, golf-playing, football-loving junior business executive, today the role model is likely to be a modish, hirsute college type. The

[9]Sociological studies of *Playboy* magazine include Gerson and Lund (1972) and Ryan (1957). Romance magazines have been dealt with by Berelson and Salter (1957), Ellis (1961), Gerbner (1958), Macfadden-Bartell (1962), Schramm (1961), and Sonenschein (1972), among others.

magazine's continuing success has in large part been the result of its ability to go hip along with the masses of young people in the late 1960s. By its liberal stand on marijuana, abortion, homosexuality, and women's liberation (the latter totally unrequited), *Playboy* continues to capture all those among us who claim to be hip without being hippies.

In sharp contrast with *Playboy* are the romance magazines. These include the Macfadden women's group of periodicals *(True Story, Photoplay, TV Radio Mirror, True Romance, True Experience,* and *True Love)* plus such magazines as *True Confessions, Real Confessions, Secrets, Intimate Story, Daring Romances,* and the *National Inquirer.* The readership of confession magazines is large. In 1962 the Macfadden group alone reached nearly 13.5 million women 15 and over. (Bogart, 1964:427). Successive content analyses (see footnote 9) have revealed that this type of publication is profoundly traditional in its ideology. Like *Playboy,* the confession magazine is an important tool of socialization. However, their readership and values are in diametric opposition. Table 6-13 contrasts the two types of publications.

In the preceding section I examined the sociological correlates of magazine readership. My conclusion must be that

diversity, rather than homogeneity, is the hallmark of the American-media-consuming population. Unlike Bogart (1964:428), Wilensky (1964), and others who focus on the conforming and integrative functions of mass media and who argue that the various subgroups of the population, as a consequence, are gradually entering the broad, homogeneous mainstream of common culture, I am struck by the persistence and possible increase in demographic and subcultural differences. American society is no melting pot; it is a mosaic.

Major trends and issues

Most of the current literature on magazines concerns either the medium's economic viability or the relationship between the content of magazines and the larger culture.[10]

Judging by the figures in Table 6-9, magazines seem to fare better than newspapers. Yet the recent demise of *Look* and *Life,* the two highly popular

[10]The first problem is examined, for example, by Root and Root (1964) and Welles (1972). The second focus is found in Baker and Ball (1969), Berelson and Salter (1957), Davis (1967), Ellis (1961), England (1960), Gerson and Lund (1972), Greene (1970), Johns-Heine and Gerth (1957), Kotok (1971), Sargent et al. (1965), Lee Smith (1972), and Sonenschein (1972), among others.

Table 6-13. *Readership of two contrasting types of publications:* Playboy *and romance magazines*

	Playboy	*Romance magazines*
Readership		
Sex	Male	Female
Marital status	Single	Married and single
Age	Young	Young and Middle-aged
Class	(Upper) middle	Working
Avowed focus	Sex	Love
Ethic	Guilt-free hedonism	Guilt-laden traditionalism
Psychology	Pleasure principle	Superego
Approved forms of behavior	Premarital sex	Virginity and marital sex
	Promiscuity	Monogamy
	Birth control and abortion	Procreation
	Occupational roles	Domestic roles
	Leisure	Work

picture magazines, indicates that the problems of mass periodicals may be as severe as those of any medium at this time. In 1967, there were four general magazines in existence in the United States, with a combined circulation of 39 million (Lyle, 1969). Today, only the *Reader's Digest* and the *Saturday Evening Post* survive. *Look* and *Life* have died, despite vast and loyal audiences. Magazines, then, seem to be of two types: the old established mass periodicals and the specialized organs aimed at specific demographic groups. The former have all but died, while the latter, in many cases, thrive.

In an incisive and prophetic analysis of the situation, Chris Welles (1972) explains the modern mass magazine's predicament. It is not that it no longer attracts a wide audience or fills a need for millions of readers—each issue of *Look* and *Life* is said to have been read by 70 million adults. The magazines' trouble lies with their other constituency, Madison Avenue. Indeed, from 1966 on, advertisers have put less money into *Life* and *Look* every year. And yet, revenue from advertising had been the lifeblood of the modern mass periodical. It cost forty-one cents to produce a copy of *Life,* but the average reader paid only twelve cents for it!

Why have advertisers lost faith in mass periodicals and administered the coup de grace to the protracted agony of such giants as *Life* and *Look?* The first reason is of course TV. The advertising cost per one thousand persons reached via *Life* was $7.71; via TV, about $3.60 (Welles, 1972:29). Thus by 1970 the four leading national advertisers—Procter and Gamble, General Foods, Bristol-Meyers, and Colgate-Palmolive—spent $434 million in TV and only $45 million in magazines (Welles, 1972:31). The second and most important cause, however, is what has been described as the dissolution of the mass. Unlike those who

maintain that American mass culture is still in the process of amalgamation and homogenization toward a broad, more or less uniform middle mass (for example, Bogart, 1964; Wilensky, 1964), Madison Avenue now recognizes an opposite tendency, the growth of specialized demographic, regional, and subcultural lifestyles and consumption patterns. This explains the success of all those publications with a distinct identity and a distinct readership: *Cosmopolitan, Ebony,* the *New Yorker, Psychology Today, Playboy, Rolling Stone.* These, then, are the mass periodicals' true competitors, and not TV. These are the media which have benefited from increasing advertising at the expense of such mass magazines as *Life* and *Look,* because Madison Avenue is convinced of the superiority of focused over "shotgun" advertising.

But what about the public's needs? Is not a combined circulation of 14 million for *Life* and *Look* prior to their demise proof that they were satisfying important needs and that their death is another case of special interests ruthlessly prevailing over public needs? To this, advertisers reply that paying twelve cents for an issue of *Life* by the average reader was no demonstration of deep need or loyalty. More significantly, a comparison of newsstand sales of mass magazines and specialized periodicals—a truer indicator of interest—shows that people will readily pay $1 for a copy of *Playboy* but are unwilling to pay thirty-five cents for *Look.* Such sales account for 80% of the former magazine's circulation, while they had become negligible in *Look*'s case (Welles, 1972:33). Thus mass magazines can clearly be said to have lost their prior popularity, while certain specialized periodicals continue to be highly viable. Madison Avenue is in part responsible, but its decisions seem to reflect rather than lead societal developments.

Perhaps the most frequent type of sociological study of magazines has been the (longitudinal) content analysis. For example, researchers have traced the changing success models found in American periodicals (Johns-Heine and Gerth, 1957), the changing treatment and position of racial and national minorities (Berelson and Salter, 1957; Kotok, 1971; Smith, 1966; Sonenschein, 1972) and their treatment of violent themes (Haskins, 1969). Most of the time, the authors have examined the magazines' contents as they reflect and relate to the changing culture at large.

Johns-Heine and Gerth (1957), for example, analyzed the content of 728 fiction stories sampled randomly from five major magazines between 1921 and 1940. In terms of the typical heroes encountered in the stories, they found a significant shift from a business model to a professional model. Heroes also generally tended to become younger, although this varied by magazine. The setting tended to be urban. In the women's magazines the main theme is love, and career orientation brings on punishment (social sanctions in middle-class publications, physical harm among the working class). Success, in the early stories, means individual Horatio Alger type business enterprise. Later, it means social recognition, esteem. The authors also note a growing secularization in the content of some of the magazines. All in all, an old but highly plausible demonstration of how mass periodicals reflect shifting cultural and social-structural developments.

An interesting longitudinal series is provided by the Berelson-Salter (1957) and Kotok (1971) studies. The first of these studies had shown, through the content analysis of 198 magazine stories from 1937 to 1943, that native WASP Americans were cast in far more favorable roles than minority Americans and foreigners. Notably, they were overrepresented among the stories' "good guys." Kotok's replication is based on eighty

stories selected randomly from more or less the same magazines, but between 1946 and 1968, thus permitting comparisons. The hypothesis underlying Kotok's study was that minorities and foreign nationals would, in many ways, receive better treatment by 1968 than had been the case earlier. In many respects the hypothesis was verified. The proportion of American minorities and foreign nationals among the heroes had increased; also, their social class standing had improved; and neither was it as frequently found necessary to explain a minority's high socioeconomic status as in Berelson's period. There was now more interethnic love and marriage, and while Berelson and Salter had found that "Americans" had more altruistic goals while minorities had more materialistic objectives, this discrepancy had declined. Finally, Kotok shows that the "slick" magazines *(Playboy, Ladies' Home Journal)* treat minorities less favorably than the "pulp" periodicals *(Argosy, True Confessions)*. This is, again, good empirical evidence of how the changing content of magazines reflects changes in the structure and culture at large.

Sex has been the other major theme found in magazines and traced by social scientists.[11] The very mention of sexual revolution has now become banal. Since Kinsey et al (1948) began, shortly after World War II, to document the gradual erosion of Puritanism in America, the flood of liberation in both sexual behavior and media treatment of sex has become diluvial. By 1960, as Ellis (1961) showed, attitudes toward extramarital sex, sex perversions, sex censorship, sex organs, and extramarital pregnancy ex-

---

[11]In footnote 9 of this chapter I listed some sociological studies of such periodicals as *Playboy* and the romance magazines. For more general discussions of obscenity, pornography, and sex in magazines, see Ellis (1961), *Playboy* (1973), Polsky (1967), Lee Smith (1972).

pressed in magazines were far more liberal than a decade earlier. His conclusions were solidly based on a longitudinal content analysis of 495 published stories and articles. A decade later, Lee Smith (1972) addressed himself to the issue under the heading "Is Anything Unprintable?" Today, the epitome in candor is perhaps most vividly represented by the classified ads found no longer only in the underground press but also in respectable periodicals like the *New York Review of Books*. For example:

> Two males guys would like to meet well hung stockie built male age 35–45 for 3 way. Send photo and phone. Will answer all. (*Berkeley Barb*, 1970).

> Stud—30—wants masculine young slaveboy. No experience necessary. Will teach. Prefer small-slender boy. (*Berkeley Barb*, 1970).

> Attractive academic couple, European, early forties, seek congenial man to make occasional New York triangle. (*New York Review of Books*, 1973).

In 1973 the United States Supreme Court moved into the breach, handing down a series of obscenity rulings affirming that local community standards were to determine censorship decisions. Since local communities could, in many cases, be expected to be intolerant of a variety of sexual, artistic, and cultural expressions, many knowledgeable observers felt that the Supreme Court had hereby opened the door to bigotry, book burning, and First Amendment abridgment.

The scholarly study of magazines has focused on additional issues. For example, Sargent et al. (1965) have contrasted the treatment accorded to racial violence by white magazines (e.g., *Life*) and their black equivalent *(Ebony)*. Haskins (1969) examined violence in magazines, noting that among the various media, magazines do not stand out for their violence content. In general, I conclude my discussion of magazines by noting, with Smith (1966), that American magazines have been remarkably beneficient as

compared to some of our other media. Far from merely providing vulgar sex and violence to their consumers, their function has frequently been to disseminate good culture to many people.

BOOKS
Historical development and current quantities

The wilderness that remained during America's colonial days and for much of the pre-Civil War period prevented the rise of a prolific autochthonous literary and scientific tradition. With the exception of an occasional book in arithmetic, poetry, or history, most Americans relied, until the turn of the nineteenth century, on pamphlets, tracts, some newspapers, and the ubiquitous almanac for their information. Insofar as they read books, these came from Europe (see Hofstadter et al., 1959, vol. 1:110-115).

During the 1840s, however, dime novels began to appear in large quantities. The American dime novel thrived until the latter part of the nineteenth century. It was the first massive book wave in this country. Some books sold a hundred thousand copies within a year (Nye, 1970:200). Editions of seventy thousand were not uncommon, and some books went through ten or more editions in one year (1970:201). Dime novels sold, to be sure, for as little as a nickel and as much as two bits. While it is a misconception to think that all dealt with the West, they did generally share a mediocrity which should, in retrospect, amuse rather than aggravate us. Nye (1970: 204) quotes the following typical dialogue between two characters who have just survived a mine slide:

> "Are you hurt?"
> "Who?"
> "You."
> "Me?"
> "Yes."
> "No."
> "Oh!"

Table 6-14. New books and new editions published in the United States, by subject*

Subject	1950	1955	1960	1965	1969	1970
Art, music, recreation, sports, travel	946	1,016	1,320	2,745	3,296	3,766
Drama, literature, poetry	1,122	1,153	1,228	2,680	3,682	4,559
Economics, sociology	515	520	754	3,242	4,462	5,912
Fiction	1,907	2,073	2,440	3,241	2,717	3,137
Juvenile	1,059	1,485	1,725	2,895	1,406	2,640
Medicine, science, technology	1,645	1,812	2,307	4,933	4,578	4,975
Philosophy, psychology	340	314	480	979	951	1,280
Other	3,488	4,216	4,758	7,880	8,487	9,802
Total	11,022	12,589	15,012	28,595	29,579	36,071

*Source. Statistical Abstracts of the United States, 1971:493.

Or the following conversation between dying bandit Burling Sharp and scout Harold Tracy:

"Who fired? Who killed me?" cried the dying man. "Oh, God, it's too late!"

"Aye, too late," cried Harold Tracy. "I fired the bullet which found your life and I shall never regret the deed!"

"Oh had I but one minute more!" groaned the dying wretch, but he did not.

As to the development of book reading in the twentieth century, one must distinguish between quantity and quality. Compared to a number of other advanced nations, America does not read very much (see Dutscher, 1957; Berelson, 1957). Compared to other leisure activities, books do not loom very large in the United States. We spend more time with the other media than with books (Opinion Research Corporation, 1957). Such facts have therefore led critical observers to describe American civilization as barbaric and functionally illiterate (Dutscher, 1957:126-127). While we shall deal with this later, let us avoid that polemic for a moment and note at the outset that recent book consumption *has* grown by leaps and bounds. Table 6-14 gives the figures from 1950 through 1970, specifying some subject categories.[12]

[12]In the introduction to this chapter I gave 62,083 as the total number of books published in the United States (in 1969). That figure includes federal government publications and doctoral dissertations. Table 6-14 does not.

Despite the many alarms about the condition of the book industry, Table 6-14 indicates the importance of books as a medium, particularly for furnishing specialized information. During the two decades covered by the table, the total annual number of publications increased more than threefold. The sharpest gains were registered in the specialized disciplines, for example, sociology and economics (elevenfold increase) and leisure and recreation (fourfold). On the other hand, traditional general areas have not kept pace with the average rate of increase. Fiction, for example, grew by a mere 1.5 factor, and juvenile literature increased only 2.5 times.

Today, the book business grosses nearly $3 billion a year, producing approximately two books for every American (based on Bogart, 1969, and Statistical Abstracts, 1971). Circulation ranges from the 125 million books sold by Erle Stanley Gardner to the self-financed one-hundred-copy anthologies published by some of my own colleagues. And in addition to book sales, there is library circulation. In 1968 our 25,000 libraries owned nearly 160 million books, checking them out at an annual rate of nearly 460 million (Statistical Abstracts, 1971:131-132).

Sociological correlates

When it comes to book reading, we must not only compare the reading

\u0000

habits of different subgroups of Americans, but also contrast the United States with other countries. Is it indeed true that we read less than most of the other developed nations? Is it indeed so that a higher proportion of our population is, for all practical purposes, unable to comprehend the content of an average book? If so, then critics may have a point—America's material wealth may not be matched by the quality of her mind.

Repeated surveys tend, indeed, to show the secondary place to which most Americans relegate book reading. The Motion Picture Association study referred to earlier (quoted in de Grazia, 1964:441-445), asking a national cross section of respondents in which leisure activities they had engaged "yesterday" found that only 18% reported having read a book, while 57% had watched TV, and 27% had read magazines. A more recent survey (cited in Lyle, 1969:196, 215) found an even lower rate of reading reported by respondents for "yesterday," a rate over five times lower for comparable demographic groups.

Men read less than women (17% vs. 19%, in the O.R.C. study), but this, again, is a function of employment. Employed women read even less than men (16% in the same study).

Similarly with age, people between 30 and 60 read much less than the young and the old because they spend more time on the job. Table 6-15 gives percentage of book reading by age.

Other studies on book reading and age

Table 6-15. *Percentage of population reading book "yesterday," by age**

15-19	21
20-29	19
30-39	17
40-49	15
50-59	15
60+	21

*From "The public appraises movies," a survey for the Motion Picture Association of America, Inc., by Opinion Research Corporation, December, 1957.

(e.g., Havighurst, 1957; Hoar, 1960; Lyle, 1969) have identified some additional patterns. For example, adults tend to read nonfiction, while children account for a greater proportion of fiction reading (as indicated by library checkouts). Furthermore, adult patronage of public libraries seems to be lower in poor neighborhoods than in affluent ones, particularly in poor black neighborhoods.

While there is, then, slight evidence that blacks may read fewer books than whites with socioeconomic status held constant, the evidence is not very conclusive. The far more relevant focus taken by sociology in this area has been to examine the rich and blossoming black literature. Outstanding black novelists of recent years include James Baldwin (*Another Country, The Fire Next Time*), Eldridge Cleaver (*Soul on Ice*), Dr. J. Denis Jackson (*The Black Commandos*) and Willard Motley (*Let No Man Write My Epitaph*). Black poets include Nikki Giovanni, Al Young, LeRoi Jones, and Clarence Major. Probably the most exciting playwright is still Imamu Amiri Baraka (alias LeRoi Jones). Also, Norman Mailer's *The White Negro* remains the classic statement on cultural and psychological convergence between blacks and countercultural whites.[13]

While this is not the place to expound on the meanings of black literature, we should note that its essential focus is on the development of revolutionary strength and consciousness through cultural nationalism (see Harrison, 1972). This is what distinguishes the modern radical black literature from the blues and other earlier and more quietistic manifestations of black culture.

Insofar as relationships have been established between book consumption and religion, they are, again, mostly spurious. Wilensky (1964), for example, found that the quality of media exposure

[13]For recent examples and discussions of black literature by radical young sociologists, see Gliner and Raines (1971:199-279) and Lewis (1972:184-223).

is highest for respondents who have no religious preference, or are inactive Protestants or Jewish, and lowest for certain groups of Catholics (1964:187). And this meant, among other things, reading (highbrow) books as against excessive TV viewing. Clearly the observed relationships between religion and book reading can in large part be traced to education and socioeconomic status. I shall deal with those correlates in a moment.

Geographic correlates of book reading are again provided by the O.R.C. study. Of the four national regions, North Central was found to read the least, the West the most, and the Northeast and the South were average. Rural-urban differences were not observed in this study, although others have established a positive relationship between book reading and urbanism (see, for example, Berelson, 1957). Also, earlier studies have shown that most books have traditionally been disproportionately concentrated in America's major cities, particularly New York, Chicago, and Los Angeles, and in the most populous states, particularly the Northeastern corridor (see, for example, Dutscher, 1957).

Turning finally to socioeconomic status, it is, of course, education which appears to be the best single predictor of book reading. This was pointed out early by Berelson (1957) and shown again in the O.R.C. study, whose findings are reproduced in Table 6-16.

More recent research led to totally different overall percentages, but a similar-ly large variance. Lyle (1969:196, 215) reports a study showing only 5.8% of the college-educated reading a book "yesterday," and only 0.9% of those with less than a high school education. I cannot account for the enormous difference between the two sources; certainly book reading did not decline that much in a decade. Both studies do, however, underscore the importance of education. And this is echoed elsewhere, for example, in Wilensky's (1964:187) finding that education is by far the most important predictor of the quality of a man's media exposure. Only among the most highly educated professionals did that author find, at last, one in four to have read a highbrow book in the last two months (1964:193).

Both Wilensky (1964) and Gerstl (1963) established the fact that occupation can, in its own right, influence the amount of book reading. Gerstl's comparison of three occupations in a similar social stratum—admen, dentists, and professors—revealed significant differences in reading habits. The proportion of professors reporting reading at least one (non-work-connected) book in the last month was one and a half times as high as it was among admen, and five times higher than among dentists (1963:160-161). Gerstl attributes this to differences in the nature of the three groups' work.

Thus, amount and type of book reading are the function of a vast variety of factors. While education accounts for most of the variance, social class, of course, also counts as an independent variable. As Bogart (1964) showed, blue-collar is generally less print oriented and more broadcast oriented than white collar. Other important factors, we saw, include sex, age, race, and subculture. Finally, America as a whole is not a book-oriented nation.

Major trends and issues

This section addresses itself to three types of questions. How large and how

Table 6-16. *Percentage of population reading book "yesterday," by education**

Less than eighth grade	12
Eighth grade	15
High school, incomplete	15
High school, complete	15
College	30

*From "The public appraises movies," a survey for the Motion Picture Association of America, Inc., by Opinion Research Corporation, December, 1957.

thriving is the book business in America today? What can be said about the quality of contemporary intellectual life in America in this context? And what major *genres* of books can be identified?

Berelson's article, "Who Reads What Books and Why?" (1957) does not provide up-to-date answers to our questions, but it states the issues in masterful simplicity: (1) Do Americans read much or little? (2) Do book readers represent the general population? (3) Has reading declined or deteriorated or both? (4) Are other media crowding out the book? (5) Do Americans read good books or bad books? (6) Do people read what interests them? (7) Do books influence people? These are indeed all the important questions, and perhaps the only important ones. Our tentative answer to the first question has been that Americans do *not* read very much. They read less than the Europeans, and spend less time reading than viewing TV or in other forms of mass culture. These facts have been established repeatedly, for example, in studies cited in Dutscher (1957) and by Wilensky (1964), and they do not seem to change very much. Berelson's second question has been answered at length when dealing with sociological correlates.

It is questions 3, 4, and 5 that cause most of the controversy encountered in the literature. Dutscher (1957), for example, argues that the condition of the book industry is wretched and that as a consequence the quality of books is getting worse. Because of skyrocketing costs and competition from the other media, the book business is not a very profitable one. Under these conditions, all the forces in the book industry push toward deterioration. Publishers, agents, best-seller listings, Book of the Month Club, bookstores, and libraries all must of necessity emphasize popularity and sales over quality. Quality works no longer get a chance to be published, as there is no demand for them (1957:128-137). Dutscher's argument seems to boil down

to the fact that the book business remains viable only by prostituting itself. Such criticism is echoed elsewhere. Hemley (1957), for example, points out that the paperback explosion should not smugly be interpreted as a cultural explosion. While it has led to the wide dissemination of "classics," it is more difficult than ever for good *contemporary* work to see the light of publication.

Thus a critical look at contemporary book production in America reveals an excessive preoccupation with monetary reward, with the "best-seller formula" (cf. Mott, 1957), and often deplorable contents characterized by blatant racism,[14] vulgarity, and violence.[15] This, then, is what has led men like Dutscher to characterize American civilization as barbaric and illiterate.

There is, however, another side to the picture. While Berelson's fifth question ("Do Americans read good books or bad books?") cannot be answered, we can try to deal with questions 3 and 4 (about changes in the quality of book reading in recent years, and the impact of other media upon book reading), pointing to some reasons why Dutscher's sharp indictment may be overdone. In the first place, book sales, library circulation, and other quantitative measures of book reading have been increasing up to three times more rapidly than the population (Toffler, 1964). And as far as the impact of other media is concerned, while there may be competition, there is also intermedia stimulation and an *additive* effect, making sometimes for more book reading by the same individuals who watch quality programs and see quality movies (Berelson, 1957). Finally, Berelson answers his last two questions ("Do people read what interests them?" and "Do books influence people?") with qualified affirmatives. Interest is, next to accessi-

---

[14]See Lewis' discussion (1972:98-100) of racism in *Airport.*
[15]For a study of the effects of violence in books, see Haskins (1969).

bility and readability, certainly a prime factor in book reading, and the great classics have certainly exerted their influence on millions of us, albeit most often indirectly.

Discussion of the major genres of books are frequently framed in the same controversial terms. For example, from the 1930s through the late 1950s, detectives were by far the most widespread kind of literature. Erle Stanley Gardner and Ellery Queen wrote ten of the nineteen best-sellers in the 1930s (Dutscher, 1957:133). In the 1950s Mickey Spillane sold more books than anyone else. The enormous popularity of that vulgar, violent, bungling hero of his, Mike Hammer, led a number of critics to worry about the overall quality of book reading (e.g., LaFarge, 1957) and about modern mass culture in general (cf. Orwell, 1957). Others have been less critical, merely trying to interpret the meaning of modern detective novels in terms of the psychological functions they perform for their readers. Thus Wilson (1957) is not overly alarmed, and Rolo (1957) feels that both Simenon's Maigret and Spillane's Mike Hammer offer us, in different ways, the vicarious opportunity to play savior; hence their popularity.

"There is no doubt," Nye (1970:268) writes, "about the permanent popularity of detective-mystery stories. . . . One of every four books . . . is a detective-mystery. Erle Stanley Gardner's books have sold upwards of 135 millions. . . . Ellery Queen [is] at 100 millions . . . Mickey Spillane at 50." The detective story provides all the entertainment value of the riddle, the puzzle, and the vicarious identification with both the criminal and the detective, without straining either the mind or the emotions. The viability of the detective as a modern mass entertainer is perhaps best indicated in the fact that in 1973, forty years after his conception, national prime-time television made room for a new Perry Mason (Monte Markham) in addition to the old (Raymond Burr).

Of course, the detective story is no longer the only enormously popular *genre* in mass literature. Significantly, whereas *Mass Culture* I (Rosenberg and White, 1957) devotes its entire fiction section to detectives, *Mass Culture* II (Rosenberg and White, 1971) only deals with spy fiction. In the 1960s Ian Fleming's James Bond replaced Spillane's Mike Hammer. Again, about 50 million copies were sold. And this time, Hollywood jumped on the bandwagon. Again, a number of sociologists (e.g., Richler, 1971; Rockwell, 1971) have deplored James Bond, the modern fiction spy, and what they represent. Unlike the sophisticated spies one finds in earlier writings by Kipling and Maugham, the contemporary heroes of le Carré and Fleming are found to embody mere ethnocentrism and xenophobia on the part of a fearful, threatened, and reactionary Western mind.

While the modern spy fiction finds few apologists among students of mass culture, science fiction, another important emerging trend, fares better. Today, many universities offer courses in science fiction, recognizing it as a legitimate area of literature. Its tradition goes back to Edgar Allan Poe and Jules Verne, and includes the excellent works of Bradbury, Huxley, and Orwell.[16] The

---

[16] Any list of major science fiction contributors must include at least the following names: Isaac Asimov (the *Foundation* trilogy), Ray Bradbury *(Illustrated Man, The Martian Chronicles, Something Wicked This Way Comes)*, Arthur C. Clarke *(2001: A Space Odyssey)*, Michael Crichton *(The Andromeda Strain, The Terminal Man)*, Robert Heinlein *(Stranger in a Strange Land)*, Frank Herbert *(Dune)*, Aldous Huxley *(Ape and Essence, Brave New World)*, Walter M. Miller *(A Canticle for Leibowitz)*, George Orwell *(Animal Farm, 1984)*, Edgar Allan Poe *(The Black Cat, The Fall of the House of Usher)*, Jules Verne *(Twenty Thousand Leagues Under the Sea, From the Earth to the Moon)*, and H. G. Wells *(The Time Machine, The War of the Worlds)*.

sociology of popular culture recognizes the social and cultural significance of science fiction. Lewis (1972:97), for example, points out that much of its theme centers around the struggle of humanism (usually embodied in an individualistic hero) against the encroachments of mechanization and bureaucracy and the dehumanizing impact of technology (often represented by the computer or the robot overtaking and neutralizing man). Nye (1970:277) sees four broad themes in science fiction: (1) space travel, (2) time travel, (3) the hazards of science and technology run out of control, and (4) the superman or super-race theme. Amplifying on Nye's typology, I feel that today there are two additional and far more pervasive science fiction themes: political doomsday prophecies predicting totalitarianism (Huxley, Orwell) and—relatedly perhaps—the collapse of our technological civilization (e.g., Miller, footnote 16).

Additional categories of books of varying socially redeeming value include the juvenile book section (see Nye, 1970), the cowboy novel (Nye, 1970), black literature (see Lewis, 1972), war books, for example, the recent spate of Vietnam novels (see Sanders, 1972), and undoubtedly numerous other genres. Each has been studied and critically appraised by sociologists, and each, of that we may be sure, reflects the needs of some segment of the American reading audience. Not all, unfortunately, function as the taste leaders, the educators, and the standard bearers of cultural progress which books might more frequently be expected to be.

COMICS

Historical development and current quantities

A comic strip, literally, is "a narrative told by a sequence of related drawings containing the necessary dialogue to advance the action" (Nye, 1970:216). There are, however, at least four related phenomena to be dealt with here: (1) the comic strip, as defined above and found in the "funnies section" of contemporary newspapers (e.g., Al Capp's "Li'l Abner"). (2) comic books appearing as separate publications (e.g., "Superman"); (3) cartoons of the single-frame joke variety (e.g., those interspersed in the pages of *Playboy,* and the political cartoons of Oliphant and others found in the daily press). (4) The various comic books, strips, and magazines spawned by Walt Disney and other organizations catering to the very young (Mickey Mouse is probably the world's best known cartoon character) (cf. Berger, 1972a; Nye, 1970). I shall use *comics* in its generic sense to cover all these phenomena, conforming thereby to established precedent (cf. Berger, 1972b:228).

According to Nye (1970:216), the first American newspaper comic strip, James Swinnerton's "Little Bears and Tigers" appeared regularly from 1892. One of the first strips that was to gain lasting memorability was "The Katzenjammer Kids," appearing in 1897. George Herriman's "Krazy Kat" lasted from 1910 to 1945. Harold Gray's "Little Orphan Annie" was born in 1924. Chic Young's "Blondie" appeared in 1930, marrying Dagwood Bumstead three years later. It eventually became the most widely syndicated of all comics (more than sixteen hundred papers). Chester Gould's supercop "Dick Tracy" began in 1931, and Al Capp launched "Li'l Abner" and the other hillbillies of Dogpatch in 1934, which was also Flash Gordon's birth year.

The late twenties and thirties were the comics' golden years (Nye, 1970:224). That era also saw the emergence of Walt Disney's cartoon characters (Mickey Mouse entering comic strips in 1928), of Elzie Segar's "Popeye" (1929) and, a little while later, the action comic book, for example "Superman," soon to be followed by "Batman," "Mandrake" and hundreds of others. World War II saw a veritable explosion of comic books. At post exchanges they outsold the major mass magazines ten to one, and the vast majority of boys and girls under 18 read them. By 1946, 60 million comic books were sold every month. A peak was reached in 1954, when about 650 different titles combined to 100 million copies per month. By 1955 the tide began to recede. Today the number of regularly appearing comic books hovers at 250, selling about 35 million copies a month. Four major categories can be discerned: (1) the kiddie comics (e.g., "Tom and Jerry"), (2) the action comics (which include the Superman-fantasy category, the war comics, and the westerns), (3) the teen scene (e.g., "Archie"), and (4) adult-aimed romance series (e.g., "Secret Hearts") (Lyle, 1969:200). The most familiar format is the thirty-two-page, twenty- or twenty-five-cent copy. The largest category is still comprised of the "Superman"-fantasy-space adventure category, including "Batman," "Aquaman," "Hawkman," "Iron Man," "Metal Man," "Spider Man," "Mandrake," "Wonderwoman," "Superboy," "Superman," the "Torch," "Captain Action," "Captain Savage," "Captain Marvel," "Flash Gordon," "Unknown," "Dr. Strange," "Unexpected," "Spectre," "Ghostly Tales," "Space Adventure," "Star Trek," "The Invaders," "Dr. Solar", "Space Family Robinson" (Nye, 1970:24).

The most significant postwar comic strips have been Charles Schulz's "Peanuts" (1943), Walt Kelly's "Pogo" (1949), Jules Feiffer's cartoons (1960), and a variety of creative strips that include Mell Lazarus's "Miss Peach," Johnny Hart's "B.C.," and Parker and Hart's "The Wizard of Id." A significant recent development in comic books has been the introduction of a whole group of modern superheroes—the "Fantastic Four," "Spider Man," the "Human Torch," and the other characters created by the Marvel Comics Group. These have greater social and artistic value than their predecessors. And there is of course the emergence of the underground comix, which represents at best profound social criticism and at worst ultrapornography. All in all, I conclude with Rosenberg and White (1957:187) that "daily and Sunday strips are part of the reading habits of more than 100 million highbrows, middlebrows, and lowbrows. Like hot dogs and popcorn, the comics are an American institution. The comic book . . . is another matter. This flamboyant medium has raised many anxieties on the part of teachers, parents, psychiatrists and lawmakers." We shall deal with the underground comix and with the moral and intellectual issues raised by the comic book in subsequent sections. Here, I conclude by reproducing the cover of a recent issue of a Marvel comic.[17]

Sociological correlates

As indicated, many social observers view comics as one of America's great collective representations. Berger (1972b:235), for example, argues that "comics are a distinctly American idiom and are one of the few things that we all have in common—one of the few things in our society that cuts across class barriers (for the most part), regional differences, ethnic distinctions—whatever you will—to give us a community of experience and of reference points."

Berger's statement is an exaggeration. The comics audience has, as that of other media, certain demographic characteristics that can be specified and shown to differ from those of other audiences. For one thing, there is unanimous agreement among students of the subject that *age* is by far the most important variable influencing reactions to comics (cf. Bogart, 1957:196). Berger (1972b:229) him-

---

[17]For more information about the history of American comics, both strips and books, see Daniels (1971) and Nye (1970).

Table 6-17. Percentage reading comic books, by age *

5-7	82
8-10	92
11-14	94
18	60

*From Asa Berger, "Comics and culture." P. 229 in George H. Lewis (ed.), Side Saddle on the Golden Calf: Social Structure and Popular Culture in America. 1972. Pacific Palisades, Calif.: Goodyear Publishing Co.

self cites figures to show this, as is apparent from Table 6-17.

The peak comic reading age is 12 to 15 years. A study of San Francisco school children shows that eighth grade boys read a median of 4.5 comic books per month, eighth grade girls only 3.3. At the sixth-grade level the corresponding figures were 3.3 books for boys and 1.4 for girls. Furthermore, a study of sixth-graders in the Rocky Mountain area produced median monthly numbers of 8.5 for boys and 4.7 for girls (Lyle, 1969:199 and 215). It is obvious, then, that boys read more comics than girls. This is as expected, in view of the fact that the vast majority of comic books are geared to males (the romance series being the exception). It also follows from those data, while more tentatively, equally plausibly, that significant regional and rural-urban differences exist, with rural and small town youngsters reading more comics than their urban counterpart.

Turning to the socioeconomic status cluster, it is now equally fashionable to argue that comics are *not* restricted to the lower class and the lower educational levels (cf. Berger, 1972b:229). This, too, is argumentative rather than exact. While it may be true that comics are becoming more popular with high school and college students, there remains a definite inverse relationship between educational level and comic book reading. As the San Francisco study cited earlier

concludes, "by the end of high school, reading [of comics] has been discontinued by most students" (Lyle, 1969:199).

The various studies linking leisure competence and taste to socioeconomic status, occupational status, and education (e.g., Gerstl, 1963; Wilensky, 1964) share a common weakness. They clearly outline and operationalize what they mean by highbrow leisure (specifying books, classical music), but they generally leave *low* leisure competence to be defined by default, that is, as some vague lack of high culture. About the only positive index of lowbrow lifestyle found in such analyses is excessive and indiscriminate TV viewing (Wilensky, 1964). I feel that studies comparing the lifestyles and leisure patterns of the various social strata must specify both highbrow and lowbrow activities, rather than defining the latter merely as the absence of the former. In that manner, one might indeed find that whereas professors read more highbrow books than dentists or blue-collar workers, they may not read as many comic books, or spend as much time with football or wrestling. My point, here, is that I suspect a definite inverse relationship between socioeconomic status and comic book reading, although this has not been examined because lowbrow leisure has generally been conceived as a residual noncategory. Note that I restrict my hypothesis to comic books. Strips are more heterogeneous, ranging from the highly sophisticated (Feiffer) to the less so ("Beetle Bailey"), and hence less amenable to generalization.

Because age is recognized to be the crucial variable for the comics audience, much of the sociological literature on comics can be grouped into two categories: articles that address themselves to comics as a youth phenomenon, and works focusing on the adult readership of that medium. Typical of the former are the sociological analyses of *Mad,* the epitome of the teenage magazine.[18] Winick's (1968) analysis, for example, focuses on the healthy role performed by that magazine and its teenage audience in a humorless America. The author's remarks were made in the early sixties, based on a content analysis and interviews with 411 typical *Mad* readers (mean age, 16.2, mostly high school). They emphasize the lack of political satire and criticism in a country that is overly preoccupied with "Americanism." *Mad*, Winick argues, provides the rare and highly needed irony and parody required for a healthy democratic system. Its young readers have the stamina and wisdom to criticize and laugh at a social system and a culture all too normlessly accepted by the parental generation.

Marshall McLuhan (1964:164-169) makes needless mental contortions trying to account for *Mad's* sudden popularity with the young in the fifties. He conceives of the magazine as a vestibule to the age of television, claiming that it is a print and woodcut form of expression. This is not a very plausible explanation. It is a clear case of ad-hocing in an effort to deal with the simultaneous rise of *Mad* and demise of other comics. McLuhan's only accurate perception in his analysis of comic books is that *Mad* portends deep changes in our culture. However, these changes have little to do with television[19]; they are the changing youth values that would subsequently culminate in the counterculture of the 1960s, a cultural revolution in its own right. Winick's re-

marks are therefore more prophetic. The generation gap, of which *Mad Magazine* was an isolated symbol in the fifties, later blossomed into a massive cultural upheaval, and today the type of irreverence it first embraced has become the pervasive force which saves us from deadly and corrupt stagnation.

Bogart (1957, 1964, 1968), on the other hand, has focused on the adult component of the comics' readership, examining the alleged psychological and social functions performed by comic strips for their adult readers. Based on a survey of 121 low-status urban workers, the author found that much adult comic strip reading tends to be "readership by inertia." That is, the strips do not function to provide significant escapist fantasy to those of us who are the most frustrated, as was widely believed, but merely provide some collective imagery and some rather superficial break in the monotony of everyday living (1957). The collective imagery and fantasies provided by the funnies offer working-class adult males something they have in common, something they share and can therefore talk about purely for sociability's sake (1968).

In sum, comics are read and discussed both by the young and by adults, and this goes for strips as well as for books. Thus far, the armed forces are alone in exploiting this fact, using the comic book format in some of their educational programs. However, schools, too, make increasing use of a variety of audiovisual aids that reduce complex abstractions to simplified visual imagery. What worries educators, intellectuals, and concerned observers is the possible deterioration of verbal aptitude and intellectual skills among young and perhaps old alike. If such a trend indeed exists, and many signs indicate that it does, then comics and their resurgent popularity may not be so funny after all. The potential erosion of literate civilization is raised in the next section.

---

[18]See, for example, Daniels (1971), Lewis (1972:225–227), Manago (1962), Winick (1968).

[19] Grand theorists cannot admit that *some* sociohistorical facts might not be related to their all-explanatory independent variable. To Durkheim, everything from religion to suicide was caused by social morphology. To Marx, the relations of production accounted for culture, consciousness, and everything else. To McLuhan, communication technology is the fundamental—and overdrawn—causal force in society.

Major trends and issues

This concluding section provides a brief characterization of the sociology of the comic. As such, it must say something about the subdiscipline's (1) assumptions, (2) its favored methodologies, (3) its tentative findings, and (4) its unresolved issues.

An assumption shared by most students of comic strips and comic books is that this pictorial device is essentially an American idiom (see Berger, 1972b; Rosenberg and White, 1957; White and Abel, 1963). This assumption is incorrect, as many other countries have a rich tradition of comic books and comic strips. While the animated cartoon was indeed mostly Walt Disney's contribution to the world,[20] comic books are generally probably superior in some European countries. Bilingual Belgium, for example, has enrichened the lives of millions of French, Flemish, and Dutch youngsters. Franquin's "Spirou" ("Robbedoes" in the Netherlands), Morris's "Lucky Luke" and Herge's "Tintin" (translated as "Kuifje" for the Dutch) are voraciously read from the North Sea to the Mediterranean, and Tintin's adventures are now available in two dozen countries around the world, including the United States. As agents of socialization, these youth heroes cannot be overestimated. Tintin and Spirou are young boys always fighting crime, always behaving according to the highest moral standards, and always triumphant. Spirou's teammate is a tall, clumsy, and somewhat ridiculous fellow by the name of Fantasio. Tintin only has his little fox terrier–type dog Milou, plus a host of recurring characters whom we meet in various parts of the globe in the young hero's consecutive adventures. Lucky Luke is a lonesome cowboy roaming the Far West, always protecting the weak

and punishing the criminals.[21] His gun is faster than those of the Dalton brothers, Jesse James, Butch Cassidy, and Billy the Kid combined, and these wrongdoers inevitably end up behind bars after they tangle with Lucky and his faithful horse Jolly Jumper. The humor, historical and political veracity and psychological sophistication of the Belgian comics are profound.

The sociology of the comics has used two types of methods: content analysis, either longitudinal, as in Barcus (1961) and Shannon (1957), or cross-cultural, as in Berger (1972a), and survey of readers, as in Bogart (1957, 1968). The two methods have been used jointly, as in Winick (1968).

The findings have not been profoundly striking. They generally show that comics reflect societal norms, or serve to socialize their readers into certain values, or represent certain moral principles or psychological needs. Thus Berger (1972a) shows that American comic strips are less authoritarian than their Italian counterpart. "Beetle Bailey," for example, expresses irreverence for the army and for authority in general, while Italian comic strips show more respect for authority.

Shannon (1957) examines "Little Orphan Annie" and finds that it serves as a tool of upper-class capitalist ideological indoctrination.[22]

Brodbeck and White analyze Al Capp's "Li'l Abner," concluding that it depicts

---

[20]We examine Walt Disney—both in movies and in print—in the next chapter. Discussions of his work include Mano (1973), Nye (1970:233–234, 383), and Schickel (1968).

[21]Americans should realize the near universality of the Far West as young boys' heroic fantasy land everywhere. To a truly incredible extent, America has exported its chivalrous heroes (who will not shoot an enemy in the back) and its ruthless villains of the Frontier to the far corners of the globe. Young boys grow up in adulation and emulation of Buffalo Bill, Davy Crockett, and Wild Bill Hickock in the outskirts of Paris, along the canals of Venice and Amsterdam, and on the playgrounds of Budapest and Moscow.

[22]For an illustrated portion of Little Orphan Annie's history, see Gray. 1970. The introduction is by Al Capp.

American life in its most typical ways. Dogpatch embodies the typical relationships found between American parents and their children, between mothers and sons, and between all types of aspiring yet stagnant individuals. Marshall McLuhan's (1964:164-169) analysis of "Li'l Abner" should also be mentioned. Some of it is nonsense ("the biggest casualty of the TV impact was Al Capp's 'Li'l Abner' "). Some is quite plausible, running along the same lines as Brodbeck and White's. "Readers have long enjoyed the fact that the Dogpatch predicament of helpless ineptitude was a paradigm of the human situation, in general. . . . It was Al Capp who discovered that . . . any degree of Scragg mayhem or Phogbound morality was accepted as funny. He put in his strip just exactly what he saw around him. But our trained incapacity to relate one situation to another enabled his sardonic realism to be mistaken for humor" (McLuhan, 1964:169).

While Capp receives high marks from a variety of authors (see also Berger, 1970), a thorough appraisal of his art would have to point to its increasingly biased, bigoted, and conservative content.

Bogart's (1957, 1968) studies of comic strips and their adult audience have already have discussed. Many additional studies and interpretations have been made. Most of the attention has been focused on the strips.

Insofar as comic books have been appraised, observers agree about their essential features, at least about those of the most widely prevailing type, the action comic. As Lyle (1969:200) notes, "there is a seemingly inexhaustible supply of evil forces," and the never-ending fight is always between pure good and unmitigated evil. There is always a black-and-white morality to the stories, and each ends on a moralistic, often guilt-laden tone. Note, for example, the conclusion of an episode where the Torch has just prevailed over an evil business-

man who has stolen and destroyed a scientific device. As he hands the culprit over to the authorities, the Torch admonishes him, "Your greed has cost science the mind of a brilliant man! And if I were you, that's a thought I couldn't live with!"

What typifies American comic books most of all, however, is their enormous violence. This, truly, is where American and European action comics differ. It is the issue of violence and more generally that of the questionable moral and intellectual quality of comics that must be dealt with under our last heading, the unresolved issues in the sociology of the comic.

As Truzzi (1968:87) notes, the "funny papers" are usually not funny, and the newspapers' "childrens' section" is usually read by adults. Action comic books are so pervasive that in some quarters, for example, the armed forces, they have at times eclipsed all other media (cf. Rosenberg and White, 1957:187). What does all this say about the quality of American cultural and intellectual life? Worry about the state of American literacy is perhaps not all that misplaced, and neither is concern about the impact of the vulgar and violent content of many comics upon their readers' minds and behavior.

One school of thought feels compelled to come to the comics' rescue. Berger (1972b) for example feels that comics often reflect youth's changing attitudes, that they are becoming more sophisticated and that they are often a progressive social force. Other apologists of comic books and comic strips, as we saw, include Bogart (1957, 1964, 1968), Brodbeck and White (1957), Lewis (1972), McLuhan (1964), Truzzi (1968), White and Abel (1963), and Winick (1968). These men ignore and minimize the negative potential of comics, focusing instead on the better examples and on innovative trends. Undoubtedly certain strips have, indeed, profound social and intellectual value. Such is the case with Jules Feiffer's cartoons,[23] Walt Kelly's "Pogo," Charles Schulz's "Peanuts,"[24] and the work of James Thurber, to name but a few. Single-frame social and political cartoons can also have important redeeming value.[25]

The comic book, however, is of much more questionable caliber. "Batman" and "Superman," whose histories are collected and illustrated in two volumes edited by E. N. Bridwell, are generally considered to be among the best examples of the genre. "Batman," in particular, has become camp even with a sophisticated adult audience since its emergence on TV in the mid-sixties. In addition, there are of course dozens of newer comics on the market, including the Marvel Comics series ("Spider Man," the "Torch") and the underground comic (see following discussion). While I do not wish to be identified with Dr. Wertham's hysteria,[26] I feel that as an instrument of socialization or cultural transmission and as an educational device, the American comic falls short of its excellent European counterpart. While American boys and girls may enjoy a quantity and variety of television offerings not available to their European age-mates, there is in this country a paucity of good, sophisticated

---

[23] For an autobiographical treatment of Feiffer's work, see Feiffer (1965).

[24] For some analyses of Schulz's work, see Short (1964) and Mendelson (1970).

[25] For an analysis of political cartoons, see Hillier (1970).

[26] Wertham (1954, 1966) is the psychiatrist who, through his book *Seduction of the Innocent,* practically single-handedly stirred up enough public anxiety to call forth Senate hearings on the impact of violence in comic books. The hearings, chaired by Senator Estes Kefauver, featured Wertham himself as star expert witness; they resulted in the Federal Comic Code of 1955. An account and appraisal of the issues involved can be found in Warshow (1970:83-104). It is interesting, twenty years later, to read about the enormous amount of parental anxiety evoked by comic books that are relatively innocuous by today's standards.

childrens' comic books. In this respect, I must therefore side with the other school of thought marking the sociology of comics, the scholars and educators who have examined the psychological and behavioral impact of the violence and vulgarity of many comic books with apprehension (see Haskins, 1969; Mussen and Rutherford, 1962; Rose, 1958; Thrasher, 1950). Haskins (1969:501), for example, reviewed the available evidence concerning the effects of violence in the printed media, concluding that "it is more likely that media-depicted violence has an undesirable 'triggering' effect than that it has a desirable 'catharsis' effect." Regarding comic books some findings suggested that delinquent boys were more interested than nondelinquent boys in reading harmful (crime) comic books (1969:497).

It is in particular with McLuhan's Pangloss-like naivete that I must sharply disagree. In his unending apology for television, for pictorial ("iconic") communication, and for the erosion of literate culture, the Canadian speculator commits one error after another. TV, he claims, has dealt a death blow to the comic (untrue); it signaled the demise of Al Capp's genre and the rise of *Mad* and similar persiflages of the advertising style (equally untrue); finally, the world of television is much more demanding than that of earlier media, claims McLuhan, and if Johnny can't read anymore it is because reading is too easy(!). The truth of the matter is that comics and comix (see following discussion) are once again highly popular and that this may indeed, along with TV, portend serious cultural and intellectual deterioration. McLuhan's attempt at redefining vices into virtues is sophistry, as is the widespread tendency among modish students of pop culture to see artistic value in a variety of mass cultural artifacts that are essentially trash.

In the final analysis, it is the entire

quality of life in the United States that is at stake. There are increasing indications that there is something drastically wrong with our socialization system, particularly insofar as the transmission of verbal, intellectual, and other cerebral skills is concerned. The national average Scholastic Aptitude Test scores among students is now considerably lower than a decade ago (*Sacramento Bee,* 1973), and this is not due to any influx of lower socioeconomic status youngsters into the school system, as that influx is now over; average college grade-point average is gradually rising, but this merely reflects eroding standards, for nothing indicates improving student performance, while much points to its deterioration; the new math, for example, is a total failure (cf. Speich, 1974); a recent study concluded that the entire American high school system was a failure and that mandatory high school should be repealed in favor of a 14-year age limit. My point is, first, that a sweeping indictment of American culture, socialization, and education may well be appropriate and, secondly, that much of the mediocrity may be due to the media we rely upon. It may be that our excessive reliance on visual pictorial devices—television, comics, photographs, motion pictures, any and all audiovisual gimmicks which will alleviate the effort required for the absorption of information—will cost us the scholarly and intellectual excellence that are the hallmark of more literate civilizations.[27]

THE UNDERGROUND PRESS AND THE INTERNATIONAL COMIX CONSPIRACY[28]

The System has not yet been budged, but the cultural revolution is being won on all fronts.

Jacob Brackman (1970)

---

[27] Further analyses of comics not yet mentioned include Becker (1959), Lupoff and Thompson (1970), Perry and Aldridge (1971), and Warshow (1970).
[28] The *comix* is simply the counterculture's comic.

Historical, quantitative, and demographic information

The twin phenomena of comix and underground press can be traced back to the birth of the counterculture itself. And since hippies emerged in the midsixties, their press can also be said to go back to about 1966. Of course, there is continuity in everything. Just as the hippies of the sixties cannot unequivocally be cut off from the beatniks of the fifties, so it may seem arbitrary to peg the birth of the underground press to a specific date. Yet, as I shall show in this discussion, cultural continuities do not mean that cultural epochs and movements cannot be distinctly demarcated. Thus in New York the underground press begins in the mid-sixties, and it includes the *East Village Other,* but excludes the *Village Voice.* The latter, started in 1955, was by the mid-sixties the voice of an older and more established generation of intellectuals.

Other newspapers that were at least originally "underground" include *Avatar* (Boston), the *Berkeley Barb,* the *Berkeley Tribe, Distant Drummer* (Philadelphia), the *Fifth Estate* (Detroit), the *Free Press* (Washington), the *Los Angeles Free Press, Movement, Open City* (Los Angeles), the *Point* (Pittsburgh), the *Oracle* (San Francisco), *Rolling Stone* (San Francisco, New York, London), and *Underground* (Los Angeles). Obviously, one finds probably more change, failure, and cooptation in this fleeting sector of popular culture than anywhere else. Thus a vast number of underground papers have had only ephemeral existence, and I probably agree with those who would question the current "underground" character of most such papers, particularly lucrative mass enterprises like *Rolling Stone* and the *L. A. Free Press.* My categorization, however, is simple. The underground press consisted originally of publications that were frequently unsanctioned by the authorities, that did not, for example, qualify for second-class mailing permits, that were often clandestine student publications put out as an alternative to the official campus paper, papers that had to be printed and circulated privately, hawked often at street corners by their own authors and publishers, and frequently exposed to censorship in the form of police raids, harassment, and confiscation of entire issues and printing plates. Eventually, "underground" became the label for any innocuous paper toying with psychedelic culture and dealing with the artifacts that are popular with countercultural youngsters, be it rock music, electronic gear, macrobiotic food, or ecology.

The countercultural comix appeared a little while later. Brackman (1970) points out that the single most significant development, here, was Robert Crumb's publication of the first issue of *Zap* (San Francisco, Spring 1968). While *Zap* had been preceded by a couple of other comix-type publications in the mid-sixties, and whereas here, too, important continuities exist, for example, between *Mad Magazine* in the 1950s and the comix of the late 1960s, we may nevertheless say that the final emergence of the latter took place in 1968.

Students of comix (Brackman, 1970; Levin and Spates, 1971; Lewis, 1972; Lyle, 1969; Pekar, 1972) agree on certain facts. Robert Crumb, his team (Rick Griffin, Victor Moscoso, and Clay Wilson), and their *Zap* are the best and most important manifestation of this form of popular culture. Furthermore, authors tracing the prelude to the "international comix conspiracy" (Brackman, 1970; Pekar, 1972) point to the same antecedents. Harvey Kurtzman's *Mad Magazine* is generally viewed as the single most significant manifestation of youth rebellion in comic form in the fifties, a direct anticipation of the comix of the late sixties. It is felt that Crumb's work and other comix were strongly influenced by

Mad. Other early comics with social significance and anticipating the comic rebellion included a number of *Mad*-like publications *(Help, Sick)*, the works of Charles Schulz and Jules Feiffer, the modish Marvel Comics Group ("Captain America," "Spider Man"), and isolated features like the *Evergreen Review's* "Barbarella." Otherwise, the comix is felt by most observers to mark the end of a decade-long dark age that produced little more than "Steve Canyon," "Dick Tracy," and other relatively trashy comics. There is, finally, a certain degree of technological determinism in some of the discussions of the phenomenon. McLuhan's ideas have already been presented (and debunked); note, in addition, the role attributed by Lazarsfeld (1971:viii) to the Xerox machine, without which no underground publication would have been possible.

It is difficult to estimate the size of the underground press and comix. These publications are rarely listed in inventories like Ayer's, and they come and go with great irregularity. In the late sixties there were two underground news agencies—the Underground Press Syndicate and the Liberation News Service. The latter used teletype machines to disseminate news to a number of underground papers estimated anywhere between fifty and two hundred. Estimates of readership vary from 300,000 to nearly 5 million (Pepper, 1972:23). The Underground Press Syndicate listed sixty underground newspapers with a combined circulation of 1 million. Some, like the *L.A. Free Press,* sold as many as seventy thousand copies, and the bestselling comix, for example, *Zap,* equaled that circulation figure.

By 1974, cooptation, repression, and commercialization had of course destroyed the counterculture. The so-called underground press had not so much disappeared as mutated into a variety of either respectable, commerical, or pornographic tabloids. In terms of sheer size, it was doing better than ever, with a paper like *Rolling Stone* enjoying a worldwide circulation of 400,000 (*Newsweek,* 1974:68). It also spawned a continuing flood of very low-quality publications, from alternative campus sheets incapable of correct spelling to comix barely readable and aimed at such diverse audiences as heroin addicts *(Junk)* and former athletes *(Big League Laffs).*

I am unaware of any study directly describing the demographics of the underground press readership. This may be approached indirectly by examining the hippie population. Those who read comix (as opposed to traditional comic books) and underground newspapers are likely to be overwhelmingly young (under 30), white, middle class in origin, urban, nonreligious or following an esoteric sectarian movement, fairly well educated, and possibly attending college. Of course, the audience of a medium ranging from hard-core pornography to dietary pamphlets and from political news to organs for transcendental meditation is likely to be extremely heterogeneous.

Major trends and issues

Here, we must deal with the major issues that have marked the evolution of the countercultural press, with the content of newspapers and comix both in terms of actual subject matter and in terms of values, and finally with the current status of these media.

The birth and background of comix cannot be divorced from the matter of censorship and the battles that have surrounded the medium from its very inception: 1955 was the year of the great purge. Psychiatrist Frederick Wertham (see footnote 27) had published a book indicting violence and horror in comic books, seeing these as causes of childrens' maladjustment. As a result, public pressure led to Senate hearings on the subject and to the creation of the Federal Comics Code Authority. Dr. Wertham was the chief expert witness at the hearings; the creators of *Archie* dominated the Comics Code Authority (Brackman, 1970:198). It all led to the legislation of a Seal of Approval which, when denied, barred access to the national distribution channels. *Mad* managed to obtain the seal, but most other mildly subversive comics did not. "Spider Man," for example, was censored because, while condemning drugs, it nevertheless discussed them (Lewis, 1972:232). Gifted men sought new havens. Kurtzman left *Mad* to join *Playboy* with his "Little Annie Fanny."

Only in the late sixties did the second comics revolution take place. What had been repressed for more than a decade now erupted with counterveiling vigor. Robert Crumb and his associates followed a conscious policy of decensoring themselves and their work, concentrating almost exclusively on sex and gore, the two taboos of the preceding decade. Others followed, for example, Rodriguez and his "Trashman," a sort of countercultural superman fighting capitalism and the establishment. Clay Wilson's contributions to *Zap* are perhaps the grossest, vividly showing "lesbians mainlining hot semen and then sprouting prodigious male organs; salami-sized penises severed by rusty cutlasses, uprooted with coiled whips; feces flung from toilets into the faces of one's family." (Brackman, 1970:330). The content of comix books can be summarized in three words: sex, violence, and drugs, and each of these is treated in unbelievably gory detail.

As offensive as the content of some comix may be, they have nevertheless been hailed as a significant cultural, artistic, and social phenomenon. Berger (1972b), Brackman (1970), Lewis (1972) and Pekar (1972) are but a few of the authors who view the comix as a creative new medium and men like Crumb as artistic geniuses. Some contributions, it should be added, are at the opposite end of Wilson's super-realism just described. Griffin and Moscoso, for example, draw nearly nonfigurative psychedelic fantasies.

The form of the underground newspaper differs from that of the comix, although its social message and cultural emphasis are similar. The four principal topics encountered in such newspapers are drugs, music, political issues approached radically, and sex. The latter subject is most vivid in the classified ads sections, where individuals seek partners for a variety of unconventional sex acts. Most underground papers are community organs. They therefore flourish in communities with a large hippie element such as Berkeley. Some, however, have achieved wealth, respectability, fame, and an international circulation. Such is the case of *Rolling Stone,* a paper essentially concerned with music that originated in San Francisco but now branches out over North America and Europe.

The values that typify the underground press are different from those of conventional society, ranging from radical militancy aimed at *political* revolution to mere alternative lifestyles and leisure activities proposed as a *cultural* revolution. Levin and Spates (1971) content analyzed 316 underground articles, comparing them with 162 articles from the *Reader's Digest.* They classified the values found in these articles as (1) instrumental, (2) expressive, and (3) other. Instrumental values included such things as the work ethic, the drive for learning, and economic values. Expressive values referred to things like self-expression through art, affiliation (friendship, love), and religion and philosophy. Other values included individualism and sex. The results of the analysis showed that 46% of the value-themes in the underground press were expressive, and only 10% instrumental. In contrast the *Reader's Digest*'s values were more

heavily instrumental (42%) than expressive (23%). Some other values were found in both types of publications, but in different contexts. For example, 20% of the underground value-themes and 10% of those in the *Digest* were classified as individualistic. However, the former tended to be an expressive individualism aimed at "doing your own thing" and immediate gratification, whereas the latter was mostly an achievement-oriented instrumental individualism.

The current fate of the countercultural press is determined by three (related) forces: (1) the commercial motive, (2) cooptation by and gravitation toward the dominant culture, and (3) qualitative deterioration and the proliferation of mediocre imitations.

To begin with, it has always been the countercultural entrepreneur's aim to create alternative business enterprises. What has been seen time after time since the mid-sixties is the creation of alternative presses, recording companies, newspapers, cooperative stores, radio stations, motion picture companies, cooperative apartment buildings, and a host of other enterprises that proclaim their independence from the existing economic system but are in fact merely the latest wave of entrepreneurial behavior in our society—with a tinge of the modish countercultural ideology to which lip service must be paid, as the financial success of any contemporary popular cultural product is predicated upon a mildly anti-establishmentarian packaging (it is the entire society which has turned radical chic). While I do not wish to deny the revolutionary and humanitarian motives that may initially have been the impetus behind the careers and enterprises of Robert Crumb, the Grateful Dead, Gerome Ragni, the Jefferson Airplane, Ken Kesey, Bill Graham, Peter Fonda, the Beatles, Bill Drake, Wolfman Jack, the organizers of Woodstock and subsequent festivals, Bob Dylan, and the hundreds of other individual as well as corporate countercultural millionaires, what I am saying is this: countercultural entrepreneurship, when highly profitable, inevitably reaches a point where it can no longer meaningfully claim to be in any way subversive or revolutionary. Today, *Rolling Stone* can no more be said to belong to the Marxian antithesis than does the *Playboy* empire (which, one should recall, also began as a subversive endeavor). So-called countercultural enterprises sooner or later become part and parcel of the capitalist system which, let us face it, constitutes our total environment.

Pepper (1972:23-26) noted that the underground press was no sooner underway than it became a mirror image of the suburban press, offering its readers juicy ads, a dogmatic ideology, and making fat profits advertising beads, drugs, or massages. The model, he explained, was New York's highly profitable *Village Voice.* "Far from representing a fundamental critique of American society, [the underground papers] are actually full-fledged participants in it." Furthermore, they have opened the door for corporate exploitation of the hippie market on a vast scale.

Commercialization is pervasive in the comix too. Back in 1968, Jack Jaxon and Gilbert Shelton started Rip Off Press in San Francisco "so they could rip off a bigger share of the profits and avoid being ripped off themselves by middlemen. Rip Off turned into a cooperative, with artists and printers splitting all revenue 50-50" (Brackman, 1970:329). Robert Crumb's *Zap* was also privately printed and distributed. But what happened to Crumb? Success led inevitably to commercialization, with the creation of full-length and highly lucrative sexual cartoons like "Fritz the Cat" (Lewis, 1972:244).

Since the summer of 1972, the Grateful Dead are the exclusive and full owners of their own record company— Grateful Dead Records, Inc. The object was to bypass retail record stores (records would be sold by direct mail and head shops) and other middlemen, in sum to avoid capitalist exploitation. Since then, the group has built a financial empire headed by former Wall Street economist Ron Rakow, consisting of a 150-member "family" whose holdings include, besides the record firm (which distributes to retail stores after all, only under its own auspices), "the Fly By Night travel agency, the Out of Town tours booking agency, the Ice-Nine publishing company, the Neal Cassady Memorial Foundation, a clothing, art, and toy store, two T-shirt manufacturers, a recording studio and a rock group." (*Rolling Stone,* 1973:5).

Along with commercialization and cooptation into the existing economic structure comes, of course, respectability. Current issues of well-known "underground" papers are generally somewhat cleaner than some years back, and there is, in many cases, a distinct establishment flavor. Leafing through earlier issues of the *Berkeley Barb* (August 8, 1969; May 1, 1970), one encounters a great deal of radical (antiwar, pro-Castro) literature and, of course, the ubiquitous sex ads in all their vivid candor. In contrast, a recent issue of the *L. A. Free Press* (December 14, 1973), while retaining a sexual classified ad section (which seems to have been somewhat cleaned up and euphemizes a great deal through such words as "massage"), also features the syndicated columns of Jack Anderson, Ralph Nader, and Nicholas Von Hoffman. Another feature is devoted to community services, and this lists not only alternative institutions but the YMCA, YWCA, and the Salvation Army as well. With some exaggeration one could say that its major remaining qualification for countercultural status is that it features an astrology section.

There is, then, a trend toward cooptation and respectability. *Rolling Stone* should again be mentioned as perhaps the most conspicuous paper that, thusly, eats its cake and has it too. And as far as the self-censorship one detects in these papers, it is quite plausible to assume that the 1973 Supreme Court obscenity rulings have something to do with this.

There is, finally, the proliferation of hosts of mediocre imitations. Productions like *Big League Laffs* (Berkeley) *Junk* and *Hog* (New Jersey) are poorly drawn and lack talent. There is, to be sure, pathos to a publication like *Junk,* which is aimed at heroin addicts and promotes the junkie liberation movement (its emblems are a gun, a hypodermic needle, and a varicose forearm), but what such comix seem to express most clearly of all, anno 1974, is the demise of the counterculture and of the creative thrust that had lit up America only so recently.

SUMMARY AND CONCLUSION

This chapter has examined one major area of mass culture—the printed media. The following five media were covered: newspapers, magazines, books, comics, and the countercultural press (including the underground comix). First, the historical growth of each area was discussed, providing quantitative statistics about current circulation, readership, and so on. Then, we looked at each medium's audience in the same way as was done for high culture, namely, tracing, insofar as possible, the sex, age, race, geographical location, religion, values, education, occupation, and social class of the various audiences. Finally, an attempt was made to discuss some of the more salient issues relating to each of the printed media.

The history of American newspapers is characterized by a steady increase in their number until about 1910, the peak year, and a slow continuing increase in circulation thereafter. In recent decades the number of newspapers has either stagnated or slowly declined.

The most significant sociological correlates of newspaper reading were found to be socioeconomic status and education. While other differences also exist (for example, per capita newspaper consumption is much higher in New England than in the Deep South), they are frequently only the indirect reflection of differences in socioeconomic status and education. Sociologists have distinguished between "print-oriented" and "broadcast-oriented" people, and they have found that the former—the "readers"—tend to be in higher occupational, educational, and socioeconomic brackets than the "watchers" and the "listeners." Also, the lower strata's newspaper reading tends to be more parochial, more focused on local rather than national and international affairs.

The following questions were raised about the newspaper world: How well is the newspaper business doing? What can be said about the current quality of newspapers? What is the nature of the triadic relationship between press, government, and business interests in our capitalist system? What, as a consequence, can be said about the press's fundamental rights (freedom of the press), obligations (fairness and accuracy in reporting), and shortcomings (bias and propaganda)? And finally, are the same monopolistic trends observable in the press as in all other sectors of big business today, and if so, to what extent?

Going back to the first question, the newspaper business was characterized as the static old giant of the media market. While the golden age of the printed press is well behind us, due of course to the advent of the electronic media, it would be wrong to conclude that the latter are replacing the former. The various media rather complement each other.

The quality of newspapers was traced to the interplay of three factors: the ideal of freedom and democracy embodied by the press, the commercial necessities of a capitalist system, and the restricting pressures of government. The Nixon administration had mounted a right-wing attack on the press, subverting the First Amendment. Watergate—ignited by the *Washington Post* and unceasingly fueled since then by the Eastern media power structure—represents the counteroffensive of a press that only becomes liberal when threatened by the extreme authoritarianism of the Nixon administration. However, the press's long-standing position is essentially conservative, for example, relative to the McCarthy-McGovern Democrats. In the final analysis, newspaper reporting is biased and propagandistic. The editor is essentially a "gatekeeper," sifting and selecting the facts as he sees fit. An increasingly accepted tenet of contemporary critical sociology is that there is no such thing as value-free science, no such thing as objective knowledge. If this is granted, then it must be admitted that the rule applies to news reporting *a fortiori*. Furthermore, the orthodox media are increasingly monolithic. Unlike half a century ago, when most American cities had several competing daily newspapers providing the population with alternative positions, the vast majority of cities today are dominated by single, monopolistic media operations. Since these growing "media baronies" comprise not only newspapers but also magazines and radio and TV stations, free competition of ideas in the opinion market is rapidly becoming a myth.

Magazines, we saw, have experienced a dual development. On the one hand, the general all-purpose family and picture magazine has not been able to withstand the onslaught of the electronic competition. *Look* and *Life* have eventually folded despite multimillion readerships. On the other hand, specialized periodicals with a focused audience have done very well indeed. Cases in point are the spectacularly successful *Playboy* and magazines like *Sports Illustrated, Ski* magazine, and *Cosmopolitan.*

With respect to magazines' sociological correlates, the major fact to remember is that this medium consists, more than any other, of a wide spectrum of specialized products, each directed at a specific demographic or sociological population. Thus we have men's magazines *(Playboy)*, women's magazines *(Playgirl)*, technical magazines *(Mechanics Illustrated)*, youth magazines for boys *(Mad)*, youth magazines for girls *(Seventeen)*, middle-class black magazines *(Ebony)*, and lower-class women's magazines *(True Confessions)*. Overall, the single most powerful predictor of magazine readership is education. While there is a positive relationship between occupational status and amount of magazine reading, and between socioeconomic status and amount of magazine reading, the strongest relationship of magazine reading is to education.

Moving on to major issues relating to magazines, we first asked ourselves why mass periodicals have all but disappeared in recent years. We saw that the major reason is not so much a loss in popularity (each issue of *Life* and *Look* is said to have reached up to 70 million Americans just prior to those periodicals' demise), but the loss of sponsors. TV advertising is simply much cheaper in terms of the number of people reached. For the rest, we saw that a favorite approach taken by sociologists to the study of magazines has been the longitudinal content analysis often used to document how magazines reflect certain aspects of the changing culture. Thus a study by Johns-Heins and Gerth (1957) showed that the typical magazine fiction hero has changed from the businessman to the professional. Bereleson and Salter (1957) and Kotok (1971) showed that the treatment of ethnics and foreign nationals in magazine stories has improved over the past three decades. Ellis (1961) and others have documented the sexual liberalization of periodicals.

Books did not loom large on the American scene until the middle of the nineteenth century. And since World War II, there has been a veritable book explosion in this country, although compared to many other developed nations (e.g., the Iron Curtain countries and most of Western Europe), America still produces and reads relatively few books. Indeed, surveys show that the book is a far less important medium than television or even the magazine.

Coming to the sociological correlates of book reading, we saw that here, even more than with newspapers and magazines, education is by far the most powerful predictor. While sex, race, religion, region, and other variables have all been shown to be related to amount and quality of book reading, those relationships are generally the spurious reflections of the more fundamental factor—education. But social class and occupational milieu also seem to exert an influence independent of education. This was shown by Gerstl (1963) and Wilensky (1964), among others.

In the final section on books, I asked three questions. What is the condition of the book business in America today? What is the quality of our book reading habits? And what are some of the major literary genres at the moment? According to several rather pessimistic sources (e.g., Dutscher, 1957; Hemley, 1957), the book business has only been able to survive by prostituting itself and by stooping to ever lower levels of intellectual and artistic quality. However, production (and presumably therefore consumption) of books has steadily increased in recent decades, and this should caution against excessive pessimism about the condition of the American book industry. Finally, the most popular genres, we saw, have included the detective story (mostly from the 1930s on), the spy fiction (since the James Bond fad in the sixties), and science fiction, which is currently gaining academic respectability.

The discussion of the conventional comic traced, first, the origin and history of comic strips a la "Peanuts" and comic books of the "Superman" variety. While strips were already found in newspapers at the turn of the century, the comic book's golden years were the twenties, thirties, and forties. During and shortly after World War II, comic books far outsold all other publications in such quarters as the armed forces.

The most significant sociological correlates of comic book reading are, predictably, age and education. The peak comic reading age, according to one study, is 12 to 15 years. Many sociologists have focused their attention on such youth comics as *Mad,* some viewing it as a symbol of youth rebellion (cf. Winick, 1968), others as an anticipation of television (cf. McLuhan, 1968). Bogart (1957), however, focuses on the comic strip's adult readership, and on that medium's social-psychological meanings.

In the final section on comics, I first questioned the widely held assumption that comics are an American idiom, providing some European examples instead. I then showed that sociologists have, through such techniques as (longitudinal) content analysis, appraised the comic's essential features, including their black-and-white morality and their enormous violence. While censorship and hysterical Puritanism like Dr. Wertham's (1954, 1966) may not be called for, I do share the worries of those who feel that the quality of American intellectual life, culture, and education may suffer from an excessive reliance on pictorial devices, including television and comics.

The underground press, including the countercultural comix, was the last area of popular culture examined in this chapter. "Underground" was defined as any alternative publication lacking solid financial and institutional backing, and often denied the postal and legal privileges granted to the orthodox press. The underground press is, of course, the press of the counterculture, the hippies. It therefore emerged in the mid-sixties, the first comix appearing about two years later at the hand of men like Robert Crumb. The size of this medium is very difficult to gauge, estimates of the readership ranging from 300,000 to 5 million in the late sixties (cf. Pepper, 1972:23). By and large, the seventies have seen the gradual demise of quality underground material, and its frequent commercialization, cooptation, and substitution by low-quality pornography.

The major issues that have marked the history of the countercultural press include censorship, the cultural revolution, and the ultimate deterioration of the medium's content and quality. The 1950s led to censorship of comic books, the Federal Comics Code, and the banning of a great many comics. Thus until the late sixties, *Mad* magazine was the only manifestation of youth rebellion. The countercultural comix which then emerged have been hailed as possessing great social significance, although their content has often been extremely obscene. Sociologists have also content analyzed the underground press, documenting its revolutionary values. Levin and Spates (1971), for example, showed that the underground press's values are much more expressive and less instrumental than those found in the *Reader's Digest*. Finally, the countercultural press's latest development has been characterized by commercialization, cooptation by middle-class culture and qualitative deterioration.

STUDY QUESTIONS

1. When it comes to the printed media, what major generalizations can be made about the quantitative trends found in (1) the newspaper business, (2) the book industry, and (3) magazines? Which area or areas, within each of these three, have grown and which ones have stagnated or declined? Why? To document your answer, use circulation figures as well as dollars and cents. Give also some cross-national comparisons, identifying America's relative position in these media. Finally, what fundamental generalization about *all* printed media has Marshall McLuhan emphasized in his writings?

2. What are, according to Raymond Nixon, the five stages in the history of American newspapers? What has characterized each stage? Give examples of papers or names of newspapermen for each era. What have been the major quantitative trends in the newspaper business during the past fifty or sixty years? Which types of publications are currently still doing well, and why?

3. Discuss the following nine sociological correlates of newspaper readership: sex, age, race and ethnicity, geography, religion, values and tastes, education, occupation, social class. Which of these are by far the most powerful predictors of newspaper reading? What are the characteristics of the "print-oriented" and the "broadcast-oriented" people? How do the different strata's reading habits differ?

4. Discuss the triadic relationship between press, government, and business. How does this relationship affect the quality and content of newspapers? Discuss also the press's rights (First Amendment), its obligations (fairness and accuracy in reporting), and its shortcomings (bias and propaganda). Evaluate the role of the gatekeeper and the monopolistic tendencies that produce ever larger media baronies. Give your overall estimation of the quality, freedom, and objectivity of the contemporary American press.

5. The recent history of American magazines has seen the decline and demise of certain types of magazines and the spectacular success of other kinds of publications. Which types of magazines are no longer viable, and which ones are? Give specific examples and explain the causes of success and failure.

6. Discuss the sociological correlates of the magazine audience covered in this chapter. With respect to sex, race, age, religion and social class, give examples of magazines targeted at specific audiences. In terms of overall magazine reading what are the best predictors of readership?

7. Discuss some of the (longitudinal) content analyses of magazines done by sociologists. What have the studies shown in terms of

changing cultural values, changing sexual attitudes, changing conceptions of ethnic and national identity, and changing folk heroes?

8. Discuss the historical as well as contemporary role of books in American society. Show that America has never been very book oriented, but that book production in this country did become a vast business as early as the mid-nineteenth century. Today, what categories of books are in greatest demand, and which ones stagnate? Can any opinion be ventured about the quality of the contemporary book business in America?

9. Which social and demographic variables predict significant differences in book reading? Discuss the concept of statistical spuriousness, and show how some of the observed statistical relationships are actually not causal, but the function of other variables. Finally, what can you say about our overall book reading habits as a nation? Do you agree with Dutscher or not? Why?

10. What are some of the major genres that have dominated the book market over the years? Discuss such areas as the detective story, the spy fiction, science fiction, the western, and the war novel. Give specific examples. What have been some of the all-time best-sellers? What criticisms have been leveled at some of these types of books by sociologists and intellectuals? How do you feel about the artistic quality and proper status of such genres as detectives and science fiction?

11. Trace the history of the American comic, with specific reference to major milestones in (1) comic strips, (2) comic books, (3) cartoon type jokes, and (4) Disney type cartoons. Which strips have lasted the longest? Which ones have been the most popular, as judged by syndication? When did action comics enjoy their greatest popularity? What are some of the most notable postwar contributions?

12. What are the most important sociological correlates of comic readership? In addition, what significance do sociologists see in the youth magazine, for example, *Mad?* Finally, what are, according to Bogart and others, some of the social and psychological functions performed by comics for their adult readers?

13. The major issue with comics is their qualitative content. What can be said about the content of contemporary American comics? What about European comics? What are the arguments for and against censorship? What is your opinion in this matter? Finally, do you agree that the way we rely on pictorial communication (comics, TV) debases the quality of cultural and intellectual life in America, or do you feel that such fear stems from ungrounded and irrational Puritan hang-ups? Be specific.

14. Trace the emergence and history of the underground press and the underground comix. Show how they belong to the counterculture of the sixties, and distinguish that wave from the beat generation of the fifties. Refer to specific publications and artists, for example, the work of Robert Crumb and his associates. How is underground press defined in this chapter? What are some estimates of the size of this press? Among which segments of the population and which demographic and socioeconomic groups are most of its readers found?

15. What has happened to the underground press and the underground comix in recent years? Document the processes of commercialization and cooptation, using examples (e.g., *Rolling Stone*), and show the qualitative deterioration of the underground press witnessed by the spate of pornographic and artistically mediocre publications now being passed off as "countercultural."

REFERENCES

Arendt, Hannah
 1951   The Origins of Totalitarianism. New York: Harcourt, Brace & World, Inc.

Atlantic Monthly Staff Writers
 1972   "The American media baronies." Pp. 103-114 in Alan Wells (ed.), Mass Media and Society. Palo Alto, Calif.: National Press Books.

Ayer, N. W. and Son
 1971   Ayer Directory of Newspapers, Magazines and Trade Publications. Philadelphia: N. W. Ayer and Son, Inc.

Baker, Robert K. and Sandra J. Ball
 1969   Violence and The Media: A Staff Report on The Causes and Prevention of Violence. Washington, D. C.: U. S. Government Printing Office.

Balk, Alfred
 1972   "Beyond Agnewism." Pp. 395-400 in Alan Wells (ed.), Mass Media and Society. Palo Alto, Calif.: National Press Books.

Banks, R. Jeff
 1973   "Current periodicals at least partly devoted to the genre." Popular Culture Methods (Summer):31.

Barcus, Francis E.
 1961   "A content analysis of trends in Sunday comics." Journalism Quarterly (Spring): 171-180.

Becker, Stephen
 1959   Comic Art in America. New York: Simon & Schuster, Inc.

Bell, Daniel
 1960   The End of Ideology: On the Exhaustion

of Political Ideas in the Fifties. New York: The Free Press.

1973   The Coming of Post-Industrial Society: A Venture in Social Forecasting. New York: Basic Books, Inc., Publishers.

Berelson, Bernard

1957   "Who reads what books and why?" Pp. 119-125 in Bernard Rosenberg and David Manning White (eds.), Mass Culture: The Popular Arts in America. New York: The Free Press.

Berelson, Bernard and Patricia J. Salter

1957   "Majority and minority Americans." Pp. 235-256 in Bernard Rosenberg and David Manning White (eds.), Mass Culture: The Popular Arts in America. New York: The Free Press.

Berger, Arthur Asa

1970   Li'l Abner: A Study in American Satire. New York: Twayne Publishers, Inc.

1972a   "Authority in the comics." Pp. 217-228 in Gregory P. Stone (ed.), Games, Sport and Power. New Brunswick, N. J.: Transaction Books.

1972b   "Comics and culture." Pp. 227-236 in George H. Lewis (ed.), Side-Saddle on the Golden Calf: Social Structure and Popular Culture in America. Pacific Palisades, Calif.: Goodyear Publishing Co., Inc.

Berkeley Barb

1970   Classified ads. (May 1–7):22.

Blumberg, Nathan B.

1971   "The 'orthodox' media under fire: Chicago and the press." Pp. 276-324 in Bernard Rosenberg and David Manning White (eds.), Mass Culture Revisited. New York: Van Nostrand Reinhold Company.

Bogart, Leo

1957   "Comic strips and their adult readers." Pp. 189-198, in Bernard Rosenberg and David Manning White (eds.), Mass Culture: The Popular Arts in America. New York: The Free Press.

1963   "Newspapers in the age of television." Daedalus (Winter):116-127.

1964   "The mass media and the blue-collar worker." Pp. 416-428 in Arthur B. Shostak and William Gomberg (eds.), Blue-Collar World, Studies of the American Worker. Englewood Cliffs, N. J.: Prentice Hall, Inc.

1968   "Adult talk about newspaper comics." Pp. 87-91 in Marcello Truzzi (ed.), Sociology and Everyday Life. Englewood Cliffs, N.J.: Prentice Hall, Inc.

1969   "How the mass media work in America." Pp. 165-186 in Robert K. Baker and Sandra J. Ball (eds.), Violence and the Media: A Staff Report to the National Commission on the Causes and Prevention of Violence. Washington, D. C.: U. S. Government Printing Office.

Boorstin, Daniel J.

1961   The Image: A Guide to Pseudo-Events in America. New York: Harper & Row, Publishers.

Bowers, David R.

1972   "The impact of centralized printing on the community press." Pp. 19-22 in Alan Wells (ed.), Mass Media and Society. Palo Alto, Calif.: National Press Books.

Brackman, Jacob

1970   "The international comix conspiracy." Playboy 17 (December):195-199, 328-334.

Bridwell, E. N.

1972   Batman: From the 30's to the 70's. New York: Crown Publishers.

1972   Superman: From the 30's to the 70's. New York: Crown Publishers.

Brinton, James E. and L. Norman McKown.

1961   "Effects of newspaper reading on knowledge and attitude." Journalism Quarterly 38(2):187-195.

Brodbeck, Arthur J. and David M. White

1957   "How to read Li'l Abner intelligently." Pp. 218-224 in Bernard Rosenberg and David Manning White (eds.), Mass Culture: The Popular Arts in America. New York: The Free Press.

Carter, Roy E.

1958   "Newspaper gatekeepers and the sources of news." Public Opinion Quarterly (Summer):133-144.

Cohn, Marcus

1972   "Subpoenas: should reporters be forced to tell what they know?" Pp. 330-334 in Alan Wells (ed.), Mass Media and Society. Palo Alto, Calif.: National Press Books.

Couperie, Pierre

1970   History of the comic strip. New York: Supergraphics.

Daniels, Les

1971   Comix: A History of Comic Books in America. New York: Outerbridge Dienstfrey.

Davis, Ethelyn

1967   "The teen magazine: a study in the sociology of fads." Proceedings of the Southwestern Sociological Association 18:84-88.

de Grazia, Sebastian

1948   The Political Community: A Study of Anomie. Chicago: University of Chicago Press.

1964   Of Time, Work and Leisure. New York: Anchor Books.

Deitch, David

1973   "Inflate and rule: the new capitalist strategy." The Nation (November 12):496-500.

Donohew, Lewis
1967 "Newspaper gatekeepers and forces in the news channel." Public Opinion Quarterly (Spring):61-68.

Durkheim, Emile
1951 Suicide (translated by A. Spaulding and George Simpson). Glencoe, Ill.: The Free Press.

Dutscher, Alan
1957 "The book business in America." Pp. 126-140 in Bernard Rosenberg and David Manning White (eds.), Mass Culture: The Popular Arts in America. New York: The Free Press.

Ellis, Albert
1961 The Folklore of Sex. New York: Grove Press, Inc.

Ellul, Jacques
1964 The Technological Society. New York: Alfred A. Knopf, Inc.

England, R. W., Jr.
1960 "Images of love and courtship in family magazine fiction." Marriage, Family Living (May):162-165.

Feiffer, Jules
1965 The Great Comic Book Heroes. New York: The Dial Press.

Feldman, Saul and Gerald Thielbar
1972 Life Styles: Diversity in American Society. Boston: Little, Brown and Company.

Gerbner, George
1958 "The social role of the confession magazine." Social Problems (Summer):29-41.

Gerson, Walter M. and Sander H. Lund
1972 "Playboy magazine: sophisticated smut or social revolution?" Pp. 80-88 in George H. Lewis (ed.), Side-Saddle on the Golden Calf: Social Structure and Popular Culture in America. Pacific Palisades, Calif.: Goodyear Publishing Co., Inc.

Gerstl, Joel E.
1963 "Leisure, taste and occupational milieu." Pp. 85-96 in Erwin O. Smigel (ed.), Work and Leisure—A Contemporary Social Problem. New Haven, Conn.: College and University Press.

Gieber, Walter
1956 "Across the desk." Journalism Quarterly (Fall):423-432.

Gieber, Walter and Walter Johnson
1961 "The city hall beat." Journalism Quarterly (Summer):289-297.

Gliner, Robert and R. A. Raines
1971 Munching on Existence. New York: The Free Press.

Gray, Harold
1970 ARF: The Life and Hard Times of Little Orphan Annie 1935-1945 (introduction by Al Capp). New Rochelle, N. Y.: Arlington House.

Greenberg, Bradley S. and Brenda Dervin
1972 "Mass communication among the urban poor." Pp. 265-272 in Alan Wells (ed.), Mass Media and Society. Palo Alto, Calif.: National Press Books.

Greene, Theodore P.
1970 America's Heroes: The Changing Models of Success in American Magazines. New York: Oxford University Press.

Harrison, Linda
1972 "On cultural nationalism." Pp. 215-217 in George H. Lewis (ed.), Side-Saddle on the Golden Calf: Social Structure and Popular Culture in America. Pacific Palisades, Calif.: Goodyear Publishing Co., Inc.

Haskins, Jack B.
1969 "The effects of violence in the printed media." Pp. 493-502 in Robert K. Baker and Sandra J. Ball (eds.), Violence and the Media: A Staff Report to the National Commission on the Causes and Preventions of Violence. Washington, D. C.: U. S. Government Printing Office.

Havighurst, Robert J.
1957 "The leisure activities of the middle-aged." American Journal of Sociology 63 (September):152-162.

Hemley, Cecil
1957 "The problems of the paper-backs." Pp. 141-146 in Bernard Rosenberg and David Manning White (eds.), Mass Culture: The Popular Arts in America. New York: The Free Press.

Hess, Stephen and Milton Kaplan
1968 The Ungentlemanly Art: A History of American Political Cartoons. New York: The Macmillan Company.

Hillier, Bevis
1970 Cartoons and Caricatures. London: Studio Vista/Dutton Pictureback.

Hoar, Jere
1960 "Book reading in the senior years: the habits and preferences of 200 Mississippians." Journal of Educational Sociology (November):137-144.

Hoffer, Eric
1951 The True Believer. New York: Harper & Row, Publishers.

Hofstadter, Richard et al.
1959 The American Republic (2 volumes). Englewood Cliffs, N. J.: Prentice-Hall, Inc.

Hoggart, Richard
1957 The Uses of Literacy: Aspects of Working-Class Life with Special Reference to Publications and Entertainments. New

York: Oxford University Press (1970 edition).

Jaffe, Carolyn
1972   "Fair trials and the press." Pp. 335-344 in Alan Wells (ed.), Mass Media and Society. Palo Alto, Calif.: National Press Books.

Johns-Heine, Patricke and Hans H. Gerth
1957   "Values in mass periodical fiction, 1921-1940." Pp. 226-234 in Bernard Rosenberg and David Manning White (eds.), Mass Culture: The Popular Arts in America. New York: The Free Press.

Judd, Robert P.
1961   "The newspaper reporter in a suburban city." Journalism Quarterly (Winter):35-42.

Kando, Thomas and Worth C. Summers
1971   "The impact of work on leisure: toward a paradigm and research strategy." Pacific Sociological Review (special summer issue):310-327.

Kinsey, A. C. et al.
1948   Sexual Behavior in the Human Male. Philadelphia: W. B. Saunders Company.

Knopf, Terry Ann
1972   "Media myths on violence." Pp. 350-356 in Alan Wells (ed.), Mass Media and Society. Palo Alto, Calif.: National Press Books.

Kornhauser, William
1959   The Politics of Mass Society. New York: The Free Press.

Kotok, Alan
1971   "Foreign nationals and minority Americans in magazine fiction: 1946-1968." Pp. 249-265 in Bernard Rosenberg and David Manning White (eds.), Mass Culture Revisited. New York: Van Nostrand Reinhold Company.

LaFarge, Christopher
1957   "Mickey Spillane and his bloody hammer." Pp. 176-186 in Bernard Rosenberg and David Manning White (eds.), Mass Culture: The Popular Arts in America. New York: The Free Press.

Lazarsfeld, Paul F.
1971   "Introduction." Pp. vii-ix in Bernard Rosenberg and David Manning White (eds.), Mass Culture Revisited. New York: Van Nostrand Reinhold Company.

Levin, Jack and James L. Spates
1971   "Hippie values: an analysis of the underground press." Pp. 266-275 in Bernard Rosenberg and David Manning White (eds.), Mass Culture Revisited. New York: Van Nostrand Reinhold Company.

Lewis, George H. (ed.)
1972   Side-Saddle on the Golden Calf: Social Structure and Popular Culture in America. Pacific Palisades, Calif.: Goodyear Publishing Co., Inc.

Lupoff, Richard and Don Thompson (eds.)
1970   All in Color for a Dime. New Rochelle, N. Y.: Arlington House, Inc.

Lyle, Jack
1969   "Contemporary functions of the mass media." Pp. 187-216 in Robert K. Baker and Sandra J. Ball (eds.), Violence and the Media: A Staff Report to the National Commission on the Causes and Prevention of Violence. Washington, D. C.: U. S. Government Printing Office.

Manago, B. R.
1962   "Mad: out of the comic rack and into satire." Add One (I):41-46.

Mano, D. Keith
1973   "A real Mickey Mouse operation." Playboy (December):199, 322-338.

Marcuse, Herbert
1964   One-Dimensional Man; Studies in the Ideology of Advanced Industrial Society. Boston: Beacon Press.

Marx, Karl
1964   Selected Writings in Sociology and Social Philosophy (newly translated by T. B. Bottomore). New York: McGraw-Hill Book Co.

MacFadden-Bartell Corporation
1962   The Women Behind the Market.

McLuhan, Marshall
1964   Understanding Media: The Extensions of Man. New York: McGraw-Hill Book Co.

Meadows, Dennis L.
1972   The Limits to Growth—A Report for the Club of Rome Project on the Predicament of Mankind. New York: University Books, Inc.

Mendelson, Lee
1970   Charlie Brown and Charlie Schulz. New York: Signet Books.

Merton, Robert K.
1957   Social Theory and Social Structure. New York: The Free Press.

Mills, C. Wright
1956   The Power Elite. New York: Oxford University Press.

Morris
1969   Daltons op Vrije Voeten. Brussels: Editions J. DuPuis & Fils S.P.R.L.

Mott, Frank Luther
1957   "Is there a best seller formula?" Pp. 113-118 in Bernard Rosenberg and David Manning White (eds.), Mass Culture: The Popular Arts in America. New York: The Free Press.

Mullins, Nicholas C.
1973 Theories and Theory Groups in Contemporary American Sociology. New York: Harper & Row, Publishers.
Mussen, P. H. and Eldred Rutherford.
1962 "Effects of aggressive cartoons on children's aggressive play." Journal of Abnormal Social Psychology 62:461-464.
Newsweek
1974 "Gathering no moss." (March 18):68-73.
New York Review of Books
1973 Classified ads. (November 29):46-47.
Nixon, Raymond B.
1972 "Trends in U. S. newspaper ownership: concentration with competition." Pp. 9-18 in Alan Wells (ed.), Mass Media and Society. Palo Alto, Calif.: National Press Books.
Nye, Russel
1970 The Unembarrassed Muse: The Popular Arts in America. New York: The Dial Press.
Opinion Research Corporation
1957 "The public appraises movies." A Survey for the Motion Picture Association of America, Inc., Princeton, N. J.
Orwell, George
1957 "Raffles and Miss Blandish." Pp. 154-164 in Bernard Rosenberg and David Manning White (eds.), Mass Culture: The Popular Arts in America. New York: The Free Press.
Pekar, Harvey
1972 "Rapping about cartoonists, particularly Robert Crumb." Pp. 236-245 in George H. Lewis (ed.), Side-Saddle on the Golden Calf: Social Structure and Popular Culture in America. Pacific Palisades, Calif.: Goodyear Publishing Co., Inc.
Pepper, Thomas
1972 "The underground press: growing rich on the hippie." Pp. 23-26 in Alan Wells (ed.), Mass Media and Society. Palo Alto, Calif.: National Press Books.
Perry, George and Alan Aldridge
1971 Penguin Book of Comics. London: Penguin Books Ltd.
Playboy
1973 "The court and obscenity." (October):60.
Polsky, Ned
1967 "On the sociology of pornography." Pp. 183-200 in Hustlers, Beats, and Others. New York: Anchor Books.
Qualter, Terence H.
1972 "The techniques of propaganda." Pp. 275-282 in Alan Wells (ed.), Mass Media and Society. Palo Alto, Calif.: National Press Books.

Reitberger, R. and Wolfgang Fuchs
1972 Comics: Anatomy of a Mass Medium. Boston: Little, Brown and Company.
Richler, Mordecai
1971 "James Bond unmasked." Pp. 341-358 in Bernard Rosenberg and David Manning White (eds.), Mass Culture Revisited. New York: Van Nostrand Reinhold Company.
Rivers, William L.
1965 The Opinion Makers. Boston: Beacon Press.
Rockwell, Joan
1971 "Normative attitudes of spies in fiction." Pp. 325-340 in Bernard Rosenberg and David Manning White (eds.), Mass Culture Revisited. New York: Van Nostrand Reinhold Company.
Rolling Stone
1973 (November 22).
Rolo, Charles J.
1957 "Simenon and Spillane: the metaphysics of murder for the millions." Pp. 165-175 in Bernard Rosenberg and David Manning White (eds.), Mass Culture: The Popular Arts in America. New York: The Free Press.
Root, Robert and Christine V. Root
1964 "Magazines in the United States: dying or thriving?" Journalism Quarterly (Winter):15-22.
Rose, Arnold W.
1958 "Mental health attitudes of youth as influenced by a comic strip." Journalism Quarterly (Summer):333-342.
Rosenberg, Bernard and David Manning White (eds.)
1957 Mass Culture: The Popular Arts in America. New York: The Free Press.
1971 Mass Culture Revisited. New York: Van Nostrand Reinhold Company.
Roszak, Theodore
1969 The Making of a Counterculture. Garden City, N. Y.: Doubleday & Company, Inc.
1973 Politics and Transcendence in Postindustrial Society. New York: Anchor Books.
Ryan, Martin
1957 "Portrait of *Playboy*." Studies in Public Communication (Summer):11-21.
Sacramento Bee
1973 "Student decline: lower aptitude scores worry educators." (December 18):A1, A14.
Sanders, Clinton R.
1972 "The portrayal of war and the fighting man in novels of the Vietnam war." Pp. 100-109 in George H. Lewis (ed.), Side-Saddle on the Golden Calf: Social Structure and Popular Culture in America. Pacific Palisades, Calif.: Goodyear Publishing Co., Inc.

Sargent, Leslie et al.
1965 "Significant coverage of integration by minority group magazines." Journal of Human Relations (fourth quarter):484-491.

Schickel, Richard
1968 The Disney Version. New York: Avon Books.

Schramm, Wilbur
1961 "Content analysis of the world of confession magazines." Pp. 297-307 in J. C. Nunnal (ed.), Popular Conceptions of Mental Health. New York: Holt, Rinehart & Winston, Inc.

Seeman, Melvin
1959 "On the meaning of alienation." American Sociological Review (December):783-791.

Shannon, Lyle W.
1957 "The opinions of Little Orphan Annie and her friends." Pp. 212-217 in Bernard Rosenberg and David Manning White (eds.), Mass Culture: The Popular Arts in America. New York: The Free Press.

Short, Robert L.
1964 The Gospel According to Peanuts. New York: Bantam Books, Inc.

Silber, Irwin
1972a "Distorted vision of despair." Guardian (Jan. 5).
1972b "Penchant for nostalgia." Guardian (Jan. 5).

Smith, Hedrick
1972 "When the president meets the press." Pp. 385-389 in Alan Wells (ed.), Mass Media and Society. Palo Alto, Calif.: National Press Books.

Smith, James Steel
1966 "America's magazine missionaries of culture." Journalism Quarterly (Autumn):449-458.

Smith, Lee H.
1972 "Is anything unprintable?" Pp. 260-264 in Alan Wells (ed.), Mass Media and Society. Palo Alto, Calif.: National Press Books.

Sonenschein, David
1972 "Love and sex in the romance magazines." Pp. 66-74 in George H. Lewis (ed.), Side-Saddle on the Golden Calf: Social Structure and Popular Culture in America. Pacific Palisades, Calif.: Goodyear Publishing Co., Inc.

Speich, Don
1974 "State may subtract new math." Sacramento Bee (May 9):A1, A22.

Srole, Leo
1956 "Social integration and certain corollaries, an exploratory study." American Sociological Review (December): 709-716.

Statistical Abstract of the United States
1971 Washington, D. C.: U. S. Government Printing Office.

Steiner, Gary A.
1963 The People Look at Television, A Study of Audience Attitudes. New York: Alfred A. Knopf, Inc.

Steranko, James
1970, 1972 History of Comics (2 volumes). Reading, Pa.: Supergraphics.

Thrasher, F. M.
1950 "The comics and delinquency: cause or scapegoat?" Journal of Educational Sociology (23):195-205.

Toffler, Alvin
1964 The Culture Consumers. Baltimore: Penguin Books Inc.
1970 Future Shock. New York: Bantam Books, Inc.

Truzzi, Marcello (ed.)
1968 Sociology and Everyday Life. Englewood Cliffs, N. J.: Prentice-Hall, Inc.

U. S. News & World Report
1972 "Leisure boom. biggest ever and still growing." (April 17):42-45.

Walker, Daniel
1968 Rights in Conflict, A Report to the National Commission on the Causes and Prevention of Violence. New York: Bantam Books, Inc.

Warshow, Robert
1970 The Immediate Experience: Movies, Comics, Theatre and other Aspects of Popular Culture. New York: Atheneum Publishers.

Waugh, Coulton
1947 The Comics. New York: The Macmillan Company.

Welles, Chris
1972 "Can mass magazines survive?" Pp. 27-34 in Alan Wells (ed.), Mass Media and Society. Palo Alto, Calif.: National Press Books.

Wells, Alan (ed.)
1972 Mass Media and Society. Palo Alto, Calif.: National Press Books.

Wertham, Frederic
1954 Seduction of the Innocent. New York: Holt Rinehart & Winston, Inc.
1966 A Sign for Cain. New York: The Macmillan Company.

White, David Manning
1972 "The 'gate-keeper': a case study in the selection of news." Pp. 191-197 in Alan Wells (ed.), Mass Media and Society. Palo Alto, Calif.: National Press Books.

White, David Manning and R. Abel
1963 The Funnies: An American Idiom. New York: The Free Press.

Wilensky, Harold L.
1960   "Work, careers and social integration." International Social Science Journal (Fall):543-560.
1964   "Mass society and mass culture: interdependence or independence?" American Sociological Review (April):173-197.
Wilson, Edmund
1957   "Who cares who killed Roger Ackroyd?" Pp. 149-153 in Bernard Rosenberg and David Manning White (eds.), Mass Culture: The Popular Arts in America. New York: The Free Press.
Winick, Charles
1968   "Teen-agers, satire and Mad." Pp. 170-185 in Marcello Truzzi (ed.), Sociology and Everyday Life. Englewood Cliffs, N. J.: Prentice Hall, Inc.

chapter 7

❧ Mass culture: cinema[1]

HISTORICAL DEVELOPMENT AND CURRENT QUANTITIES

In 1891, Thomas Edison patented his rudimentary motion picture camera, the kinetoscope. This was the birth of cinema in the United States. However, as all other major inventions in history, motion picture was the product of many minds. Across the Atlantic, the aptly named brothers Lumière had also invented a motion picture camera; the film strips used in the kinetoscope had been developed by Eastman; much of Edison's camera was the work of his assistant William Dickson; others, in turn, succeeded in projecting moving pictures onto a screen; and none of this would have been possible without the prior contributions of Daguerre, Niepce, and the other pioneers of photography.

No sooner was the kinetoscope invented than it became a marketable commodity. The first penny arcade opened in New York in 1894, soon followed by others. For a penny, an individual could glue himself to one of these internal movie projectors

Photoworld

[1]Portions of this chapter were written in collaboration with Tom Wilson.

and watch a thirty-second peep show unfold. Arcades consisted of the rows of kinetoscopes necessary to accommodate large numbers of individuals, one at a time for each device.

A breakthrough was accomplished the next year, however, with the first external motion picture projection. This led to the immediate and spectacular rise of the cheap, early movie theater—the nickelodeon. The first ones were built in 1895; by 1910 there were at least thirteen thousand, attended by as many as 7 million people every day. For a nickel initially, a dime or fifteen cents later on, one could now be part of an entire audience, watching multireel movies lasting as long as thirty minutes.

It is generally understood (see, for example, Dulles, 1965:291, and Nye, 1970:364) that cinema began as a distinctly lower-class form of entertainment, at least in the United States. Movies were first popular with the masses, only later with the middle and upper classes, in contrast with many other leisure activities, particularly sports. Indeed, whereas the general diffusion pattern of leisure and recreation has been downward, cinema represents a notable exception. The nickelodeons were the first wave of mass culture and mass leisure in American history. They proliferated in the tenement districts, providing cheap recreation to a rapidly industrializing society and its growing urban masses.

Most early films were plotless and simple, with perhaps one major slapstick event, a hose spraying a gardener, or the ubiquitous chase motif. Then in 1903 Edwin S. Porter, cameraman for Thomas Edison, made *The Great Train Robbery,* the first full-fledged movie with story, plot, violence, action, characters, and all the other necessary ingredients of the modern action film.

In 1909, Mack Sennett went to Hollywood, where he organized the *Keystone Cops* two years later. And in 1911 Jesse

Lasky filmed *Squaw Man,* also one of the first pictures made in that location. This, then, was the birth of Tinsel City, California.

Another milestone was D. W. Griffith's *Birth of a Nation,* in 1914. This was the first of the big productions. At $100,000, its cost far exceeded any other film made thus far. It was eventually to earn $18 million, an unprecedented profit margin.

From then on the trend was toward big, feature-length productions, often the filmed version of well-known books. The 1910s produced *Uncle Tom's Cabin, Oliver Twist, Romeo and Juliet, Ben-Hur, Moses, Samson, Joan of Arc, Quo Vadis, Queen Elizabeth* (starring Sarah Bernhardt). By 1918, Hollywood produced 841 feature-length films annually (Nye, 1970:365), 97% of the world's movies. They were shown in 21,000 theaters across the nation, with admission prices ranging up to $1.50. Motion pictures had now established a solid middle-class following, no longer attracting the lower classes only. The movie industry was now the fifth largest in the United States. During the next decade, actors like Charlie Chaplin and Douglas Fairbanks would earn as much as $25,000 to $30,000 weekly. The star system was born.

The trends of the 1910s acquired further momentum in the twenties, the decade of the super colossals (Nye, 1970:367). Cecil B. De Mille's first *Ten Commandments* came out in 1923. Typically, classics were filmed repeatedly: *Uncle Tom's Cabin* and *Oliver Twist* three times, and *Michael Strogoff, Carmen, Rip Van Winkle, Ivanhoe,* and *Robinson Crusoe* each twice.

From 1912 through the thirties and particularly between 1914 and 1926, the serials flourished. *The Perils of Pauline* (1914), *Tarzan* (1928), *Flash Gordon* (1936), and innumerable others were produced in twenty, forty, or sometimes more than one hundred episodes (Nye, 1970:368-370).

The roaring twenties were culturally in many ways similar to our own era today. The hedonistic, glamorous, and make-believe world dangled before the masses by the media and always at the core of American mass culture found its first massive manifestation half a century ago. Crass materialism, blatant sexuality, the cult of youth, the illusory pursuit of excitement and success, these were the dominant values of the twenties, as they are today. The twenties' films bore titles like *Money! Money! Money!,* glamorizing "jazz babies" and showing champagne baths. Contemporary social critics (cf. Daniel Boorstin, 1961; Herbert Marcuse, 1964; Marshall McLuhan, 1964) have shown us the role of pseudoevents, illusions, and myths in our lives; they point out that we live in a never-never land, drugged by the media and the power-elite into total social and political unconsciousness, blind to our true condition; they explain how we identify with the glamorous and nonexistent world of Madison Avenue presented on television while actually leading drab, impoverished, and exhaustingly harsh lives, chasing a lifestyle of excitement, pleasure, wealth, sex, youth, and luxury that is simply not there to anyone but a select few. What these critics fail to point out is that this psychological enslavement goes back to the beginnings of mass consumption and that the roaring twenties were, to use a current colloquialism, the first time "Madison Avenue laid its trip on us."

It was thus in the twenties that we built the monstrous mass theaters required to accommodate the 7 to 10 million Americans who went to see a movie every day, establishments providing the masses with a cheap and synthetic experience of lavish, exotic pomp. Huge theaters were erected in America's major population centers. New York's Roxy could accommodate 6,214 visitors; it had three organs, a 110 piece orchestra, and 125 ushers (Nye, 1970:378). The architectural style of these massive movie halls was a garish mishmash of Moorish, Gothic, and neoclassic elements that would have made the designers of the Parthenon, the Alhambra, and Notre Dame turn in their graves.

The major technological milestone of the 1920s was, of course, the introduction of sound. While the first sound films were made as early as 1923, it was not until Al Jolson's *The Jazz Singer* (1927/8)[2] that the talkies were on their way to total supremacy. By 1930 the takeover was nearly complete. One of the last few silent films deserves mention because of its excellence—Chaplin's *City Lights* (1931).

Sound gave another impetus to movies' exponential growth. By 1929, "weekly attendance jumped to an estimated 110 million—the equivalent of four fifths of the entire population going to a show once a week throughout the entire year" (Dulles, 1965:299).[3]

The rise of the talkie resulted in an array of new genres: whereas the silent movie had been an eminently appropriate vehicle for comedy (pantomime) and adventure (fast-moving visual action), sound led to the birth of horror films, musicals, sound comedies, singing westerns, and "social message" movies.

Horror films began with classics like *Dracula* (Bela Lugosi) and *Frankenstein* (Boris Karloff), and they have remained popular, as Hollywood still produced one hundred such films annually as recently as in the early sixties. The origin of movie

[2]Dulles (1965), Nye (1970), and Schickel (1964), my major sources for this historical sketch, are often at variance in their dates and figures. Here, for example, Dulles and Schickel assign *The Jazz Singer* to 1928, Nye a year earlier.
[3] Again, different sources give grossly different data. Here, Nye (1970:379) is in obvious error, claiming a gross income of $110 million for the movie industry in 1929, one-tenth Dulles's estimate. Nye may have misread the weekly attendance figure of 110 million (see Dulles, 1965:299) for annual receipts of $110 million.

musicals is tied to two names and two names only—Fred Astaire and Ginger Rogers. These films also remained viable for a long time, as evidenced by the fact that *The Sound of Music* (1965) was the most lucrative film ever made up to that time. The sound comedy departed from the earlier pantomime in that humor now needed to be verbal, not merely facial. Masters of visual comedy (e.g., Chaplin) were supplanted by the masters of the wisecrack: Jimmy Durante, Bob Hope, the Marx Brothers. In a rare instance an actor had sufficient talent of both kinds to successfully make the transition to talkies even though he had been an established star of the silent movies: such was the case of W. C. Fields (Nye, 1970:381). The singing westerns of Gene Autry and Roy Rogers also go back to the first sound decade, and so do several of John Ford's excellent films, for example, *Grapes of Wrath* (1939, Henry Fonda). Other memorable films from the last prewar decade include Hitchcock's *39 Steps* (1935), Capra's *You Can't Take It with You* (1938), Selznick's *Gone With the Wind* (1939, until then the most lucrative film ever) and Welles' *Citizen Kane* (1941).

The thirties were also the decade of the cartoon, specifically Walt Disney's cartoons. Although the genre goes back to 1912 (Winsor McKay's *Gertie the Dinosaur*), it was not until the late twenties and thirties that Disney moved into the area, first with *Mickey Mouse* (1928), later with feature-length cartoons beginning with *Snow White and the Seven Dwarfs* (1937). Disney's supremacy has remained virtually uncontested even after his death, despite an occasional challenge such as Stephen Bosustow's *Mr. Magoo* (1940s).[4]

The second and last peak in the history of the motion picture occurred in 1939.

After the 1929 crash, attendance and receipts had steadily regained ground until by 1939 an estimated 85 million Americans once again saw one movie per week. However, it was also in 1939 that the first television sets reached the consumer market.

The conquest of America by the one-eyed monster was temporarily postponed by World War II. Thus by the end of the war weekly attendance was still as high as 90 million, keeping twenty thousand theaters in business. Then, motion picture's sharpest decline set in. By 1965 the total number of theaters had gone down to thirteen thousand, and this included four thousand new drive-ins. Over eleven thousand four-wall theaters had had to close since the war. If population growth is taken into account, the decline was even more spectacular. In 1945 we had had one movie theater per seven thousand population; by 1965 only one for every fifteen thousand. Television was, of course, responsible. As Fig. 5 shows, the rise of TV has been simultaneous with the decline of the movie theater.

Responding to the challenge of television, the motion picture industry has introduced a number of new and costly devices in its effort to hold on to its audience. The drive-in theater had been in existence since 1933, but only after the war was it perceived as a tool in the struggle for survival. It took until 1948 to build the first eight hundred of them, but six years later their number had multiplied fivefold (Statistical Abstracts, 1973:210). Today, nearly one third of all theaters are of the drive-in variety.

Other initatives included the production of ever more expensive "blockbusters," from *My Fair Lady* (1952, $5.5 million) to *Cleopatra* (1963, $37 million, four and a half long hours), and the introduction of techniques like Cinemascope, Cinerama, Circarama, Vista-Vision, Todd-A0, Panavision, three-dimensional cinema, and double features. Through all

---

[4] For a recent discussion of the Disney empire, see Mano (1973).

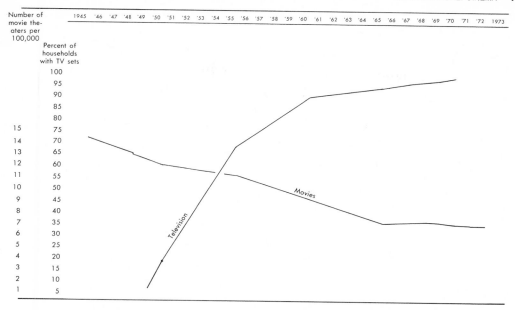

Fig. 5. *The fall of the movie theater and the rise of television: two simultaneous and related phenomena. (Sources of statistics on television sets from Statistical Abstracts of the United States, 1973:210, 499; Bogart, 1972:15.)*

Table 7-1. *Trends in the motion picture industry since World War II**

	1945	1950	1955	1960	1965	1968	1969	1970	1971	1972
Number of theaters										
Four-wall	20	18	15	12	10	10	10	11	11	11
Drive-in	0	1	4	4	4	4	4	4	4	4
Total (thousands)	20	19	18	16	13	14	14	14	14	14
Receipts (billions)		1.38	1.33	0.951	0.927	1.05	1.09	1.16	1.21	
Average admission price (dollars)		0.44	0.55	0.65	0.85	1.31	1.42	1.54	1.65	1.70
Weekly number of admissions (millions)	95	60	45	41	25			19		
Number of films made in Hollywood	370		200		180					

*Sources: Bogart (1972:412), Lyle (1969:204), Nye (1970:385), Statistical Abstracts of the United States (1971:202, 1973:210).

this, the industry managed to hold on to a fraction of its former audience, and by sharply increasing prices it stabilized its annual receipts at slightly over $1 billion. Table 7-1 shows these postwar developments through a variety of indicators.

Much of the recent literature argues that the decline of motion pictures has come to a halt and that the industry has finally turned the corner. Thus Schickel (1964:183) wrote that "the panic in Hollywood" had finally been stopped, and Lyle (1969:204) saw hope in the fact that the proportion of domestic films released in the country had again been rising (from a low of 28% in the early sixties to 39% in 1967). Yet one wonders how wishful such thinking may be. Schickel's all-time low weekly attendance of 36 million (1964:164) was, as may be seen from Table 7-1, to be surpassed by even more dismal figures in subsequent years. It is not clear whether the quantitative decline of motion picture attendance has hit rock bottom. "Right now . . . there seems to be a resurgence of the movie business in numbers of patrons and dollars" (Michener, 1974:44). It may indeed be that the consumer, due to fuel shortages and inflation, is experiencing a curtailment of his mobility and substituting short trips to the movie theater for distant outdoor leisure activities. However, such a trend, if it exists, cannot yet be established at this time.

The quality of American movies (to which I shall address myself again in a moment) is subject to debate and controversy. Perhaps sex, violence, and gore have, by the 1970s, reached unprecedented proportions as the industry's survival gasps drive it to produce works like *Deep Throat,* a film whose overhead costs consist of little more than a supply of Chap Sticks for "star" Lovelace's sore lips, yet is capable of mustering a $5 admission fee wherever it plays, thus demonstrating the enormous profitability of all-out sex.

In all fairness, one must recall that the industry has, from its very inception, always produced four or five B-grade pictures for every first-rate film coming out of Hollywood. And while expensive productions remain hazardous, some spectacular financial successes have recently been scored. *The Godfather* is expected to break the records set by *Gone With the Wind* (Zimmerman, 1972) and *The Sound of Music,* and independently financed (and advertised) pictures like *Billy Jack* and *Easy Rider* have also produced profits of millions. Most importantly, the quality of American cinema has vastly improved over earlier decades, as it is no longer a monolithic industry dominated by a few giant studios in Hollywood. From a fi-

Table 7-2. *Percentage of population going to see movie "yesterday," by sex and age**

Sex	
Men	4
Women	5
All	5
Age	
15-19	15
20-29	8
30-39	5
40-49	3
60+	1
All	5

*From "The public appraises movies," a survey for the Motion Picture Association of America, Inc., by Opinion Research Corporation, December, 1957. The O.R.C. data distinguished between regular theaters and drive-ins. I have combined the figures.

nancial standpoint, the future of American cinema appears a mixed bag at best. However, it is safe to say that as an art form, cinema has successfully withstood the onslaught of television. It now assumes, instead of its earlier preponderant position, a stable and permanent place in the vast and diversified American entertainment market.[5]

SOCIOLOGICAL CORRELATES

Today's motion picture audience is as heterogeneous as the movies that are produced, and it is constantly changing. Unlike the docile television audience, moviegoers are capricious and unpredictable (Jarvie, 1970). Furthermore, the cinema audience has not been well researched. "We have few, if any, figures on the population as a whole" (Jarvie, 1970:108).

Let us, again, begin with sex and age. Table 7-2 reproduces the Opinion Research Corporation's findings on the relationship between these two variables and frequency of movie attendance.

[5] Additional information about the history of motion pictures may be obtained from Hampton (1931), Mast (1971), and Quigley (1948).

According to Table 7-2, men and women do not differ very markedly in frequency of movie attendance. This makes sense. Most movie going is done by couples, frequently married. Indeed, other studies show that less than 20% of movie attendance is done alone (Jarvie, 1970:108), and that 59% of moviegoers are married, against 41% unmarried (Jarvie, 1970:114). Interestingly, the O.R.C. study found employed women to attend movies twice as often as those not employed. Furthermore, unmarried women have been found to attend movies much less frequently than unmarried men (Jarvie, 1970:114).

Age is, of course, much more strongly related to movie attendance than sex. Table 7-2 clearly indicates that the movie audience is quite young. All sources concur on this. According to a more recent source (Nye, 1970:386), 70% of all moviegoers are under 30, 52% under 20, and the vast majority of them are between 16 and 22. Jarvie (1970:117), who documents the youth of moviegoers both in the United States and in Britain, concludes that "the hard core is mainly the young and the unmarried who want to escape home and television."

When it comes to race and ethnicity, indications seem to be that movies are becoming more popular among blacks and other minorities. Certainly the recent spate of black violence coming out of Hollywood indicates that the studios sense a rising market in the inner city. In addition, we now also have Oriental, feminist, and other minority violence as the theme of large numbers of B-grade films. From *Shaft, Superfly, Black Godfather* and the subsequent series of black violence through the *Kung Fu* and the *Chinese Connection* (Bruce Lee) to the karate black-belted oriental female heroine (!) pictures, we are now plagued by a stream of counter-cultural and subcultural violence that merely follows a tradition as old as the movie industry

Table 7-3. *Percentage of population going to see movie "yesterday," by region and urban-rural residence* *

Region	
Northeast	5
North Central	5
South	6
West	4
All	5
Rural-urban	
Rural	3
Below 100,000	6
100,000-999,999	6
1 million +	7
All	5

*From "The public appraises movies," a survey for the Motion Picture Association of America, Inc., by Opinion Research Corporation, December, 1957.

itself. Not all of this, to be sure, is unmitigated trash. Some of the musical scores are fine (for example, Isaac Hayes' and Curtis Mayfield's contributions to the black movies), and pictures like *Superfly* even take a sort of perverted sociophilosophical stance.[6] However, the new minority violence is, as a whole, no more redeeming than the earlier B-grade pictures.

For geography and the rural-urban variable, we go back to the O.R.C. study. Table 7-3 reproduces that study's findings with respect to those two variables.

While the regional differences in Table 7-3 do not appear conclusive, there is a clear positive relationship between urbanism and movie attendance.

Finally, what about education and the socioeconomic cluster of variables (social class, occupation, etc.)? Table 7-4 gives the O.R.C.'s findings on education.

Table 7-4 does not reveal a clear-cut relationship between education and movie attendance, and the same O.R.C. study is equally inconclusive with regard to income (cf. de Grazia, 1964:443), except

---

[6]For discussions of black art and black movies see Lewis (1972) and Michener (1972).

Table 7-4. *Percentage of population going to see movie "yesterday," by education**

Less than eighth grade	4
Eighth grade	3
High school, incomplete	5
High school, complete	5
College	4
All	5

*From "The public appraises movies," a survey for the Motion Picture Association of America, Inc., by Opinion Research Corporation, December, 1957.

David Brody/Editorial Photocolor Archives

for the below $3,000 income bracket, where movie attendance is, understandably, significantly lower. However, a study by Clarke (1958), distinguishing between five occupational prestige levels, found that movie attendance was most frequent at the highest prestige levels. Generally, it would seem that socioeconomic status and education are somewhat positively correlated with movie attendance, but the more important fact is that the different social, educational, and ethnic-subcultural strata each see different *kinds,* rather than amounts, of movies. Thus college students and professors may frequent art theaters located at the outskirts of University campuses or at the center of the largest cities, theaters which show primarily classics (Chaplin, W. C. Fields, Eisenstein) and contemporary foreign films (Antonioni, Bergman, Godard, Truffaut) at reduced prices. Meanwhile the domestic industry, while experiencing at this time a remarkable renaissance of quality films, continues to cater to the population's lowest drives by cranking out productions that reach, year after year, ever greater depths of horror, violence, and tastelessness.[7]

---

[7]For additional information about the movie audience and its demographic correlates, see Anast (1967), Bogart (1964), and Lewis (1972). For a study of urban-small town differences, see Schramm et al. (1961). For information about the British audience, see Jarvie (1970:83-117).

MAJOR TRENDS AND ISSUES

I cannot, within the framework of this book, devote adequate attention to the sociology of the cinema and its many problems. I must resign myself to a mere enumeration of some of the most salient issues, suggesting some of the readings that have come to my attention.

Perhaps the very first problem to mark the history of motion pictures was the complex issue of sex, sensationalism, pornography, and censorship. This is traced historically by Dulles (1965) and Nye (1970), and Lewis (1972) reproduces parts of the recent Report by the President's Commission on Obscenity and Pornography. The debate about the sexual (and violent) content of movies is as old as the industry itself. Pressure from (conservative) public opinion eventually led to self-regulation, the industry wisely choosing that over the worse evil of governmental intervention. Of course, the hard-core pornography of the sixties and seventies is not bound by the Motion Picture Association's Code. While the pornography battle now rages in local courts as a result of the Supreme Court's decision to relegate the responsibility to the local community, Lewis and others (see Lewis, 1972:88-95) show that the pornography patron is not, generally, a deviant.

Walt Disney is another area dealt with by a variety of authors, Nye (1970) and Schickel (1964) among others. In addition, Mano (1973) and Schickel (1968) focus more sharply on the financial aspects of the Disney-Disneyland-Disneyworld empire. These and other recent sources belong to a growing body of accusatory books and articles blaming the Disney organization for everything from ecological plunder (e.g., of the Florida Everglades) to the capitalistic exploitation of its personnel (e.g., at Disneyland and Disneyworld). There is now a tendency in some quarters to view the Disney empire as a symbol of corporate capitalism and the evils of that system.

By far the greatest amount of writing on cinema has been devoted to "the great debate," the question of motion picture's artistic status. From the very first moment, cinema has embodied both the good and the bad, both prostitution to commercial interests and artistic excellence. And, concomitantly, the great debate about cinema's merits has been upon us from the form's very inception. Nye (1970:372-373), for example, notes that as early as 1912 a National Education Association study of movies took a highly critical stance, while *The Nation,* only a year later, came out strongly in favor of the new medium, viewing it as a force for democracy. Other general evaluative and critical works include Kuhns (1972), Schickel (1964), Warshow (1970), Wolfenstein and Leites (1970), and Wood (1973). Schickel's book is rather optimistic, and it specifies in detail the industry's more notable contributions. Thus Kazan *(On the Waterfront),* Kubrick *(Lolita, Dr. Strangelove, 2001:A Space Odyssey, A Clockwork Orange)* and Wilder *(The Apartment, Irma la Douce)* are noted to be among the best American directors of the day, and the author also gives excellent coverage of the international scene, from Eisenstein *(Potemkin, Ivan the Terrible),* through the French New Wave (Resnais, Godard, Truffaut), to the postwar Italian (De Sica, Fellini, Antonioni), English (Richardson, Schlesinger) and Swedish (Bergman) directors. I concur that most of these works have substantial artistic merit. For example, on the domestic scene Stanley Kubrick is certainly one of the most talented directors at this time. In *Dr. Strangelove,* he explodes, through humor, the pompous and monstrous idea of safety-through-nuclear-balance-of-terror. In *A Clockwork Orange,* he provides a prophetic and not all that futuristic depiction of our emerging jungle society in which only the immoral and the violent survive with any degree of success. *2001:A Space Odyssey* is an outstanding piece of science fiction entertainment, a pleasure to the eye. Overall, however, it is the foreign film industry which has produced the overwhelming majority of socially and artistically redeeming works. The no longer so new French New Wave discussed by Schickel, for example, has produced such classics as *The 400 Blows, Jules and Jim* (Truffaut), *Breathless* (Godard) and *Hiroshima, Mon Amour* (Resnais). Such films are small-budget, black-and-white features characterized by powerful acting and masterful realism in depicting human interaction and experience. *Breathless* deals in death and violence, *The 400 Blows* is about childhood and pain, *Jules and Jim* is about love and death, as is *Hiroshima, Mon Amour.* While these and the many other outstanding films produced by the French Nouvelle Vague all contain tragedy, they do no more so than life itself, and in the end it is this fact—their accurate rendition of the human experience—which distinguishes them so sharply from Hollywood. It is inescapably true, Schickel concludes, that foreign cinema has been an art form while Hollywood has been (big) business.

Additional discussions of cinema as an art form may be found in Atlas (1972), Bremond (1961), Dienstfrey (1962), and Hurley (1957). Atlas interviews Arthur Penn, one of America's outstanding new directors *(Alice's Restaurant, Bonnie and Clyde, Little Big Man),* Bremond describes the French New Wave, Dienstfrey deals with the New American Cinema, and Hurley discusses the cinema of tomorrow.

Still under the heading of critical appraisals, I must now turn to sources that review specific pictures. By way of examples, let me mention Beck (1972), Kando and Willis (1970), Larrabee and Riesman (1957), Silber (1972a), Trilling (1971), Willis (1970) and Zimmerman (1974). Larrabee and Riesman review *Executive Suite,* an older picture with features that are nevertheless relevant for the contemporary scene; the authors find in it both Veblenian and populist overtones. Kando, Trilling, and Willis review *Easy Rider* and related films; while Trilling addresses herself to the new morality of such a film (emphasizing that it is, indeed, an alternative morality rather than the mere absence of one), Kando and Willis are at each other's throat with respect to the picture's implications for women's liberation. Beck and Zimmerman both review *A Clockwork Orange* (and such related films as *Strawdogs* and *The Boy Friend*). They are both highly critical of such pictures, although for different reasons. Both deplore the ultraviolence, but only Silber, an English Marxist, views it as the manifestation of capitalism's death throes. Zimmerman's review of *Magnum Force,* the latest in the Dirty Harry series, explains, in addition to indicting the continuing ultraviolence, how as a result of Watergate and the liberal winds blowing in 1974, even fascism

has gone mod. Clint Eastwood continues his murderous rampage, but now killing overzealous policemen rather than plain criminals. Hollywood wastes no time jumping on bandwagons.

Sources that address themselves more generally to the problem of violence in motion pictures include Albert (1957), Berkowitz and Rawlings (1963), Berkowitz and Green (1966), Blumer (1933), and Morgenstern (1972). Morgenstern, as well as increasing numbers of others, seems to feel (and deplore the fact) that movie violence is increasing.

More general appraisals of Hollywood or some of its aspects include Kracauer (1957), Elkin (1957), Powdermaker (1957), Soderbergh (1965-1966), Steele (1971), and White et al. (1957). Kracauer documents, through content analysis, Hollywood's treatment of national types, for example, the English and the Russians. Elkin traces the way Hollywood portrays god and religion. Powdermaker provides a caricature of Hollywood, the dream factory. Soderbergh discusses Hollywood's treatment of the South. Steele points out, as was done above, that Hollywood is quick in jumping on promising sociopolitical trends. Here, the author shows how the industry went mod in the early seventies, trying to emulate *Easy Rider*'s success and to cash in on the hippie syndrome (to little avail). White et al. analyze Hollywood's newspaper advertising. All in all, film criticism and analysis is one of the richest and most interesting areas of popular culture. For a useful discussion of the sociology of film criticism, see Jarvie (1970).

A further area of interest to students of cinema has been the audience—its role and nature. Gans (1957, 1964) and Jarvie (1970) are among the sociologists who have dealt with this, Gans, in particular, focusing on the reactive effect of the audience (through the so-called audience image) upon the nature and quality of motion pictures.

There is, finally, a certain body of literature whose rallying point is nothing but nostalgia for cinema's golden age and, more generally, for anything that happened more than ten years ago. Typical of this tendency is the growing number of films taking place just ten, twenty, thirty, or fifty years ago: *American Graffiti, Summer of '42, Paper Moon, The Way We Were, Bonnie and Clyde, The Sting, The Great Gatsby.* The nostalgia is manifest in Croce (1973), Kael (1973), Knox (1973), Koch (1973), Lambert (1973), Mankiewicz (1973), Mankiewicz and Welles (1973), all books that deal with oldies but goodies like *Gone With the Wind, Citizen Kane, Casablanca,* and *An American in Paris.* Wood (1973), who reviews this series of books, dissociates himself from the nostalgia. Rodgers (1972) also described the tendency recently, tracing it both in motion picture ("Marilyn Monroe is still part of the American Dream") and other areas of leisure.

In sum, there is a vast and fascinating area of popular culture to be dealt with under the sociology of the cinema. Jarvie (1970) provides a useful beginning for the new discipline, approaching the subject matter the way Berelson and others approached other media two and three decades ago, applying role-theoretical and other basic sociological concepts to the problems. The four questions that sociology must answer, Jarvie suggests, are (1) Who makes films and why? (2) Who sees films, how and why? (3) What is seen, how and why? and (4) How do films get evaluated and why? The author also provides an enormous annotated bibliography. Here, I have merely outlined some of the phenomenon's dimensions. As cinema becomes more art and less mass entertainment in the coming decades, it is hoped that it will receive the attention it so richly deserves on the basis of its artistic and creative potential, and not merely be appraised from a quantitative and financial perspective.

SUMMARY AND CONCLUSION

This chapter has provided a cursory discussion of cinema as one major area of popular culture. Following my established format, I first traced the motion picture's history and its current magnitude, then provided some of the form's major sociological correlates, and finally touched upon some of the most salient issues one finds discussed in the literature on movies.

From Thomas Edison's kinetoscope (1891) through the first decade of the twentieth century, movies were a highly popular but predominantly cheap, lower-class urban form of mass entertainment. Initially, this took the form of penny arcades and nickelodeons—the first type of movie theater. Hollywood was born between 1909 and 1911, with the creation of the *Keystone Cops* and *Squaw Man.* In 1914, Griffith's *Birth of a Nation* set the tone for the big expensive productions of the next decades. During the roaring twenties, movie production and attendance reached staggering proportions with over 21,000 theaters showing the nearly one thousand feature-length films produced in Hollywood annually, most of these exuding materialism, glamour, sexuality, youth, and success. Sound was introduced in 1927-1928. After a decade of depression, movies reached a second peak in 1939—the year of *Gone With the Wind.* That, however, was also the year when the first television sets reached the market. Thus the postwar period ushered the steady decline of cinema in favor of television. Despite the introduction of Cinemascope, Cinerama, doublefeatures, drive-ins, a variety of other gimmicks and ever more expensive "blockbusters," by 1965 the number of theaters had declined to thirteen thousand. And weekly attendance, which has exceeded 100 million in the twenties and again approached that figure just after World War II, declined to 19 million in 1970. Finally there were some indications by 1974 that movies were again gaining in popularity, perhaps as a side-effect of the energy shortage.

While the movie audience is less predictable than that of, say, television, we saw that it was younger, more urban, and probably better educated and of higher socioeconomic status than the population at large. In addition, the film audience, as we saw, consists of a heterogeneous collection of ethnic, social, and subcultural groups, each consuming a different *genre* of films.

The major issues touched upon in this chapter included the matter of sex, violence, pornography, and censorship, and. the question of cinema's artistic status. With regard to the first question, the two major recent developments to be noted are the relegation of the pornography debate to the local level by the Supreme Court and, meanwhile, the ever increasing amount of ultraviolence and hardcore pornography presented on the screen. As to the social, artistic, and intellectual quality of contemporary films, it is still true, generally, that Hollywood is a business enterprise while the foreign cinema is an art form. However, there is also a recent resurgence of low-budget quality domestic films, and it can be argued that the American cinema has, in recent years, amply made up in quality for what it has lost in quantity.

STUDY QUESTIONS

1. Trace the history and growth of cinema in the United States. What were some of the major milestones in that history. When did Hollywood become the industry's headquarters? What were the peak years and the peak decades in terms of the medium's productivity and popularity? What have been the typical characteristics of movies produced at different times, for example, during the roaring twenties? What have been some of the most memorable, most expensive, and most lucrative films? Finally, show the direct inverse relationship between the advent of television and the postwar trend in motion pictures. What gimmicks has the motion picture industry tried in its efforts at stemming the tide? Have they helped? Could it be that the decline has finally hit rock bottom? Why?

2. What are some of the motion picture audience's main demographic characteristics? Historically, what can you say about movies and social class? Today, what are some of the target audiences which some of Hollywood's products are directly aimed at? What does this suggest in terms of the changing socioeconomic and ethnic composition of the movie audience?

3. Discuss the issues of sex and violence in motion pictures. What have been the major trends with respect to hard-core pornography and ultraviolence during the past decade? How is the Supreme Court's pornography ruling likely to affect future trends? Discuss the pros and cons of censorship, self-regulation, and governmental intervention. Overall, has American cinema improved or deteriorated in recent years? Why?

4. Discuss the artistic and cultural quality of contemporary movies on both sides of the Atlantic. Give specific examples of significant American and foreign films, significant both for their excellence and their poor taste. What typifies a group like the French New Wave? What are the main trends operating in Hollywood at this time? Discuss for example such trends as the new nostalgia, the ultraviolence, and the new permissiveness. Overall, what would still be the main difference between Hollywood and foreign cinema? Do you see this changing?

REFERENCES

Albert, R. S.
   1957   "The role of mass media and the effect of aggressive film content upon children's aggressive responses and identification choices." Genetic Psychology Monographs 55:221-285.

Anast, Phillys
   1967   "Differential movie appeals as correlates of attendance." Journalism Quarterly (Spring):86-90.

Atlas, Jacoba
   1972   "A conversation with Arthur Penn." Pp. 120-127 in George H. Lewis (ed.), Side-Saddle on the Golden Calf. Pacific Palisades, Calif. Goodyear Publishing Co., Inc.

Beck, Bernard
   1972   "Violent search for heroism." Society, (Nov.-Dec.):39-47.

Berkowitz, Leonard and Russell G. Green
1966 "Film violence and the cue properties of available targets." Journal of Personal Social Psychology 3:(May):525-530.

Berkowitz, Leonard and Edna Rawlings
1963 "Effects of film violence on inhibitions against subsequent aggression." Journal of Abnormal Social Psychology 66:405-412.

Blumer, Herbert and Philip Hauser
1933 Movies, Delinquency and Crime. New York: The Macmillan Company.

Bogart, Leo
1964 "The mass media and the blue-collar worker." Pp. 416-428 in Arthur B. Shostok and William Gomberg (eds.), Blue-Collar World. Englewood Cliffs, N. J.: Prentice-Hall, Inc.
1972 The Age of Television. 3rd ed. New York: Frederick Ungar Publishing Co., Inc.

Boorstin, Daniel J.
1961 The Image: A Guide to Pseudo-Events in America. New York: Harper & Row, Publishers.

Bremond, Claude, et al.
1961 "The heroes of the New Wave films." Communications 1:142-177 (French).

Clarke, Alfred C.
1958 "Leisure and occupational prestige." Pp. 205-214 in Eric Larrabee and Rolf Meyersohn (eds.), Mass Leisure. Glencoe, Ill.: The Free Press.

Croce, Arlene
1973 The Fred Astaire and Ginger Rogers Book. New York: E. P. Dutton & Co., Inc.

de Grazia, Sebastian
1964 Of Time, Work and Leisure. New York: Anchor Books.

Dienstfrey, Harris
1962 "The new American cinema." Commentary 33(June):495-504.

Dulles, Foster Rhea
1965 A History of Recreation: America Learns to Play. New York: Appleton-Century-Crofts.

Elkin, Frederick
1957 "God, radio, and the movies." Pp. 308-314 in Bernard Rosenberg and David Manning White (eds.), Mass Culture. New York: The Free Press.

Gans, Herbert J.
1957 "The creator-audience relationship in the mass media: an analysis of movie making." Pp. 315-324 in Bernard Rosenberg and David M. White (eds.), Mass Culture. New York: The Free Press.
1964 "The rise of the problem-film, an analysis of changes in Hollywood films and the American audience." Sociological Abstracts Bi, B-3683, p. 1393, 1964-V, 12.

Hampton, Benjamin B.
1931 A History of the Movies. New York: Arno Press.

Hurley, Neil P.
1957 "The cinema of tomorrow." Social Order 7(May):207-214.

Jarvie, I. C.
1970 Movies and Society. New York: Basic Books, Inc., Publishers.

Kael, Pauline
1973 The Citizen Kane Book: Raising Kane. Boston: Atlantic-Little Brown.

Kando, Thomas M. and Ellen Willis
1970 "Exchange on women's liberation and the movies." New York Review of Books (February 26).

Knox, Donald
1973 The Magic Factory: How MGM Made "An American in Paris." New York: Praeger Publishers, Inc.

Koch, Howard
1973 "Casablanca," Script and Legend. Woodstock, N. Y.: The Overlook Press.

Kracauer, Siegfried
1957 "National types as Hollywood presents them." Pp. 257-277 in Bernard Rosenberg and David Manning White (eds.), Mass Culture. New York: The Free Press.

Kuhns, William
1972 Movies in America. Dayton, Ohio: Pflaum Press.

Lambert, Gavin
1973 GWTW: The Making of Gone With the Wind. Boston: Atlantic-Little Brown.

Larrabee, Eric and David Riesman
1957 "Company-town pastoral: the role of business in 'Executive Suite,' " Pp. 325-337 in Bernard Rosenberg and David Manning White (eds.), Mass Culture. New York: The Free Press.

Lewis, George H. (ed.)
1972 Side-Saddle on the Golden Calf: Social Structure and Popular Culture in America. Pacific Palisades, Calif.: Goodyear Publishing Co., Inc.

Lyle, Jack
1969 "Contemporary functions of the mass media." Pp. 187-216 in Robert K. Baker and Sandra J. Ball (eds.), Violence and the Media: A Staff Report to the National Commission on the Causes and Prevention of Violence. Washington, D. C.: U. S. Government Printing Office.

Mankiewicz, Joseph L.
1972 More about "All About Eve." New York: Random House, Inc.

Mankiewicz, Herman J. and Orson Welles
1973 The Shooting Script in the Citizen Kane Book: Raising Kane, Pauline Kael. Boston: Atlantic-Little Brown.

Mano, D. Keith
 1973   "A real Mickey Mouse operation." Play-
        boy (December):199, 322-338.
Marcuse, Herbert
 1964   One-Dimensional Man: Studies in the
        Ideology of Advanced Industrial Society.
        Boston: Beacon Press.
Mast, Gerald
 1971   A Short History of the Movies. New York:
        The Bobbs-Merrill Co., Inc.
McLuhan, Marshall
 1964   Understanding Media: The Extensions of
        Man. New York: McGraw-Hill Book Com-
        pany.
Michener, Charles
 1972   "Black movies." Newsweek (October):74-
        81.
 1974   "The great Redford." Newsweek (Febru-
        ary 4): 44-50.
Morgenstern, Joseph
 1972   "The new violence." Newsweek (February
        14):66-69.
Nye, Russel
 1970   The Unembarrassed Muse: The Popular
        Arts in America. New York: The Dial
        Press.
Powdermaker, Hortense
 1957   "Hollywood and the U. S. A." Pp. 278-293
        in Bernard Rosenberg and David Man-
        ning White (eds.), Mass Culture. New
        York: The Free Press.
Quigley, Martin, Jr.
 1948   Magic Shadows: The Story of the Origin
        of Motion Pictures. Washington, D. C.:
        Georgetown University Press.
Rodgers, Jonathan
 1972   "Back to the 50's. Newsweek (October
        16):78-82.
Schickel, Richard
 1964   Movies: The History of an Art and an In-
        stitution. New York: Basic Books, Inc.,
        Publishers.
 1968   The Disney Version. New York: Avon
        Books.
Schramm, Wilbur, Jack Lyle and Edwin B. Parker
 1961   Television in the Lives of Our Children.
        Stanford, Calif.: Stanford University
        Press.

Silber, Irwin
 1972a "Distorted vision of despair." Guardian
        (Jan. 5).
 1972b "Penchant for nostalgia." Guardian (Jan.
        5).
Soderbergh, Peter A.
 1965-66 "Hollywood and the South." Mississip-
        pi Quarterly 19(Winter):1-9.
Statistical Abstracts of the United States
 1971   Washington, D. C.: U. S. Government
        Printing Office.
 1973   Washington, D. C.: U. S. Government
        Printing Office.
Steele, Robert
 1971   "Art, youth culture, and the movies." Pp.
        222-232 in Bernard Rosenberg and David
        Manning White (eds.), Mass Culture Re-
        visited. New York: Van Nostrand Rein-
        hold Company.
Trilling, Diana
 1971   " 'Easy Rider' and its critics." Pp. 233-248
        in Bernard Rosenberg and David Man-
        ning White (eds.), Mass Culture Revisit-
        ed. New York: Van Nostrand Reinhold
        Company.
Warshow, Robert
 1970   The Immediate Experience: Movies, Com-
        ics, Theatre and other Aspects of Popular
        Culture. New York: Atheneum Publish-
        ers.
White, David M., Robert S. Alpert and R. Allan
Seeger
 1957   "Hollywood's newspaper advertising: ste-
        reotype of a nation's taste." Pp. 443-451
        in Bernard Rosenberg and David M.
        White (eds.), Mass Culture. New York:
        The Free Press.
Willis, Ellen
 1970   "See America first." New York Review of
        Books (January 1):20-22.
Wolfenstein, Martha and Nathan Leites
 1970   Movies, A Psychological Study. New
        York: Atheneum Publishers.
Wood, Michael
 1973   "Movie crazy." New York Review of
        Books (November 29):6-10.
Zimmerman, Paul D.
 1972   " 'The Godfather': triumph for Brando."
        Newsweek (March 13):56-61.
 1974   "Slippery Harry." Newsweek (January
        7):60-61.

chapter 8

Mass leisure: sports, outdoors, and travel

Ata Kando

A comprehensive sociology of leisure text can only in part be devoted to sports. But it must be recognized that the sociology of sport is itself a booming subdiscipline, spawning national research centers like Jack Scott's Institute for the Study of Sport and Society, international organizations like the International Committee on the Sociology of Sport, journals like the *International Journal of Sports Sociology,* vast numbers of articles, and a proliferation of textbooks and readers[1] used in the growing number of physical education and recreation, sociology, psychology, kinesiology, and other academic departments which somehow consider sport part of their business. In addition, book racks from coast to coast display increasing numbers of autobiographical, critical, biographical, patriotic, radical, and other varieties of paperback accounts of great professional athletes, coaches,

[1]Edwards (1973), Hart (1973), Loy and Kenyon (1969), and Talamini and Page (1973) are among the most widely used recent texts in the subdiscipline.

and teams. One channel of occupational mobility that has recently become available to former athletes is, for those sufficiently prominent, the published disclosure of private and personal information about the world of big sport. Much of this literature consists of complaints about the financial, social, racial, and political practices in big sport; it may be characterized as radical muckraking of variable quality and as stemming, in some but by no means all instances, from a pecuniary motive (cf. Bouton, 1970; Meggyesy, 1971; Shaw, 1972). Some of this literature, however, is favorable to big sport (see, for example, Sayers and Silverman, 1970). One should add that this new best-seller formula is now being exploited not only by former athletes, but by journalists, novelists, and sociologists as well.[2]

The emergence of a vigorous sport sociology and a multiplying popular literature dealing with sports, along with the enormous time and money devoted by the media to this category of leisure, reflect an important sociocultural trend. About the growth of sport in some form or another there can be no doubt.

The question, however, is what *kind* of sport is now so massively a part of American social structure and popular culture? The growth of sport in modern society apparently refers to the growth of *institutionalized, organized, professionalized,* and *commercialized* sport. This, then, must be the major theme of our discussion, as it must be central to any sociology of sport.

The institutionalization of sport in modern society has many facets, and it is the identification and evaluation of those facets that lead to dispute and controversy. It is possible to discern at least

two factions in this regard. On one side are those who deplore the nature of contemporary organized sport, viewing it much like the vulgar bread and circuses provided two thousand years ago by the Roman state to a passive mass of mere spectators (in contrast with the healthy, spontaneous games characterizing Greek civilization). To this camp belong, as indicated above, many of the muckraking authors currently providing us with inside information about big-time football, baseball, and basketball. Here also are the more detached philosophers and social scientists, for example, de Grazia (1964), Huizinga (1949), and Stone (1958, 1972a). On the other side are those who are firmly committed to existing sport structures, all the way down from the International Olympic Committee through college coaches to athletes themselves and the millions among us who view in the National Football League, the National Basketball Association, and the World Series symbols of the American dream. I shall examine how various authors have approached these matters, myself assuming a somewhat critical yet positive attitude toward contemporary American sports. I shall show that the basic underlying trend I speak of is undeniable and that it ties in with some of the most fundamental historical processes in Western civilization.

While this chapter will, as the preceding ones, be primarily issue oriented and focus most of all on the institutionalization of sport in modern society, I must first cover some of the historical, economic, and sociological aspects of major sports. As in previous chapters, I shall first deal with sport historically and quantitatively, and a second section will present some of sports' contemporary sociological correlates. To these ends, certain conceptual categories had to be established. The magnitude of baseball, for example, is one thing when talking about how many millions watched this year's

---

[2]Examples of the genre include Bouton (1970), Chapin and Prugh (1973), Edwards (1973), Hoch (1972), Kahn (1971), Meggyesy (1971), Plimpton (1965), Sayers and Silverman (1970), and Shaw (1972).

World Series on television and how large the combined budgets of the American and National Leagues are; it is another when asking how many children play little league baseball. Sport, then, is a recreational activity for (1) spectators and (2) participants. Furthermore, participants may be (3) amateurs, or they may be (4) professionals, and in our society there is also that ambiguous in-between category, (5) the college athlete. So, some attention will have to be paid to each of these five groups, for they, together, make sport one of the most important elements of contemporary American mass culture and mass leisure.

HISTORICAL DEVELOPMENT AND CURRENT QUANTITIES
History

Sport's historical origin and literal definition are closely related. The word stems from the Middle English word *disport,* meaning "to divert oneself." This etymology suggests that sport's original meaning—diversion—was not too distant from that of play, game, recreation, and leisure.[3] However, today's standard dictionary definition of sport is "an athletic activity requiring skill or physical prowess and often of a competitive nature." *(Random House Dictionary of the English Language).* As Edwards (1973: 55ff.) explains, contemporary sports have little to do with diversion, games, and play. They inevitably involve physical exertion, most of the time in a competitive setting.

In primitive societies, sport had not yet been reduced to a physical contest. Generally, primitive sports were games representing vestiges of warfare, a residual activity no longer economically useful (e.g., archery), or derived from religion (Kraus, 1971:130). As McIntosh (1963:4) observes, "The Tailteen Games in Ire-

land, wrestling among the Aztecs, the team game of Tlachtli by Maya people in Central America, and ju-jitsu practiced by the Samurai Warriors of Japan all had religious significance. In Britain, too, the early history of some games of football suggests that fertility rites were involved."

It is safe to assume, as McIntosh does, that "throughout the last two thousand years religious observance and competitive sport have constantly impinged upon each other."

As with so much of our civilization, the modern concept of sport finds its origin in Graeco-Roman antiquity. Our word athletics comes from the Greek $\alpha\vartheta\lambda o\sigma$, which means contest. And indeed, today, sport and athletics are virtually synonymous. The Greeks institutionalized athletic competition into a variety of sacred festivals. Athletic games were held in half a dozen different cities annually, most notably in Olympia. While such contests and festivals are known to have been held in Olympia as early as 1300 B.C., thus going back to the archaic Neolithic culture, it is in the fifth century B.C., during Pericles' golden rule over Athens, that the Olympic ideal came to full fruition. The games enabled major Greek cities to compete peacefully and symbolically. The principal contests comprised running, horse and chariot racing, wrestling and boxing, and throwing the discus (Kraus, 1971:136). Through the substitution of symbolic competition for real warfare, the Panhellenic games integrated a larger area covered by otherwise dissenting city states. As McIntosh observes, to Olympia "came competitors and spectators from all over the Greek world to meet under the protection of a sacred truce, whatever wars might rage" (1963:16). The fact that the Greeks' wisdom did not prevail does not deter from its significance.

Most important for us is the meaning of Greek sports. Martindale (1960b) has

---

[3]See the conceptual discussion of these four terms in Chapter 2.

explained the centrality of both physical and intellectual contest to Greek civilization; Socrates' dialectic method of reasoning and Aristotle's syllogism meant that henceforth truth criteria were to be sought within the thought process itself. That is, ideas were to stand upon their own merit (Martindale, 1960b:7); by inventing rational logic, the Greeks moved mankind up from theology and superstition to philosophy and wisdom. But the democracy of ideas meant a democracy of men as well; "may the best idea prevail" had its corollary in "may the best man win." Ideally, then, Greek sport represented contest in its purest form. No free citizen was excluded from athletic competition, and all participants were amateurs, preferably partaking in a variety of skills rather than specializing in one. Today's decathlon event reminds us of this classical ideal.

The gradual deterioration of the Olympic ideal commenced in Greece itself, imperial Rome merely extending the trend. From Alexander the Great on, athletic specialization, commercialization, and professionalization began to weaken the earlier form. "Gradually, sports, along with other forms of performing activity . . . were performed only by highly skilled specialists before crowds of admiring spectators. Chariot races became more popular, and hippodromes were built for huge crowds" (Kraus, 1971:139).

Rome, then, magnified the process already well under way in Hellenistic Greece. In Rome, sports and games were supported "chiefly for utilitarian rather than aesthetic or spiritual reasons" (1971:139). The ideals of spontaneous play and leisure declined, and so did culture. Sport was valued "chiefly because of its practical (e.g., medical) benefits" (1971:139). The performance of culture, music, theater, the performing arts, was mostly relegated to foreigners. Gradually, more than half the calendar year became holidays. Eventually, the urban

masses were offered nearly two hundred days of games and spectacles a year. Leisure became a passive spectator activity. Baths, athletic clubs, gymnasia, and ball courts were popular, but the more typical activities were watching acrobats, athletes, and fighters perform and maim each other. The athletes themselves were now full-time professionals, specialized and organized into unions, led by coaches and trained in designated schools.

> Competitive sport . . . had become completely commercialized and professionalized. To maintain political popularity and placate the bored masses, the . . . senate provided great parades . . . bankrupting both the public treasury and private fortunes. . . . Audiences sometimes totaled half the adult populations of their cities. The . . . games were a visible dramatic illustration of lust for power, as well as preoccupation with brutality and force. . . . Shows were often lewd and obscene, leading to mass debauchery, corruption, and perversion of the human spirit. Over all, their vulgarity, cruelty, and lack of humanity reflected the spirit of the . . . people. . . . Historians have concluded that a major reason for the downfall of (the civilization) was that it was unable to deal with leisure; its citizens grew physically weak and spiritually corrupt. Although they were great engineers, soldiers, builders and administrators, they did not have the coherent philosophy of life that the ancients . . . had. When faced by the challenge of excess wealth, luxury and time, as a nation, they responded by yielding to corruption—and ultimately lost the simple virtues that had made them great as a nation [Kraus, 1971:141-142].

The similarity between Rome and America has to be one of history's most remarkable inescapabilities. I suggest that the reader go over Kraus's quote once again, mentally inserting "America" wherever "Rome" was meant. Not one passage will be inappropriate. It has been said before, and it must be repeated vigorously, the American empire has devolved from the Europeans in a manner inescapably similar to the way the Romans followed the Greeks.[4] Whether

---

[4] For a brief anthology of writings about the fall of Rome, including passages from Gibbon's magnum opus, see Chambers (1963).

or not one subscribes to any kind of cyclical determinism, the uncanny similarity cannot fail to strike us as some sort of handwriting on the wall.

The historical analogy can be further extended. Just as today a rallying point of any revolutionary counterculture is an ascetic antimaterialism, so too the medieval Christian morality that was heir to Roman civilization centered around asceticism, self-deprivation, hard work, and monastic withdrawal from worldly and bodily gratification.

Still, the Catholic church did not entirely ban sports and games. During the Dark Ages, hunting was the favorite sport of both clergy and nobility. Hawking was also extremely popular. And by the twelfth century, when a certain degree of stability had once again been established over Europe, the chivalrous culture of the Middle Ages had developed. Tournaments in which mounted knights attempted to unhorse each other were no longer merely for military training; they were contests, sport, and spectacles. The peasantry, in addition to attending such jousting matches, also had its ball games, bear-baiting, and cockfights (Kraus, 1971:146). In addition, archery and early variations of football, tennis, billiards, and other contemporary sports and games were being played in England, France, Northern Italy, and other parts of medieval Europe.

The Renaissance is that period of Western history when cultural and scientific progress resumed its forward course. The sixteenth century saw the further elaboration of a variety of sports, for example, tennis among the English nobility, football among the nobility of Italy and later among all strata in England, and cockfighting and archery enjoyed by most people everywhere (Kraus, 1971:149). Monarchs like Henry VIII of England and Francis I of France promoted sports for the nobility. Henry built bowling alleys and tennis courts, and the two kings are said to have engaged in friendly wrestling matches with each other (Henry's amorous leisure life is said to have cost him the victory). Schools opened up, training men in riding, fencing, running, and jumping. Most popular among the coaches and fencing masters were the Italians, as sports had been refined to greatest perfection in that part of the world. The general affluence had a democratizing effect. Despite royal edicts prohibiting various activities to the lower strata, the downward diffusion of sports was inevitable. Football, initially a noblemen's sport, was soon played at Oxbridge and then among the masses (McIntosh, 1963:38-39).

The Renaissance and the Age of Reason brought about a revival of classical philosophy. Men like Rabelais, Montaigne, and later Locke and Rousseau rejected the mind-body dualism that had been central to medieval Christian doctrine, reviving the classical ideal of human unity. As Montaigne wrote, "It is not a mind, it is not a body that we are training; it is a man and he ought not to be divided into two parts" (quoted in McIntosh, 1963:47).

According to McIntosh (1963:53), "the writer who did more than any other to change social attitudes to sport was Jean Jacques Rousseau." The Frenchman's philosophy for sport, as found in *Emile* (1762) and in *Considerations on the Government of Poland* (1773), was a naturalistic one: "The training of the body, though much neglected is . . . the most important part of education not only for making children healthy and robust, but even more for the moral effect, which is generally neglected altogether or sought by teaching the child a number of pedantic precepts that are only so many misspent words" (quoted in McIntosh, 1963:54).

Thus, early Renaissance philosophers like Montaigne (1533-1592) freed the body from its subordination to the mind,

206 LEISURE AND POPULAR CULTURE IN TRANSITION

a subordination that was inherent in medieval Catholicism's mind-body separation, its asceticism, its other-worldly orientation, and its view equating the body with sin and evil. Later, educators such as Rousseau (1712-1778) contributed the notions of freedom, spontaneity, and self-realization through games, sport, and play. Sport, as Rousseau saw it (cf. McIntosh, 1963:54), should satisfy the desires and aspirations of the growing individual at each particular stage of development.

The Protestant Reformation led to a new Puritanism which undid much of the progress scored by sport and leisure during the Renaissance. Luther (1483-1546) and Calvin (1509-1564) may *chronologically* antedate the philosophers of the Renaissance, the Age of Reason, and the neoclassic revival, but their impact must nevertheless be treated as the next stage in Western cultural history. "The Reformation had within it the seeds of a new asceticism," writes McIntosh (1963:42). First, however, came the liberal wind just discussed, permitting the arts, sport, games, and leisure to flourish. Only gradually was there a return to a philosophy of asceticism inherently hostile to sport and leisure. Besides, sectarian, regional, socioeconomic, and political variations make it quite clear that neither liberalism nor Puritanism ever got an unchallenged upper hand over the other. For one thing, Luther had not been hostile to sport and games. This was mostly a feature of Calvinism, and of its Anglo-Saxon variant—Puritanism. Secondly, sports and games may have gradually declined in Protestant regions (England, New England, Germany), but this certainly did not happen in Mediterranean Europe (and neither do Brueghel's paintings suggest a very austere life among the Flemish Protestants). Furthermore, the new Puritanism became a feature of some social strata, legitimating their economic behavior,[5] but it was shared neither by the elite nor by the lower class. Indeed, in the seventeenth century, sport became a political issue (McIntosh, 1963:42), favored by the courtiers (e.g., James I of England) but condemned by the Puritans.

All in all, sport and leisure were definitely on the defensive during this period. For the time being, Puritanism was making vigorous inroads into the liberalism which a while earlier had seemed to put a definitive end to medieval asceticism. The Puritans' condemnation of sports and games was indeed reminiscent of early Catholicism. In England, Sunday football and tennis were banned, and other such "devilish pastimes" as dancing, gambling, bowling, bear-baiting, cockfighting, hawking, and hunting were severely condemned by the religious authorities (Kraus, 1971:153).

America was born during the age of Puritanism. The history of sports and recreation in this country inevitably reflects this. As I indicated in Chapter 2, the first settlers, particularly the New England Puritans, created a colonial society based on the work ethic. Rugged frontier conditions necessitated this. In the South, to be sure, slavery plus a relatively clement ecology led to the early development of a leisure class. There, hunting and fishing were soon sports to be leisurely enjoyed, not merely the work activities of a subsistence economy.

By the end of the seventeenth century the Northern colonies also began to relax their attitude toward leisure, and there, too, sports like hunting, fishing, and bowling, as well as target shooting, footraces, and wrestling, became popular. A major sport event in many towns was training day, where as many as a thousand men would come together to drill,

---

[5]This, of course, is the theme of Max Weber's *The Protestant Ethic and the Spirit of Capitalism*. See our discussion of this in Chapter 1.

The Bettmann Archive

practice shooting, and celebrate. As Sarah Knight described this when she traveled through Connecticut in 1704: "On training dayes the Youth divert themselves by Shooting at the Target, as they call it, (but it very much resembles a pillory,) when hee that hitts nearest the white has some yards of Red Ribbon presented him, which being tied to his hattband, the two ends streaming down his back, he is led away in Triumph, with great applause, as the winners of the Olympiack Games" (quoted in Dulles, 1965:29).

Many ball games were played in colonial America, for example, bat and ball games that would eventually develop into baseball, bowling (popular mostly in the Dutch settlements of New York), and early forms of football. Bentley, an early observer of this rude game, described it as "rather disagreeable to those of better education, who use a hand ball, thrown up against a house or fence instead of the Foot Ball, which is unfriendly to clothes as well as safety" (quoted in Dulles, 1965:33).

Regional differences were important. The more rigidly stratified social structure of the South was reflected in its lei-

sure life. Horse racing was far more popular in Virginia than in Massachusetts, but it was frequently a spectator sport enacted by the aristocratic elite and watched by the peasantry. In general, spectacles like cockfights, bull-baitings, and bear-baitings were more common in the South. In the North the accent was on participation, for example, sleighing in the winter and swimming in the summer (Dulles, 1965:33). Ethnic differences also existed, as with skating, which was most popular with the Dutch population settling in New York.

Frontier life after independence remained tough. The importance of physical skills and strength in a pioneering existence explains the proliferation of a variety of sports during that period. In addition to horse racing, hunting, fishing, and the other sports already popular in colonial America, the nineteenth century saw the emergence of such sports as horseshoe pitching, tomahawk hurling, rail flinging, and bullet throwing (Dulles, 1965:73). The brutality of frontier life is, of course, represented to us daily in contemporary mass media. It is not a myth. By far the most pervasive sports were shooting and fighting, and as every child knows from the innumerable fights he has seen televised from the fictitious bars, ranches, taverns, streets, and cowtowns that seem to represent the totality of the Old West's architecture, no holds were barred from the brutal leisure activities of the violent men on the frontier. Life was cheaper than today, in a society which would have looked upon contemporary football as a tame affair.

What has been said thus far about American sports is preliminary. Sport, in its modern sense, connotes two developments which were only incipient during most of the nineteenth century, and which have yet to reach their full fruition even today. (1) Sport is an organized activity and (2) it is generally witnessed by spectators. In this sense, it did not loom large on the American scene until the middle of the nineteenth century, and even then, as a form of mass leisure, sport was first a spectator activity. Only several decades later did it begin to enlist the participation of the masses. If every bar brawl, hunting trip, or other physical activity in our early history is considered sport, then people have always participated in sports. However, in its true sense, participant sport cannot be said to have been widespread until the emergence of such organizations as the YMCA, the German turnverein, and other athletic clubs and until the inclusion of physical exercise into the scholastic curriculum.

The only spectator sport to go back to colonial days was horse racing. During the decades immediately following independence, trotting and running races remained the only popular spectator sport. Then, during the first decades of the nineteenth century, rowing, sailing regattas, and foot races also began to attract substantial crowds (Dulles, 1965:137). The runners (*pedestrians,* they were called) were all professionals, and they were heavily gambled on. The professionalization and commercializa-

tion of sport were on their way. Prizefighting was still outlawed in this period, as it was a bloody bare-knuckle unregulated affair going for up to eighty and one hundred rounds, or as long as necessary for one of the contestants (or both) to collapse of exhaustion and mutilation. Even so, the illegal activity attracted growing masses of spectators. Once gloves were substituted for bare fists and the Marquis of Queensberry rules (devised in 1867) had been adopted, prizefighting became legal and enormously popular.

The growing masses of a continent undergoing rapid population and urbanization were dependent on spectator activities as long as they lacked the mobility to leave the cities or to even frequent urban gymnasia. Only toward the end of the nineteenth century would streetcars and railroads begin to provide the masses access to the outdoors.

As Dulles (1965:182 ff.) explains, because of gradual urbanization, the period preceding the Civil War had witnessed the decline of informal country sports in the East without a compensatory emergence of organized participant sports as we know them today. That, then, was the spectator-oriented era I just spoke of. Finally, in the 1860s a variety of athletic activities got Americans moving again. The populous urban East was no longer hunting, fishing, and horseback riding. Instead, gymnastics, roller skating, bicycling, and baseball were fast becoming national pastimes.

The origin of baseball goes back to England, where in the seventeenth and eighteenth centuries a variety of bat and ball games (rounders, townball) were practiced. As with so many other elements of European culture, these games underwent a bifurcate development, one variant becoming English cricket and the other one, brought over by the early settlers, developing into contemporary American baseball.

According to Dulles (1965:186), modern baseball was born in 1842, when a group of New York businessmen founded the Knickerbocker Club—the first formal baseball organization. Gradually, professionalism developed. This first took the form of paid tours, bonus fees, and such fringe benefits as better paying jobs for expert players. The first recorded game with gate receipts (fifty cents admission) took place in 1858. Then, in 1869, the Cincinnati Red Stockings were hired for a country-wide tour. This was the first professional team. Seven years later the National League of Professional Baseball Clubs was founded. The American League was founded in 1899, and the first World Series was held in 1903. During the first decades of the twentieth century, baseball unquestionably established itself as the national recreational pastime, particularly as a spectator sport. No serious challenge to its supremacy developed until World War II.

In a mosaic-like society such as nineteenth-century America, there were of course many varieties of sports and regional and subcultural leisure activities. While organized sport began to dominate the East, the West was still on its gambling, drinking, fighting, and shooting spree. In the East, then, some sports were introduced from England for the high society, for example, lawn tennis; some games, like croquet (also from England), became social occasions bringing the sexes together; and then there were crazes like bicycling (introduced primarily from France) and roller skating that soon engulfed millions of Americans of all social backgrounds, all ages, and both sexes.

The role of colleges in the history of American sports is inseparable from football. Only in the latter part of the nineteenth century did intercollegiate football develop, and for decades it remained virtually the only significant contribution made by the campuses to the world of sports. Like baseball, football grew out of a variety of old English games. It shares a common ancestry with rugby and association football (soccer). These brutal games were traditionally played by common men only, and kings tried to outlaw them from their very inception. As early as 1314, Edward II decreed that "for as much as there is great noise in the city, caused by hustling over large balls from which many evils arise which God forbid; we forbid such game to be used in the city in the future" (quoted in Dulles, 1965:197). And in the United States, while colleges played some variants of the game throughout the country's history, its excessive roughness also led to frequent prohibitions. Finally, in 1869, Rutgers and Yale played the first official intercollegiate football game (with fifty men on the field!). Soon thereafter, rules were finalized, distinguishing American football once and for all from rugby, soccer, and other foreign relatives. For some decades the game was dominated by the big three —Harvard, Yale, and Princeton. And by its nature, it immediately developed into a spectator sport. Unlike baseball, the game is primarily for boys, depending "upon brute force" and satisfying "atavistic instincts as could no other modern spectacle except the prize-fight" (Dulles 1965:198).

It is in the twentieth century that sport assumed the proportion of a national obsession. The growth of sports at all three levels, professional, amateur, and college—high school, since 1900 pales all preceding developments. A glance at the big three, football, baseball and basketball, will show this.

Intercollegiate football was destined to become the country's most popular spectator sport. First, however, severe difficulties had to be ironed out. Under the old rules the game was so rough that its 1903 death toll reached forty four (Dulles, 1965:347). During Teddy Roose-

velt's presidency, therefore, rules were devised that saved the game by making it both safer and more interesting. The reforms included the forward pass, the on-side kick, and separation of the rush lines. From then on, football's popularity never ceased to grow. Universities built stadia accommodating 70,000 to 100,000 fans. From the Ivy League, football power gradually moved West. In 1920 the American Professional Football Association was formed. After World War II the familiar process of social mitosis led to the formation of the competing AFL (1960), later to be incorporated into the NFL (1969). The jet age finally gave the sport a truly national scope, as teams could now be matched from universities and clubs thousands of miles apart at little inconvenience. With the proliferation of preseason and postseason games (college bowls and professional championships), the football season encroached ever deeper on baseball, basketball, and other sports. Superbowls were watched on television by 90 million Americans and by an additional 100 million Europeans and Latin Americans via satellite. In 1974 the World Football League was created.

Baseball's twentieth-century history has been somewhat less spectacular. As a spectator sport it had already become our national pastime at the turn of the century. The subsequent rise of competing sports—football, basketball, boxing, automobile racing—could only weaken its hegemony. Attendance figures did not keep up with population growth, and college baseball never became popular. And then, of course, came television. While television has kept millions of people away from all sorts of leisure activities, its impact on baseball has been particularly severe. Unlike the case with football, for example, those who stay away from live games do not massively follow them on television. On this, Bogart (1972), Dulles (1965), Howe (1957), McLuhan (1964), and others agree. As to why, McLuhan's theory plausibly argues that television and our entire new gestaltist culture call for new sports, new forms of leisure; today, the Canadian explains, baseball is becoming an anachronism rooted in the age of linear rationality; hence its relative decline. With this, we should note that baseball is by no means dead, or even moribund. There is to the grand old man of American sports a lore, a tradition, a symbolism and an emotionalism that may be richer than those found anywhere else in American mass leisure. The sentiment and nostalgia evoked by the Brooklyn Dodgers (who never really left Brooklyn), Jackie Robinson, and Willie Mays (who never really left New York) surpass other manifestations of fandom and loyalty (see, for example, Kahn, 1971). The love for the Mets and the hatred for the Yankees, the immortality of Babe Ruth (whom Hank Aaron in spite of topping the Babe with home runs batted in will never really beat), Stan Musial, and Joe DiMaggio, all these remind us that baseball is more than just a matter of attendance figures. It is fortunate that the clumsy New York Mets are capable of mustering the enthusiasm which eludes robotlike football teams like the Miami Dolphins. Slick, technocratized sport, then, has not yet rooted out old-fashioned fun, McLuhan notwithstanding.

Thus the twentieth century has been sport's golden age. Boxing was another mass spectacle to emerge in the early part of the century. As with football, the sport's worst features first needed polishing up. Prior to the introduction of the Queensberry rules, boxing's object was simply to pummel the other fellow into oblivion, by whatever means. Bare knuckles were sometimes covered with a cestus of leather-covered bronze so as to increase physical punishment. The new regulations, then, prescribed five-ounce padded gloves, prohibited wrestling, limited the number of rounds, and gave the

sport legitimacy. Prizefighting's gold era began with Dempsey's reign as world heavy weight champion (1919-1920). Jack Dempsey, Gene Tunney, Joe Louis, and the other colorful champions of that period commanded million-dollar gates. After the war, the sport lapsed into disrepute, and less than a decade ago observers bemoaned its demise (cf. Dulles, 1965:353). This may have been premature. In the 1970s, record-breaking amounts were once again paid to see not only world championships, but even the rematch of contenders Joe Frazier and Muhammad Ali. The latter man, draft-dodger, black militant, poet, and clown besides boxer, was, perhaps single-handedly, responsible for prize fighting's revival.

Basketball, along with football and baseball, is considered to be one of America's big-three spectator sports. It is unique in that it is the sole popular American game not derived from some English sport. It was invented by James Naismith, an instructor at a Massachusetts YMCA training college, in 1891. Its function was to provide an indoor activity for the winter as a practical substitute for baseball and football. Today, the game rivals football as one of college's most popular varsity sports; its two professional leagues are as much a part of the world of high finance as major baseball leagues; in addition, high-school basketball is, in some parts of the country, practiced as assiduously and followed as obsessively as college sports everywhere. In Indiana, Minnesota, and other midwestern states, the high-school basketball championships are of the utmost importance to the public. And for the masses of youngsters trapped in the central cities, basketball is one of the few outlets available in the asphalt jungle. The Harlem Globe Trotters are not the only top-notch players to represent the ghetto. From Wilt Chamberlain to Kareem Abdul-Jabbar the teeming slums have produced disproportionate numbers of superstars.

Another spectator sport that dates back to the turn of the century is automobile racing. The first motorcar race on record ran from Paris to Rouen and was won by the Marquis de Dion at an average speed of 11.9 miles per hour. A year later, in 1895, the United States entered the field with a fifty-two-mile race in Chicago. The winner of that contest completed the course in a little over 10.5 hours. While European racing has tended to remain an elite affair (Formula I racing) for participants and spectators alike, the United States Auto Club and National Association for Stock Car Auto Racing events have become a true form of mass leisure. Today, Indianapolis attracts annual crowds of 300,000, and Daytona, Riverside, Watkins Glen, and other American circuits are each known to pack up from 100,000 people for any single event. As the oil shortage becomes more critical, American automobile racing can be expected to further develop into a mass spectacle in which only a few well-sponsored participants can enter.

The list of spectator sports that flourished during the first half of the twentieth century is endless. While horse racing had been popular since colonial days, it, too, partook in the general boom. Golf, tennis, hockey, track and field events, greyhound races, and six-day bicycling also gained either temporary or lasting popularity. The 1920s were the golden age of all sports, but particularly spectator sports. Prior to that, big sport has yet to be established as an efficient, full-time, nationwide enterprise. After that, the electronic media began to keep increasing numbers of people away from live events.

The enormous growth of spectator sports in the twentieth century led to the well-known concern about spectatoritis. However, the truth of the matter is that spectatorship did not grow at the expense of participation, but *in conjunction with it.* While the American and the National Baseball Leagues, the ABA, NBA, AFL, and NFL attracted ever larger masses, the same population was also ever more actively taking advantage of the outdoors, swimming pools, golf courses, ski slopes, bowling lanes, and baseball diamonds across the country. At least during the first half of the century, there was a general boom in sports involving both participation and spectatorship.

Participant sports that gained most of their adherents after the turn of the century include, in addition to some of the games already discussed, golf, tennis, skiing, bowling, softball, volleyball, badminton, handball, shuffleboard, billiards, gymnastics, roller skating, ice skating, hockey, most water sports, hunting, motorcycling, lacrosse, trapshooting, table tennis, and skydiving.

Golf, tennis, and skiing have remained upper-class or upper-middle-class sports, largely due to the cost factor. However, the growing national affluence meant that increasing millions of nouveaux riche could, as early as 1920, join the status-seeking conspicuous consumers then already moving out to the suburbs, joining country clubs that were eventually to number more than five thousand. Massive addiction to skiing began somewhat later, but it, too, persisted even in the face of growing gasoline and energy shortage, as the consumer society began to devise cheap, collective means of transportation that would permit it to continue to visit the slopes.

Meanwhile, the lower middle class and the working class had bowling and softball. Bowling had been imported to the United States as early as the eighteenth century, becoming an indoor game soon thereafter. The contemporary rules and format of tenpin bowling were adopted in 1895, with the foundation of the American Bowling Congress. Once automatic pinsetters were introduced in the 1940s, the game was on its way to becoming the most popular organized amateur sport of them all.

Softball originated with the organization of the Amateur Softball Association of America in 1933. It was, of course, the amateur version of baseball, a game that began to attract millions of women and children as well as men. By 1938 the softball association boasted that there were eight thousand softball diamonds in the country, with up to 10 million players. Today, little league baseball carries on a tradition and socialization functions for American youngsters without which our society would not be the same.[6]

The growth of outdoor recreation is mostly the result of increased affluence and increased mobility—the car. In addition, cultural change explains the increasing popularity of such activities as

[6]For some recent studies of little league baseball, see Watson (1973, 1974) and Watson and Kando (1974).

water sports. From the 1920s onward, as Victorianism gave way to more enlightened attitudes toward leisure, women's rights, sexual etiquette, and life in general, swimming gained ever greater popularity. As the least expensive of all sports, it is available to all, and consequently the most popular outdoor activity by far. Other water sports that have attracted growing masses include fishing, boating, waterskiing, skin diving, scuba diving, and surfing. Since the 1930s the Army Corps of Engineers has built more than 263 artificial lakes and reservoirs. This, in addition to conservation measures, the stocking of rivers and lakes, and the expansion of the national and state parks systems has, until recently at least, provided the facilities required by a swelling consumer class. Until the 1970s limits to recreational use of the environment were not envisioned by anyone seriously except the rare radical ecologist, and his doomsday prophecies were dismissed by a society that was as voracious in its consumptive habits as

Mike Dobo/Editorial Photocolor Archives

it was shortsighted in its environmental utilization. The series of ecological and economic crises that began to plague our world from 1973 onward, while overall unpleasurable, nevertheless had a certain number of positive latent functions. Inflation and gasoline shortage led to the declining utilization of parks, mountains, beaches, and deserts. The environment, at least, was given a breathing spell. And it was to be hoped that Americans would, perforce, learn alternatives to mindless material consumption and physical mobility as their sole form of recreation. Of course, the storm gathering over the West would perhaps merely lead to the gradual impoverishment of the middle masses, increasing inequality, and thus a general deterioration in the quality of life. But this is a political matter I wish to postpone for the concluding chapter.

The growth of participant and spectator sports has been cursorily traced. To repeat, there can be no doubt about the fact that sport's enormous growth is a modern phenomenon. But what, besides quantity, are some of contemporary sport's most typical features?

The key word to a sociological understanding of the meaning of sport today is *institutionalization.* Page (1973) outlines the five pervasive themes in the sociology of sport, and the two major ones among these refer precisely to what I am speaking of—sport in mass society, and the organization of sport: the thrust of bureaucracy (Page, 1973:14-37). As we move on toward the twenty-first century, as massive technocracies with anonymous populations into the hundreds of millions become the typical geopolitical unit, as the emerging brave new world becomes one of increasing rationalization, scientific management, and technocratic human manipulation (cf. Ellul, 1964; Roszak, 1973), sport loses the element of play to assume all the rational utilitarian features of a bureaucratized scientific human technique.

School sports programs are a case in point. In Europe, gymnastics, athletics, and other physical education requirements were first introduced as drill-like activities not dissimilar in function to military training. Among the states to first emphasize this facet of school sports was, perhaps inevitably, Germany. As the Prussian Minister of Public Worship and Instruction "ordered" in 1882: "The school must foster play . . . along with increase in physical strength and skills . . . and this must be done not merely now and then, but as a matter of course and in a systematic way" (quoted in Kraus, 1971:176).

In the United States, colleges were not in the forefront of organized athletic development. Until the turn of the century the fraternities' intramural activities (from the 1840s on) and varsity football (from 1869 on) were about the extent of their contribution. At that time, organized amateur sport was carried primarily by nonacademic clubs like the YMCA and, again, the German imported turnverein. Eventually, however, American schools became the arena for keen professionalized and commercialized physical competition. College football practically became an occupation and a rich source of revenue. Athletic scholarships, fat coaches' salaries, and fancy buildings are among the better-known manifestations of the commercialization of American scholastic athletics. Today, some universities are little more than physical education institutions and training grounds for future professional athletes. For basketball, the scouts and recruiters' hunting grounds include high schools as well, to which the commercial interest has also spread. In many high schools, physical prowess may well be *the* fundamental criterion of prestige, status, and reward ascription, a value system that has contaminated students and staff alike. In our society, to be a high school teacher is less than prestigious, but to be a high school football coach is worthy of

Table 8-1. Years in which national sports associations were founded*

	Germany	U. S. A.	Sweden	Britain
Association football (soccer)	1900	–	1904	1863
Swimming	1887	1878	1904	1869
Cycling	1884	1880	1900	1878
Rowing	1883	1872	1904	1879
Skating	1888	1888	1904	1879
Athletics	1898	1888	1895	1880
Lawn tennis	1902	1881	1906	1886
Skiing	1904	1904	1908	1903

*From Peter McIntosh. 1963. Sport in Society. London: C. A. Watts Co.

display. Thus in America today we have professionalism and amateurism, and in the shrinking no-man's-land in between are the schools. The increasing institutionalization of sport is perhaps most noticeable at that level. As Edwards (1973), McIntosh (1963), Scott (1971), Shaw (1972), and others have shown, the growing emphasis on discipline, competition, winning, and technique has become the hallmark of college and even high school athletic programs. Thus the play element wanes and sport becomes just another form of work.

The institutionalization of amateur sports has been equally noticeable on the international scene. McIntosh (1963:85) informs us about the foundation dates of major national sport associations in four Western countries. His data are reproduced in Table 8-1.

The modern Olympic Games are no exception to the trend of which I speak. In 1894, Baron Pierre de Coubertin convened delegates from fourteen nations at the Sorbonne to revive the classical Olympic Games. The International Olympic Committee was formed. De Coubertin's motives seem to have been less than purely idealistic. French chauvinism and a deep hostility toward Germany (no delegates from across the Rhine were invited) were part of it. Since then, the games have been plagued by creeping professionalism and nationalism. East of the Iron Curtain, any distinction between professionalism and amateurism is ludicrous. And in the West, commercialism is threatening at the gate in the form of fees, advertisements, and promotions. An occasional gesture like barring ace skier Karl Schranz from Olympic competition for accepting promotional fees seems more symbolic than effective. Retired I.O.C. head Avery Brundage's pessimism about the Games' future is well taken. The total politization of the Olympics was epitomized in 1972, when Israel's team was decimated by Arab terrorists. Throughout their history, the Games have been dominated by those nations that, by virtue of their culture or their political regime, needed most badly to hoard goal medals. Thus American competitiveness accounts for our perennial presence in the top group, Soviet nationalism does likewise for theirs, and so does East Germany's authoritarian tradition. That small country's incredible performance has more to do with its *Junker* tradition than its current social system. The Olympic Games, far from embodying national health and international cooperation, are merely a quadrennial barometer of the vigor of chauvinism in the world.

Today, then, sports are a grimly serious business everywhere. While they may have evolved out of play initially, they no longer have anything to do with

Table 8-2. *Selected spectator sports: 1950 to 1972**

	1950	1960	1965	1969	1970	1971	1972
Major league baseball attendance (thousands)	17,659	20,261	22,806	27,498	29,000	29,544	27,330
Professional basketball attendance (thousands)	n.a.	1,986	2,750	5,891†	7,113	8,724	9,431
Football attendance (thousands)							
College	18,962	20,403	24,683	27,626	29,466	30,455	30,829
Professional	2,008	4,153‡	6,497	9,334	9,913	10,560	11,096
Boxing (gross receipts from professional matches, $thousands)§	3,800	5,902	8,264	8,422	10,642	10,237	11,847
Horse racing attendance (thousands)	29,291	46,879	62,887	68,099	69,704	73,619	70,795
Greyhound racing attendance (thousands)	6,083	7,924	10,865	12,006	12,660	13,666	13,760
Total spectator sports expenditures ($millions)	222	290	389	487	524	537	n. a.

*Source: Statistical Abstracts of the United States (1973:208, 209).
†ABA founded.
‡AFL founded.
§Excludes closed-circuit television receipts.

it, as Edwards (1973:55) explains. They always involve physical exertion, formal structure, organization and rules, and explicit role relationships; they are always rational, formal, and goal directed (utilitarian). They are, in sum, an institution.

Current quantities: spectator sports

Table 8-2 gives an indication of the rapid increase in attendance at major spectator events since 1950.

Depending on the measure used—attendance figures or receipts—spectator sports have, over the period shown, increased their popularity by 118% to 141%. Either way, this far surpasses population growth, which amounted to 37% over the same period.

Table 8-2 reveals some interesting trends. Major league baseball is the grand old man among American spectator sports, increasing its attendance more slowly than the other major sports. Still, even baseball's 55% increase in at-

tendance exceeds population growth, indicating that until the seventies, at least, major league baseball has been able to hold its own. The minors are, of course, another matter. In football, it is the professional sector which grew by a staggering 453%. Intercollegiate football, represented today by 620 National Collegiate Athletic Association teams, increased its attendance by a "mere" 63%. Despite the fact that football players, unlike basketball and baseball players, cannot be expected to play daily, that game manages to attract the most people. The bulk of this is still at the college level (as it was in 1950). Professional football's attendance figures are still far behind those of major league baseball. The same applies to professional basketball, whose growth has been extremely rapid, but only recent. This game is undoubtedly the sport of the future. As urbanization, population, ghettoization, and the ecological crisis prevent increasing numbers of youngsters from participating in roomy

outdoor recreation, basketball will pick up further adherents. Finally, in Table 8-2, one of the most striking facts is that racing continues to draw more spectators than all other major sports combined, as they have since colonial days! One measure of the incentive is the amount of money bet on the animals, up from $1.805 billion in 1950 to $7.279 billion in 1972 (Statistical Abstracts, 1973:209). Another expression of the cash nexus in American mass leisure.

Not listed in Table 8-2, yet second only to horse racing, is automobile racing. In 1968, 40 million Americans paid to watch some type of auto race. Internationally, there are probably another 50 million paying customers every year, making auto racing the second most popular spectator sport in the world, next to soccer. Formula One racing—the Grand Prix circuit leading to the world cup—is the main foreign variety. There, crowds of nearly half a million have been known to attend events like the twenty-four hours of Le Mans. In America, the Indianapolis 500 is the most popular event, but other circuits also pack in crowds in

excess of 100,000 for any single event. Unlike the Europeans, we have made car racing into a veritable mass leisure. From the prestigious Can-Am races down through semiprofessional and amateur stock car races, drag races, autocross and demolition derbies all the way to the illegal street races held in Watts and Harlem (Lewis 1972:36-37), car racing as a form of recreation is of the essence of Americana. Tom Wolfe's fascination with the demolition derby, for example, is part of a wider concern for the meaning of American popular culture: "The nature of their appeal is clear enough. Since the onset of the Christian era, no game has come along to fill the gap left by the abolition of the purest of all sports, gladiatorial combat. . . . Since then, no game, not even boxing, has successfully acted out the underlying motifs of most sports, that is, aggression and destruction" (Wolfe, 1966:27).

Nowhere else, of course, could such junkyard romantique develop. Only in a nation that owns in excess of 100 million automobiles could thousands of cars each year be reduced, in status and function,

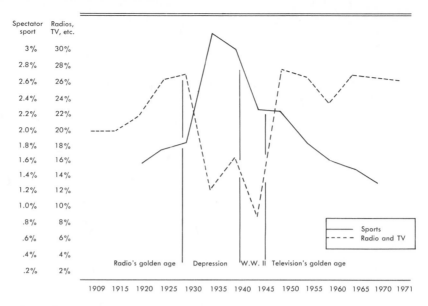

Spectator sport	Radios, TV, etc.
3%	30%
2.8%	28%
2.6%	26%
2.4%	24%
2.2%	22%
2.0%	20%
1.8%	18%
1.6%	16%
1.4%	14%
1.2%	12%
1.0%	10%
.8%	8%
.6%	6%
.4%	4%
.2%	2%

Radio's golden age   Depression   W.W. II   Television's golden age

——— Sports
- - - - Radio and TV

1909 1915 1920 1925 1930 1935 1940 1945 1950 1955 1960 1965 1970 1971

Fig. 6. Percentage of consumer expenditures for spectator sports and for radios, televisions, and musical instruments, 1909-1971. (Sources of statistics: de Grazia, 1964:433-435; Statistical Abstracts of the United States, 1973:208.)

to firecrackers. And those who, by 1974, anticipated the end of the extravagance because of the gasoline shortage overlooked the fact that earlier civilizations had also opted for circuses over bread.

Additional millions attend such spectacles as hockey, golf, track and field events, tennis, and a variety of other sport events. The list cannot be exhausted. However, one important question must be raised before concluding this section: in the preceding discussion of the growth of spectator sports, nothing has been said about the role of the media.

It is television, most of all, which has had the dual impact of both magnifying the sport audience factorially and stimulating added interest in a variety of sports, while at the same time eroding live attendance. The proportion of their disposable income spent by people on spectator sports over the years clearly reflects this. As Fig. 6 shows, the percentage of recreational expenditures devoted to live attendance of spectator sports has

steadily declined since the late thirties, while conversely the proportion spent on radios, televisions, and related items has increased, receiving its first big boost with the introduction of radio in the early twenties and reaching a second peak with the advent of television after World War II.

Television's impact on spectator sports has been examined by Bogart (1972) and Johnson (1973) among others. A number of surveys taken during television's early years indicated that the medium often stimulated interest in sport events in which little interest had existed before, for example, wrestling and roller derby (Bogart, 1972:172-173), but that it also led to declining live attendance, particularly at football and baseball games. Hardest hit were the minor league baseball teams, whose number fell from 448 in 1949 to 127 in 1969, attendance dropping from 42 to 10 million (1972:416). On the other hand, it was estimated in 1969 that 8% of all television households watched the average professional baseball game, 21% watching the World Series, 9% the typical NBA game, 13% the average college football game on ABC, over 10% the average professional football game, and 40% the Super Bowl (1972:415). Thus, in a literally *remote* sense, television has vastly increased the popularity of spectator sports. There is, of course, something repugnant about a new leisure format which further undermines community by reinforcing privatism and social withdrawal.

Current quantities: participant sports, outdoor recreation, and travel[7]

While live attendance at spectator sports has not held its own in comparison with the general increase in leisure spending, participation in sports and outdoor recreation has. Table 8-3 shows the growth of a selected number of such activities since 1950.

Table 8-3 gives figures for organized and officially recorded activities. In addition, countless millions of Americans partake in a variety of unorganized forms of physical and outdoor recreation. Table 8-4 provides some estimates for such activities.

Sports not listed in Table 8-4, but also attracting millions of adherents every

---

[7]Written in collaboration with Tom Wilson.

year include table tennis, croquet, lacrosse, gymnastics, badminton, and many others. Table tennis has recently gained political significance as a diplomatic bridge to China. This may enhance its popularity, particularly among Chinese Americans. Tennis, too, may gain additional adherents, as it was recently converted from a sport into a social issue when feminism and male chauvinism, personified in Billie Jean King and Bobby Riggs, clashed. It may become the first major sport to carry out total sexual equalization (cf. *Newsweek*, 1972).

Not listed anywhere is swimming, a sport so vastly more popular than any other that the number of swimmers is hard to estimate. There are at least 400,000 swimming pools in the United States, and probably more than 100 million swimmers. Another popular water sport is boating (see Table 8-3), engaged in by at least 27 million Americans in 1972 (Statistical Abstracts, 1973:208), using fifty-five hundred docks and marinas across the nation.

The popularity of fishing is also impressive. Stone (1958, 1972) has observed that many activities which were formerly work have, in modern society, become play, whereas former play has often become work. While baseball and football have developed from play into grim pro-

Table 8-3. Selected participant sports: 1950 to 1972*

	1950	1960	1965	1960	1970	1971	1972
Amateur softball teams (thousands)	355	378	560	791	794	706	847
Golfers (thousands)	3,215	4,400	7,750	9,500	9,700	10,000	10,400
Golf courses	4,931	6,385	8,323	9,926	10,188	11,174	11,374
Tenpin bowling lanes	52,488	107,908	159,079	143,029	141,492	139,483	139,023
Membership (thousands)	1,937	5,538	8,010	7,907	7,733	7,610	7,863
Outboard motors in use (thousands)	2,811	5,800	6,645	7,101	7,215	7,300	7,400
Average horsepower	69	27.4	28.2	33.1	31.0	35.6	38.1

*Source: Statistical Abstracts of the United States (1973:209-210).

Table 8-4. Estimated number of participants in selected recreational activities (millions)*

	1946	1956	1961	1966	1971/1972
Cycling	–	–	–	59	–
Volleyball	–	–	20	40	–
Camping	–	–	5.5	37	43
Fishing	13.1	25	30.3	36.2	38
Roller skating	–	–	15	25	–
Billiards	–	–	–	23	–
Hunting, archery	–	14	18	20	22.2
Shuffleboard	–	–	5	10	–
Waterskiing	–	–	6	9.1	8.5
Tennis	4.1	6.6	7.5	9.1	8.6
Horseshoes	–	–	–	9	–

*Sources: Kraus (1971:321), Statistical Abstracts of the United States (1973:207-208), *U. S. News & World Report* (1972).

fessions, hunting and fishing, being no longer the subsistence activities of an agrarian society, are now play. However, even colonial Americans sometimes fished just for the fun of it, as did Cotton Mather; Samuel Sewall tells of the time when the stern old Puritan went out with line and tackle and fell into the water (Dulles, 1965:25). Other emerging water sports include waterskiing (tried by at least 11 million people by 1971), skin and scuba diving (5 million in 1964), and surfing (1.5 million in 1967).

Winter sports that deserve mention include skating (14 million in 1972), skiing (7.2 million), and snowmobiling (7.2 million). A great deal of money is involved in these activities. Between equipment, food, lodging, lift tickets, and entertainment, skiiers spent at least $1.5 billion in 1972. There were over 1 million snowmobiles in 1970, and this number increased by 400,000 each year. At an average price of $1,000 and a top speed of fifty miles per hour, these vehicles were as lucrative to the industry as they were harmful to the environment and the consumer.

The popularity of camping, hunting, and fishing is not accurately reflected in official campground permits and hunting and fishing licenses. Records indicate, for 1971–1972, 25 million campers, 23 million hunters, and 32 million fishermen. Actually, more than 40 million people camped, and at least 38 million fished.

Passive outdoor recreation is possibly even more popular than the activities discussed so far. This includes walking for pleasure (54.2 million in 1972), nature walks (26.7 million), driving for pleasure (54.2 million), sightseeing (59.8 million), picnicking (74.4 million), bird watching (8.5 million), and wildlife photography (7 million) (Statistical Abstracts, 1973:208; *U. S. News & World Report,* 1972).

More active outdoor sports not yet mentioned include mountain climbing (8.6 million), horseback riding (8.7 million), and flying (1 million) (Statistical Abstracts, 1973:208; *U. S. News & World Report,* 1969).

The postwar boom in outdoor sport and recreation has been impressive. Perhaps the best single indicator for this is the increase in *sporting occasions,* that is, *the number of single participations in any sport by one person,* per year. In 1965 the Bureau of Outdoor Recreation of the Department of the Interior reported a total of 6.5 billion such occasions, which included everything from hiking to hockey, from swimming to skating. The figure was predicted to reach 10 billion by 1980 and 17 billion by the year 2000 (Kraus, 1971:324). This was, of course, before the energy crunch and before Nixonomics had begun to effectuate the first general decline in consumer buying power in our history. By 1973, indications were that outdoor leisure had peaked. Long-distance travel and vacations were being curtailed. The National Park System had been visited (in more than one sense) by an all-time record 212 million tourists in 1972 (Statistical Abstracts, 1973:202). But a year later, according to the National Park Service, attendance at major national parks such as the Grand Canyon was significantly down. Yellowstone and the Grand Canyon were no longer as easily accessible, and the cause was not energy shortage (that crisis only set in at the end of 1973), but plain national impoverishment.

It is worthwhile to take a glance at the vast national recreation system which has, since the nineteenth century, hosted the urban exodus to the great outdoors. The system is essentially composed of federal, state, county, municipal, and private parks and facilities. In 1972 the National Park System consisted of 297 areas that included thirty-eight national parks, added up to nearly 39 million acres, and were run at an annual cost of $187 million. The increasing popularity and accessibility of the national parks had, until then, been unquestionable—33 million visitors in 1950, 212 million in 1972. In addition, there is the National Forest System, controlling over 187 million acres of land and providing recreational facilities for millions of campers, hunters, fishers, and tourists. In 1972, 184 million visitor-days were spent in the National Forest System's recreational facilities. Furthermore, the Army Corps of Engineers administers over 8 million acres of federal land and 8 million acres of lakes and reservoirs which

it has constructed over the years. These facilities are also visited by millions of people every year. The Bureau of Indian Affairs controls about 53 million acres, containing nine thousand lakes, ponds, and reservoirs. These reservations provided over 11 million visitor-days in 1971. The Bureau of Reclamation has created a number of recreational projects that add up to about 6 million acres. The Tennessee Valley Authority project contributes another million acres of recreational land. The Fish and Wildlife Service operates a chain of nature preserves totaling 27 million acres. Overall, the federal government owns 760 million acres, one third of the country. While the purpose of this land ranges from forest conservation and grazing to navigation and military training, recreation is certainly among its prime explicit functions.

Similarly, the states operate a vast system of recreational areas. In 1950 there were 1,725 state parks with a total of 4,657,000 acres. By 1970 this had nearly doubled. Total visits to state parks and state recreational facilities increased from 114 million in 1950 to 483 million in 1970. At the municipal and county level, we had (in 1970) another 31,000 areas for a total of nearly 1 million acres.

This list is not exhaustive. Private recreational facilities have not been mentioned, for example, the nation's five thousand country clubs, the ski resorts, and private beaches. If we tally all federal land set aside for tourism and conservation, add to that state and local parks and throw in 2 million acres to account for all private recreational facilities, we get approximately 540 million acres of real estate that is neither residential nor commerical, that is, primarily recreational. This exceeds the combined area of France, Japan, Italy, Germany, Great Britain, Greece, Portugal, Austria, Denmark, Switzerland, the Netherlands, and

Belgium, countries with a combined population of 400 million people.

Speaking of foreign places, we must now complement our discussion with some data on foreign travel. As Table 8-5 reveals, increase in foreign travel since World War II has been even steeper than domestic travel.

In twenty-five years the number of Americans traveling abroad has multiplied by sixteen, the amount they spent on such trips by eleven. In 1947, over half of all foreign travel was by ship; today 99% is by air. Although no area has declined in popularity, Europe has become the uncontested mecca for an affluent people in search of its ancestral identity. Only 34% of foreign travelers thought they could afford Europe in 1947. In 1972, 57% crossed the Atlantic. In that year, twenty-six times as many Americans traveled to Europe as in 1947. Air travel, often of the cheap charter variety, had made shorter trips for more people worthwhile. While per diem expenditure in Europe had gone up from $12.00 in 1950 to $18.00 in 1972,[8] the average cost of a transatlantic journey had declined because people did not stay as long. The average European vacation took sixty-four days in 1950, twenty-seven days in 1972. By the beginning of the seventies, the character of American overseas travel had been injected with a new element. A new homo americanus was now flocking to the far corners of the globe, an ugly American different from the one described by Lederer and Burdick (1958). Instead of the wealthy, contemptuous personification of American capitalism, our tourists included increasing numbers of long-haired draft-dodgers and dope peddlers roaming the slums of

[8]A best-selling fairy-tale throughout the 1960s was entitled *Europe on Five Dollars a Day.*

Table 8-5. *Foreign travel, 1947-1972**

	1947	1950	1955	1960	1965	1968	1969	1970	1971	1972
Travelers to										
Europe	149	302	482	832	1,405	1,937	2,363	2,898	3,202	3,843
Latin America	272	261	556	712	1,018	1,684	1,945	1,912	1,990	2,330
Other	14	13	37	90	200	264	315	450	475	617
(thousands)										
Total†	435	676	1,075	1,634	2,623	3,835	4,623	5,260	5,667	6,790
Expenditures ($million)	716	1,022	1,612	2,623	3,768	4,730	5,382	6,169	6,633	7,716

*Source: Statistical Abstracts of the United States, (1971:205, 1973:213).
†Figures exclude travel to Canada and Mexico, Vietnam, military, and other government travel and cruises.

the world and languishing in jails from Innsbruck to Istanbul.

But let us return to the domestic scene. As we saw, there is in the United States an enormous area and a huge market for outdoor recreation. And as we have been told incessantly during the past few decades, Americans have massively flocked to the great outdoors, spending vast sums of money on recreational and consumer goods and leading some business sectors to ecstasy. Time and again during the 1960s and the early 1970s publications would document America's "leisure boom," its "recreation explosion," and its "leisure time bonanza."[9] The success stories of industries catering to the leisure market were offered as proof. AMF, manufacturer of skis, motorcycles, golf balls, and other leisure products, registered huge increases in profits, so did Winnebago industries, the leading motor home producer, when its shares on the New York Stock Exchange rose 1,000% over a two-year period. Holiday Inns, American Express, and other travel businesses were all among the winners. Sociologists and businessmen alike foresaw an endless leisure expansion, questioning neither their narrow conception of leisure nor the ecological limits to such gluttony. The massive twenty-seven volume study of the Outdoor Recreation Resources Review Commission (1962) did not base its inventory of national recreational resources and its extrapolations to that inevitable year 2000 on a possible dip in leisure, consumption, discretionary spending, and the standard of living. From David Riesman (1950, 1951, 1958) to Daniel Bell (1960, 1973) postindustrial society was predicted to ever closer approximate the leisure society, the affluent society, the society of high mass consumption.

And indeed, Americans were responding, like lemmings, to the seductive call

[9]For example, Kazickas (1972), Toffler (1964), and *U. S. News & World Report* (1969, 1972).

of the advertisers. One of the epidemic's most notable manifestations was the spread of recreational vehicles. At the risk of hopeless financial bondage, millions of workers bought trailers, campers, semis, pick-up trucks, motor homes, motor boats, motorcycles, dune buggies, and snowmobiles, only to leave them to rust in a garage as most spare time would be spent moonlighting to meet the payments, or at best to be used in smog-bound weekend traffic jams. This, one was told by television and the neighbors, was the good life. The number of recreational vehicles skyrocketed. California, which made the transition from pristine purity to junkyard more rapidly than other regions of the world, multiplied its recreational vehicles more than tenfold between World War II and 1972. By then, there were 4 million such vehicles in the country, grossing a fat $2 billion for the industry annually.

Similarly, motor home sales tripled from 1968 to 1972, mobile home construction nearly tripled between 1965 and 1972 (Statistical Abstracts, 1973:684), and second homes, which are also included in the "leisure market," increased each year by 150,000 to reach 2 million in 1972, a value of $2 billion. (*U. S. News & World Report,* 1972). The land development game was more lucrative than ever. In 1965, $7 billion worth of vacation land and lots was sold. Four years later, the figure had nearly doubled. As part of the sales pitch, extravagant recreational functions were promised, from private golf courses, beaches, tennis courts, and swimming pools to weekly fox hunts and wolf hunts.

Having meandered from professional football through the National Park System to European travel and finally second homes and vacation lots, let us now stress the underlying unity to all this. This discussion has been about participant sports, outdoor recreation, and travel. Table 8-6 provides a final set of fig-

Table 8-6. *Percentage of consumer expenditures for participant recreation and sport equipment, 1909-1971**

	Participant recreation			Sports equipment		
	Commercial participant amusements†	Pari-mutuel net receipts‡	Total	Nondurable toys and sport supplies	Wheel goods, durable toys, sports equipment, boats, and pleasure aircraft	Total
1909			2.6			16.6
1914			2.5			18.6
1919			2.5			17.3
1925			5.1			14.5
1930	5.7	0.2	5.9	7.9	4.9	12.8
1935	6.2	1.2	7.4	9.6	6.0	15.6
1940	6.0	1.7	7.7	9.3	7.7	17.0
1945	5.4	2.9	8.3	10.4	7.6	18.0
1950	4.6	2.4	7.0	13.9	8.8	22.7
1955	4.9	3.0	7.9	14.6	11.1	25.7
1960	6.3	2.8	9.2	13.2	11.5	24.7
1965	5.7	2.8	8.5	13.1	11.2	24.2
1968	4.9	2.6	7.5	14.0	11.7	25.7
1969	4.7	2.6	7.3	14.4	12.2	26.6
1970	4.5	2.5	7.1	14.5	12.1	26.5
1971	4.6	2.5	7.0	14.4	12.0	26.4

*Sources: de Grazia, (1964:434-435), Statistical Abstracts of the United States (1973:208).
†Includes billiard parlors, bowling alleys, dancing, riding, shooting, skating, swimming places, amusement devices and parks, daily-fee golf course greens fees, golf instruction, club rental, caddy fees, sightseeing buses and guides, and private flying operations.
‡Gambling, betting on horses and greyhounds.

ures to indicate aggregate trends in some of these activities.

Wall Street's jubilance over the booming leisure market finds some basis in Table 8-6. However, the euphoria may be premature or altogether misplaced. During the twentieth century, a temporary historical anomaly has permitted the North American people to privatize their mode of transportation, to motorize their lives and to plunder their environment as no other civilization has ever done before. The binge came to an abrupt end during the winter of 1973. Americans awoke to the realization that public transportation was in a state of total neglect, carrying one fourth as many passengers as it had only a quarter of a century earlier, that their sprawling cities, massive freeways, 100 million automo-biles, and additional millions of recreational vehicles constituted a dangerous overextension. Our postindustrial society, far from entering the age of leisure and high mass consumption, was undergoing gradual impoverishment through inflation, energy depletion, and food shortages. Skeptics like de Grazia (1964) and neo-Malthusians like Ehrlich (1968) and Meadows (1972) turned out to be better prophets than naive technocrats like Bell (1960, 1973) and Toffler (1964, 1970) and shallow consumption sociologists like Riesman (1950, 1951, 1958) and Kaplan (1960). A sobering reappraisal was in order.

For the future a number of scenarios could be conceived. One hope was that America would become a sensible ecology-minded civilization, developing cheap collective transportation and returning to healthy physical activities combining work with play, like bicycling. Along with that, it was to be hoped that our leisure would evolve back to a more spiritual and participatory type of activity as envisioned by de Grazia. However, an alternative possibility was that people would become increasingly immobilized and isolated from one another by economic dislocation, confined to ever heavier doses of spectatoritis as during the days of early urbanization, but now in its aggravated private form of universal addiction to the one-eyed monster. Play, then, as Stone (1958) suggested, would be entirely replaced by display. Finally, if our collective urge for self-obliteration (cf. Howe, 1957) proved strong enough, it was also possible that the nation would carry on its devastating consumptive spree for another decade or two, facing then a crisis the magnitude of which was said to be an exponential function of the time by which it was being delayed (cf. Meadows, 1972). The likeliest prospect, in my opinion, was a combination of elements. For example, it could be expected that ecological plunder would, at first, proceed unrelentingly, followed by a foot-dragging and belated slowdown during which public transportation, conservation, and sound ecological policies would receive the minimum attention necessary for societal survival, and during which mass spectatoritis would reach new records. Only much later could the people be expected to carry out a Platonic leisure ideal directing all men toward spiritual creativity and true wisdom.[10]

SOCIOLOGICAL CORRELATES

A pervasive sociological theme in the study of sport, as Page (1973:18-32) points out, is that of social differentiation. This includes such things as tracing

---

[10]For a recent diagnosis of the state of mankind stemming from the heart of one of the great contemporary economists, see Heilbroner (1974).

the social class and demographic correlates of sports, and it is what I intend to focus on in this section. In line with the organization of the material thus far, I shall first examine some correlates of spectator sports, secondly those of participant sports, and finally other physical and outdoor activities, including travel. I shall, as in previous chapters, look at the following variables: sex, age, ethnicity and religion, geography, and the socioeconomic status cluster, including education, occupation, and social class.

Spectator sports

For a look at some demographic correlates of spectator sports, we go back to the O.R.C. study reproduced in de Grazia (1964:441-444). Submitted to a national probability sample of 5,021 persons representing the total United States population 15 years old and over, the interview asked what leisure activities the respondents had engaged in yesterday. Table 8-7 reproduces some of that study's findings.

Men, as Table 8-7 shows, attend sport events more than twice as much as women. When women are separated into employed and nonemployed, 4% of the former went to see a sport, against only 1% of the latter. Thus working women attended spectator sports nearly as often as men, housewives only one fifth as much.

Age appears to be inversely related to spectator sport attendance. Regionally, Southerners watched sports the most, followed by Midwesterners. Here, stereotypes are confirmed. Rural people watched sports the least, probably because of unavailability. The relationship of spectator sports to education turned out positive, perhaps a surprise in view of existing stereotypes as well as sporadic findings (e.g., Gerstl, 1963) supporting the familiar jock-egghead antithesis. The figures in Table 8-7 indicate that high schools and colleges are spectator sport's

Table 8-7. *Percentage of population who went to see a sport event "yesterday," by personal characteristics**

All	4
Sex	
Men	5
Women	2
Age	
15-19	7
20-29	4
30-39	4
40-49	4
50-59	4
60+	2
Region	
North East	3
North Central	4
South	5
West	3
Rural-Urban	
Rural	3
Below 100,000	4
100,000-1,000,000	5
1,000,000+	4
Education	
Less than eighth grade	1
Eighth grade	3
High school, incomplete	4
High school, complete	4
College	4
Income	
Lower	3
Lower middle	4
Upper middle	5
Upper	5

*From "The public appraises movies," a survey for the Motion Picture Association of America, Inc., by Opinion Research Corporation, December, 1957.

major locus in our society, watched there by those who are affiliated with the institutions.

The sociology of sport has paid more attention to the socioeconomic status cluster than to any other variable. Lewis (1972), Page (1973), Stone (1958, 1972a), and others have been concerned with the social stratification of sport. Table 8-7 re-

veals that the relationship between income and spectator sport attendance is positive. More important, to many sociologists, has been the relationship between social class and *specific* sports. Clarke (1958), for example, distinguishing between five occupational prestige levels, found that attending football games was relatively popular among high-prestige groups (not far behind concert and theater attendance), whereas baseball games were most popular among the lowest prestige levels. Robinson (1967) corroborated this fact, and Edwards (1973:270) suggests that it reflects the contrast between the aggressive instrumental goal orientation of the middle class and the more relaxed attitude of the lower class. Watson (1973) and Watson and Kando (1974), examining little league baseball, noted that the social disorganization at these events was so severe that the line separating participants (children) from spectators (parents) became blurred, most of all in lower-class leagues.

Auto racing is another spectacle which assumes different characteristics depending on its social class setting. Iniguez (1974) shows how car competition can be stratified into seven social classes: Formula One (Grand Prix) racing is strictly upper-class business, both as a participant and as a spectator sport. It is the glamour sport of the international jet set (cf. Stewart, 1972). For the American upper strata, we have another prestigious race, the Canadian-American Challenge Cup. As Iniguez (1974) writes, "Such events as the Can-Am of Watkins Glen are social events of some importance to the people of upstate New York. The spectators who buy the expensive grandstand seats go to the events to be seen as well as to see the race. The people who view these events are part of the upper group of society. They must have some knowledge of the cars, which are terribly complex, as well as the teams and drivers. Rich auto making families, business executives, and celebrities are frequent attendants at these events."

A third prestigious form is American Formula 5000 racing. Below this we find car racing's middle class: the USAC Indianapolis type cars, the NASCAR stock cars, and drag racing. "These are truly American forms of auto racing," writes Iniguez, "USAC and NASCAR events are run almost entirely on oval tracks and not on road courses. . . . Drag racing is run on quarter-mile strips with only two cars competing against each other. . . . If one wanted to get a view of middle America, he should attend one of these events. Campers, hot dogs, beer cans, long-haired mini-skirted girls, pot-bellied tee-shirted men sitting on lounge chairs, the smell of barbecue mixed with engine exhausts, loud music, marching bands, floats, and wild parties are all part of the scene."

NASCAR and drag racing began as illegitimate sports. NASCAR is said to have been born in the forties when a group of backwoods moonshiners began to race on an old dirt track. Drag racing was introduced when hot-rodding teen-agers were forced onto an abandoned Florida airfield by an annoyed citizenry. These origins still show. The social class differences between European Grand Prix racing and the typical American event is well illustrated in the following passage from Iniguez: "After winning the 1968 Indy 500, Bobby Unser went to a local Indianapolis bar and drank beer with fellow drivers and friends until early morning. In contrast to this, Jackie Stewart, after winning the 1973 Monaco Grand Prix, attended a small cocktail party given by Prince Rainier of Monaco which was also attended by other royalty. The purse of the Monaco Grand Prix is barely one-quarter of the Indianapolis purse. . . . The American fan," Iniguez continues, "is basically from middle America. The thrill of brute power, of

drivers forcing and pushing their way to the lead, of a group of cars charging into a turn with no one giving an inch is what the American fan enjoys best." In contrast, Formula One racing is smooth and slick, demanding the finest man-machine coordination and a skill and delicate balance which Grand Prix fans appreciate.

At the bottom of the heap, finally, are the bush league dirt tracks, where the modified hard tops bump and grind around quarter-mile clay and asphalt circuits. This is local lower-class leisure, with little professionalism, a personal relationship between fans and racers, and all the gemeinschaft that is typical of prole sports (cf. Lewis, 1972; Wolfe, 1966).

Participant sports

We begin, once again, with the O.R.C. study (de Grazia, 1964:441-444), reproducing in Table 8-8 the percentages of people it found participating in sports among various demographic categories.

Table 8-8 shows, first, that 8% of the respondents report participation in some sport. This is twice the percentage reporting attending some spectator sport (Table 8-7), a noteworthy fact when discussing allegations of spectatoritis. Men were, predictably, found to participate in sports much more than women (twice as much), and employed women participated more than housewives (5% vs. 3%). The strong inverse relationship between age and sport participation was predictable. Regional and urban-rural differences seemed to converge; rural areas like the South were low in sport participation, urban areas like the Northeast high. Education and income were both positively related to sport participation, those in the upper-income class and those who had attended college reporting three to four times more sport participation than the lowest education and income class.

In sport participation, it is once again

Table 8-8. *Percentage of population engaging in some sport 'yesterday," by personal characteristics**

All	8
Sex	
Men	8
Women	4
Age	
15-19	26
20-29	8
30-39	8
40-49	7
50-59	3
60+	2
Region	
North East	11
North Central	9
South	6
West	8
Rural-Urban	
Rural	7
Below 100,000	10
100,000-1,000,000	8
1,000,000+	9
Education	
Less than 8th Grade	3
8th Grade	4
High School, Incomplete	5
High School, Complete	7
College	9
Income	
Lower	3
Lower Middle	8
Upper Middle	10
Upper	11

*From "The public appraises movies," a survey for the Motion Picture Association of America, Inc. by Opinion Research Corporation, December, 1957.

the socioeconomic status cluster of variables which has received the largest amount of attention.[11] Looking at education, Schafer and Armer (1972) raise the oft alleged antagonism between athletic and educational values; they refute the notion that athletes are inferior students, further undermining the folk belief in an inverse relationship between education and sport participation. Gerstl (1963), however, does show that the sport participation of professors is far lower than that of other occupations of similar income but lower education; professors' sport participation, in that study, consists of little more than an occasional hike or swim, while dentists and admen play golf, swim, fish, bowl, and ski for an average of three to four times as many sporting occasions as the academicians (Gerstl, 1963:151).

Dulles (1965), Lewis (1972), Stone (1958, 1972c), Talamini and Page (1973), and others discuss the essentially upper-class origin of sport, explaining that most sports gradually undergo downward social diffusion as part of their historical development.

Clarke (1958) (who, like the O.R.C. study, found that participatory activities far exceed spectatorship, even when including television and movies, thus casting further doubt on the spectatoritis thesis) showed that the middle occupational levels spend nearly twice as large a proportion of their leisure time as passive spectators as either the lower or the upper strata, where active participation is far more prevalent.

As with spectator sports, the literature in the area of sport participation is mainly devoted to specific sports. Clarke's

[11]The relationship between socioeconomic status and sport is examined by Anderson and Gordon (1964), Clarke (1958), Dulles (1965), Edwards (1973), Emrie (1970), Gerstl (1963), Lewis (1972), Schafer and Armer (1972), Shostak and Gomberg (1964), Stone (1958, 1969, 1972a to c), and Talamini and Page (1973), to mention but a few sources.

(1958) study fits here again, as it ranks a number of leisure activities by occupational prestige. Golf is, predictably, found to be most popular among the relatively higher prestige levels, while fishing and driving for pleasure are most popular among the lowest prestige groups. In addition to social class, sex also differentiates outdoor sports. Three out of four fishers are men, although the two sexes' participation in this sport converges with age. As they become older, women fish more, men less. Stone and Taves (1958) have interpreted the meaning of outdoor activities, offering social-psychological explanations in terms of sexual identity. The rugged outdoor experience may be functional to male ego and identity in an otherwise emasculated urbanized society.

An interesting variable is physical size. Scott (1969) deals with this, pointing to its importance to the jockey.

Ethnicity is, of course, very much "in" as a central concern of sport sociologists. Orr (1973) discusses black boxing, Loy and McElvogue (1971) discuss the role of race in professional football and baseball, and no recent book in the sociology of sport fails to address itself to problems of alleged racism and the condition of the black athlete in the world of modern sport (cf. Edwards, 1972; Hoch, 1972; Loy and Kenyon, 1969; Meggyesy, 1971; Scott, 1971; Talamini and Page, 1973). I shall address that matter in a moment. Here, I can only raise questions, for not much research has been done and few attempts have been made to explain the different patterns of sport participation among the various ethnic groups. Why are Jews underrepresented in so many sports? Is the black overrepresentation in professional sports indeed due to the fact that sport has been one of the few channels of upward mobility open to them? Kraus (1968:44) found that black participation in outdoor activities which are direct, casual, and inexpensive is high, but that it is low in activities which involve the purchase of equipment, the payment of special fees, or a high-social-class identification. Thus over 40% of blacks participate in picnicking and fishing, but only 1.4% ski. However, if black participation in sports were only a function of economics, then why do they partake so little in all winter sports, even inexpensive ones like skating (one third the rate of whites), and why do black women skate as much as white women? And northern blacks fish only one sixth the rate of northern whites, but in the South they fish more. Is fishing still a subsistence activity to some rural southern blacks? And why do nonwhites hunt more than whites?

What, then, is the role of culture, economics, and natural environment in the relationship between sport and ethnicity? What can be said about karate among Orientals, soccer among Europeans and Latins, jai alai among Cubans and other similar subcultures? And in cases like hockey in Canada, speed skating and skiing in Scandinavia, skiing in the Alpine region, surfing and swimming in the Pacific basin, basketball in cities, fishing and hunting in the southern and western United States, skating in the Netherlands and Minnesota, geography may be the major determinant, but there surely is more to it than that. Culture, tradition, race, and environment have all worked together to produce a myriad of sport subcultures around the world, and much of this rich material is still terra incognita to the social scientist.

Other outdoor recreation and travel

I conclude this discussion with some correlates of a few remaining recreational activities.[12]

---

[12]My sources, again, include Kraus (1968, 1971), the National Recreation Survey (Ferris, Abbott et al., 1962), the O.R.C. study (de Grazia, 1964:441-444), Statistical Abstracts of the United States (1971, 1973), and *U. S. News & World Report* (1969, 1972).

Camping, predictably, is done more by men than by women (50% more), except from 25 to 44 years, when women camp slightly more than men. It is over-whelmingly a white activity. Westerners camp the most, three times the national average. In the West, too, the proportion of nonwhite campers increases, although even there it only reaches half that of whites. There is a positive and linear as-sociation between camping and income. Professionals, technical workers, and craftsmen camp more than managers, of-ficials, and proprietors.

Picnicking is done slightly more by women than by men, and for men the rate declines at an earlier age than for women. Picnicking is the most popular outdoor activity among blacks, although even in this respect blacks are underrep-resented (54% white participation vs. 45% black), except in the West, where their participation equals that of whites. The rural rate equals that of the nation as a whole, but among urban areas the rate goes up with city size. There is a positive association between picnicking and education and between picnicking and income up to the middle income bracket, after which the relationship levels off. It is more popular among craftsmen and technical, professional, and white-collar occupations than among laborers and service workers.

Driving for pleasure has been found to be nearly as popular among men as among women. The relationship to age was an inverse one, with respondents under 19 reporting pleasure driving more than twice as often as those 50 and over. Regional differences were not sharp, but more pleasure driving was reported in middle-sized cities than in ei-ther rural areas or cities of over 1 mil-lion. The association with education was positive, and so was it to income.

Domestic travel has been a vast and growing business, swallowing $25 billion in 1965, $35 billion in 1969, and $40 bil-lion in 1972. Until the energy crisis, 80% of all travel was by car, 13% by air. A national travel survey in 1967 found the most frequent purpose to be visiting friends and relatives (40%) followed by pleasure driving (36%). Americans drove 300 billion miles in 1972 for nonwork re-lated reasons. The relationship of domes-tic travel to education is positive, as it is to occupational level, although there is no clear association with income.

Overseas travel has consistently in-volved a slightly higher proportion of men than women. The age of overseas travelers has declined. In 1959, less than 10% were students; ten years later the figure had gone up to 26%. The propor-tion of independent businessmen and professionals had also sharply increased over that decade, from 10% to 30%. Over-seas travel is obviously strongly associat-ed with the socioeconomic status cluster, and also with the urban-rural variable (in 1969, 62% of all passports were is-sued in the thirty-one major metropol-itan areas) and with race and region (westerners are more cut off from inter-continental travel; far more passports are issued, proportionally, in New York than in Los Angeles).

MAJOR ISSUES IN SPORT SOCIOLOGY

Page (1973:14-37) detects five major themes in contemporary sport sociology: (1) sport, society, and culture, (2) sport in "mass society," (3) sport and social dif-ferentiation, (4) the organization of sport: the thrust of bureaucracy, and (5) the culture of sport. The first of these is hardly a theme, as it really sums up what the sociology of sport itself is all about. Theme 3—the social differentia-tion of sport—is what the entire preced-ing discussion attempted to deal with: so-cial class, demographic and economic cor-relates of sports. Theme 5—the culture of sport—is an interesting area which this book can alas not probe; it ap-proaches the world of sport as a subculture, or as a number of subcultures, studying its own structures and meanings the way ethnographers have developed an understanding for non-Western or deviant subcultures.[13] This leaves us with themes 2 and 4—sport in "mass society" and the organization of sport: the thrust of bureaucracy. My conceptualization of the subject matter leads me to view these two themes as being part of one and the same problem, and to view that problem as *the fundamental and essential problem of contemporary sport when viewed as a sociological phenomenon.* I refer to *the institutionalization of sport.*

The institutionalization of sport

Every evening millions of harried breadwinners plop into their favorite chair, daily paper in hand. Headlines and front pages bombard them, day after day, with a barrage of news conveying nothing less than the prelude to World War III, the collapse of Western Civilization, and the extinction of mankind itself. Yet most of them, totally disregarding such trivia, go straight for the sport section. They are the lay sport audience of America. In addition, an increasing minority of athletes, novelists, sociologists, and other participant observers probe into sport with a concern for something more than just daily scores. What both laymen and serious students of sport have in common is an awareness that words like professionalization, specialization, rationalization, bureaucratization, commercialization, organization, and institutionalization grasp well some of modern sport's most central tendencies. Other words may be used, as, for example, when Ingham and Loy (1973) speak of reification and objectivation, but there is, I argue in this discussion,

an underlying unity to a phenomenon of which these and undoubtedly additional concepts are mere outcroppings. I suggest that the most *generic* of these concepts is *institutionalization,* as it appears to have logical and perhaps causal primacy over such derivative trends as commercialization, rationalization, bureaucratization, and professionalization. In any event (and I shall not insist on this theoretical point), it is under that heading that I propose to discuss all major sociological and political issues affecting contemporary sport.

By anchoring my analysis in the concept of institutionalization, I recognize that modern sports develop within and reflect larger societal processes. Indeed, sport's twentieth-century history cannot be viewed apart from the most fundamental changes that have affected Western society at large. I refer, of course, to the complex process of modernization signaled already by the nineteenth-century evolutionists, a modernization that Tonnies chose to view as a trend toward gesellschaft, Durkheim considered to lead to organic solidarity, Maine viewed as producing contract, and Weber later approached from the standpoint of rationality, Cooley from the concept of secondary group, and Linton from the standpoint of status achievement, to mention but a few of the men who addressed the question. The development of contemporary sports fits those classic evolutionary schemes perfectly, as it also fits in with the more recent macroanalyses of such scholars as Arendt (1951), de Grazia (1948), Ellul (1964), Galbraith (1958), Kornhauser (1959), Marcuse (1964), Martindale (1960a), Mills (1951, 1956), Riesman et al. (1950), Roszak (1969, 1973), Whyte (1956), and Stone (1958, 1972a), again to name but some. The society, according to many of these observers, is now a technocracy, a "social form in which . . . society has reached the peak of its organizational integration . . .

[13]Some examples of this type of work include Kahn (1971), Meggyesy (1971), Plimpton (1965), Polsky (1972), Scotch (1961), Sillitoe (1959), and Stone (1972c).

and in which those who govern justify themselves by appeal to technical experts who, in turn, justify themselves by appeal to scientific forms of knowledge" (Roszak, 1969:5, 8). The technocracy is characterized by the ever increasing scale of its institutions, the individuation (Riesman et al., 1950) and massification (Arendt, 1951; Kornhauser, 1959; Mills, 1956) of its population, the depersonalization of social relationships, and the eclipse of polity and community. It is, at the same time, affluent (Galbraith, 1958) sensate (Mills, 1951; Sorokin, 1947), materialistic, and indolent.

With this, we grasp the larger societal trends within which sport's institutionalization proceeds. Some aspects of this process have been welcomed; some have been viewed with apprehension. Page (1973:27) stresses the desirable:

> The sharp decline of exclusionism in sport has been and continues to be related to professionalization. . . . And as it has emerged as a major part of mass entertainment, sport has become big business, marked by the principal features of such enterprise: long-range planning, large capital investment, such efficiency practices as cost accounting and market forecasting, and formalization of employee-management relationships. These innovations carry implications for the "democratization" of sport: they go hand in hand with the replacement of personalistic and sentimental considerations by the rational calculation of modern business enterprise and the consequent employment of athletic laborers on the basis of performance and potential irrespective of their social credentials. This sketchy depiction of an important trend should not obscure persistent nonrational elements in professional sport: traditionalism; cronyism; sentiment-based decision making, ethnic, racial and sexual discrimination, and so on. But these elements, understandably stressed by the muckrakers of sport, have been, and continue to be, substantially weakened by the rational calculation of big business.

To Page, then, the modernization and commercialization of relations in the world of sport mean democratization and the application of what Parsons called universalistic criteria, in one word: progress. However, not all sociologists equate the trends we speak of with progress. Stone (1958:262), for one, is skeptical about the direction modern sports are taking:

> The game (play), inherently moral and ennobling of its players, seems to be giving way to the spectacle, inherently immoral and debasing. With the massification of sport spectators begin to outnumber participants in overwhelming proportions, and the spectator, as the name implies, encourages the spectacular - the display. In this regard the spectator may be viewed as an agent of destruction as far as the dignity of sport is concerned.

The problem, as Stone views it, is the massification and commercialization of American sport. His comments were written two decades ago, but today, play has lost out to display even more. The analogy between American mass consumption and mass spectacles and the Roman bread and circuses drawn by Stone is apter than ever, as the two societies, separated by two thousand years, nevertheless seem to share an increasing number of structural, political and cultural features.

We may think of contemporary sport's constituency as consisting of three groups: the amateur participants, the spectators, and the professionals and aspiring professionals. The growth of professionalism and spectatorship has been rapid, and it has been at the expense of amateur participation. Each of the three sectors of modern sport's constituency has its distinct set of problems, and sociology has made contributions to each area.

Sport's three constituencies

Children and adults, you and I, have been playing sports and games since the dawn of history, and we continue to do so today. This—the amateur participant—is one population of interest to sport sociologists.

I have come across at least five major approaches in the sociology of participant sport, three of which are in some way functionalist in focus. The first of these is the rich social-psychological tradition which goes back to Mead (1934) and Piaget (1932) and is currently carried on by such research as Roberts and Sutton-Smith (1969), Avedon and Sutton-Smith (1972), Inbar (1972), Iona and Peter Opie (1969), and Watson and Kando (1974). Here, sports and games are examined for the functions they may perform toward the socialization of youngsters and novices into society, culture, and institutions. Mead stressed the development of role-taking capability and the internalization of the generalized other, using baseball as his paradigm and distinguishing between the simple play and the more complex game. Piaget focused on the emergence of morality and rule-following behavior in children, using marbles for an illustration and distinguishing between an early egocentric stage and a later stage of autonomy. Current research in this tradition views sport mostly as a microcosm in which learning, rehearsal, and preparation for the real world take place, and as an important experience in human development (cf. Page, 1973:15).

A second interest of the sociology of participant sport has been that of the functional relationship between sport (along with leisure in general) and work. Havighurst (1957), Kando and Summers (1971), and Wilensky (1960) are among those who have examined the mutual impact of work on leisure and leisure on work. Leisure activities may, for example, compensate for work-related deprivations, or they may, on the contrary, be a spillover from work in the sense that they have the same characteristics as one's work (Kando and Summers, 1971). Other examples of this kind of functionalism include Steele and Zurcher (1973) and Zurcher (1968, 1970). These authors use the concept of ephemeral role to examine the immediate needs that sports may fulfill for their participants.

Third, participation in sport and leisure has also been approached in a macrofunctionalist fashion, as when Gross (1963) proposes a Parsonian framework to examine leisure's system-maintaining functions. How, Gross asks, does leisure contribute to the adaptation, goal-attainment, integration, and pattern-maintenance needs of social systems?

Sport may also, of course, be viewed as recreation. Examples of this fourth approach may be found in Talamini and Page (1973:361-412). Here, the emphasis is on the ludic features of sports, the play element, the end-in-itself aspect.

Finally, some theoretical work attempts to establish typologies of sports and sport players. Caillois' seminal classification of play fits here (1961). The Frenchman distinguished between games of competition (football), chance (betting), pretense (theater), and vertigo (mountain climbing). Recently, Ingham and Loy (1973) established a typology of sport players. Following Merton's classic typology of deviant adaptations to anomie, these authors produce nine types from the intersection of two dimensions (sport's form and its content): the good-sport (the conformist) accepts both sport's form and its content; the bad-sport (Merton's rebel or retreatist, perhaps) rejects both; the wet-blanket rejects form but is indifferent to content; the agnostic is indifferent to both; the cheat rejects form but embraces content; the hustler, on the contrary, accepts form but not content; the spoil-sport rejects content but is merely indifferent to form; the game addict accepts the form but is indifferent to content—he is the ritualist; the gamesman, finally, accepts content with indifference to form.

In the preceding paragraphs, five approaches to the sociology of participant sport have been summed up. They are neither mutually exclusive (Piaget and Mead, for example, are concerned both with sport's socializing functions and its ludic aspects), nor exhaustive, but they do recur with sufficient persistence to be noted in even the most cursory survey.

A second population of interest to sport sociology is that of the spectators. Here, a relatively rich sociology of fandom has been spawned by men like Beisser (1966), Edwards (1973), Stone (1958, 1969), and Thompkins (1971), among others. The central question raised by these authors concerns the functions of fandom and spectatorship. At least five types of functions have been proposed.

Among the earliest theories about fandom and its functions is Stone's (1958) suggestion that sports provide for their followers a sense of order and continuity which is absent from the chaos of the real world. In addition, the author argues, sport consumption may provide continuity to personal life, as one follows the careers and achievements of beloved stars and teams to which allegiance and loyalty was developed during adolescence. Subsequently, Stone (1969) presented data about fandom and sport consumption among various social and demographic strata.

A second function sport has often said to perform for its consumers is the legitimate outlet it provides for cathartic-expressive behavior and for the pent-up frustrations which would otherwise lead to (more) serious violence. Thompkins (1971) offers an example of such an interpretation: "The ability to exhibit feelings or emotions of any kind has very low priority and acceptance in a technical world. . . . Modern society has gradually closed off avenues for discharge of those energies and for getting emotional assurances. But sport . . . allows those outlets" (quoted in Edwards, 1973:240).

Third, sport is said to engender a feeling of belonging, identification, and group integration for an otherwise increasingly atomized and alienated urban mass. This has been hypothesized by Beisser (1966) and Thompkins (1971).

Edwards (1973:237-272), however, who reviews these competing hypotheses, dismisses them all in favor of a fourth one, a political one. Spectatorship, the black sociologist argues, functions essentially to "reaffirm the established values and beliefs defining acceptable means and solutions to central problems in the secular realm of everyday societal life" (1973:243).

In addition, Edwards also documents a fifth explanation of spectator sports. They may be a functional equivalent of traditional religion (1973:261-263). Thus the author's interpretation of fandom and spectatorship combines a radical neo-Marxism with sociological functionalism. In effect, Edwards is saying that sport serves both as society's normative pattern maintenance mechanism (Parsons) and as religion-like opium for the masses (Marx). This double-barreled theory does justice to a good deal of earlier research. Stone (1969) found significantly less fanaticism among women than among men; Clarke (1958), Robinson (1967), and others found that football was more popular with the middle class, baseball more with the working class, and that the former is encroaching upon the latter. Much of this falls into place, Edwards shows, with the realization that those who play instrumental roles and are imbued with the achievement syndrome—men and the middle class—are also those who empathize with aggressive sport. The author hypothesizes that "the more aggressive the sport, not counting pseudosports such as commercial wrestling and roller derby, the greater . . . the proportion of middle-class to lower-class clientele" (1973:270). Achievement motivation, then, and middle-class ethos would account for football's inroads into baseball, not the electronic media, as McLuhan argued.

The various functions assigned to fandom and spectatorship may not be mutually exclusive. Edwards' political interpretation may be reconcilable with the psychologistic explanations advanced by Beisser, Stone, and Thompson.

A second major area examined by the sociology of spectator sport has been its relationship to the mass media. This is done, for example, by Bogart (1972), Cantwell (1973), Cozens and Stumpf (1973), Johnson (1973), McLuhan (1964), and Stone (1958). Here, the focus has been on technology and how it has affected spectatorship, sometimes stimulating new interests (Bogart, 1972), often eroding live attendance,[14] and sometimes substituting new sports for old ones by virtue of their inherent format (McLuhan, 1964). What is being noticed above all is the enormous commercialization of sport by the mass media, particularly television. By the late sixties, the three major networks alone spent more than $150 million on sports annually. Big sport had become an extension of Madison Avenue. Among those to suffer the most from this were local clubs, minor leagues (Bogart, 1972), and American education.

Two decades ago Stone wrote that "perhaps one of the most pressing problems facing the social science analyst of sports in America is the problem of how the spectator becomes caught up in the dignity of the game he witnesses to the extent that his consumership of sport is ennobling rather than debasing. Only when that problem is solved and the solution is applied will play become a legitimate ethical alternative to work in America" (1958:262-263). Today, the massification and commercialization of spectator sports proceed at an accelerated pace. Exclusive prize-fights were at one time accessible to 145,000 live spectators, as when Tunney successfully defended his title at Chicago's Soldiers Field, and the rest could at least listen in by radio. Today, we have placed so

many echelons—each representing an additional moneyed interest—between the event and the spectator that the 1974 Ali-Frazier rematch was not only inaccessible for most people via closed-circuit television, but that the only immediate round-by-round account available to the public on the night of the fight was a third-hand local radio broadcast based on information wired by the Associated Press out of Madison Square Garden! When mass sport has reached this level of depersonalization, the question is no longer even one of brutalization and debasement, as Stone and Edwards stress, although that remains an issue. The question is whether the distance between audience and superstar has become intolerable. As far as the spectator is concerned, passively absorbing cultural drugs in his television cubicle, Muhammad Ali may not really exist. Indeed, fiction becomes reality and reality becomes fiction, so that it can be plausibly argued that the superstar has no more of an empirical existence than Henry Kissinger, the alleged moon walks, Ben Cartwright, Batman, or Mickey Mouse.

Professionals and college athletes constitute the third major group in the triadic world of sport. The sociology of sport approaches this sector with an array of feelings comparable to that found in the discussion of spectatorship. The increasing institutionalization of sport in modern society has brought about professionalization, commercialization, and specialization, and observers have both welcomed and rejected these tendencies.

The large and powerful camp on the side of big sport includes some authors and some sociologists, but most of all the coaches, men like Darrell Royal, Ara Parseghian, Vince Lombardi, the owners, perhaps a majority of reporters, and a large but shrinking segment of the athletes themselves.

On the other hand, there is a growing number of observers who view the world

[14]See the data on this in the preceding discussion.

of organized sport with increasing misgivings. The virulence with which big sport has been indicted in recent years for its racism, dehumanization, and commercialization is perhaps a function of the strength of those processes themselves. The athletic revolution which began around the 1968 Mexico Olympics may be the dialectic antithesis evoked by the system itself. As professionalization, commercialization, and institutionalization reach excessive heights, there is a concomitant increase in the amount of doubt and criticism from without and desertion from within the rank and file. I hold it to be a self-evident truth that social change is a dialectic process and that every system contains within itself the seeds of its negation. Lewis' (1972) analysis of popular culture follows this Hegelian format, and it seems to me eminently appropriate to do likewise for sport. From a dialectic standpoint, there is cause for optimism, since that perspective implies that no historical excess will remain unchallenged. The spokesmen of the athletic revolution and the growing number of muckrakers provide a collective force against what they term "fascist sport" (cf. Hoch, 1972).

On the far right, then, are those deeply committed to organized sport in its current form and to the traditional values it supports. This is the American sports creed so aptly described by Edwards (1973:71-130). Its major ingredients include nationalism, religiosity, discipline, competition, and success at any cost. An early statement linking organized sport to nationalism is provided by Curtis (1904:264):

> The team [effort] represents the earliest form of organization of society and is one of nature's own methods of leading the youth into patriotism. . . . What does it matter if a leg is broken now and then? It is worth a thousand broken legs if you can teach your boy to be a hero and a patriot.

Bob Pettit, former basketball super-star with the St. Louis Hawks, voices the relationship between sport and religiosity:

> In 1958 I was part of a team—the St. Louis Hawks; the greatest group of athletes I have ever been associated with in my life. We ate together, we slept together, we traveled together, we won together, we lost together, as a unit. A tremendous group of men. . . . We didn't have the talent that a lot of ball clubs have, but we had something else, we had desire and pride and we played as a team, we were a team. We went ahead and beat the Boston Celtics in six games and won the world's championship. . . . There is another team also of which I am a part . . . and that's the team of Christianity. I am on Christ's team. . . . I also hope that you'll be a part of this ball club. . . . We are playing for the victory of Christ.

And Paul Dietzel, West Point Coach, draws the same line:

> To be a champion athlete takes real guts and training; to be a real Christian takes real guts and training.

The discipline and competition aspects of organized sport are stressed by Jess Hill, athletic director at the University of Southern California:

> Athletics develop dedication and desire to excel in competition, a realization that success requires hard life and that life must be lived according to rules. An athlete learns a sense of loyalty and a respect for discipline, both of which are lacking in this country today [quoted in Edwards, 1973:71].

And the emphasis on winning can best be illustrated through a quote from (who else?) Vince Lombardi:

> Running a football team is no different from running any other kind of organization—an army, a political party, a business. The problems are the same. The objective is to win.

In a recent televised football game between Alabama and Mississippi, reporter Chris Schenkle commented on the air that "these two teams epitomize the spirit of sport and fair play and brotherhood in America" (quoted in Hoch, 1972:167). This sums up the majority feeling toward big sport in this country.

On the left, however, is the growing dissidence from the established attitudes documented in the preceding paragraphs. This includes sociologists (Edwards, 1973; Hoch, 1972; Scott, 1971) and muckraking novelists (Bouton, 1970; Meggyesy, 1971; Shaw, 1972), both of whom are frequently former athletes. While questions have been raised about some of these authors' motives (no doubt some have benefited from what has been a new best-seller formula), they provide an insiders' view with a great deal of credibility.

There are many issues pitting the radical wing against organized sport. I conclude this chapter with a brief discussion of some of these.

The first and still major cause of the athletic revolution has been race. The history of American sport has been characterized by racial discrimination. The entry of Jackie Robinson, and with him the Negro, into major league baseball in 1945 is invariably cited as a milestone. Since then, black athletes have gradually acquired their just share of athletic positions, and then some. Sociologists agree that the current preeminence of blacks in professional sports is the product of sociocultural forces and not inherent racial differences. This area has been one of the few channels of upward mobility open to blacks. Because desegregation has, as a consequence, proceeded further in the world of sport than in other occupations, a certain smugness has developed. To quote Olsen (1968:7), "Every morning the world of sport wakes up and congratulates itself on its contributions to race relations. The litany has been so often repeated that it is believed almost universally. It goes: 'Look what Sports has done for the Negro.' "

Yet evidence suggests continuing discrimination, albeit in subtler forms. A study by Loy and McElvogue (1971) indicates that racial segregation in professional team sports is positively related to

Table 8-9. *A comparison of race and position in major league baseball in 1967**

Position	White	Black
Catcher	27	1
Shortstop	17	1
First base	18	7
Second base	16	4
Third base	16	6
Outfield	38	36
Total	132	55

*Source: Loy and McElvogue (1971:117).

Table 8-10. *A comparison of race and position in major league football in 1968 (offense)**

Position	White	Black
Center	26	0
Quarterback	25	1
Right guard	24	2
Left guard	25	1
Right tackle	21	5
Left tackle	19	7
Tight end	20	6
Split end	18	8
Fullback	15	11
Halfback	10	16
Flankerback	17	9
Total	220	66

*Source: Loy and McElvogue (1971:119).

Table 8-11. *A comparison of race and position in major league football in 1968 (defense)**

Position	White	Black
Middle linebacker	24	2
Right linebacker	25	1
Left linebacker	23	3
Right end	18	8
Right tackle	20	6
Left tackle	17	9
Left end	19	7
Right safety	17	9
Left safety	17	9
Right cornerback	8	18
Left cornerback	4	22
Total	192	94

*Source: Loy and McElvogue (1971:120).

centrality. What the authors mean or imply is that the most strategic, prestigious, promising, and lucrative positions —for example, catcher in baseball, quarterback in football—rarely accrue to black players. Tables 8-9 to 8-11 reproduce some of the authors' findings. Figs. 7 to 9 are included to refresh the reader's mind on basic positions.

Loy and McElvogue go to great lengths to explain the dynamics of racial discrimination in baseball and football.

However, the validity of the centrality concept can be questioned. Only if locational centrality translates into socioeconomic advantage is it a meaningful measure of social discrimination. That location is not even related to prestige is proven by the low-prestige center position (with, incidentally, not a single black occupant in 1968).

Overall, it must be pointed out that in 1968, 40% of all first string major league baseball players were black or latin, one third of professional football players were black, and so was a staggering 60% of the NBA (Talamini and Page, 1973:224). One may continue to focus, as do the radicals, on the absence of black managers, black quarterbacks, and on the other ways in which full equality has not yet been accomplished. By the same token, a rigid racial quota approach becomes ludicrous, as it would for example demand that we fire 80% of the black basketball players!

Space does not permit me to deal with other controversial issues at equal length. Sex, for example, has now become as important as race has been since the 1968 Olympics. As women's liberation followed the black power movement by a couple of years, so the equalization of the sexes follows desegregation. Billie Jean King's pioneering efforts in the tennis world deserve special mention (*Newsweek,* 1972).

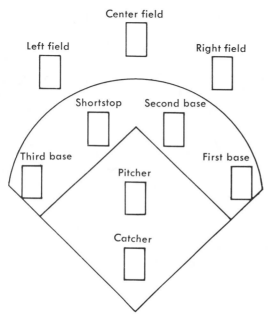

Fig. 7. *Field positions in professional baseball.*

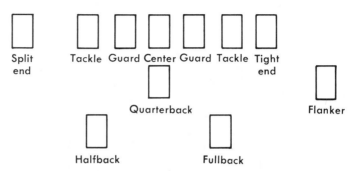

Fig. 8. *Field positions in professional football (offense).*

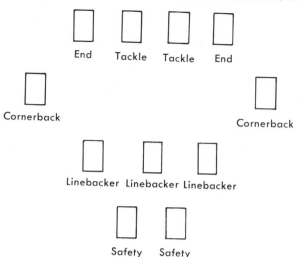

Fig. 9. *Field positions in professional football (defense).*

The issue of professionalization and commercialization has already been touched upon. Here, too, radical reform is demanded with increasing vigor. Scott (1971:89-103) deplores the state of amateurism, explaining that it is a luxury only the wealthy can afford. Stone (1958) points out that the economic structure of sport resembles an inverted pyramid, with a small minority of athletes doing the actual sporting and an enormous appendage of sponsors, reporters, coaches, managers, commentators, media men, equipment specialists, doctors, promoters, agents, and other personnel reaping far greater profits than the athletes themselves. Hoch (1972:40-69), Bouton (1970), Stone (1958), and innumerable others have documented the fact that professional sport is a voracious business which devours its boxers, athletes, and ball players. Having fattened the purses of his parasites, many an aging athlete finds himself sliding into a life of poverty and degradation.

With the professionalization taking place at the college level as well, all sorts of psychological costs are incurred. As Ogilvie and Tutko (1973) show, some athletes suffer from success phobia. This is merely one of the many ways in which sport has lost its spontaneous ludic element.

As sport becomes less play and more display or spectacle, it loses its ennobling character. Boxing was perhaps the first major sport to go. According to Dulles (1965:353), it has degenerated into a sorry, corrupt mess. From this vantage point, Muhammad Ali's current antics merely further reduce the sport to circus. Prole sports in general (wrestling, roller derby, demolition derby) exhibit many of the features of the debasing spectacle. They are unsophisticated displays of faked or genuine violence, black-and-white drama without nuance. However, radical sociologists have not only failed to criticize the vulgarity of proletarian display, they have actually seen in it the charm, creativity, and raw vitality of the populace (cf. Lewis, 1972; Wolfe, 1966; Stone, 1958). This is no doubt because of the radical intellectual's sentimental sympathy for the lower class.

Finally, radicals view in contemporary organized sport an embodiment of militaristic patriotism and authoritarian discipline, in brief, fascism itself (Hoch, 1972).

To be sure, not all students and chron-
iclers of sport can be pegged along a political spectrum. Men like Dwight
Chapin and Jeff Prugh (1973), Roger
Kahn (1971), George Plimpton (1965),
and Gale Sayers and Al Silverman
(1970) have written entertaining and relatively apolitical albeit sarcastic books
about the world of big sport. Then, too,
the scientific sociology of men like Loy
and Kenyon (1969) can hardly be termed
political. It prides itself on being value-
free in the best Weberian sense. Alas,
this is where it has been most severely
attacked by the radicals (cf. Hoch,
1972:xii-xiii; Scott, 1971:41). It is the in-
tolerance of value-free science which,
more than anything, indicates the politi-
cization and polarization of a realm of
life that should be just fun and play.

SUMMARY AND CONCLUSION

This chapter has examined sports, outdoor activities, and travel, with most of
the emphasis on the first. As in previous
chapters, I first traced the phenomenon's history, then provided some facts
and figures about its current magnitude,
then covered its major sociological correlates, and finally discussed some important issues centered around it. When it
comes to sport, I noted at the outset,
the two most important observations are
(1) the enormous growth of the phenomenon, in all forms, and (2) its increasing
institutionalization and professionalization.

Tracing the history of sport we saw,
first, that tribal society's sports were
mostly a mixture of gamelike and religious elements. It was in ancient Greece
that sport acquired its modern meaning
of athletic competition. The ancient
Olympic Games were held as early as
1300 B.C. The Olympic ideal initially embodied by the Greek games meant the
free and democratic participation in the
contests by any citizen amateur. However, Rome perverted that tradition, turn-

ing play into display and spontaneous
and genuine contest into contrived mass
spectacle, providing bread and circuses to
the masses of passive spectators in the
form of gladiator combat and other dehumanizing spectacles. The dehumanization and massification of society and culture which took place from Greece to
Rome seems to be replicated when, in
modern history, the focus shifts from
Europe to America. After the fall of
Rome there followed an era of asceticism; sports and games declined during
the Middle Ages. And as with other
areas of culture, it was the Renaissance
which caused the revival of those activities. While the Renaissance and philosophers like Rousseau did much to free
man's body from the Puritan straightjacket of medieval Catholicism, the Protestant Reformation set the development
of sports and games back by centuries.
Because of the Puritanism inherent in
the doctrines of men like Calvin, leisure
and sports were not permitted to flourish
as they had begun to do during the Renaissance.

Since America was born during this
period, our country's initial attitude
toward sport and leisure was inevitably
negative. However, by the end of the seventeenth century a certain relaxation
began to set in; the more aristocratic
South had already enjoyed horse racing
and a variety of other spectacles, and
now even the Puritan North ventured
into such activities as target shooting,
wrestling, and other sports. Then, from
the beginning of the nineteenth century
on, true spectator sports began to
emerge, for example, rowing, sailing,
foot races, and prizefighting. While the
latter sport remained outlawed until
after the Civil War, all these activities
already involved paid professionals. For
a while the growing urban masses were
reduced to passive spectatorship, urbanization having proceeded without the
concomitant development of adequate

means of mass transportation. However, from the 1860s on, indoor participant sports like gymnastics and roller skating became popular, and baseball, which had been officially created in 1842, was fast becoming the national pastime, a position that would remain uncontested until after World War II. Football, now baseball's prime competitor, was first played between Yale and Rutgers in 1869. After the game's excessive violence had been ironed out at the beginning of the century, it rapidly became the major college spectacle, and in 1920 the American Professional Football Association was formed. The financial empire of professional football was still continuing to expand in 1974, with the newly formed World Football League anticipating the creation of at least a dozen new franchises. The inroads made by football into baseball over the years have been attributed to a variety of causes. According to Marshall McLuhan (1964), this process is due to television, a medium which lends itself more to football than to baseball. According to Harry Edwards (1973) it is, rather, the outcome of the growth of aggressive, competitive, middle-class values among the population. I argue that Edwards' explanation is the more plausible of the two, and I, along with that author, deplore the trend.

Whatever the specific trends are, there can be no doubt that the twentieth century has been sport's golden age. Other mass spectacles of the twentieth century include boxing, basketball, automobile racing, horse racing, golf, tennis, hockey, and track and field events. Although the enormous growth of spectator sports in the twentieth century has led to concern about *spectatoritis,* it should be kept in mind that *participant* sports have grown at least as spectacularly. Thus the upper and middle classes now participate by the millions in such activities as golf, tennis, and skiing, while the lower-middle and working classes have sports like

bowling and softball. Furthermore, general affluence, mobility (the universality of the private car), and the demise of Victorianism and changing sexual etiquette have made swimming and other water sports the most popular activity by far.

Tracing the history of (modern) sport, we finally arrived at an ultimate characterization to which most contemporary trends seem to lead: the institutionalization and "technocratization" of modern sport, which seem to be manifest in all its areas, not only in the professional sphere. School programs, for example, increasingly emphasize the utilitarian and competitive aspects of athletic activities, rather than spontaneity and fun. The modern Olympic Games, while supposed to uphold the ideal of amateurism, have of course also degenerated into a sorry commercialized, professionalized, and—worst of all—politicized spectacle. And as far as amateur sports are concerned, for example, outdoor activities such as hunting, camping, skiing, and fishing, numerous authors discern an increasing emphasis on technical gadgetry, fancy gear, and concern with skill, efficiency, and physical comfort rather than the spontaneous experience of nature itself.

The figures on the growth of spectator sports indicated that it has far exceeded that of the population. In baseball, attendance at major league games has not suffered, but the minors have suffered severe losses. In football, the professional sector increased its audience by an incredible 453% from 1950 to 1972. More popular than either football or baseball are, in terms of paid attendance figures, horse racing and automobile racing. Overall, paid attendance of live sports events has declined as a proportion of *total consumer expenditure* since the 1930s. This, I showed, is clearly related to the rise of the electronic media, particularly television. Indeed, there has been an inverse relationship between the dissemination of radio and television on the one hand, and percentage of income spent on live game attendance on the other.

As far as amateur participant sports and travel are concerned, the figures indicated that these activities, unlike spectator sports attendance, had increased at least as rapidly as overall leisure spending. Frequencies were given for a variety of activities, including softball, cycling, swimming, fishing, waterskiing, winter sports, camping, and hiking. The broken-down composition and size of the total outdoor recreational system available to Americans was also presented. It includes the national, state, and county parks systems, plus the National Forest System and portions of such areas as the Tennessee Valley Authority and the Indian lands, as well as private facilities, for example, the nation's five thousand country clubs. All in all an area of perhaps 540 million acres. Postwar increase in foreign travel was also documented. It was shown that European travel has experienced the sharpest increase. And returning to the domestic scene, I indicated that what optimistic business-oriented sources dub a "leisure boom" has in fact generally been an odious spree of consumerism, a response by the population to the advertiser's call to spend every last penny and ounce of its energy on recreational vehicles, motor homes, vacation lots, and second homes. Finally, by 1974, with the energy shortage and the ecological crisis assuming ever more immediate urgency, it became apparent that the so-called "leisure boom" was in for a drastic reappraisal.

The discussion of sport's sociological correlates began with spectator sports. According to the O.R.C. study reproduced by de Grazia (1964:441-444), men attend sport events more than twice as often as women, although working women's attendance is nearly as frequent as that of

men. Age turned out to be inversely related to sport attendance, and there were also regional and socioeconomic status differences. The latter were documented through a discussion of auto racing, showing the neat status stratification of that sport, from the elite Formula-One type down to the dirt tracks where modified hardtops grind out their stock car races before a predominately lower-class public.

Some of the sociological correlates of participant sports were similar to those of spectator sports. Again, men and young people were found to participate significantly more than women and older people. In addition, urban participation was found to be higher than that in rural areas. As far as the socioeconomic status cluster is concerned, sources concur that most sports are of upper-class origin, subsequently diffused downward in the social structure. The various social strata differ more in terms of the *kinds* of sports in which they engage than in terms of *amounts.* Racial differences also abound (e.g., blacks fish and picnic in large numbers but hardly participate in winter sports), and each ethnic and regional subculture has, of course, its major sport, be it soccer, jai alai, hockey, skating, skiing, or surfing. The study of sport subcultures is one of the most promising areas of sociology.

As to outdoor recreation and travel, it was shown that men tend to camp more than women while women do slightly more picnicking and that there is a positive association between many outdoor activities (camping, picnicking) and travel on the one hand, and education, income, occupation, and other socioeconomic status variables on the other. Blacks' most popular activity in this area is picnicking, and overseas travel is done the most by the wealthy, men, urbanites, easterners, and, increasingly, the young.

The third discussion in this chapter addressed itself to the major issues in sport sociology. It was argued that the most crucial sociological problem in contemporary sport is its *institutionalization,* and under that label such processes as professionalization and commercialization are also referred to. It was suggested that by following these tendencies, contemporary sport merely follows and reflects larger societal trends, namely the trends toward gesellschaft, mass society, technocracy, rationalization, and away from community and primary relations noted by sociologists from Tonnies to Kornhauser and from Sorokin to Roszak. Thus the world of sport is actually merely a microcosm of the larger society, and its changing character reflects the various aspects of what may, for better or worse, be called social progress. Page (1973) and others have emphasized the gains, for example, the decline of exclusionism, of racial discrimination, and of personal favoritism, that is, the substitution of universalism for particularism. Indeed, the rational properties of bureaucratization and institutionalization noted by Weber have blessed modern man with at least one benefit that can no longer be questioned: the emergence of universalism, a cornerstone of egalitarian democracy. Modernization has, however, been a two-edged sword. Its other prime feature—in sports as elsewhere—has been *dehumanization,* and it is that feature which we find indicted in much of the literature. As in ancient Rome, the spontaneous play and the morality of the game have, in contemporary America, gradually been replaced by the contrived display (Stone, 1958) and the cash nexus.

Under a separate and final heading, sport's three constituencies—the amateur participants, the spectators, and the professionals—were discussed. The sociology of participant sports, we saw, has produced at least five major theoretical-empirical approaches: the social-psychological socialization focus based on the tradition of Mead and Piaget, the study of the functional relationship between sports and other areas such as work, the macrofunctional analysis of sport as an institution, sport viewed purely for its ludic elements, and finally the establishment of sport typologies such as Caillois' (1961). The sociology of fandom and spectatorship has focused mostly on the functions of these behaviors, providing competing psychologistic (Thompkins, 1971) and political (Edwards, 1973) explanations. It also examines the role of the mass media in the performer-spectator relationship. Professional sport, finally, has been approached by two groups with radically different perspectives—those who see in big sport the embodiment of the most profound American traditions, and those who view it as a dehumanized, commercialized, racist, and even fascist institution. The former camp, then, feels a deep commitment to the American sports creed, including nationalism, religiosity, discipline, competition, and success, while the other consists primarily of muckraking novelists and radical sociologists. One area where the controversy comes to a head is race. While some students (e.g., Loy and McElvogue, 1971) tenuously attempt to show the persistence of racial discrimination in professional sports, the total integration and in fact enormous overrepresentation of blacks in many areas of sports can no longer be ignored. With respect to the racial issue, the radicals' position is weak, and one suspects that many of their other accusations are ideological and rhetorical rather than factual.

STUDY QUESTIONS

1. What is the central theme in this chapter on sports? Show how this process goes hand in hand with the emergence of big sport, and how it reflects the same complex of processes in the society at large. What analogy have I drawn between contemporary American civilization and Graeco-Roman antiquity? Discuss the three camps whose writings and opinions are covered

in this chapter—the value-free sport sociologists, the radical muckrakers, and the big sport establishment—and show, with specific references, how each approaches the world of sport.

2. Discuss the etymology, origin, and history of sport, beginning with tribal society, tracing the origin of the Olympic Games in ancient Greece, the deterioration of that ideal in Rome, the eclipse of sports during the Middle Ages, its revival during the Renaissance, the obstacles placed before its development by Protestant Puritanism, and the birth and development of sports in the United States, from the colonial period to today. When did such sports as horse racing, boxing, football, foot races, rowing, basketball, automobile racing, golf, and hockey originate in the United States? When did professionalism first manifest itself? According to many social critics, what are some of the undesirable characteristics both amateur and professional sports have recently been taking on? Do you agree with this or not? Why?

3. Discuss the twentieth-century growth of spectator sports. How does this compare with population growth and with total leisure spending? What has been the role of television? How has baseball fared? How about football? What, then, are currently the most popular spectator sports? What competing hypotheses have been offered for the enormous growth in football's popularity at the expense of baseball? Which of these hypotheses is the most plausible to you? Why?

4. Discuss the twentieth-century growth of participant sports. Has this been greater or smaller than growth in spectator sports? Which areas are now particularly popular? What is the estimated domestic acreage that is totally or primarily devoted to recreation? What are the main components of this total? Discuss also the extent and growth of foreign travel. Finally, what can be said about the alleged outdoor-recreational

boom? Why has this chapter expressed criticism of the vast sums of consumer dollars poured into such things as recreational vehicles, second homes, and vacation lots?

5. Discuss the main sociological correlates of (1) spectator sports and (2) participant sports. Focus particularly on the significance of such variables as sex, age, and employment status for *overall* sport participation and attendance. Then, show that variables like race and socioeconomic status make a difference in the *kinds* of sports consumed, rather than in the amounts. Finally, discuss a number of sport subcultures, either some of those suggested in this chapter, or any other known to you from experience.

6. This chapter has argued that the central problem in contemporary sport is the phenomenon of institutionalization. Show what was meant by that. What are some of the trends I subsume under that term? Show how those trends are operating in the society at large, of which sport is a mere reflection. What have been the main benefits of those processes, and what have been the costs? Which of the two weigh the heaviest, according to the sources quoted, and according to you?

7. The final section of this chapter discusses sport's three constituencies—the amateur participants, the spectators, and the professionals (including the aspiring professionals in college and high school). What are the five major theoretical-empirical approaches I identified in the sociology of participant sports? Second, what are some of the problems focused on by the sociology of fandom and spectatorship? Finally, what two ideological camps exist vis-a-vis professional sports? What are some of the arguments raging between these two camps with respect to such things as race, sex, money, ideology, and values in the world of sports? What is your own position and why?

REFERENCES

Anderson, Charles and Milton Gordon
    1964   "The blue-collar worker at leisure." Pp. 407-416 in Arthur B. Shostak and William Gomberg (eds.), Blue-Collar World: Studies of the American Worker. New York: Prentice-Hall, Inc.

Arendt, Hannah
    1951   The Origins of Totalitarianism. New York: Harcourt, Brace and World.

Avedon, Elliott M. and Brian Sutton-Smith
    1972   The Study of Games. New York: John Wiley & Sons, Inc.

Beisser, Arnold R.
    1966   The Madness in Sports. New York: Appleton-Century-Crofts.

Bell, Daniel
    1960   The End of Ideology: On the Exhaustion of Political Ideas in the Fifties. New York: The Free Press.
    1973   The Coming of Post-Industrial Society. New York: Basic Books, Inc., Publishers.

Bogart, Leo
    1972   The Age of Television. 3rd ed. New York: Frederick Ungar Publishing Co., Inc.

Bouton, Jim
    1970   Ball Four. New York: Dell Publishing Co., Inc.

Caillois, Roger
    1961   Man, Play and Games. New York: The Free Press.

Cantwell, Robert
1973 "Sport was box-office poison." Pp. 441-453 in John T. Talamini and Charles H. Page (eds.), Sport and Society. Boston: Little, Brown and Company.
Chambers, Mortimer
1963 The Fall of Rome—Can it be Explained? New York: Holt, Rinehart & Winston, Inc.
Chapin, Dwight and Jeff Prugh
1973 The Wizard of Westwood: Coach John Wooden and His UCLA Bruins. New York: Warner Books.
Clarke, Alfred C.
1958 "Leisure and occupational prestige." Pp. 205-214 in Eric Larrabee and Rolf Meyersohn (eds.), Mass Leisure. Glencoe, Ill.: The Free Press.
Cozens, Frederick W. and Florence Scovil Stumpf
1973 "The sports page." Pp. 418-431 in John T. Talamini and Charles H. Page (eds.), Sport and Society. Boston: Little, Brown and Company.
Curtis, Henry S.
1904 "A football education." The American Physical Education Review (December).
de Grazia, Sebastian
1948 The Political Community: A Study of Anomie. Chicago: University of Chicago Press.
1964 Of Time, Work and Leisure. New York: Anchor Books.
Dulles, Foster Rhea
1965 A History of Recreation: America Learns to Play. New York: Appleton-Century-Crofts.
Edwards, Harry
1972 "Preface to The Revolt of the Black Athlete." Pp. 304-307 in M. Marie Hart (ed.), Sport in the Socio-Cultural Process. Dubuque, Iowa: William C. Brown Company, Publishers.
1973 Sociology of Sport. Homewood, Ill.: Dorsey Press.
Ehrlich, Paul R.
1968 The Population Bomb. New York: Ballantine Books, Inc.
Ellul, Jacques
1964 The Technological Society. New York: Alfred A. Knopf, Inc.
Emrie, William J.
1970 Recreation Problems in the Urban Impacted Areas of California. Sacramento, Calif.: State of California Department of Parks and Recreation.
Ferriss, Abbott et al.
1962 National Recreation Survey. Washington, D. C.: U. S. Government Printing Office.
Galbraith, John Kenneth
1958 The Affluent Society. Boston: Houghton Mifflin Company.

Gerstl, Joel E.
1963 "Leisure, taste and occupational milieu." Pp. 85-96 in Erwin O. Smigel (ed.), Work and Leisure—a Contemporary Social Problem. New Haven, Conn.: College and University Press.
Gross, Edward
1963 "A functional approach to leisure analysis." In Erwin O. Smigel (ed.), Work and Leisure: A Contemporary Social Problem. New Haven, Conn.: College and University Press.
Hart, M. Marie
1972 Sport in the Socio-Cultural Process. Dubuque, Iowa: William Brown Company, Publishers.
Havighurst, Robert J.
1957 "The leisure activities of the middle-aged." American Journal of Sociology 63 (September):152-162.
Heilbroner, Robert
1974 "The human prospect." New York Review of Books (January 24):21-34.
Hoch, Paul
1972 Rip Off The Big Game. New York: Anchor Books.
Howe, Irving
1957 "Notes on mass culture." Pp. 496-503 in Bernard Rosenberg and David Manning White (eds.), Mass Culture—The Popular Arts in America. New York: The Free Press.
Huizinga, Johan
1949 Homo Ludens: A Study of the Play Elements in Culture. London: Routledge and Kegan Paul.
Inbar, Michael
1972 "The socialization effect of game playing on pre-adolescents." Journal of Health, Physical Education and Recreation (June).
Ingham, Alan G. and John W. Loy, Jr.
1973 "The social system of sport: a humanistic perspective." Quest 19 (January):3-23.
Iniguez, Richard
1974 Car Racing. Unpublished term paper. California State University, Sacramento.
Johnson, William
1973 "TV made it all a new game." Pp. 454-472 in John T. Talamini and Charles H. Page (eds.), Sport and Society. Boston: Little, Brown and Company.
Kahn, Roger
1971 The Boys of Summer. New York: The New American Library, Inc.
Kando, Thomas and Worth C. Summers
1971 "The impact of work on leisure: toward a paradigm and research strategy." Pacific Sociological Review (special summer issue):310-327.

Kaplan, Max
   1960   Leisure in America. New York: John Wiley & Sons, Inc.
Kazickas, Jurate
   1972   "America's leisure time bonanza." Sacramento Union (February 24).
Kornhauser, William
   1959   The Politics of Mass Society. New York: The Free Press.
Kraus, Richard
   1968   Public Recreation and the Negro. A Study of Participation and Administrative Practices. New York: Center for Urban Education.
   1971   Recreation and Leisure in Modern Society. New York: Appleton-Century-Crofts.
Lederer, William J. and Eugene Burdick
   1958   The Ugly American. Greenwich, Conn.: Crest Books.
Lewis, George H. (ed.)
   1972   Side-Saddle on the Golden Calf: Social Structure and Popular Culture in America. Pacific Palisades, Calif.: Goodyear Publishing Co., Inc.
Loy, John W. and Joseph F. McElvogue
   1971   "Racial segregation in American sport." Pp. 113-127 in Sociology of Sport: Theoretical Foundations and Research Methods (Magglinger Symposium). Basel, Switzerland: Birkhauser Verlag.
Loy, John W., Jr. and Gerald S. Kenyon
   1969   Sport, Culture and Society: A Reader on the Sociology of Sport. New York: The Macmillan Company.
Marcuse, Herbert
   1964   One-Dimensional Man: Studies in the Ideology of Advanced Industrial Society. Boston: Beacon Press.
Martindale, Don
   1960a   American Society. New York: Van Nostrand Reinhold Company.
   1960b   The Nature and Types of Sociological Theory. Boston: Houghton Mifflin Company.
McIntosh, Peter C.
   1963   Sport in Society. London: C. A. Watts & Co., Ltd.
McLuhan, Marshall
   1964   Understanding Media: The Extensions of Man. New York: McGraw-Hill Book Company.
Mead, George Herbert
   1934   Mind, Self and Society. Chicago: University of Chicago Press.
Meadows, Dennis L.
   1972   The Limits to Growth. New York: Universe Books.
Meggyesy, Dave
   1971   Out of Their League. New York: The Paperback Library.

Mills, C. Wright
   1951   White Collar—The American Middle Classes. New York: Oxford University Press.
   1956   The Power Elite. New York: Oxford University Press.
Newsweek
   1972   "Tennis: a triumph for women's lob." (June 26):56-63.
Ogilvie, Bruce and Thomas Tutko
   1973   "Success phobia." Pp. 188-201 in John T. Talamini and Charles H. Page (eds.), Sport and Society. Boston: Little, Brown and Company.
Olsen, Jack
   1968   The Black Athlete - A Shameful Story. New York: Time, Inc.
Opie, Iona and Peter Opie
   1969   Children's Games in Street and Playground. Oxford: Clarendon Press.
Orr, Jack
   1973   "The black boxer: exclusion and ascendance. Pp. 240-260 in John T. Talamini and Charles H. Page (eds.), Sport and Society. Boston: Little, Brown and Company.
Outdoor Recreation Resources Review Commission
   1962   Commission's report in 27 volumes, Washington, D. C.: U. S. Government Printing Office.
Page, Charles H.
   1973   "Pervasive sociological themes in the study of sport." Pp. 14-36 in John T. Talamini and Charles H. Page (eds.), Sport and Society. Boston: Little, Brown and Company.
Piaget, Jean
   1932   The Moral Judgment of the Child. New York: Harcourt, Brace, and World.
Plimpton, George
   1965   Paper Lion. New York: Harper & Row, Publishers.
Polsky, Ned
   1972   "Of pool playing and poolrooms. Pp. 19-54 in Gregory P. Stone (ed.), Games, Sport and Power. New York: E. P. Dutton & Co., Inc.
Riesman, David
   1951   "Leisure in urbanized America." In P. K. Hatt and A. J. Reiss (eds.), Reader in Urban Sciology. Glencoe, Ill.: The Free Press.
   1958   "Leisure and work in post-industrial society." Pp. 363-385 in Eric Larrabee and Rolf Meyersohn (eds.), Mass Leisure. Glencoe, Ill.: The Free Press.
Riesman, David, Nathan Glazer and Denney Reuel
   1950   The Lonely Crowd. New Haven, Conn.: Yale University Press.
Roberts, John M. and Brian Sutton-Smith
   1969   "Game involvement." Pp. 116-135 in John

W. Loy and Gerald S. Kenyon (eds.), Sport, Culture and Society. New York: The Macmillan Company.

Robinson, John
1967 "Time expenditure on sports across ten countries." In The International Review of Sport Sociology. Warsaw: Polish Publishers.

Roszak, Theodore
1969 The Making of a Counterculture. Garden City, N. Y.: Doubleday & Company, Inc.
1973 Politics and Transcendence in Post-Industrial Society. New York: Anchor Books.

Sayers, Gale and Al Silverman
1970 I Am Third. New York: Bantam Books, Inc.

Schafer, Walter E. and J. Michael Armer
1972 "Athletes are not inferior students." Pp. 97-116 in Gregory P. Stone (ed.), Games, Sport and Power. New Brunswick, N. J.: Transaction Books.

Scotch, N. A.
1961 "Magic, sorcery and football among urban zulu: a case of reinterpretation under acculturation." The Journal of Conflict Resolution 5:70-74. Also Pp. 230-235 in Marcello Truzzi (ed.), Sociology and Everyday Life. Englewood Cliffs, N. J.: Prentice-Hall, Inc.

Scott, Jack
1971 The Athletic Revolution. New York: The Free Press.

Scott, Marvin B.
1969 "The man on the horse." Pp. 424-438 in John W. Loy and Gerald S. Kenyon (eds.), Sport, Culture and Society. New York: The Macmillan Company.

Shaw, Gary
1972 Meat on the Hoof: The Hidden World of Texas Football. New York: Dell Publishing Co., Inc.

Shostak, Arthur B. and William Gomberg (eds.)
1964 Blue-Collar World: Studies of the American Worker. New York: Prentice-Hall, Inc.

Sillitoe, Alan
1959 The Loneliness of the Long Distance Runner. New York: Signet Books.

Sorokin, Pitirim
1947 Society, Culture and Personality. New York: Harper & Row, Publishers.

Statistical Abstracts of the United States
1971 Washington, D. C.: U. S. Government Printing Office.
1973 Washington, D. C.: U. S. Government Printing Office.

Steele, Paul D. and Louis A. Zurcher
1973 "Leisure sports as 'emphemeral roles.'" Pacific Sociological Review (July):345-357.

Stewart, Jackie
1972 "A candid conversation with Grand Prix racing's two-time world champion." Playboy (June):77-80, 82, 84, 86, 88, 90, 92, 94, 194.

Stone, Gregory P.
1958 "American sports: play and display." Pp. 253-263 in Eric Larrabee and Rolf Meyersohn (eds.), Mass Leisure. Glencoe, Ill.: The Free Press.
1969 "Some meanings of American sport: an extended view." Pp. 5-16 in Gerald S. Kenyon (ed.), Proceedings of C.I.C. Symposium on the Sociology of Sport. Chicago: The Athletic Institute.
1972a "Some meanings of American sport: an extended view." Pp. 155-167 in M. Marie Hart (ed.), Sport in the Socio-Cultural Process. Dubuque, Iowa: William C. Brown Company, Publishers.
1972b Games, Sport and Power. New Brunswick, N. J.: Transaction Books.
1972c "Wrestling: the great American passion play." In Eric Dunning (ed.), Sport: Readings from a Sociological Perspective. Toronto: University of Toronto Press.

Stone, Gregory P. and Marvin J. Taves
1958 "Camping in the Wilderness." Pp. 290-305 in Eric Larrabee and Rolf Meyersohn (eds.), Mass Leisure. Glencoe, Ill.: The Free Press.

Talamini, John T. and Charles H. Page
1973 Sport and Society: An Anthology. Boston: Little, Brown and Company.

Thompkins, William G.
1971 Cited in David Hendlin "Footballitis: a contagious, incurable disease." Fremont News-Register (October 29):29.

Toffler, Alvin
1964 The Culture Consumers. Baltimore: Penguin Books Inc.
1970 Future Shock. New York: Bantam Books Inc.

U. S. News & World Report
1969 "83 billion dollars for leisure—now the fastest-growing business in America." (September 15):58-61.
1972 "Leisure boom. biggest ever and still growing." (April 17):42-45.

Watson, G. G.
1973 Game Interaction in Little League Baseball and Family Organization. Unpublished doctoral dissertation. University of Illinois, Urbana-Champaign (October).
1974 "The meaning and social functions of the game for middle- and working-class little leaguers." (mimeograph) California State University, Sacramento.

Watson, G. G. and T. M. Kando
1974 "The meaning of rules and rituals in little league baseball, or what happens when parents meddle in their childrens' affairs."

Pacific Sociological Association, San Jose, California (March 28-30).

Weber, Max
1958   The Protestant Ethic and the Spirit of Capitalism. New York: Charles Scribner's Sons.

Whyte, William H., Jr.
1956   The Organization Man. Garden City, N. Y.: Anchor Books.

Wilensky, Harold L.
1960   "Work, careers and social integration." International Social Science Journal (Fall):543:560.

Wolfe, Tom
1966   The Kandy-Kolored Tangerine-Flake Streamline Baby. New York: Pocket Books.

Zurcher, Louis A.
1968   "Social-psychological functions of ephemeral roles." Human Organization (Winter):281-297.

1970   "The friendly poker game: a study of an ephemeral role." Social Forces (December):173-186.

chapter 9

Youth, culture, and social change

So far, only conventional forms of leisure and recreation have been dealt with. My objective in writing this book would not be accomplished if social and cultural change and their most potent source—youth—were not discussed.

This chapter examines youth culture in two ways. Following one of sociology's most basic dichotomies, it focuses first on culture and then on structure. Leisure belongs primarily to culture, and politics to structure. While this book is mostly about leisure, it should be clear by now that it is also about politics. I follow Aristotle, Marx, and lesser men in believing that little if anything in human life is apolitical, certainly not leisure. Therefore I have examined the kinds of changes currently going on both from a cultural and from a political standpoint. As the issue is so often phrased, Is the revolution to be cultural or social?

Under the heading of cultural change, the discussion of youth will begin with the 1950s. At that time, youth rebellion, insofar as it existed at all, took the innocuous form of satire a la *Mad Maga-*

Joshua Aronson/Editorial Photocolor Archives

zine, moderate amounts of illicit sex, drinking and delinquency, expressive behavior at jazz concerts, and fraternity type pranks like goldfish swallowing and jamming people in telephone booths. While few could see social significance in all this, it nevertheless constituted the earliest rumble of youth dissent. Lonely and quixotic were men like Paul Goodman and Herbert Marcuse who detected justification for youth rebellion even then, although none manifested itself as yet, which led to the dominant assumption that this generation had overwhelmingly found bliss in unprecedented affluence. Daniel Bell's *The End of Ideology* (1960) were the famous last words written just before the onset of the most vigorous ideological movement since Marxism—the counterculture.[1]

The mid-sixties suddenly thrust a massive youth movement upon America. This was the product of both long-term social-structural trends like accelerated bureaucratization, urbanization, and rationalization (cf. Davis, 1971) and specific historical events (the Vietnam war).

The hippies, of course, did not come out of the blue. They extended, magnified, and diluted what the beat generation of the 1950s had begun. I shall trace this continuity.

Analyses of the counterculture abound.[2] The sixties may have been the decade of the counterculture, but the era immediately following it was undoubtedly the age of counterculture analysis. Young and not so young sociologists in search of hot material—to be published mostly in *Transaction*—were not the last to benefit from hippies. While I do not intend to cover a terrain already trampled to death (but occasionally brilliantly covered, as by Roszak, 1969), I must, nevertheless, explicate those features of the counterculture which have relevance to our subject—leisure and culture.

The key word to the counterculture has been liberation. The movement proposed liberation from and alternatives to existing forms at three levels—psychological, social, and cultural. At the psychological level, two themes—consciousness and affect—are discussed. At

[1]With that kind of a batting average in social forecasting, one has to admire Bell's chutzpa as he continues to venture into the crystal ball. No doubt his latest futurological effort (1973) will be as dismally off the mark as were his earlier attempts.
[2]General analyses of the counterculture include Barry (1970), Berger (1967, 1971), Berger and Berger (1971), Braden (1970), Brustein (1971), Davis (1967, 1971), Douglas (1970b), Einhorn (1972), Eisen (1971), Feuer (1969), Gliner (1973), Gliner and Raines (1971), Hedgepeth and Stock (1970), Hunter (1972), Illich (1971), Jones (1971), Laing (1967), Lewis (1972), Lipset (1971), Melly (1971), Nobile (1971), Reich (1970), Roszak (1969, 1973), Rubin (1970), Simmons and Winograd (1966), Sontag (1966), Ten Have (1972), Thoenes (1967), Todd (1971), Toffler (1970), Watts (1971), Widmer (1971), Wolfe (1968), and Yablonsky (1968).
Works dealing with the counterculture's music include Belz (1969), Braun (1969), Denisoff and Peterson (1972), Eisen (1969, 1970), Gillett (1972), Horowitz (1971), Maracotta (1973), Marcus (1971), Meltzer (1970), Nanry (1972), Oberbeck (1969), Orth (1974), Parachini (1971), Ragni et al.(1968),

Robinson and Hirsch (1972), Roxon (1969), Taylor (1968), and Thompson (1971).

Countercultural drug use is the topic of Alpert and Cohen (1966), Blum et al. (1964), Davis and Munoz (1968), Holmes (1970), McGrath and Scarpitti (1970), *Newsweek* (1971), Pearlman (1970), Suchman (1968), Sutter (1970), and Watts (1971).

The New Left and student protest are discussed in Alinsky (1969), Anderson (1969), Becker (1970), Bettelheim (1969), Flacks (1972), Goulet (1971), Hallie (1971), Harris (1971), Jencks (1969), Jencks and Riesman (1968), Keniston (1968), Marin (1971), Martin (1972), *New York Times* (1972), Scott and Lyman (1970), Skolnick (1969), Spender (1969), Trow (1968), Wilkinson (1971), and Zinn (1969).

Communes are the subject of Ald (1970), Fairfield (1972), Kanter (1972), Kovach (1971), and Melville (1972).

My analysis of the counterculture will be based on many of these works and on additional sources as well. This footnote should, if nothing else, document the bandwagon character of the topic at hand.

the social level, gemeinschaft structures are dealt with; that is, it is shown that the counterculture has tried to recreate community and primary relationships. At the cultural level, finally, leisure, life-style, art, and the communication of ideas are examined.

In the following discussion I move to the political implications of the counter-culture. First, the theories and theorists behind the new politics, for example, Herbert Marcuse, are examined. Follow-ing this, the New Left's politics, are dis-cussed, both for their substantive objec-tives and for the form which they propose to take. Form and content, means and ends—the New Left departs from conventional politics in both re-spects. The substantive reforms that make up the counterculture's platform include peace, equality, institutional re-form of the educational system, legal re-form in regard to victimless crimes such as marijuana smoking, ecology, and local autonomy. In addition to these substan-tive issues, the New Left adds another element to conventional politics. As Laing (1967), Scott and Lyman (1970), and others (see footnote 2) have ex-plained, the new politics have at times become an end in themselves, a theatri-cal game, a collective public experience which requires no extrinsic justification. (Politics as a form of leisure?). This con-trasts sharply with conventional politics, which are, by definition, means to ulteri-or ends. An examination of the American New Left, the Dutch Provos and Ka-bouters, and the French student uprising of June 1968 substantiates this point. In concluding the discussion of the counter-culture I contrast its two inherent ten-dencies: liberation and enslavement, or, to use Merton, retreatism combined with ritualism on the one hand, and innova-tion combined with creative rebellion on the other. Both the potential for the age of Aquarius and for a return to the dark ages are indicated. In the end I argue,

like Lewis (1972) and unlike the Marx-ists, that culture is not epiphenomenal and irrelevant to historical change, witness the impressive success of the New Left in realizing its political objec-tives, and the unprecedented cultural diffusion from the counterculture into the larger society.

The final discussion addresses itself more generally to the question of social change. First, recent changes in the dom-inant social character, particularly as they affect attitudes toward work and leisure are discussed. Then, I analyze the major areas in which industrial civiliza-tion has been indicted by the critical school of sociologists. The case against technology, bureaucracy, capitalism, and consumerism is examined. Finally, I take a tentative step into futurology, discuss-ing first four alternative scenarios for so-ciety at large and along with each the leisure pattern most likely to prevail. One possibility, I argue, is the extension of current technocratic trends, with a concomitant technocratic leisure. An al-ternative possibility is ecological disaster with, in leisure and culture, a return to the dark ages, a revival of the sinister, the occult, and the irrational in all its negative meaning. A third possibility is the gradual deterioration in the quality of life as capitalism breaks down perma-

nently. The leisure most likely to accompany this is an increasing amount of passive participation in cheap and increasingly mediocre culture. Finally, there is a leisure ideal whose seeds have been lying dormant through history, cultivated and brought to flourish on occasion, as was done with partial success by the counterculture. This ideal will require the reintegration of work and leisure, body and mind, activity and passivity, society and the individual, man and nature, a return to active peace and dynamic harmony.

CULTURE, YOUTH, AND THE NEW LEISURE
The quiet before the storm

"The generation of the 1950's," as Manning and Truzzi explain, "was called the silent or apathetic generation, faulted for its conservatism, its careerist future plans, and its stodgy and stable view of the world" (1972:5). And as late as 1963, Friedenberg wrote that the American adolescent was essentially not political and that he could not be (1972:35). Others felt that the teenager of the 1950s was not even concerned with jobs or studies—"he was not preparing for The Good Life, he was living it" (Malone and Roberts, 1971).

As a conceptual category, the teenager was Madison Avenue's invention in the face of postwar consumer expansion. The infusion of money into the economy had helped to create the affluent leisure class of the American teenager. Teenage magazines, teenage music, and teenage commodities were produced to exploit this sector of the consumer market. Youth, as Friedenberg (1972) explains, was a silent minority economically exploited, socially discriminated against, and feared and niggerized as no other minority was.

A lone and early symbol of teenage rebellion, then, was *Mad*, which "transferred the world of ads into the world of the comic book" (McLuhan, 1964:166).

Sociologists wondered whether youth was tame or wild, especially with regard to sex. While Kingsley Davis (1940) and Talcott Parsons (1942) argued that adolescents were irresponsible, impulsive, and antiadult, Ira Reiss (1961) felt that the youth of the fifties was "not only not extreme but . . . quite conservative and restrained in the area of premarital sexual codes and behavior." Hollingshead's famous study of Elmtown's youth (1949) also gave evidence of the conservatism of postwar youth, for example, in the areas of status consciousness and conformity.

Popular music has been a favorite barometer by which sociologists have periodically gauged the mood of the younger generation. Popular music is culturally linked to dancing and meeting the other sex. The overwhelming proportion of it devoted to love and courtship themes leaves no doubt about that (cf. Hayakawa, 1957; Horton, 1957; Nye, 1970; Riesman, 1957a). And although it has become fashionable to advocate more sex for the elderly, sex, mate selection, and reproduction are, by virtue of the life-cycle itself, the problems of the young and not those of the old, hence a logical association between popular music and youth culture (with all due overlap granted). Riesman's (1957a) early discussion of this relationship was perceptive, for it noted both the apathy characteristic of the majority of teenagers and the incipient youth movement already present among a rebellious minority. The majority indiscriminately accepted all popular music and the superficial mediocrity and social conformity it entailed. The minority rebelled against the commercial and the mediocre, listening to exclusive jazz rather than "sweet" music and thus combining art and ideology by empathizing with the Negro and other outcastes. This was the birth of what Norman Mailer would call the white Negro.

In 1964, New Zealand psychologist

A. J. W. Taylor did a study of teenage music fans in action (1968). He interviewed 346 Beatles fans to determine correlations between "beatlemania" (defined as screaming, hysterical, and involuntary behavior) and personality instability. The sample was divided into "enthusiasts" and "Beatles resisters," those high and low on beatlemania. Then, the two groups were compared for such things as neuroticism and instability, as measured by psychological tests like the Minnesota Multiphasic Personality Inventory, which measures a respondent's behavior and personality traits. Taylor found some correlations (girls, for example, who were high on beatlemania were more unstable), but overall he saw no cause for alarm as no one in the experimental groups was found to be exceptionally rebellious or antisocial. The New Zealander's study represents, I feel, a surprisingly late left-over of the mood of the fifties. It deals with the Beatles, a group whose historical significance has been said—by those lapsing into an opposite extremism—to exceed that of Jesus Christ (cf. Lewis, 1972:xi). Yet it persists in viewing in youth culture little more than psychoneurotic behavior. This is pseudoscience at its worst.

In the fifties and early sixties, then, youth was relatively tame and apolitical, and society liked it that way. Insofar as incidents occurred, they were viewed as isolated pranks or acts of delinquency. College fraternities might engage in panty raids or "mooning," and teenagers might go on a joy ride. No political or social significance was attached to such actions. In retrospect, those who viewed youth culture as turbulent and subversive even then may have been writing about a preceding era, or merely about their own unsubstantiated fears. The mood of that era has been well depicted in recent films like *Summer of '42* and *American Graffiti*. And it was precisely from that mood that much of the rock

movement of the 1960s (cf. the Mothers of Invention) explicitly wished to depart. As Frank Zappa and other "hippies" later complained, the American adolescent was notoriously immature and incapable of intellectual reflection, political consciousness, aesthetic appreciation, and social innovation.

The troublemakers

As Aries (1968) showed with respect to childhood, one can similarly show that the identity of teenage adolescents has been the social construction of a specific historical epoch; there have been no teenagers and adolescents among the Trobrianders or among the Zunis, or in medieval Europe. It is only in recent Western history that youth became more than a mere demographic category. As Davis (1971) shows, the increasing rate of technological change, urbanization, massification, and specialization in post-industrial society has produced certain problems peculiar to the young only. These include identity loss, fear of failure, and a sense of personality fragmentation. And as sociology teaches us, human beings who share common problems develop common cultures to cope with them, hence the recent emergence of youth culture in Western society. Youth became, along with other categories sharing common life chances, a social class.

Now social classes have historically always first been merely *an sich* (of themselves), and only later *fur sich* (for themselves). This was Marx's way to say that a social class is first a group of people merely sharing common life chances —an objective entity—and only later developing subjective class consciousness, that is, an awareness of itself and of its political and economic interests. To put it succinctly, existence always precedes consciousness.

The history of youth culture is no exception. And as with other social classes, consciousness did not develop until it was triggered by outside agitators, intellectuals, catalysts if you will. As Marx and Engels descended into the lower class so as to ensure the self-fulfillment of their prophecies, so youth rebellion was fueled by several consciousness raisers. Let us trace the role of some of these troublemakers.

Ironically, Madison Avenue was among the first culprits. To tap the rich consumer market that developed among suburban youth after World War II, the concept of teenager was launched. This was to be a harmless label, handy perhaps for the economic and social manipulation of a totally disfranchised minority (cf. Lewis, 1972). However, it soon helped to fuse a new social identity meaningful not only to its millions of youthful occupants, but also to novelists, educators, and sociologists who began to inquire into the human condition behind the label. Thus Madison Avenue may well have contributed a conceptual prerequisite for the emergence of youth class consciousness.

When J. D. Salinger immortalized the adolescent's plight in *Catcher in the Rye,* he tapped a strong ground swell of empathy among the nation's young and not so young. In the late fifties, there was already a restlessness on campus indicating that students would not live by football alone. Something was astir, a quest for more. Poetry anthologies were reported circulating in fraternities.

The beat generation had been operating for a decade. Itself, it consisted initially of men in their twenties and thirties, not boys—war veterans, writers, artists, misfits. Nevertheless, it has been recognized as the first wave of youth rebellion in postwar America, if not in its own membership at least for the inspiration it gave to subsequent youth rebellion and for the example it set for subsequent radicalism. Jack Kerouac's *On the Road* was as great a hit among disaffiliated students as *Catcher in the Rye.* It

symbolized freedom, gut-level experience, rebellion against the regimentation of a bureaucratized society and against Madison Avenue and consumerism. It was the first book that lured masses of young people to the pleasures of drugs, primarily marijuana at that point.

Other members of the beat generation included poets Gregory Corso, Lawrence Ferlinghetti, and Allen Ginsberg. Their work voiced mostly disaffiliation from American materialism, a rebellion that was spiritual rather than militantly political, and above all the pain of artists who had visions of America's ugliness. Ginsberg's *Howl* (1956) begins as follows:

> I saw the best minds of my generation destroyed by madness, starving hysterical naked,
> dragging themselves through the Negro streets at dawn looking for an angry fix,
> angelheaded hipsters burning for the ancient heavenly connection to the starry dynamo in the machinery of night,
> who poverty and tatters and hollow-eyed and high sat up smoking in the supernatural darkness of cold-water flats floating across the tops of cities contemplating jazz

The poem raves angrily on, page after page of sheer pain and suffering. And then comes the indictment of America:

> What sphinx of cement and aluminum bashed open their skulls and ate up their brains and imagination?
> Moloch! Solitude! Filth! Ugliness! Ashcans and unobtainable dollars! Children screaming under the stairways! Boys sobbing in armies! Old men weeping in the parks!
> Moloch! Moloch! Nightmare of Moloch! Moloch the loveless! Mental Moloch! Moloch the heavy judger of men!
> Moloch the incomprehensible prison! Moloch the crossbone soulless jailhouse and Congress of sorrows! Moloch whose buildings are judgment! Moloch the vast stone of war! Moloch the stunned governments!
> Moloch whose mind is pure machinery! Moloch whose blood is running money! Moloch whose fingers are ten armies! Moloch whose breast is cannibal dynamo! Moloch whose ear is a smoking tomb![3]

---

[3]Copyright © 1956, 1959 by Allen Ginsberg. Reprinted by permission of City Lights Books.

Norman Mailer was an off-and-on fellow traveler, his major contribution to beat culture being *The White Negro* (1957), an essay that has remained a classic despite Mailer's customary aberrations. In it, the author argued that the American Negro must function as a role model for the white hipster.[4] The Negro has suffered, and he is stronger and wiser than the white man. His artistic creativity is superior to that of the degenerate Western mind, as shown most clearly in his jazz music. Mailer and the beats subscribed to a reverse racial prejudice, and they proposed a coalition with black America. The effort failed because of black militancy's increasingly separatist stance in the sixties.

Jazz, marijuana, poetry, and disaffiliation with the system were the most salient cultural elements the beat generation transmitted to the counterculture. In addition, the Zen-inspired Eastern spiritualism that would permeate the youth culture of the sixties was also present among the early hipsters. Jack Kerouac's *Dharma Bums* (1958) is one example. More profound, perhaps, was Alan Watts' contribution in this regard. The former Anglican counselor wrote half a dozen books dealing with Zen and mysticism. While some have accused him of vulgarizing Zen for mass Western consumption (cf. Roszak, 1969:132), he was undoubtedly responsible for bringing to America and to its youth some of the philosophy of peace, harmony, and wholism so inherent in Eastern doctrines and so absent from our competitive culture. In addition, Watts was among the first to experiment with psychedelic drugs, and he contributed to the counterculture not only a philosophy of consciousness but LSD insights as well (cf. Watts, 1962). In this, he was not alone. Huxley (1954) before him and Timothy Leary (1965) after both developed philo-

[4]Beat, beatnik, and hipster are synonyms. The word hipster reveals the link between the beat generation of the fifties and the hippies of the sixties.

sophies of which the psychedelic drug experience was to be a cornerstone (see Watts, 1971).

In Europe, Hermann Hesse also made the journey to the East quite early, in fact earlier by far than any of the men discussed thus far. With books like *Siddhartha* and *The Glass Bead Game,* the Nobel Prize winner succeeded where no one else had in invalidating Kipling's classic observation that East and West would never meet. Hesse's genius transcended culture and brought the beautiful mind of India into the heart of the West. But his contribution to the counterculture was posthumous, for his visions were, as those of all great men, ahead of their time.

Apart from everyone else stands the lone figure of Paul Goodman. The angry utopian's acerbic diagnosis of American society is of the utmost relevance here, for it addresses itself directly to the problems of youth. In *Growing up Absurd* (1960) and elsewhere, Goodman dissociates himself from movements like the beat generation. He emphatically concurs that contemporary youth suffers from a meaninglessness and nihilism engendered by a monstrously materialistic society, but he views the productions and the lifestyle of the beatniks as a symptom of the disease rather than as a cure for it. "The beat generation," he writes, "are those who have resigned from the organized system of production and sales and its culture" (1960:170). Goodman felt that World War II, Korea, and the draft in general were the disorganizing forces which swelled the ranks of disaffiliated youth. This was prophetic, for the Vietnam war would, of course, create additional millions of hippies. One may predict that future wars and conscription will further contribute to the manpower of revolutionary youth.

Be this as it may, Goodman explicitly reviews and rejects the philosophy and the existence of men like Kerouac, Ginsberg, and Mailer. In a review of *On the*

Road (1960:279-284) he deplores "the blank of experience in which these poor kids generally live." Their "racing-across-the continent . . . is the woeful emptiness of running away from even loneliness and vague discontent. . . . In our economy of abundance there are also surplus people, and the fellows on the road are among them." Again, there is prophecy here, as Goodman's words apply *a fortiori* to today's street people. And as far as Norman Mailer's "White Negro" is concerned, the author feels that it is mostly idiotic (1960:173).

The beat generation, then, is seen as a pathological reaction to basic societal problems, along with juvenile delinquency and the organization man. What, then, is the problem? The central thesis in *Growing up Absurd* is "that the accumulation of the missed and compromised revolutions of modern times, with their consequent ambiguities and social imbalances, has fallen, and must fall, most heavily on the young, making it hard to grow up" (1960:217) and that what is essentially lacking in America today is a sense of community. It is in this light that Goodman's critique of contemporary youth must be viewed, for, paradoxically, he has few kind words for a youth which he so desperately wishes to save. The kids are empty and nihilistic, lacking patriotism; they suffer only from too much affluence; they lack character and strength; all the beatnik needs is a healthy hunger pang; healthy patriotism in the form of community identification is also needed; what the young need is more real man's work like farming and building houses and less parasitic effeminate activity like advertising; our top-heavy bureaucratized technocracy seems to reward occupations in a ratio that is inverse to their real utility. Man's work, useful and meaningful work, is discouraged by the reward system—teaching is a case in point.

Goodman seems to see few redeeming qualities in contemporary youth, but so-ciety is to be blamed for that. Because of this stance, the utopian critic has been labeled a *mea culpa* apologist of youth dissent (cf. Davis, 1971:5-6), that is, someone who blindly blames himself and his generation for contemporary youth problems. I fail to see Davis's point, as Goodman's perspective in basic sociology. He simply locates the problem in the dominant culture and in the socialization process, in the social system rather than within the young individual himself. Davis's irritation reflects the sociologist's typical noncommittal stance. Goodman, on the other hand, does not stop at analysis; he suggests solutions, and these do not entail a blind acceptance of youthful weaknesses. The philosopher's ideas mix conservatism and radicalism. His critique of the beat generation undoubtedly applies even more to the indolent hippies of the sixties. Yet he became, as Roszak (1969:178-204) shows, the counterculture's willing champion.

The truth of the matter is that, as the Goodman brothers knew,[5] the solutions required to halt the moral and physical decay of our society must be radical and imaginative, transcending old cliches. Thus Goodman does not propose mere "liberation," which so often is a euphemism for permissiveness, and he does not condone the negative retreatism of beatniks and hippies. To divide all educators into a *mea culpa* camp (liberal youth apologists like Goodman and Spock, allegedly) and a *"spoiled brat"* camp (for example, conservative psychologist Bettelheim), as does Davis, is to reduce the complexity of Goodman's analysis to a cliché. In fact, he convinces us that nothing short of a revolutionary change in our entire approach to work, and to life itself, will be sufficient. As it is, young people merely learn to do the wrong things for the wrong reasons. They learn that selling is better than

---

[5]See also *Communitas,* a utopian study of urban planning by Paul Goodman and his architect brother, Percival.

producing, advertising and packaging better than creating, that what counts is whether a product or commodity is profitable, not whether it is useful. And when youth rebellion finally manifests itself—in the form of delinquency—society reacts by not taking it seriously. The adolescent is said to act up because of poor socioeconomic background, alcoholic father, and so on. The policy is to neutralize and desexualize aggressive youth, and psychiatry and other manipulative techniques are supposed to be the appropriate means to that end. Thus the society tries to control its explosive young by robbing them of their last vestiges of pride, dignity, and manhood, rather than by attempting to provide them with work and lives that are meaningful.

Goodman's analysis was the most incisive at the time. It was soon echoed in various forms by other educators and sociologists. In 1963, Friedenberg (1972), for example, wondered whether enough people in America want real freedom to accommodate youthful idealism. And the concern for community first expressed by the Goodman brothers has gradually become a major theme in both conventional urban sociology (cf. Stein, 1960; Swanson, 1970) and radical urban philosophy (for example, Bierman, 1973; Jones, 1971). It is therefore understandable that the movement back to community, a movement of which the counterculture was such a salient part, derived much of its inspiration from Paul Goodman.

The counterculture

The preceding discussion has traced some of the counterculture's philosophical foundations. The continuity between the beatniks and the hippies has been shown.[6] Both subcultures have fol-

lowed a lifestyle of material asceticism combined with sensual and sexual epicureanism; both used and advocated the use of drugs for pleasure and for enlightenment. The beats stayed mostly with marijuana, although they also experimented with peyote, mescaline, and other heavier hallucinogens. The hippies' drug became, more than any other, LSD-25 (acid). The beats listened to jazz, the hippies rock. Thus the beats reached out to the blacks, while the hippies never really built that bridge. Both subcultures borrowed from Zen and other Eastern sources (I Ching divination became a favorite hippie pastime). While both were essentially *artistic* subcultures, the beats were more cerebral, thus relying on the written forms of prose and poetry, while the hippies' primary medium became music. Finally, there was a generational difference. The hippies represent, to use Roszak's (1969:134) term, the adolescentization of American youth rebellion. A hippie, quite literally, is a little hipster.[7] All in all, the beats were more mature than the hippies. But about their interconnectedness there can be no doubt. Even some of the counterculture's membership was a transfusion of former beatniks, as in the case of Allen Ginsberg, and also Jack Kerouac's semimythical hero Dean Moriarty who suddenly emerged a decade later as Neal Cassady, then a member of the Ken Kesey-Grateful Dead family.

Let us now turn to the counterculture.

---

[6]The bohemian tradition goes back much further, of course. I arbitrarily chose to restrict my analysis to the postwar era. Bennett Berger (1967) traces the tradition to its early nineteenth century manifestations.

[7]A note on terminology is perhaps long overdue. The hippie emerged in the mid-sixties as a direct derivation from the hipster, and denoting the younger kid who began to emulate the drop-out music- and drug-centered subculture of the older hipster. Furthermore, hippie generally refers to the retreatist wing of the counterculture, which also includes the activist New Left and possibly other elements. While I recognize and use this distinction in the following pages, I have sometimes used hippies and counterculture interchangeably. As my conclusion will show, it is ultimately the apolitical hippie who is at the hard core of the counterculture.

Youth culture is made up of many sub-cultures (e.g., the fraternity system) and contracultures (e.g., delinquent gangs). As Matza (1961) showed, many of these embody values like courage, justice, and freedom, values which have become increasingly neglected and derided by the dominant majority in the course of our country's history, and which have therefore become the dominant middle-class culture's *subterranean* counterpoint. The counterculture is one such contraculture. It emerged in the mid-sixties and is distinct in that it, alone, has a total and coherent alternative world view. While there is, within the counterculture, an ambivalence between retreatism (the hippies and the cultural revolution) and rebellion (the radical students of the New Left and the political revolution; see footnote 6), at least it *has* ideology. Other youth movements have lacked ideology, and social movements without ideology are doomed to ineffective and ephemeral existences. Because of its strong ideological underpinning, the counterculture has been and will continue to be the most significant social movement since Marxism.

Although sociologists have assembled long lists of "core hippie values," including immediacy, spontaneity, egalitarianism, communalism, feeling, tribalism, intuition, awareness, spiritualism, love, expressiveness, primitivism, naturalness, and many more (cf. for example, Berger, 1967; Davis, 1971; Roszak, 1969; Yablonski, 1968), they agree that one concept more than any other is the key to the counterculture's ideology—freedom. Liberation is advocated at the psychological, sociological, and cultural levels.

Psychological liberation has been identified as the counterculture's most distinguishing feature, as it is in this respect that it is said to depart from earlier revolutionary movements (cf. Roszak, 1969). Hippies differ from the Old Left in their goals as well as in their means. They re-

ject Marxist's objective of class liberation, opting for individual psychic liberation instead; they reject organized politics and violence as revolutionary means.[8] As Roszak sums it up, the counterculture is faced with a choice between Marx and Freud, and its response ranges from the political neo-Marxian stance of the New Left to the psychologistic and apolitical attitude of the hippies, who merely advocate cultural revolution. And each wing derives its ideological inspiration from sources accordingly—the New Left heavily relying on Herbert Marcuse (1962, 1964), whose attempt at synthesizing Marx and Freud remains more political than psychological, and others on apolitical sources such as Norman Brown (1959). Insofar as the counterculture opts for psychic liberation, it is because it considers modern man's central problem to be *alienation,* not economic exploitation.

Psychic liberation means, first, consciousness expansion, awareness and self-exploration. This is accomplished through a variety of means, including Zen, transcendental meditation, yoga, and other Eastern methods, as well as drugs like LSD. Hunter (1972:23) speaks of the mental mutation which perennial LSD users may already have undergone. Speaking of acid freaks, some literally mean a new breed of man—a breed to which, according to Hunter, television may have contributed as much as has LSD.[9]

---

[8] It is interesting to note the left's reaction to the kidnapping of the Hearst daughter—a nearly unanimous rejection of such revolutionary methods by the various New Left organizations.

[9] Analogies between the impact of LSD and television are not uncommon. Whether it be viewed with optimism as by McLuhan (1964) and Hunter (1972), or with disgust as by Rosenberg (1971), there is a fairly widespread tendency to attribute both to television and to LSD such things as the emergence of wholistic consciousness and of gestaltist perception. Future research may determine whether the theory is as absurd as it appears to be.

Second, psychic liberation means the blossoming of emotion, affect, feeling, sentiment, and love, in other words, that which civilization, as Freud stressed, forces man to repress. It is this aspect to which the stereotype of the hippie alludes, a stereotype that places excessive emphasis on the sexual, irrational, and anti-intellectual features of hippie mentality. Related to this is a value which, according to Davis, (1971:14) is perhaps as central to the counterculture as freedom itself—expressiveness. Psychic liberation also means the spontaneous expression, in behavior, in art, and in word, of inner motives. In sum, psychic liberation is the complex social-psychological and cultural change which has been described by so many authors in recent years, either rhapsodically, as did Reich (1970) with his consciousness III, or apprehensively, as did the dominant conservative majority.

At the sociological level—and my distinctions are, of course, merely heuristic (they serve analytical purposes but are artificial)—the counterculture's central import is, in one word, community. Whereas typical features of conventional society are the large-scale organization and the depersonalized secondary group, the counterculture offers a return to primary relationships and intimacy; whereas the dominant interpersonal attitude is instrumental, utilitarian, and egotistical, the counterculture stands for communalism and for relationships based on intrinsic value rather than ulterior payoff. Simmel's (1971) notion of sociability for its own sake, Schmalenbach's (1961) sociological category of communion, and of course Tonnies' (1971) gemeinschaft type grasp well some of the counterculture's central features. The counterculture's return to the natural, to the primitive, and to the communal has been described as neotribalism. McLuhan (1964), Hunter (1972), Widmer (1971), and others see electronic technology and countercultural values blending into a new tribalism that simultaneously goes back to man's primitive past and forges into the twenty-first century. *Hair* (1968) was the counterculture's tribal love rock musical. Tribal families like Ken Kesey's Merry Pranksters (cf. Wolfe, 1968) and Jerry Garcia's New Riders of the Purple Sage (the renamed Grateful Dead), and utopian communes (cf. Kanter, 1972 ; Zablocki, 1971) are representative of the counterculture's social structure. As Eisen (1969:xiv) explains, "rock people have groped for ways to reconstitute the sense of community."

One of the first targets of the counterculture, then, has been the monogamous family, a symbol of middle-class conformity. Rock music is replete with songs that repudiate that institution. For example, one of the sixties' top hits, the Beatles' "When I'm Sixty-four" (1967), speaks derogatorily of valentine cards, domestic chores, gardening, and marriage proposals. The song shows the derision and contempt in which conventional marriage, old age, and petty bourgeois lifestyle are held. Conversely, a song like the Jefferson Airplane's "Triad" (1968) is a profoundly subversive proposal to experiment with alternative forms of sexual bond. Grace Slick's seductive alto invites two lovers to establish a simultaneous family of three. Why not, the song asks, when all love one another? Is this not better than the possessive and exclusionary monogamous Western family?

With this, we are touching upon the third major area in which the counterculture advocates total liberation—culture and leisure. Perhaps the very cornerstone of the counterculture's world view is its opposition to science and technology, opposition which therefore leads it to religion and spiritualism. Davis's (1971) excellent analysis of hippies bears the title "An Expressive-Religious Reaction to the Technocratic

Order," revealing that he considers those elements to be indeed central. And Roszak (1969) devotes more attention to this theme than to any other.

C. P. Snow (1959) coined the concept of the two cultures—one scientific and the other humanistic. Since then, scholars and laymen have struggled with the idea. The struggle has been particularly marked in sociology, a discipline which inherently straddles the distinction, a field where the scientists (quantitative methodologists, positivists, "abstract empiricists," survey researchers, experimentalists, operationalists) are pitted against the humanists (qualitative methodologists, participant observers, interactionists, phenomenologists, ethnomethodologists). With the relatively vigorous comeback of qualitative sociology in recent years, an increasing number of authors have had to choose sides or, at least, to address the issue (cf. Berger, 1963; Blumer, 1969; Bruyn, 1966; Cicourel, 1964; Douglas, 1970a; Filstead, 1970; Gouldner, 1970; Mills, 1959; Zetterberg, 1965). In general, the human disciplines are of course still under the firm control of the positivists.

When historian-sociologist Roszak examines the counterculture, then, it is with the sympathy of the humanist who has long suffered the isolation of the minority man in an overwhelmingly scientific academia. He makes no bones about his hostility toward the technocracy and what he terms "the myth of objective consciousness" (1969, Chapter vii and Appendix; 1973, passim).

The hippies' stance goes further, of course, free as they are from the rationalistic impediments of the academic intellectual. Not only does the counterculture reject science, technology, and philosophical materialism (the notion that ultimate reality resides in the realm of the material and not that of the spiritual), but it goes beyond this, into religious spiritualism. The crucial question divid-

ing philosophers of science and young hippies alike is, What is the nature of truth, and how is it apprehended? The counterculture's answer is that truth cannot be apprehended scientifically and analytically, that it must be experienced through faith, intuition, and wholistically. Hence the popularity of Eastern mysticism, hence also the revival of sectarian religion, the occult (cf. Demerath, 1974; Tiryakian, 1972), and the cult of Christ himself, as illustrated by the rock opera *Jesus Christ Superstar.*

Kingsley Widmer (1971) has pointed out another way in which the counterculture liberates culture and leisure from the grasp of the technocracy. With their strobe lights, Day-glo paints, synthetic materials applied to art, quadraphonic music, and amplified synthesizers, the rock generation has, in some instances, reduced technology to play and thus disarmed and accepted it.

Related to this is another cultural innovation, one that is central to this book. The counterculture has rejected the dominant society's two major economic principles—work and consumption—in favor of a leisure alternative not unlike that advocated by de Grazia and the Epicureans. This is where it becomes obvious that only an affluent postindustrial society could produce a hippie generation, something which is recognized by Marcuse and Roszak (1969:109): "As the excuse of scarcity wears thin, as work discipline with the coming of cybernation relaxes, the performance principle and the domination regimes it supports are called radically and obviously into question. Like Marx in *Capital,* Marcuse takes 'the shortening of the working day' to be the fundamental premise on which the 'true reality of freedom' is founded."

Thus the revolution advocated by the counterculture would "call in question not only capitalist society but industrial society. The consumer's society must perish of a violent death. The society of alienation must disappear from history. We are inventing a new and original world. Imagination is seizing power" (French 1968 revolutionary student manifesto, quoted in Roszak, 1969:22).

In Davis's (1971) conventional sociologese, two of the hippies' major cultural innovations have been their rejection of middle-class compulsive consumption and middle-class deferred gratification. Their "time scale of experience" has been the now and not the future. Work in the traditional sense is rejected, and leisure is the ideal, although it is a creative and active leisure.

Indeed, a fourth element of the counter*culture* has been its rejection of conventional leisure as well, the kind of leisure which consists of passive recreation, consumption, and spectatorship (cf. Davis, 1971). Instead of spectatorship and the worship of entertainment stars, the counterculture opts for a participatory culture in which the star-audience distinction fades (1971). This goes back to the 1950s, when men like Jack Gelber introduced the Living Theater, to the artistic happening in which all those present may participate in the creative process, and even to the traditional jam session in jazz. As Eisen (1969:xii) explains, since the 1950s the art-circuses stratification and the audience-performer barrier have been eroded. The be-ins, love-ins, pop festivals, and street and guerilla theaters of the 1960s were all further extensions of the new participatory conception of art and culture. "Poetry and culture were back in the hands of the people" (1969:xii). Thus the counterculture produced a leveling or democratization of culture. "Part of the rebellion of youth in the 1960s," Eisen continues, "has involved the attempt to move away from hero worship . . . towards greater independence, not greater dependence on charismatic figures" (1969:xiii).

A fifth crucial element of the counter-culture, then, has been its music—perhaps the most conspicuous example of their participatory conception of leisure and culture. The combination of sexual and artistic rebellion contained in the rock music of the past decade was traced by Mooney (1969:25) to a combination of historical trends, including the infusion of "the horde of highly permissive and hedonistic lower classes entering the record market." While middle-class morality was indeed one of the rock culture's casualties, it must be kept in mind that the counterculture's membership has been overwhelmingly of middle-class origin.

Related to this is the youth rebellion's persistent inability to join hands with the other minority—the blacks. This failure may be inevitable in view of the former group's rejection of conventional success values and the latter's desperate belief in them (see, for example, Davis, 1971:26). The downward social mobility of one group and the upward thrust of the other has prevented political coalition between the two against a white power structure which could potentially be defined as a joint enemy.

At the cultural level the cleavage manifests itself in the separation between electronic psychedelic music, which "has been primarily confined to white musicians," and jazz, soul, and blues, which are the black forms (cf. Eisen, 1969). The blues is a musical form—a particular twelve-bar progression of harmonies—and a mood. The mood is rooted in a scale not unlike the classical minor key, and it is therefore similarly melancholic. The blues' inherent sadness is said to reflect the Negro past. Soul is a more generic term. It has been defined as "feeling what you are doing." It is not necessarily sad. James Brown and Isaac Hayes have soul. Whether the adoption of the blues by whites has been successful is the subject of much debate, and so is the question of how much soul there is in psychedelic music. Perhaps the racial barrier cannot be transgressed, but then, does not a song like Donovan's *Abraham, Martin and John* have soul?

Today, rock is in a state of disarray. Since the 1960s the cooptation of the counterculture's music has reached grotesque forms. Used-car television commercials use Santana for background music, ABC's "Wide World of Sports'" background accompaniment is *Jesus Christ Superstar,* and the United States Marine Band's repertoire includes numerous Beatles' songs, songs whose original meaning is the glorification of LSD.

In the seventies, nostalgia is as characteristic of the world of music as it is of other sectors of popular culture. Nothing comparable to the creative thrust of the 1960s is being produced. The typical current teenage star has been Alice Cooper, who, perhaps more than anyone else, sets the tone of the seventies. "His stage show is an elaborate vaudeville of titillating adolescent fantasies, leaning toward sadomasochism and homosexuality . . . . He is a cartoon figure of bizarre appearance and indeterminate sex. Thousands of teenagers emulate him" (Maracotta: 1973). Thus there is a nostalgic falling back on the music of the sixties, as Bob Dylan makes a successful comeback (Orth: 1974), the ex-Beatles continue to hit the charts, and "Great Hits of the Sixties" albums flood the market of the seventies.

Another area of leisure and culture on which the counterculture has put its permanent imprint is sex. As Eisen explained, the rock movement and the counterculture took it upon themselves to subvert the sexually repressive society and the value system on which it has been based since the Enlightenment (1969:xiv). The movement freed the libidinal, that which could be potentially disruptive. Of course, the counterculture has no monopoly on sex. As Kinsey (1953) already reported more than two

decades ago, less than one human copulation in a thousand results in pregnancy. Today with the pill up and the birthrate down, that rate is obviously much lower yet. Nelson Foote (1958) discusses such facts under the heading "Sex as Play," explaining that one of the fundamentally distinguishing features of homo sapiens is that sex, to him, is not merely a biological imperative but, perhaps more significantly, a form of leisure. While this fact can, in our sexually liberated society, no longer sensibly be questioned, it is only the counterculture which developed sex into a true art form. Alan Watts (1971) has described in detail some of the ways in which sex might develop into an elaborate form of leisure and culture, borrowing, for example, from the *Kama Sutra.* As we shall see in a moment, the cultural diffusion to the larger society which has characterized so many of the counterculture's innovations is probably most pronounced with respect to sexual liberation. While it may be argued that in 1975 the counterculture is long dead and gone, there can be no doubt about the permanent contribution it has made to the demise of Puritan sexual morality in the culture at large.[10]

A seventh element in the counterculture's leisure has been more controversial—drugs. This is not the place for an

---

[10]Sexual liberation has, of course, no longer much to do with political liberation. In fact, participation in "avant-garde" or deviant sexual activities may often go hand in hand with extreme conservatism in other realms. Bartell's (1972) paper on swingers, Humphreys' (1970) book on covert homosexuality, and Kando's (1973) study of transsexualism are among the works showing that such groups may often be conservative, suburban, law-and-order, and Republican in their composition, supporting candidates like George Wallace and favoring racial discrimination. The mate-swapping key clubs operating at various air force bases are also illustrative of how permissiveness may be coopted by groups that are otherwise the very antithesis of any kind of liberation movement. It will be seen in a moment that all this falls into place under Marcuse's concept of *repressive desublimation.*

exposition on the use and misuse of drugs by contemporary youth (see footnote 2 for some references on this). However, note should be made that the counterculture has not advocated the indiscriminate use of any and all drugs. There are essentially seven classes of "drugs": (1) stimulants (coffee, tea, tobacco), (2) inebriants (alcohol, marijuana, hashish), (3) psychedelics (LSD, mescaline), (4) sedatives (sleeping pills, tranquilizers), (5) stimulant narcotics (amphetamines, speed, pep pills, weight pills), (6) strong narcotics (hard drugs, heroin, cocaine, opium) and (7) technical poisons ("sniffers," glue) (Hansen and Jensen, 1971:121-122). While the counterculture eventually contributed to the spread of hard drugs, those are actually foreign to its avowed lifestyle, as foreign as are tobacco and alcohol. Stimulants like alcohol and cigarettes are identified with the dominant society and therefore are rejected on that basis (as well as in the context of the organic food–ecology ideology). Hard drugs belong much more to the ghetto subculture. Speed and amphetamines belong to delinquent subcultures like the Hell's Angels. Despite increasing overlaps and the diffusion of all sorts of drugs among all types of subcultures, only two drugs can be said to be central to the counterculture and its lifestyle—marijuana and LSD. Marijuana's function has been mostly recreational, but LSD has also had ideological significance, tying in with the counterculture's philosophy of consciousness. Huxley's (1954:21-22) concept of the *Mind at Large* is relevant here:

Reflecting on my experience, I find myself agreeing with the eminent Cambridge philosopher, Dr. C. D. Broad, "that we should do well to consider much more seriously than we have hitherto been inclined to do the type of theory which Bergson put forward in connection with memory and sense perception. The suggestion is that the function of the brain and nervous system and sense organs is in the main *eliminative* and not productive. Each person is at each moment capable of remembering all

that has ever happened to him and of perceiving everything that is happening everywhere in the universe. The function of the brain and nervous system is to protect us from being overwhelmed and confused by this mass of largely useless and irrelevant knowledge by shutting out most of what we should otherwise perceive or remember at any moment, and leaving only that very small and special selection which is likely to be practically useful." According to such a theory, each one of us is potentially Mind at Large. But in so far as we are animals, our business is at all costs to survive. To make biological survival possible, Mind at Large has to be funneled through the reducing valve of the brain and nervous system.

By experimenting with mescaline, a psychedelic drug similar in effect to LSD, Huxley came in touch with his Mind at Large—with the universe. One of the most intriguing claims of the counterculture and of those who have experienced drug-induced consciousness expansion is that *collective consciousness,* one very different from Durkheim's mechanistic kind, is a possibility. Robert Heinlein, for example, in his science fiction novel *Stranger in a Strange Land,* uses the theme of group mind. He terms it the ability to grok, and means by it a sort of telepathic extrasensory perception which transcends verbal communication and physical barriers. Many youngsters report having had such an experience when taking acid, at a massive pop festival, or under other conducive conditions. It is not clear at this time whether the phenomenon is to be dismissed as a form of collective behavior and an unfounded return to the cult of the occult caused by increasing mental and social stress in our society. The fact is that inexplicably accurate nonverbal communication *has* been observed in such settings as musical groups, social gatherings, and artistic happenings. Musical, physical, and creative group processes are sometimes coordinated so perfectly that the overall rhythm, harmony, and timing cannot be viewed as the mere product of rigorous rehearsal, particularly in so much of modern art, where spontaneous creation supersedes rigorous technical expertise. No easy mechanistic explanations exist for sociocreative processes that are apparently based on intuition, yet in which individualities mesh into perfect wholes. Future science may have to acknowledge the existence of additional communicative levels.[11]

The counterculture has made its innovative contributions in various other areas of leisure and culture as well. In popular culture, music has not been its only area of artistic creativity. It was seen in Chapter 6 that comix and the underground press were, at least for a while, vigorous indicators that the print was by no means dying among the younger generation, as claimed by McLuhan. The plastic, decorative, and figurative arts have all been revolutionized, too. The movement's innovations in the areas of sport, health, and the outdoors should also be touched upon. The ecological movement is a logical outgrowth of the counterculture's philosophy of oneness with the environment and peaceful harmony with nature. Bicycling is its logical cheap and unpolluting mode of transportation. For additional physical exercise, yoga, meditation, and other Eastern forms are proposed, rather than competitive Western athletics. This, too, is in line with a philosophy of peace and harmony instead of Western competitiveness. And in the realm of food, the macrobiotic and health food movements represent a rejection of the increasingly complex and potentially harmful chemical processing to which modern food is subjected, and a return to the organic.

In sum, there can be no doubt that the counterculture of the 1960s produced a vast range of innovations, revolutionizing culture, leisure, and the lifestyle of not only thousands of youngsters and committed hippies, but through a

process of cultural diffusion, millions of middle-class Americans who otherwise remained firmly committed to the established order of things. What remains to be done, now, is to see whether the impact has been merely cultural, or political as well, and if so to what extent.

POLITICS AND THE NEW SOCIETY
More troublemakers

We have argued that the counterculture contains at least two strands—one apolitical (the hippies) and one highly political (the New Left). The preceding section has dealt with the hippie wing and the sources from which it drew its inspiration.

The New Left derived its theoretical and intellectual base from the social criticism of men like Ellul (1964) and Roszak (1973), from communists like Angela Davis, Regis Debray (1967), Che Guevara (1962), and Mao Tse-tung (1962), and above all from the critical sociology of Herbert Marcuse (1962, 1964).

In *One-Dimensional Man* (1964), Marcuse provides a debunking analysis of contemporary technocratic society. Today's domination regime, he begins, is based on technology rather than on terror as in an earlier era. We live in a one-dimensional society, in the sense that "ideas, aspirations, and objectives that, by their content, transcend the established universe of discourse and action are either repelled or reduced to terms of this universe. They are redefined by the rationality of the given system and of its quantitative extension" (1964:12). Thus one-dimensional society is a society no longer capable of qualitative change. The political universe has been closed, as even the working class is integrated into the technocratic system (1964:22-34), thus precluding revolution or dialectic social change. In the realm of culture, "technological rationality is liquidating the oppositional and transcending elements of the 'higher culture' " (1964:56).

---

[11]My thanks, here, to George Harmon for providing the inspiration (grokking?) for some of these ideas.

There is a "wholesale incorporation (of cultural values) into the established order," for example, "through their reproduction and display on a massive scale" (1964:57). Through such a process of cooptation, culture is robbed of its true function, which is to provide a genuine alternative. This is one part of what Marcuse calls repressive desublimation. The other part is sexual permissiveness, which results in the immediate gratification of the *sexual* while denying the truly erotic. "Institutionalized desublimation thus appears to be only an aspect of the conquest of transcendence achieved by the one-dimensional society. Just as this society tends to absorb opposition in the realm of politics and high culture, so it does in the instinctual sphere. The result is the atrophy of the mental organs for grasping the contradictions and the alternatives and, in the one remaining dimension of technological rationality, the *Happy Consciousness* comes to prevail" (1964:79).

The alternative to one-dimensional society is, of course, dialectic history. One-dimensional society is a closed ahistorical system in which past and future are ignored so as to lock in a timeless present. Positivistic social engineering is the appropriate discipline in such a technocracy.

Beyond this, Marcuse provides an analysis of the dominant mode of *thinking* in one-dimensional society. While both pretechnocratic and technocratic societies have had domination regimes, only in the latter do we see personal dependence and the logic of domination becoming rationalized as "dependence on the objective order of things," that is, scientifically justified (1964:144 ff.). Thus potential protest is neutralized, negative thinking turns into positive, and one-dimensional philosophy (e.g., linguistic analysis) replaces the dialectic (1964:170 ff.).

Marcuse is not optimistic about the chances for successful alternatives. Having coopted all potential negation at the social, cultural, and sexual levels, the technocracy makes everyone "happy" and thereby disarms potential protest. However, the very conditions likely to be accomplished by the technocracy—the total automation of repressive labor and the liberation of man for true leisure—are the prerequisites for transcending the technocratic order (1964:231). Furthermore, the critical theorist, Marcuse himself and his like, is there to enunciate the "absolute refusal" (1964:255) and to reject empirical sociology, the pseudo-objectivity of technocratic science, and the quasihappiness of the technocratic order. In the final analysis, Marcuse (and disciples like Angela Davis) seems to rely on an act of faith not unlike that of Camus' existential philosophy. When all else has failed, man is still a rebel; his freedom and dignity are guaranteed in the ontological fact that he can refuse, refuse life itself. There is no determinism.

It is his strong gut-level indictment of the technocratic order which has made Marcuse one of the counterculture's prime spokesmen. But he was not alone. In France, Ellul (1964) had voiced very similar feelings, and recently Roszak (1973) has once again mounted an attack against the enemy, this time arguing that the entire world consists of four types of technocracies—the suave technocracy (America, Europe), the vulgar technocracy (the Soviet orbit), the teratoid technocracy (fascist regimes), and the comic opera technocracy (the third world). Collectively, men like Ellul, Marcuse, and Roszak have provided the intellectual and theoretical base for the New Left's activism.

Political revolution

The counterculture, then, was not merely a retreatist cultural revolution. It was also a political movement, departing from conventional politics both in the *substance* of its objectives and in the *form* of its actions. With respect to substance, the movement has had a clear political platform, pursued vigorously and, as I shall prove, highly successfully. The first item on the New Left's agenda was peace. While the counterculture's vicissitudes have been inextricably intermeshed with the Vietnam episode (sparked and fueled by the escalation and diffused by our disentanglement), the cause of peace antedates Vietnam, as evidenced by the early peace songs of Bob Dylan, Phil Ochs, Donovan, Buffy St. Marie (her unforgettable "Universal Soldier"), and a host of other early folk singers.

The New Left's platform has, secondly, always included the demand for social and racial equality. From the earliest freedom rides to the current Berkeley scene, the radical youth movement has always pursued the political goal of equality. Related to this is a third programmatic point, the New Left's insistence on local autonomy (cf. Bierman, 1973; Jones, 1971). A fourth type of institutional reform demanded by radical youth has been the overhaul of the educational system. Demands for relevance, alternative curricula, and self-governance have been hurled at faculty and administration ad nauseam since the mid-sixties, and while the results have been of mixed benefit to the various parties involved, the point here is that the counterculture's impact on academia has been profound.

A fifth point on the counterculture's political agenda has been legal reform, notably the decriminalization of the so-called victimless crimes, especially marijuana. Finally, there is, of course, the entire ecology movement, again an example of radical political and institutional change for which the counterculture bears much of the initial responsibility.

With respect to form, the New Left's most radical departure from conventional politics has been its opposition to *structure.* Since technocratic bureaucracy and the alienation inherent in mass society are the targets (rather than material poverty or class exploitation), the new politics must, above all, never loose their *participatory experiential* character. The intrinsic reward of the political experience itself remains as important as the extrinsic objective. This is why the meaning of the new politics has often been viewed as that of a game, or an adventure (cf. Laing, 1967; Scott and Lyman, 1970). If the purpose of such labeling is to trivialize student protest, it is misplaced. On the other hand, it is an undeniable fact that such activism has meant, among other things, a shared, self-rewarding and spontaneous experience not unlike the happening. And this conception of politics finds its justification in the need to destructure and personalize the political process. Thus from the beginning of the Provo movement in Amsterdam and Berkeley (cf. Thoenes, 1967), through the activities of Rudi Dutschke and the Students for a Democratic Society in Berlin, the June uprising in Paris, the student movement in Prague, the Free Speech and People's Park episodes in Berkeley, to the recent Amsterdam Kabouters and the current radlib political coalitions in Berkeley and Madison, every manifestation of the new politics has made it a point to dissociate itself as much from communism as from capitalism, because it considers both systems to be bankrupt oppressive regimes. This is why the counterculture and the New Left are the most significant social movements since Marxism. As Servan-Schreiber (1969:18) explains, we are arriving at the end of the long religious war which has, for a century or more, divided the world into capitalists and communists. For the first time since

Marx a significant new world movement is under way, a movement which is as contemptuous of Moscow communists as it is of bourgeois democrats. When in June of 1968 the French Communist party leaders came to join the student rebellion at the Sorbonne, Daniel Cohn-Bendit said, "Here come those filthy Stalinists!" (quoted in Servan-Schreiber, 1969:16). It is Mao Tse-tung and his cultural revolution which provided one of the left-wing cornerstones of the youth movement in the West. The little red book—a new bible for millions of youngsters in the West—had indeed predicted that the Chinese cultural revolution would affect the world at large, undermining the technocratic order everywhere, threatening "all the dominant classes from the Moscow and Peking bureaucrats to the millionaires of Washington and Tokyo" (Servan-Schreiber, 1969:17).

Conclusion: the age of Aquarius, or a return to the dark ages?

The ultimate question about the counterculture is, of course, whether it promises true liberation—the Aquarian age—or a new sort of enslavement instead. Both tendencies are clearly discernible.

Liberation has often been a euphemism for permissive hedonism, sexual promiscuity, and deadly or at least debilitating drug abuse. Leisure could be a mere euphemism for laziness, indolence, and parasitism. The antiempirical ideational stance has often become an excuse for ignorance and superstition. In education, this has manifested itself in a growing contempt for facts and knowledge, and in the society at large there has been a revival of the occult (cf. Demerath, 1974; Tiryakian, 1972) and of astrology, a proliferation of encounter type pseudo-religions led by opportunistic quacks, and the madness of black magic and exorcism. Here, then, are some of the more sinister alternatives to the scientific-

technocratic order emanating from the counterculture.[12]

To the internal enslavement to drugs, placebos, and imbecile beliefs must be added the external enslavement to the commercial interests, disc jockeys, and music impresarios like Bill Graham, Bill Drake, and Tom Donehue (cf. Shearer, 1969), the $2 billion a year record industry, and all the other interests growing rich on the hippie (cf. Pepper, 1972). As Eisen (1969:xiii) noted, "the entertainment industry and its satellites exist not to further the revolution, but to make money, and they exist largely through cultural debasement and the crassest form of exploitation. . . . They'll sell antiwar songs and good poetry just as eagerly as they'll sell the shlock."

Furthermore, disaffiliation with the system has often been a cop-out for total political apathy. Indeed, it could be argued that the counterculture has, by its very nature, to be apolitical. Since politics mean power, organization, and violence, it is foreign to the countercultural ideology. Since, as I showed, psychic liberation was to take precedence over social liberation and since truth, to the New Left, meant personal and biographical experience rather than theoretical doctrine (Roszak, 1969), the movement has focused on remodeling itself, its way of life, its perceptions and sensitivities rather than on society's institutions. The objective of the hippies has been self-consciousness, not class-consciousness. This became clear in rock music. From an early concern with political causes, for example, Pete Seeger, Joan Baez, early

---

[12]This theme was cleverly exploited in *The Omega Man,* a science fiction film about the post-World War III struggle between a lone surviving scientist (Charlton Heston) and the new breed of hippielike antitechnology mutants created by radioactivity. The film is unmitigated fascism, showing Charlton Heston—with God and Christ on his side—weeding out the mutants as if they were no more than vermin.

Dylan, the trend moved toward psyche-delic surrealism and aestheticism, for ex-ample, Crosby, Stills and Nash, late Beatles, late Dylan. Themes of social and racial injustice became less prevalent. Thus the counterculture was unable to build bridges to the young blacks, to fac-tory workers, to the wretched of the earth. As Roszak succinctly pointed out, the movement's major weaknesses were its inability to ally itself with the disad-vantaged, and its vulnerability to exploi-tation as a sideshow of the swinging soci-ety.

At worst, then, the counterculture be-came a case of retreatism and ritualism, in the Mertonian sense. Trachtenberg (1971) voiced a prevalent opinion among intellectuals when he described much of the movement as hedonistic, nihilistic, apolitical, and anti-intellectual. And by the mid-seventies, many felt that youth had come full circle, back to the political apathy and the careerism of the fifties. For the first time in years fraternities were flourishing and youth once again engaged in faddish pranks like "streak-ing," that is, suddenly dashing naked through public places, (cf. *Newsweek*, 1974), a reminiscence of the 1950s. Uni-versity life in 1974 was described under such titles as "The Calm After the Storm" (Solochek, 1974:6-9) and "Where are the 'Rads' of Yore?" *(Newsweek, 1974:32-33)*. And those few youngsters who did not make it back into the system degenerated into a new generation of hoboes. The street people now drifting into Berkeley were a sorry group of winos, beggars and bums, a new skid row generation and nothing more (cf. Mc-Ginn, 1973:El).

However, there is also a brighter side to the picture. While the counterculture did not bring about the age of Aquarius, it did move society toward greater free-dom and equality. At its best, sexual lib-eration has permitted the feelings of closeness and affection hitherto con-strained by a repressive culture to flourish. In its positive sense the new lei-sure has been an active and creative so-cial process, a participatory artistic or recreational activity whose departure from traditional recreation and passive mass spectacle is wholesome. Similarly, the counterculture's critique of positiv-ism has often been beneficial, suggesting constructive alternatives and comple-ments to the narrow scope of Western science.

And in the realm of the political, the counterculture has by no means been re-duced to total impotence. Even in the music, there continues to be a vigorous element of political engagement. Much but not all of rock became apolitical. The Mothers of Invention's music often re-mained engage, as one of Frank Zappa's frequent complaints was the hippies' lack of political consciousness. Chicago is another group whose music continues to reflect concern for the social question. For example, in "Dialogue" (1972) Terry and Peter argue politics. The former is socially conscious and tries to awaken the latter, who is apathetic. In the end both agree to change the world.

There has been a tendency to dismiss the counterculture's impact upon society as ephemeral and minimal. The reaction to Reich's (1970) *Greening of America* was typical of this, as scores of sociolo-gists (cf. Berger, 1971; Nobile, 1971) im-mediately felt called upon to reassure us (and their gnawing anxieties) that the hippies were not about to take over. That was knee-jerk defensiveness. Today, there is a smugness based on the feeling that, thank god, the battle against the hippies has been won. Hence the many articles about the "calm after the storm" and about the quiet campuses of the sev-enties. But let us take stock of some of the movement's direct and indirect politi-cal accomplishments to date. Between the McCarthy and McGovern campaigns, it literally took over the Democratic party, forced an end to the Vietnam war, and retired Lyndon Johnson from office. It has, since then, indirectly been responsible for immobilizing Nixon's drive toward a police state. It has contributed to far-reaching reforms in the educational and occupational structures, instituting ethnic studies, women's studies, alternative studies, and an affirmative action program now imposed upon us by the Washington power structure—thereby literally turning the tables on the dominant conservative majority! It is in large part responsible for the ecology and conservation movements, movements powerful enough to slow down, if not halt, the march of international corporate capitalism. It has elected hundreds of local and national politicians, from the Mayor of Madison to the Berkeley city council to increasing numbers of sympathetic congressmen, an impressive list of accomplishments as it stands. But in addition, who is to say that the current lull in American history is not comparable to those occurring after 1905 in Russia and 1848 in Europe? Is history not replete with temporary restoration periods? Is the Kissinger era not reminiscent of that of Metternich? I suggest that the disposition of the counterculture and the New Left be held in abeyance.

Finally, if one takes into account the *cultural diffusion* emanating from the counterculture, its impact has been truly awesome. Today, the musical market remains under the uncontested domination of rock 'n roll—good and bad. The multifaceted sexual liberation movement, from gay lib to women's lib and from mate swapping to communal marriages, is in large part the product of the counterculture. The lifestyle, hairdo, and attire now characteristic of a world wide uniculture can also be traced back to the first long-haired kids. Similarly, the cult of feeling, love, sensitivity, and spiritualism initiated by the counterculture has become institutionalized in hundreds of

Esalen type encounter groups, a multimillion dollar growth sector in psychology today to which thousands of middle-class housewives and junior executives flock. On the negative side, another wave rippling out from the counterculture is drug use. Marijuana is now smoked in executive suites, at police headquarters, and in elementary schools. Its use will, in some form or another, become legal before the end of the decade. Finally, even our eating habits are undergoing revolutionary change, as more and more people adopt some of the recommendations of the organic health food movement. In sum, I conclude with Lewis (1972) that culture can indeed be a powerful "independent variable," a *cause,* rather than a mere reflection of social change.

THE CHANGING SOCIETY
Changing personality and changing values

As we saw in chapters 1 and 4, there is considerable consensus in the literature on some of the basic features of the cultural and personality changes that are taking place in twentieth century Western society. The study of national character is a slippery area, and generalizations can degenerate into prejudicial stereotypes. However, as Martindale (1967:30) explains, "when pluralities interact in national collectivities they develop common suppositions, pursue conjoint objectives, and measure performance against similar ideas: they form in short, national characters." What I wish to argue in this final section is that the technocratic conditions currently prevailing in Western society—and most of all in the United States—produce a specific type of man and a distinct system of values and attitudes. I am concerned, of course, primarily with attitudes toward work and leisure. Having traced the typical postindustrial social character with particular emphasis on lifestyle preferences, my concluding effort in this book will be to deal with social and cultural change. I shall ask where we are going, as an economic system, as a people, and as a species whose most fundamental needs include self-actualization through creative leisure.

Contemporary American national character has been described and its development has been traced by numerous authors.[13]

Riesman et al. (1950) set much of the tone of the discussion when coining the tradition-directed, inner-directed, and other-directed personality types. One of *The Lonely Crowd*'s interesting and overlooked contributions was the relationship it tried to establish between character and communication media. Long before McLuhan, Riesman noted the essential role of the print in the development of the dominant character under industrialism (1950:87 ff.), the inner-directed personality.

Today, of course, inner-directed man is said to have been superseded by the other-directed personality. This change

---

[13]Some relevant sources in this area include Brameld (1968), Charlesworth (1968), Demone (1968), Ellul (1964), Goodman (1947), Gorer (1940), Leys (1968), Lifton (1972), Marcuse (1962, 1964), Martindale (1967, 1968), Mead (1955), Mills (1951), Ogburn (1922), Riesman (1954, 1967), Riesman et al. (1950), Reich (1970), Sibley (1968), Skinner (1970), Toffler (1970), Turner (1920), Vanderbilt (1968), Wheelis (1958), Whyte (1956).

Papers dealing with American physical character include Theobald (1968) and Zais (1968).

Works dealing with the relationship of character to art, culture, and the media include Clark (1968), McLuhan (1964), and Riesman et al. (1950).

Social character in the context of urbanism is examined by Bacon (1968), Gans (1963), Riesman (1957b), and Simmel (1971).

Consumption and status seeking as dominant character traits are the topic in Packard (1959), and Veblen (1899).

Hedonism, sexuality, and the "fun morality" are the subjects of Ellis (1968), Mills (1940), Sorokin (1947), and Wolfenstein (1958).

Attitudes toward work and leisure are examined by de Grazia (1964), Dulles (1965), Lenski (1963), Riesman (1958), Riesman et al. (1950), and Weber (1958).

has been observed and often deplored since the 1950s. Mills' *White Collar* (1951) and Whyte's *Organization Man* (1956) are among the well-known critiques of the emerging breed. The trend toward the social and away from the individual was, in fact, perceived by Paul Goodman as early as 1947, when that author predicted a future religion of *sociolatry*. Goodman was also among the first to use the concept of technocracy (cf. 1960:218).

Another early analysis along similar lines was provided by Allen Wheelis (1958). It was that psychologist, in fact, who formulated long before Toffler (1970) the thesis that the logarithmic rate of technological change was making increasingly severe demands on human adaptability and the human nervous system. According to Wheelis, today's dominant social character has become the smooth, adaptable role-player, the individual quickly able to alter his values and his reactions. Whereas in the nineteenth century hard work and thrift were important personality traits, today flexibility, warmth, and adjustment are the features with greatest survival value.

Other similar typifications include Reich's (1970) consciousness II, Lifton's (1972) protean man, and many others. Different authors focus, of course, on different variables. Contemporary sociologists have often described the other-directed consumer whose consumption's function is primarily "impressive." This is the generalization of the conspicuous consumption syndrome already noted by Veblen (1899) among the elite. The sensate, hedonistic, and sexual components of the new character structure have been noted by Mills (1940), Sorokin (1947, 1956), and Wolfenstein (1958). The need for adaptability, role playing, and instant decision making is the topic of a book like Toffler's *Future Shock* (1970).

Out of the vast amount of literature in

this elusive realm, certain features relevant to our topic begin to emerge. There seems to be a general consensus that the work ethic of the self-reliant, frugal, and moral Protestant is now an anachronism. The relationship between work and religion postulated by Weber (1958) has been invalidated by Lenski (1963). The theories I have just surveyed and empirical evidence (cf. Dubin, 1963; *Newsweek,* 1973; Seligman, 1965) both indicate that work no longer serves as a source of meaning and identity for a majority of the population. For most industrial workers and for lower-echelon service workers, the focus of life has shifted from work to nonwork. These two realms of life may be conceived of as communicating vases: as work is gradually depleted of its content, psychic value is cathected into nonwork. Alienation from work becomes the rule, with the notable exception of the hard-working and highly motivated vanguard professions described by Wilensky (1963, 1964).

But what does the nonwork side of the equation entail? From the sources I have surveyed, the major characteristics of the new culture are (1) material consumption, (2) social status comparison, (3) group belongingness, and (4) physical pleasure. Today's leisure is a clear reflection of these four fundamental values. What is conspicuously absent from the new leisure, just as it was absent from the previous industrial epoch, is the value of the mind—philosophy and spiritual activity as forms of art and recreation.

The case against the technocracy

In the extensive discussion of the counterculture and of men such as Herbert Marcuse, the case against the technocracy has already been made, particularly from the standpoint of a rebellious youth. Here, I wish to bring together in a brief final formulation the major *scholarly* arguments which have been leveled

at the technocracy, and at the personality, culture, and leisure just discussed. Again, the literature is vast, and the best way to deal with it is to bunch it into groups. The following five categories provide one possible classification: (1) the critical school and the neo-Marxists,[14] (2) the counterculturalists,[15] (3) the aristotelians,[16] (4) the antibureaucrats,[17] and (5) the neo-Malthusians.[18]

These five groups are merely a tentative way to organize the material. While each group focuses on a different aspect of the dominant social system, they all criticize its weaknesses. The critical neo-Marxist position was dealt with earlier when discussing Marcuse. To this group, the problem is not with the technological society in toto, but with capitalism. Alienation (Schacht, 1971), abstraction (Zijderveld, 1971), exploitation (Deitch, 1973), and domination (Marcuse, 1962, 1964) are features endemic to capitalism. This system is in its death throes, however (Schroyer, 1971), and history will, dialectically, bring about a better society. While this group has little sympathy for contemporary Russia, its analysis of history is largely inspired by Marx, and temperamentally, it is on the side of scientific socialism, not the counterculture.

On the other hand, the counterculturalists' indictment of the technocratic order is apolitical. According to Toffler (1970:326), technology itself is at the root of our problems (as it creates an overload in human decision making), and to men like Hunter (1972) and Roszak (1969, 1973), socialism is as outdated a

[14]For example, Deitch (1973), Habermas (1970), Marcuse (1962, 1964), Schacht (1971), Schroyer (1971), and Zijderveld (1971).
[15]For example, Hunter (1972), Jones (1971), Roszak (1969, 1973), and Toffler (1970).
[16]Including Bierman (1973), de Grazia (1964), and Stone (1958).
[17]Men like Ellul (1964), Mills (1951, 1959), and Whyte (1956).
[18]Including Ehrlich (1968), Heilbroner (1974), and Meadows (1972).

concept as capitalism. These men's vision of the new society departs from anything known today, both East and West of the iron and bamboo curtains. They see little value in the Marxian rhetoric, in fact they reject all theory, opting for experience instead.

De Grazia may be termed an Aristotelian, in the sense that his critique of contemporary society stems from ideals first formulated by that Greek philosopher. The good life, according to de Grazia, is the leisure life. Men should cultivate their minds, play music together, and personally act out the life of their community. Bierman (1973) voiced similar feelings, advocating a return to community and to city-state autonomy, and Stone (1958) deplored the massification and depersonalization of both Roman and contemporary spectacles. These men are critical of contemporary mass leisure, mass consumption, and mass politics.

The antibureaucrats' focus is somewhat different. Mills' white-collar worker (1951) and his cheerful robot (1959) and Whyte's organization man (1956) are the product of the bureaucratic ethos and, more generally, of the introduction of *technique* to all areas of life, including human organization (Ellul, 1964). The decline of individualism and the depersonalization of interpersonal relationships are among the technocratic features stressed and deplored by these men.

Finally, there is a group that may be termed neo-Malthusian, as it emphasizes the ecological and demographic limits to industrial growth, limits which mankind, they fear, may already have reached. Ehrlich's alarming report (1968) on the population problem, the Club of Rome's extrapolations of resource utilization over the next century (Meadows, 1972), and analyses like Heilbroner's (1974) recent one all seem to point to ecological Armageddon. The problem, as these men view it, is not political but ecological. While the socialist system may outlast the West by one hundred years because of its superior organizational capability (Heilbroner, 1974), the eventual collapse of the world industrial order is practically inevitable. The technocracy is doomed. The sad part of this scenario is not the inevitability of the end of high mass consumption; one can easily come to terms with a return to more modest consumption, more gemeinschaft, less bureaucracy, more public transportation, more bicycling. No, the frightening part of the neo-Malthusian script is the inevitability of catastrophic conflict and suffering *before* society is forced to mend its ways.

A venture into futurology

With the neo-Malthusian script, I have touched upon the final point on my agenda: a tentative forecast into the future, an effort to see what forms work, leisure, culture, and lifestyle might take during the next century. As I now make my modest contribution to futurology, I must maintain the same healthy skepticism found in Mullins' (1973) discussion of this thriving new branch of sociology. Indeed, it is not clear whether the "Commission on the Year 2000," which includes such perennial would-be prophets as Daniel Bell, Herman Kahn, Margaret Mead, and David Riesman (Mullins, 1973:165) is a farce or not. As a theory group, the futurologists lack both intellectual leadership and social organization (1973:155). Their research centers include the Hudson Institute and the Rand Corporation, organizations which epitomize technocratic one-dimensional thinking. Here, I wish to discuss the future under four distinct possibilities, only one of which is a technocratic extension.

The first extrapolation, then, is the technocratic one. Typical of this kind of futurology is Daniel Bell's *The Coming of Post-Industrial Society* (1973), Herman Kahn's (1962) work on alternative war scenarios, Leonard C. Lewin's *Report from Iron Mountain on the Possibility and Desirability of Peace* (1967), and Skinner's behavioristic brave new world (1970). Bennis (1970), Michael (1970), Skedgell (1970), and Webber (1970), too, depict various aspects of future technology, for example, the information explosion, postbureaucratic leadership, and some political effects of computers. And Veblen had, of course, already hinted at the advent of the technocratic meritocracy more than half a century ago (1914). Many observers are not only aware of where the technocracy is leading us, but also of the pitfalls, problems as well as potentialities of this tendency. Gouldner (1970), Keniston (1970), McLuhan (1964), and Toffler (1970) belong to those who have critically examined some of the predictable consequences—both positive and negative—of scientific human manipulation, electronic communication, and bombardment by consumer requirements.

The technocratic extrapolation implies technocratic leisure. Max Kaplan's Center for the Study of Leisure has produced a film typical of this perspective— *Living with the 20-hour Workweek*. It predicts that each decade will see the average workweek decline by four hours, to a twenty-hour week by the year 2000. It suggests that the postindustrial society will be even more overproductive that ours is today. The decades ahead will see a veritable leisure explosion. Billions of dollars will be invested in the creation of fantastic Caribbean, Mediterranean, and Pacific leisure resorts and in pleasure islands in the remotest corners of the globe. Thousands of people will jet to such places; millions will ski from the Sierra Nevada to the Himalayas. Space tourism will be as common as transatlantic travel is today. The hedonistic pleasures of the flesh will become a way

of life. The film is, in one word, nothing but a fraudulent commercial.

In sum, one scenario frequently encountered in the literature is the technocratic one. Here, the prediction is simply for more, much more of the same. Leisure, consequently, will continue to be nothing but material consumption (in varying degrees of luxury, depending on one's social class), and it will remain sharply separated from work. There are two problems with this script. First, it is one-dimensional, in Marcuse's sense; it is a mere quantitative extension of our current lifestyle, promising therefore no solution to such endemic problems as alienation. Second, it may not be realistic, as it is predicated on continued rapid economic growth. If the incipient decline in the standard of living becomes long-term, then the future society promises not more, but even less technocratic leisure than currently enjoyed by the masses.

This brings us to the second prognosis, in my view a much more likely one. According to neo-Marxists (Deitch, 1973; Marcuse, 1962, 1964; Silber, 1972) and some other economists as well (Dowd, 1974; Heilbroner, 1974), the most important historical fact toward the year 2000 will be the gradual deterioration and eventual demise of capitalism. As economic conditions deteriorate, with inflation and unemployment rising simultaneously, shortages spreading to all areas of the market and organized labor losing more and more of the ground gained since the 1930s, things will get worse before they get better. Internally, the poor will become poorer and the rich will become richer, as wealth, far from being redistributed, flows to banking and corporate interests. Never again will interest rates go below 8% or 10%. Internationally, there will be a certain redistribution as the multinationals, owing no allegiance to the United States, transfer capital and indeed profits to the pockets of Middle-Eastern monarchs and share-holders the world over. The gradual impoverishment of the great American middle class will polarize our society. We shall resemble England, with an elite and a working class. No longer will America be an exceptionally middle-class society, as the internal and the international working classes will more and more resemble each other. The internationalization of American corporate wealth will have been at the expense of the American people.

In the realm of leisure, then, mass culture will become even more "mess culture." As long as society remained relatively affluent, it could afford the luxury of high culture. Now, with the trimming of the fat and the tightening of the belt, high culture, art, and the humanities will receive even lower priorities. As can already be seen in education, subject matter which has no immediate survival value is gradually eliminated in favor of courses in vocational training, applied research, vocational rehabilitation, police science, criminology, social work, welfare work. In junior colleges, paraprofessional staff is prefered to Ph.D's, because it is cheaper and because it trains for short-term action rather long-term knowledge. With the massification of education, the deterioration of literacy, language, and thought itself, high culture will be weeded out of leisure, leaving only impoverished mass spectacle and vulgar display of cathartic violence. With the declining standard of living, fewer people will be able to travel and take advantage of the great outdoors. The material extravagance of American recreation and consumption will be toned down, and our lifestyle will resemble the grim ways of countries like Poland and the Soviet Union. This will be the last chapter of capitalism, a chapter with no immediate foreseeable end, but whose major characteristic is the slow deterioration of the quality of life.

A third script is ecological Armageddon. While the consequences of this would differ from scenario 2—the collapse of capitalism—only quantitatively, the conditions it predicts would be far worse, and the causes it blames are entirely different. We must therefore deal with it separately. The neo-Malthusian doomsday prophecies differ from those of the neo-Marxists in that they are apolitical. The causes of the imminent collapse of our civilization are considered to be primarily demographic (Ehrlich, 1968) and ecological (Heilbroner, 1974; Meadows, 1972). Ehrlich, for example, offers us three alternative scenarios for the 1970s (1968:72-80). In each, the world is viewed as an interdependent system in which population pressure, politics, war, and resource depletion are in mutual interaction. The crucial variable is, of course, population. According to Ehrlich, it is both the key to and the cause of the world's ills. The Club of Rome's report (Meadows, 1972) extrapolates five variables—population, pollution, food production, and industrial and natural resources. It predicts, through the computer simulation of allegedly *all* possible combinations of factors, inevitable collapse before the year 2100 at the latest, probably much earlier. Heilbroner (1974) is similarly fatalistic, attributing to the socialist system a temporary advantage (of no more than a century) due to its organizational superiority, but eventually predicting catastrophic decline for the entire world.

Leisure, culture, and lifestyle would, under these conditions, be unrecognizable. Not only would creative participatory leisure and high culture vanish, but so would passive mass leisure and spectacles, as social and personal disorganization would become pervasive. There would be a return to the dark age of ignorance and illiteracy. Social organization would perhaps be of the fragmented feudal type, based on agrarian tribalism and isolated, self-sufficient communities. Life would be cheap and unsafe both within and outside such groups. One element of which the future belief system would be an extension is already present: the growing popularity of astrology, satanism, exorcism, and other occult beliefs. Under scenario 3, whatever "culture" might deserve that name would be essentially the triumph of these elements.[19]

Finally, let me outline a fourth scenario, my favorite one.[20] Predictably, perhaps, it is an extrapolation of many elements found in the counterculture. The postindustrial utopia, as envisioned by a number of idealistic philosophers, will be a *cooperative* economic system (cf. Warbasse, 1972), a *Communitas* (cf. Goodman and Goodman, 1947) based on a subsistence economy in which each individual will work one year out of seven. It will be an autonomous city-state (Bierman, 1973), not a cog in a mass society. It will be an extension of the experiments in local control, consumer cooperation, and community action currently under way in places like Berkeley (cf. Jones, 1971).

The key word to an understanding of work, leisure, and lifestyle under scenario 4 is integration. In the literature on cultural change, one finds an increasing number of statements about integration and vanishing distinctions. Thus Riesman et al. (1950) and Stone (1958) already noted a blurring between age categories, social classes, and even the sexes. These various demographic groups no longer constitute distinct cultural and social-psychological entities. Middle-aged men are "boys," both sexes blur into unisex, and everyone becomes a middle-class consumer. Similarly, Stone (1958) pointed out, work and play are in increasing interpenetration. For example, for increasing numbers of professionals and white-collar workers, work is as much at home as at the office, and the business luncheons, committee meetings, and golf-course negotiations are as much leisure as work. Then there is the interpenetration of cultural form and content, medium and message, applauded by McLuhan (1964) and deplored by Boorstin (1961). Also, mass production has erased much of the distinction between the lifestyle of the mass and that of the elite. The difference between owning a Lincoln Continental and owning a Chevrolet is not as great as that between owning an automobile and owning a mule. Yet that is how class distinctions and status symbolism now manifest themselves. These, then, are some of the culture-integrative tendencies noted by sociologists in recent years.

For our purpose, the most important integrative trend is that between work and leisure. A distinction traditionally central to our culture has been that between work and nonwork, production and consumption. The production process has been alienating, demanding, and from eight-to-five. The consumption process has been the passive consumption of commodities or culture after-hours. The two have not intermeshed. Today, however, an increasingly widely accepted tenet of the sociology of work and leisure is that *the solution to both problems of work—alienation—and problems of leisure—passivity—must be sought in their mutual integration.* The traditional active-passive dichotomy must fall.

---

[19]Walter Miller's *Canticle for Leibowitz* and the aforementioned film *The Omega Man* are two recent science fiction visions of what I have in mind under scenario 3.

[20]My distinction between the four alternative scripts presented is, of course, merely heuristic. A fifth and most probable prognosis is pluralism, or a combination of elements from the various models. This would perhaps be a regional pluralism, with different parts of the world approximating the different situations I have described. Davis's (1971) idea of a trifurcated future society is akin to this: according to that vision, the technocracy, the hippies, and the third world people will coexist.

As Parker (1971:116) indicates, there are essentially two philosophies in this respect. On the one hand, we have "those who advocate the differentiation of work and leisure as the solution to at least some of the problems in either sphere," and they do so "on the assumption . . . that the segmentation of spheres is a characteristic and desirable feature of modern industrial society." Representatives of the differentiation school include industrial sociologists Robert Dubin in the United States and Georges Friedmann in France. On the other hand, we find those who advocate the *integration* of work and leisure on the basis of the recognition that leisure cannot be made more creative unless work is also creative. Today, there is overwhelming evidence to suggest that this is the correct position (see, for example, Havighurst and Feigenbaum, 1959; Meyersohn, 1972; Parker, 1971). Sociologists who advocate work-leisure integration include Ellul (1964), Parker (1971), and Seligman (1965), as well as Riesman, who originally opposed it (cf. Parker, 1971:120). In a recent anthology titled *Work and Nonwork in the Year 2001* (Dunnette, 1973:9) all authors agree that work and nonwork will become less differentiable, as opportunities for increased work fulfillment become more numerous. Gabor (1964), who views the age of leisure as one of the three major threats to our civilization (along with nuclear war and overpopulation), also stresses the need to transcend the work-leisure dichotomy, and so does Greenberg (1958). The consensus, then, seems widespread.

We thus arrive at a prognosis and an ideal. It seems probably that work and nonwork will become increasingly integrated, and that this will be the key to many current problems in both spheres. Our leisure ideal borrows from de Grazia's Aristotelian concept and from the counterculture. Ideally, the future society will provide freedom for creativity. The work-leisure distinction will vanish, and so will that between audience and performer, between passive spectatorship and active participation. Music, games, and entertainment will become *happenings,* permitting the free democratic participation by all. Art will become public again (Heckscher, 1968). Education, too, will become a creative participatory process involving all, not merely the teacher. Such freedom will not preclude learning and growing, as gurus, teachers, coaches, and facilitators will continue to gently and firmly show the way to greater perfection. As Davis (1967) predicted, some day we shall all be hippies.

SUMMARY AND CONCLUSION

This final chapter has dealt with social and cultural change from an intergenerational perspective. Focusing on youth, dissent, and countercultural innovations in the realm of leisure and popular culture, I concluded the book with a number of alternative scenarios for the remainder of the twentieth century. Throughout this chapter I have emphasized the dual and inseparable nature of the subject matter: leisure is not only a cultural but also a political phenomenon.

The first discussion, then, focused on culture. First, a brief characterization was given of the quiet fifties, when campuses and youth in general exhibited little turmoil but also little creativity. Then, the first rumbles of criticism, youth dissent, and cultural innovation were traced. The beat generation of the fifties was discussed and identified as the major progenitor of the counterculture of the sixties. Allen Ginsberg (*Howl,* 1956), Norman Mailer (*The White Negro,* 1957), and Jack Kerouac (*On the Road,* 1957; *The Dharma Bums,* 1958) were among the beats' main spokesmen. Others who were to exert a profound influence upon the youth culture of the sixties include Aldous Huxley (*The Doors of*

Perception, 1954), Alan Watts, Timothy Leary (the cult of LSD), and Hermann Hesse (Eastern culture and philosophy). Of particular importance was Paul Goodman (*The Empire City,* 1947; *Growing up Absurd,* 1960), whose social criticism is more political than cultural. Inspired by such sources, triggered by the Vietnam war, and responding to such long-term macrostructural trends as massification and bureaucratization, the under-thirty generation of the sixties began to gravitate toward a new ideology, representing the most significant social movement since socialism. The generic term for this youth movement is counterculture, and the hippie is its most obvious symbol, although he, as we saw, only represents the retreatist wing of a movement which also includes a strong rebellious faction. Just as all forms of socialism, communism, and Marxism rally around one word—equality—so the countercultural groups found in the various industrial nations (while the movement has been an international phenomenon, it is a manifestation of affluent, postindustrial civilization, absent from the underdeveloped world), rally around freedom, liberation. In this analysis, I examined the specifics of countercultural liberation at three levels: psychological, social-structural, and cultural.

At the psychological level the counterculture's cult of consciousness expansion and its return to affect and sentiment was documented.

At the social level the counterculture, we saw, advocates a return to community (gemeinschaft) and communal lifestyles as opposed to the conventional monogamous nuclear family.

Culturally, we examined the counterculture's position in terms of C. P. Snow's two cultures—the scientific and the humanistic orientations. It was noted that the counterculture is firmly on the side of the humanistic value-orientation. In addition, its core cultural values include mysticism, leisure over work, specifically an active, participatory, and creative kind of leisure rather than one characterized by a sharp spectator-performer distinction. Music has been the counterculture's main form of expression, but I have argued that the hippies failed to culturally reach out to the members of the third world community, and the recent deterioration of rock was also noted. Sexual liberation has been another noticeable contribution of the counterculture, a contribution which has probably been coopted by the dominant society more than any other element. It was noted that the ultimate perversion of this process, leading as it does to mate-swapping, pornography, massage parlors, and other forms of "liberated" sexuality embraced by groups that could, ideologically, not be further removed from the counterculture, groups that have mechanized sex and emptied it of the very element emphasized the most by the counterculture—love. Drugs, we saw, are a further important element of the countercultural lifestyle, along with the speculations about heightened interpersonal sensitivity (telepathy?). Finally, the counterculture's innovations in the realms of sports (yoga, transcendental meditation), eating (organic food), and man's relations to nature (ecology) were also noted.

The second discussion in this chapter dealt with the political facet of the counterculture. First, men like Herbert Marcuse (*One-Dimensional Man,* 1964) and Theodore Roszak (*The Making of a Counterculture,* 1969; *Politics and Transcendence in Post-Industrial Society,* 1973), who inspired, or recorded, much of the counterculture's political position were discussed. It was then noted that the New Left—the political wing of the counterculture—departs from conventional politics both in *form* and in *content.* With respect to form, the new politics emphasize the participatory and the experiential, as against the structured and the organizational aspects typical of conventional politics. Thus countercultural politics have sometimes been viewed as a game, an adventure, an intrinsically rewarding activity, departing from conventional politics, which are, by definition, means to ulterior ends. With respect to substance the New Left's agenda includes peace, social and racial equality, local autonomy, educational reform (student governance), the decriminalization of victimless crimes, and the cessation of environmental plunder by corporate interests. The main point of these pages was to emphasize the counterculture's dual constituency. It consists, in the Mertonian sense, of a retreatist wing (the hippies) and a rebellious one (the New Left). At the conclusion of this discussion, we examined the counterculture's potential both for enlightened liberation and for a return to the most sinister forms of barbarism. Drugs, ignorance, disregard for empirical facts, commercial cooptation by the dominant society, retreatism from the society at large, and chaotic social relations due to an absence of structure and patterned behavior are among the movement's most notable weaknesses. However, the counterculture has already had a permanently wholesome impact upon the larger society. From peace in Vietnam to Watergate and from ecology to art and fashion, there is hardly an area in which the youth movement of the sixties has failed to put its progressive imprint. And as to whether the cultural revolution is dead or not, the current lull could indicate either the permanent restoration of the ancien regime, or merely an episode comparable to that following so many abortive but merely preliminary revolutions in the past.

The final discussion in this chapter attempted to deal with social and cultural change in a larger perspective. First, I traced again the recent changes in American national character noted by so many sociologists—from inner-direction to other-direction, from work to consumption orientation, from consciousness I to consciousness II. The typical contemporary American, observers concur, is the organization man, the bureaucrat, the conformist, the status seeker, the adaptable role-player. This is all the outcome of industrialization and bureaucratization—in short the advent of the technocracy. In the subsequent pages, therefore, the major arguments found in the literature against the technocracy were once again summed up and categorized. The arguments of the critical neo-Marxists, the counterculturalists, the Aristotelians, the antibureaucrats, and the neo-Malthusians were distinguished and discussed. While the arguments differ, they all point to alleged deficiencies in the lifestyle of the typical contemporary advanced society. Finally, I concluded this book with a tentative series of social forecasts. The future may be a further accentuation of technocratic capitalism; it may be the gradual deterioration of capitalism; it may come to total ecological disaster; or it may, finally, bring about the true leisure society. Whichever of these four scenarios turns out to be the final script (and they are, of course, not mutually exclusive), each carries with it clear indications of what leisure and lifestyle will be. In terms of probabilities, current indications point most strongly toward further technocracy as well as worsening contradictions in our economic system and the end of limitless environmental abundance. Thus the advent of the Aristotelian leisure ideal is perhaps—while the most desirable—the least likely prospect. Yet it is a dialectic fact of history that decline leads to growth, problems contain their solutions, and crisis produces victory. Thus I propose, with some faith, that the stormy chapter with which Western society seems to be bent on concluding the twentieth century may also contain the seeds of a new age of tranquility, wisdom, and happiness.

STUDY QUESTIONS

1. Trace the continuity between the isolated cases of youth dissent manifesting themselves during the quiet fifties, for example, the beat generation, and the massive counterculture of the sixties. Who were the beats' main spokesmen? What other important figures were responsible for spreading the cult of LSD, consciousness expansion, Eastern philosophical ideas, and radical communalism among the under-thirty generation? Who were some of the political ideologues who inspired the politics of the New Left?

2. Discuss the background, origin, and composition of the counterculture as follows: trace the specific historical events and the long-term sociological trends that finally led to massive youth dissent. Then, show how the counterculture has actually been a dual social movement, consisting of a retreatist wing that advocates, at best, cultural revolution (the hippies), and a rebellious activist wing that proposes political revolution (the New Left).

3. Discuss the counterculture's innovations at the psychological, social-structural, and cultural levels. Show how, in each case, the focus is on liberation from existing forms and patterns of behavior. Show what the cultural revolution means, with specific reference to the following areas: philosophical orientation, religion, work and leisure, music, sexual behavior, drugs, sports, diet, and living within the natural environment. Show also the shortcomings and perversions to which many of these innovations have led.

4. Discuss the counterculture's political wing—the New Left—with reference to the two ways in which the new politics propose to depart from conventional politics. It has been said that the new politics differ from the old not only in content but also in *form*. Explain and elaborate this point. Then, discuss the main *substantive* reforms that are on the New Left's agenda.

5. Appraise the counterculture's contributions to society, the positive as well as the negative side of the balance sheet, and estimate the influence it has exerted on the dominant society thus far as well as its potential for significant future influence. What major *political* developments can, directly or indirectly, be traced back to the counterculture? How about the movement's *cultural* impact? What are some of the more destructive tendencies found in the new "liberation"? Finally, what should we conclude at this point about the final disposition of the (cultural) revolution?

6. Go, once again, over the main arguments that have been made against the technocracy, that is, the type of social system currently dominant in the world. Explain, specifically, what has been said by critical sociologists (the neo-Marxists), the counterculturalists, the Aristotelians, the antibureaucrats, and the neo-Malthusians. Give specific names of authors classified in each of these groups, and explain why they have been so pegged. What fundamental assumption do all these schools share? Finally, which, if any, of these arguments are you in greatest sympathy with? Why?

7. Discuss the four forecasts I propose for the conclusion of the twentieth century. Describe the kind of leisure that is most likely to accompany each scenario. Which of these predictions is most likely to come out, according to this book, and according to you? Do you see alternative possibilities not covered in this book? Which ones?

REFERENCES

Ald, Roy
1970   The Youth Communes. New York: Tower Publications, Inc.

Alinsky, Saul D.
1969   Reveille for Radicals. New York: Random House, Inc.

Alpert, Richard and Sidney Cohen
1966   LSD. New York: The New American Library, Inc.

Anderson, Walt
1969   The Age of Protest. Pacific Palisades, Calif.: Goodyear Publishing Co., Inc.

Aries, Phillip
1968   Centuries of Childhood. New York: Vintage Books.

Bacon, Edmund N.
1968   "American homes and neighborhoods, city and country." Annals of the American Academy of Political and Social Science (July): 117-129.

Barry, Thomas
1970   "Why there can't be another Woodstock." Look Magazine (August 25):28-30.

Bartell, Gilbert D.
1972   "Group sex among the mid-Americans." Pp. 292-303 in Joann S. DeLora and Jack R. DeLora (eds.), Intimate Lifestyles— Marriage and Its Alternatives. Pacific Palisades, Calif.: Goodyear Publishing Co., Inc.

The Beatles
1967   Sgt. Pepper's Lonely Hearts Club Band. Capitol Records (SMAS 2653).

Becker, Howard S.
1970   Campus Power Struggle. Chicago: Aldine Publishing Co.

Bell, Daniel
1960   The End of Ideology: On the Exhaustion of Political Ideas in the Fifties. New York: The Free Press.

1973   The Coming of Post-Industrial Society: A Venture in Social Forecasting. New York: Basic Books, Inc., Publishers.

Belz, Carl
1969   The Story of Rock. New York: Oxford University Press.

Bennis, Warren G.
1970   "Post-bureaucratic leadership." Pp. 33-56 in Donald N. Michael (ed.), The Future Society. New Brunswick, N. J.: Transaction Books.

Berger, Bennett M.
1967   "Hippie morality: more old than new." Transaction (December): 19-27.
1971   "Audiences, art and power." Transaction (May): 27-30.

Berger, Peter L.
1963   Invitation to Sociology. New York: Anchor Books.

Berger, Peter L. and Brigitte Berger
1971   "The blueing of America," New Republic (April 3):20-23.

Bettelheim, Bruno
1969   "Student revolt: the hard core." Vital Speeches (April 15):405-410.

Bierman, A. K.
1973   The Philosophy of Urban Existence. Athens, Ohio: Ohio University Press.

Blum, R. et al.
1964   Utopiates: The Use and Users of LSD 25. New York: Atherton Press, Inc.

Blumer, Herbert
1969   Symbolic Interactionism, Perspective and Method. Englewood Cliffs, N. J.: Prentice-Hall, Inc.

Boorstin, Daniel J.
1961   The Image: A Guide to Pseudo-Events in America. New York: Harper & Row, Publishers.

Braden, William
1970   The Age of Aquarius. Chicago: Quadrangle Books, Inc.

Brameld, Theodore
1968   "The quality of intellectual discipline in America." Annals of the American Academy of Political and Social Science (July):75-82.

Braun, D. Duane
1969   Toward a Theory of Popular Culture: The Sociology and History of American Music and Dance, 1920-1968. Ann Arbor, Mich.: Ann Arbor Publishers.

Brown, Norman
1959   Life Against Death. Middletown, Conn.: Wesleyan University Press.

Brustein, Robert
1971   Revolution As Theatre. New York: Liveright.

Bruyn, Severyn T.
1966   The Human Perspective in Sociology.

Englewood Cliffs, N. J.: Prentice-Hall, Inc.

Charlesworth, James C. (ed.)
1968   The changing American people: are we deteriorating or improving? Annals of the American Academy of Political and Social Science 378 (July).

Cicourel, Aaron V.
1964   Method and Measurement in Sociology. New York: The Free Press.

Clark, Wesley C.
1968   "The impact of mass communication in America." Annals of the American Academy of Political and Social Science (July):68-74.

Davis, Fred
1967   "Why all of us may be hippies some day." Transaction (December): 10-18.
1971   On Youth Subcultures: The Hippie Variant. New York: General Learning Corporation.

Davis, Fred and Laura Munoz
1968   "Heads and freaks: patterns and meanings of drug use among hippies." Journal of Health and Social Behavior ix (June):156-164. Also pp. 137-147 in John H. McGrath and Frank R. Scarpitti (eds.), Youth and Drugs: Perspectives on a Social Problem. 1970. Glenville, Ill.: Scott, Foresman and Company.

Davis, Kingsley
1972   "The sociology of parent-youth con-
(1940)   flict." Pp. 93-104 in Peter K. Manning and Marcello Truzzi (eds.), Youth and Sociology. Englewood Cliffs, N. J.: Prentice-Hall, Inc.

Debray, Regis
1967   Revolution in the Revolution? New York: Grove Press, Inc.

de Grazia, Sebastian
1964   Of Time, Work and Leisure. New York: Anchor Books.

Deitch, David
1973   "Inflate and rule: the new capitalist strategy." The Nation (November 12):496-500.

Demerath, N. J., III
1974   A Tottering Transcendence: Civic vs. Cultic Aspects of the Sacred. Indianapolis, Ind.: The Bobbs-Merrill Co., Inc.

Demone, Harold W., Jr.
1968   "Mental illness, alcoholism and drug dependence." Annals of the American Academy of Political and Social Science (July):22-33.

Denisoff, R. Serge and Richard A. Peterson
1972   The Sounds of Social Change. Chicago: Rand McNally & Co.

Douglas, Jack D.
1970a   Understanding Everyday Life. Chicago: Aldine Publishing Co.
1970b   Youth in Turmoil. Washington, D. C.: U. S. Government Printing Office.

Dowd, Douglas F.
1974 "Structural instability." Society (January-February):15-18.

Dubin, Robert
1963 "Industrial workers' worlds: a study of the central life interests of industrial workers." Pp. 53-72 in Erwin O. Smigel (ed.), Work and Leisure—A Contemporary Social Problem. New Haven, Conn.: College and University Press.

Dulles, Foster Rhea
1965 A History of Recreation: America Learns to Play. New York: Appleton-Century-Crofts.

Dunnette, Marvin D.
1973 Work and Nonwork in the Year 2001. Belmont, Calif.: Wadsworth Publishing Co., Inc.

Ehrlich, Paul R.
1968 The Population Bomb. New York: Ballantine Books, Inc.

Einhorn, Ira
1972 78-187880. New York: Anchor Books.

Eisen, Jonathan
1969 The Age of Rock. New York: Random House, Inc.
1970 The Age of Rock 2. New York: Random House, Inc.
1971 Twenty-Minute Fandangos and Forever Changes (a reader). New York: Vintage Books.

Ellis, Albert
1968 "Sexual promiscuity in America." Annals of the American Academy of Political and Social Science (July):58-67.

Ellul, Jacques
1964 The Technological Society. New York: Alfred A. Knopf, Inc.

Fairfield, Richard
1972 Communes, USA—A Personal Tour. Baltimore: Penguin Books, Inc.

Feuer, Lewis S.
1969 The Conflict of Generations. New York: Basic Books, Inc., Publishers.

Filstead
1970 Qualitative Methodology: Firsthand Involvement with the Social world. Chicago: Markham Publishing Co.

Flacks, Richard
1972 "Social and cultural meanings of student revolt: some informal comparative observations." Pp. 325-343 in Peter K. Manning and Marcello Truzzi (eds.), Youth and Sociology. Englewood Cliffs, N. J.: Prentice-Hall, Inc.

Foote, Nelson N.
1958 "Sex as play." Pp. 335-339 in Eric Larrabee and Rolf Meyersohn (eds.), Mass Leisure. Glencoe, Ill.: The Free Press.

Friedenberg, Edgar Z.
1972 "The image of the adolescent minority." Pp. 30-38 in Peter K. Manning and Marcello Truzzi (eds.), Youth and Sociology. Englewood Cliffs, N. J.: Prentice-Hall, Inc.

Gabor, Dennis
1964 Inventing the Future. London: Pelican Books.

Gans, Herbert
1963 "Effects of the move from city to suburb." Pp. 184-198 in Leonard Duhl (ed.), The Urban Condition. New York: Basic Books, Inc., Publishers.

Gillett, Charles
1972 "The black market roots of rock." Pp. 274-281 in R. Serge Denisoff and Richard A. Peterson (eds.), The Sounds of Social Change. Chicago: Rand McNally & Co.

Ginsberg, Allen
1956 Howl and other Poems. San Francisco: City Lights Books.

Gliner, Robert
1973 American Society as a Social Problem. New York: The Free Press.

Gliner, Robert and R. A. Raines
1971 Munching on Existence. New York: The Free Press.

Goodman, Paul
1947 The Empire City. New York: The Macmillan Company.
1960 Growing Up Absurd. New York: Random House, Inc.

Goodman, Paul and Percival Goodman
1947 Communitas: Means of Livelihood and Ways of Life. New York: Random House, Inc.

Gorer, Geoffrey
1940 The American People. New York: W. W. Norton & Company, Inc.

Gouldner, Alvin W.
1970 The Coming Crisis of Western Sociology. New York: Basic Books, Inc., Publishers.

Gouldner, Helen P.
1970 "Children of the laboratory." Pp. 115-131 in Donald N. Michael (ed.), The Future Society. New Brunswick, N. J.: Transaction Books.

Goulet, Denis
1971 "The troubled conscience of the revolutionary." Pp. 56-75 in Irving Louis Horowitz (ed.), The Troubled Conscience: American Social Issues. Palo Alto, Calif.; James E. Freel and Associates.

Greenberg, Clement
1958 "Work and leisure under industrialism." Pp. 38-42 in Eric Larrabee and Rolf Meyersohn (eds.), Mass Leisure. Glencoe, Ill.: The Free Press.

Guevara, Che
1962 In The Marxists, by C. Wright Mills. New York: Dell Publishing Co.

Habermas, Jurgen
1970 Toward a Rational Society: Student Protest. Science and Politics. Boston: Beacon Press.

Hallie, Phillip P.
1971 "Justification and rebellion." Pp. 247-264 in Nevitt Sanford and Craig Comstock (eds.), Sanctions for Evil. San Francisco: Jossey-Bass, Inc., Publishers.

Hansen, Soren and Jesper Jensen
1971 The Little Red Schoolbook. London: Stage 1.

Harris, David
1971 "On the necessity of revolution." Pp. 149-155 in W. Ron Jones (ed.), Finding Community: A Guide to Community Research and Action. Palo Alto, Calif.: James E. Freel and Associates.

Havighurst, Robert J. and Kenneth Feigenbaum
1959 "Leisure and life-style." American Journal of Sociology (January)396-404.

Hayakawa, S. I.
1957 "Popular songs vs. the facts of life." Pp. 393-403 in Bernard Rosenberg and David Manning White (eds.), Mass Culture: The Popular Arts in America. New York: The Free Press.

Heckscher, August
1968 "Changing styles in art and entertainment." Annals of the American Academy of Political and Social Science 378 (July):109-116.

Hedgepeth, William and Dennis Stock
1970 The Alternative. New York: The Macmillan Company.

Heilbroner, Robert
1974 "The human prospect." New York Review of Books (January 24):21-34.

Heinlein, Robert A.
1961 Stranger in a Strange Land. New York: Berkeley Medallion Books.

Hesse, Hermann
1951 Siddhartha. New York: New Directions Publishing Corp.
1969 The Glass Bead Game. New York: Holt, Rinehart & Winston, Inc.

Hollingshead, August B.
1949 Elmstown's Youth. New York: John Wiley & Sons, Inc.

Holmes, Douglas
1970 "Selected characteristics of hippies in New York City: an overview." Conference on Drug Usage and Drug Subcultures, Asilomar, Calif.: (February).

Horowitz, Irving Louis
1971 "Rock on the rocks, or bubblegum, anybody?" Pp. 459-465 in Bernard Rosenberg and David Manning White (eds.), Mass Culture Revisited. New York: Van Nostrand Reinhold Company.

Horton, Donald
1957 "The dialogue of courtship in popular song." American Journal of Sociology (May):569-578.

Humphreys, Laud
1970 Tearoom Trade. Chicago: Aldine Publishing Co.

Hunter, Robert
1972 The Storming of the Mind. Inside the Consciousness Revolution. New York: Anchor Books.

Huxley, Aldous
1954 The Doors of Perception. New York: Harper & Row, Publishers.

Illich, Ivan D.
1971 Celebration of Awareness. A Call for Institutional Revolution. New York: Anchor Books.

Jefferson Airplane
1968 Crown of Creation. RCA Victor (LSP 4058).

Jencks, Christopher
1969 "Limits of the New Left." Pp. 360-367 in Judson R. Landis (ed.), Current Perspectives on Social Problems, 2nd ed. Belmont, Calif.: Wadsworth Publishing Co., Inc.

Jencks, Christopher and David Riesman
1968 The Academic Revolution. New York: Doubleday & Company, Inc.

Jones, W. Ron
1971 Finding Community: A Guide to Community Research and Action. Palto Alto, Calif.: James E. Freel and Associates.

Kahn, Herman
1962 Thinking About the Unthinkable. New York: Avon Books.

Kando, Thomas
1973 Sex Change. Springfield, Ill.: Charles C Thomas, Publisher.

Kanter, Rosabeth Moss
1972 "Communes." Pp. 114-120 in Peter K. Manning and Marcello Truzzi (eds.), Youth and Sociology. Englewood Cliffs, N. J.: Prentice-Hall, Inc.

Keniston, Kenneth
1968 Young Radicals: Notes on Committed Youth. New York: Harvest Books.
1970 "How community mental health stamped out the riots." Pp. 77-94 in Donald N. Michael (ed.), The Future Society. New Brunswick, N. J.: Transaction Books.

Kerouac, Jack
1957 On the Road. New York: The Viking Press, Inc.

1958   Dharma Bums. New York: The Viking Press, Inc.

Kinsey, Alfred C. et al.
1953   Sexual Behavior in the Human Female. Philadelphia: W. B. Saunders Co.

Kovach, Bill
1971   "Communes — the road to utopia." San Francisco Chronicle (January 4):6.

Laing, R. D.
1967   The Politics of Experience. New York: Ballantine Books, Inc.

Leary, Timothy
1965   "The religious experience: its production and interpretation." Pp. 191-207 in G. Weil (ed.), The Psychedelic Reader. Hyde Park, N. Y.: University Books, Inc.

Lenski, Gerhard
1963   The Religious Factor. Garden City, N. Y.: Anchor Books.

Lewin, Leonard C.
1967   Report from Iron Mountain on the Possibility and Desirability of Peace. New York: The Dial Press.

Lewis, George H. (ed.)
1972   Side-Saddle on the Golden Calf: Social Structure and Popular Culture in America. Pacific Palisades, Calif.: Goodyear Publishing Co., Inc.

Leys, Wayne A. R.
1968   "Ethics in American business and government: the confused issues." Annals of the American Academy of Political and Social Science (July):34-44.

Lifton, Robert Jay
1972   "Protean man." Pp. 386-396 in Peter K. Manning and Marcello Truzzi (eds.), Youth and Sociology. Englewood Cliffs, N. J.: Prentice-Hall, Inc.

Lipset, Seymour Martin
1971   "New perspectives on the counterculture." Saturday Review (March 20):25-28.

Mailer, Norman
1957   The White Negro. Dissent (autumn).

Malone, Michael E. and Myron Roberts
1971   From Pop to Culture. New York: Holt, Rinehart & Winston, Inc.

Manning, Peter K. and Marcello Truzzi (eds.)
1972   Youth and Sociology. Englewood Cliffs, N. J.: Prentice-Hall, Inc.

Mao Tse-tung
1962   In The Marxists, by C. Wright Mills. New York: Dell Publishing Co.

Maracotta, Lindsay
1973   "Images, mirages, and nostalgia." Penthouse ( ):72-74.

Marcus, Greil
1971   "Who put the bomp in the bomp de-bomp de-bomp?" Pp. 423-443. Bernard Rosenberg and David Manning White (eds.),

Mass Culture Revisited. New York: Van Nostrand Reinhold Company.

Marcuse, Herbert
1962   Eros and Civilization. New York: Vintage Books.
1964   One-Dimensional Man: Studies in the Ideology of Advanced Industrial Society. Boston: Beacon Press.

Marin, Peter
1971   "The open truth and fiery vehemence of youth: a sort of soliloquy." Pp. 122-154 in Irving Louis Horowitz (ed.), The Troubled Conscience: American Social Issues. Palo Alto, Calif.: James E. Freel and Associates.

Martin, Peter W.
1972   "The draft card burners." P. 272 in Harry C. Bredemeier and Jackson Toby (eds.) Social Problems in America: Costs and Causalities in an Acquisitive Society. New York: John Wiley & Sons, Inc.

Martindale, Don
1967   "National character in the perspective of the social sciences." Annals of the American Academy of Political and Social Science (March).
1968   "Timidity, conformity and the search for personal identity." Annals of the American Academy of Political and Social Science (July):83-89.

Matza, David
1961   "Subterranean traditions of youth." Annals of the American Academy of Political and Social Science (November):102-118.

McGinn, Art
1973   "New hobo generation drifts into Berkeley." Sacramento Bee (December 23):E1.

McGrath, John H. and Frank R. Scarpitti (eds.)
1970   Youth and Drugs: Perspectives on a Social Problem. Glenville, Ill.: Scott, Foresman and Company.

McLuhan, Marshall
1964   Understanding Media: The Extensions of Man. New York: McGraw-Hill Book Company.

Mead, Margaret
1955   Cultural Patterns and Technical Change. New York: The New American Library, Inc.

Meadows, Dennis L.
1972   The Limits to Growth — A Report for the Club of Rome Project on the Predicament of Mankind. New York: University Books, Inc.

Melly, George
1971   Revolt Into Style—The Pop Arts. New York: Anchor Books.

Meltzer, Richard
  1970   The Aesthetics of Rock. New York: Something Else Press, Inc.
Melville, Keith
  1972   Communes in the Counterculture. New York: William Morrow and Company, Inc.
Meyersohn, Rolf
  1972   "Leisure." Pp. 205-228 in Angus Campbell and Philip E. Converse (eds.), Human Meaning of Social Change. New York: Russell Sage Foundation.
Michael, Donald N.
  1970   The Future Society. New Brunswick, N. J.: Transaction Books.
Miller, Walter M., Jr.
  1961   Canticle for Leibowitz. New York: Bantam Books, Inc.
Mills, C. Wright
  1940   "Situated actions and vocabularies of motives." American Sociological Review (October):904-913.
  1951   White Collar—The American Middle Classes. New York: Oxford University Press.
  1959   The Sociological Imagination. New York: Oxford University Press.
Mooney, H. F.
  1969   "Popular music since the 1920s; the significance of shifting taste." Pp. 9-29 in Jonathan Eisen (ed.), The Age of Rock. New York: Vintage Books.
Mullins, Nicholas C.
  1973   Theories and Theory Groups in Contemporary American Sociology. New York: Harper & Row, Publishers.
Nanry, Charles
  1972   American Music: From Storyville to Woodstock. New Brunswick, N. J.: Transaction Books.
Newsweek
  1971   "The polemics of pot. "(May 3):109.
  1973   "The job blahs: who wants to work?" (March 26):79-89.
  1974   "Where are the 'rads' of yore?" (January 14):32-33.
New York Times
  1972   "Student disruption of the University of Chicago." P. 277 in Harry C. Bredemeier and Jackson Toby (eds.), Social Problems in America: Costs and Causalities in an Acquisitive Society. New York: John Wiley & Sons, Inc.
Nobile, Philip (ed.)
  1971   The Con III Controversy: The Critics Look at the Greening of America. New York: Pocket Books.
Nye, Russell
  1970   The Unembarrassed Muse: The Popular Arts in America. New York: The Dial Press.

Oberbeck, S. K.
  1969   "Roxon's rock." Newsweek (Nov. 10):127.
Ogburn, William Fielding
  1922   Social Change with Respect to Culture and Original Nature. New York: B. W. Huebsch.
Orth, Maureen
  1974   "Dylan—rolling again." Newsweek (January 14):46-49.
Packard, Vance
  1959   The Status Seekers. New York: David McKay Co., Inc.
Parachini, Allan
  1971   "Donovan sings a different tune." San Francisco Examiner.
Parker, Stanley
  1971   The Future of Work and Leisure. New York: Praeger Publishers, Inc.
Parsons, Talcott
  1972   "Age and sex in the social structure of the United States." Pp. 136-147 in Peter K. Manning and Marcello Truzzi (eds.), Youth and Sociology. Englewood Cliffs, N. J.: Prentice-Hall, Inc.
Pearlman, Samuel
  1970   "Drug use and experience in an urban college population." Pp. 40-50 in John H. McGrath and Frank R. Scarpitti (eds.), Youth and Drugs: Perspectives on a Social Problem. Glenville, Ill.: Scott, Foresman and Company. Also in American Journal of Orthopsychiatry xxxviii (April 1968):503-514.
Pepper, Thomas
  1972   "The underground press: growing rich on the hippie." Pp. 23-26 in Alan Wells (ed.), Mass Media and Society. Palo Alto, Calif.: National Press Books.
Ragni, Gerome, Galt MacDermot and James Rado
  1968   Hair, the American Tribal Love-Rock Musical. RCA Record (LSO 1150).
Reich, Charles A.
  1970   The Greening of America. New York: Random House, Inc., and Bantam Books, Inc.
Reiss, Ira L.
  1961   "Sexual codes in teen-age culture." Pp. 21-30 in John N. Edwards (ed.), Sex and Society. Chicago, Ill.: Markham Publishing Co.
Riesman, David
  1954   Individualism Reconsidered and other Essays. Glencoe, Ill.: The Free Press.
  1957a "Listening to popular music." Pp. 408-417 in Bernard Rosenberg and David Manning White (eds.), Mass Culture. New York: The Free Press.
  1957b "The suburban dislocation," Annals of the American Academy of Political and Social Science 314 (September):124-146.

1958 "Leisure and work in post-industrial society. Pp. 363-385 in Eric Larrabee and Rolf Meyersohn (eds.), Mass Leisure. Glencoe, Ill.: The Free Press.

1967 "Some questions about the study of American national character in the twentieth century." Annals of the American Academy of Political and Social Science (March):36-47.

Riesman, David, Nathan Glazer and Denney Reuel
1950 The Lonely Crowd. New Haven, Conn.: Yale University Press.

Robinson, John P. and Paul M. Hirsch
1972 "Teenage response to rock and roll protest songs." Pp. 222-232 in R. Serge Denisoff and Richard A. Peterson (eds.), The Sounds of Social Change. Chicago: Rand McNally & Co.

Rosenberg, Bernard
1971 "Mass culture revisited." Pp. 2-12 in Bernard Rosenberg and David Manning White (eds.), Mass Culture Revisited. New York: Van Nostrand Reinhold Company.

Roszak, Theodore
1969 The Making of a Counterculture. Garden City, N. Y.: Doubleday & Company, Inc.
1973 Politics and Transcendence in Post-Industrial Society. New York: Anchor Books.

Roxon, Lillian
1969 Rock Encyclopedia. New York: Grosset & Dunlap, Inc.

Rubin, Jerry
1970 Do It! New York: Simon & Schuster, Inc.

Salinger, J. D.
1951 Catcher in the Rye. Boston: Little, Brown and Company.

Schacht, Richard
1971 Alienation. New York: Anchor Books.

Schmalenbach, Herman
1961 "The sociological category of communion." Pp. 331-347 in Talcott Parsons et al. (eds.), Theories of Society. New York: The Free Press.

Schroyer, Trent
1971 "The critical theory of late capitalism." Pp. 297-321 in George Fisher (ed.), The Revival of American Socialism. New York: Oxford University Press.

Scott, Marvin B. and Stanford M. Lyman
1970 The Revolt of the Students. Columbus, Ohio: Charles E. Merrill Publishing Co.

Seligman, B. B.
1965 "On work, alienation and leisure." American Journal of Economics and Sociology 24 (October):337-360.

Servan-Schreiber, Jean-Jacques
1969 The American Challenge. New York: Avon Books.

Shearer, Harry
1969 "Captain pimple cream's fiendish plot."

Pp. 357-384 Jonathan Eisen (ed.), The Age of Rock. New York: Vintage Books.

Sibley, Mulford Q.
1968 "Anonymity, dissent, and individual integrity in America." Annals of the American Academy of Political and Social Science (July):45-57.

Silber, Irwin
1972 "Distorted vision of despair." Guardian (Jan. 5).

Simmel, Georg
1971 On Individuality and Social Forms, Chicago, Ill.: The University of Chicago Press.

Simmons, J. L. and Barry Winograd
1966 It's Happpening. Mare-Laird.

Skedgell, Robert A.
1970 "How computors pick an election winner." Pp. 19-32 in Donald N. Michael (ed.), The Future Society.

Skinner, B. F.
1970 Beyond Freedom and Dignity, New York: Alfred A. Knopf, Inc.

Skolnick, Jerome
1969 The Politics of Protest. New York: Simon & Schuster, Inc.

Snow, Charles P.
1959 The Two Cultures and The Scientific Revolution. Cambridge: Cambridge University Press.

Solochek, Beverly
1974 "The calm after the storm." Parade (February 10):6-9.

Sontag, Susan
1966 Against Interpretation. New York: Farrar, Straus & Giroux, Inc.

Sorokin, Pitirim
1947 Society, Culture and Personality. New York: Harper & Row, Publishers.
1956 The American Sex Revolution. Boston: Porter Sargent, Publisher.

Spender, Stephen
1969 The Year of the Young Rebels. New York: Vintage Books.

Stein, Maurice R.
1960 The Eclipse of Community. Princeton, N. J.: Princeton University Press.

Stone, Gregory P.
1958 "American sports: play and display." Pp. 253-263 in Eric Larrabee and Rolf Meyersohn (eds.), Mass Leisure. Glencoe, Ill.: The Free Press.

Suchman, E. A.
1968 "The 'hang-loose' ethic and the spirit of drug use." Journal of Health and Social Behavior 9:146-155.

Sutter, Alan G.
1970 "Worlds of drug use on the street scene." Pp. 74-87 in John H. McGrath and Frank R. Scarpitti (eds.), Youth and Drugs: Perspectives on a Social Problem. Glen-

ville, Ill.: Scott, Foresman and Company. Also Pp. 802-814, 826-829 in Donald R. Cressey and David A. Ward (eds.), Delinquency, Crime, and Social Process. New York: Harper & Row, Publishers.

Swanson, Bert E.
1970   The Concern for Community in Urban America. New York: Odyssey Press.

Taylor, A. J. W.
1968   "Beatlemania—the adulation and exuberance of some adolescents." Pp. 161-170 in Marcello Truzzi (ed.), Sociology and Everyday Life. Englewood Cliffs, N. J.: Prentice-Hall, Inc.

Ten Have, Paul
1972   "The counterculture on the move: a field study of youth tourists in Amsterdam." Paper presented at the 1972 ASA meetings, New Orleans.

Theobald, Robert
1968   "The implications of American physical abundance." Annals of the American Academy of Political and Social Science (July):11-21.

Thoenes, Piet
1967   "Rebels from affluence: the provos of Holland." The Nation (April 17):494-497.

Thompson, Toby
1971   Positively Main Street: An Unorthodox View of Bob Dylan. New York: Coward, McCann & Geoghegan, Inc.

Tiryakian, Edward A.
1972   "Toward the sociology of esoteric culture." American Journal of Sociology (November):491-512.

Todd, Richard
1971   "Alternatives." Pp. 466-473 in Bernard Rosenberg and David Manning White (eds.), Mass Culture Revisited. New York: Van Nostrand Reinhold Company.

Tönnies, Ferdinand
1971   On Sociology: Pure, Applied and Empirical. Chicago, Ill.: University of Chicago Press.

Toffler, Alvin
1970   Future Shock. New York: Bantam Books, Inc.

Trachtenberg, Alan
1971   "Culture and rebellion: dilemmas of radical teachers." Pp. 120-130 in Bernard Rosenberg and David Manning White (eds.), Mass Culture Revisited. New York: Van Nostrand Reinhold Company.

Trow, Martin
1968   "Conceptions of the university." The American Behavioral Scientist (May-June):14-21.

Turner, Frederick Jackson
1920   "The significance of the frontier in Amer-

ican history. In The Frontier in American History. New York: Henry Holt & Company, Inc.

Vanderbilt, Amy
1968   "Bad manners in America." Annals of the American Academy of Political and Social Science (July):90-98.

Veblen, Thorstein
1899   The Theory of the Leisure Class. New York: The Macmillan Company.
1914   The Instinct of Workmanship. New York: The Macmillan Company.

Warbasse, James P.
1972   Consumer Cooperation. New York: Thomas Y. Crowell Company.

Watts, Alan
1962   The Joyous Cosmology. New York: Pantheon Books.
1971   "The future of ecstasy." Playboy 18 (January):183-184, 212, 239-241.

Watts, W. David, Jr.
1971   The Psychedelic Experience. Beverly Hills, Calif.: Sage Publications, Inc.

Webber, Melvin M.
1970   "The politics of information." Pp. 11-18 in Donald N. Michael (ed.), The Future Society. New Brunswick, N.J.: Transaction Books.

Weber, Max
1958   The Protestant Ethic and the Spirit of Capitalism. New York: Charles Scribner's Sons.

Wheelis, Allen
1958   The Quest for Identity. New York: W. W. Norton & Company, Inc.

Whyte, William H., Jr.
1956   The Organization Man. Garden City, N.Y.: Anchor Books.

Widmer, Kingsley
1971   "The electric aesthetic and the short-circuit ethic: the populist generator in our mass culture machine." Pp. 102-119 in Bernard Rosenberg and David Manning White (eds.), Mass Culture Revisited. New York: Van Nostrand Reinhold Company.

Wilensky, Harold L.
1963   "The uneven distribution of leisure: the impact of economic growth on 'free time'." Pp. 107-145 in Erwin O. Smigel (ed.), Work and Leisure—A Contemporary Social Problem. New Haven Conn.: College and University Press.
1964   "Mass society and mass culture: interdependence or independence?" American Sociological Review (April):173-197.

Wilkinson, John
1971   "On the revolutionary potential." Pp. 45-56 in Irving Louis Horowitz (ed.), The

Troubled Conscience: American Social Issues. Palo Alto, Calif.: James E. Freel & Associates.

Wolfe, Tom
1968 The Electric Kool-Aid Acid Test. New York: Farrar, Straus & Giroux, Inc.

Wolfenstein, Martha
1958 "The emergence of fun morality." Pp. 86-95 in Eric Larrabee and Rolf Meyersohn (eds.), Mass Leisure. Glencoe, Ill.: The Free Press.

Yablonsky, Lewis
1968 The Hippie Trip. Indianapolis, Ind.: Pegasus.

Zablocki, Benjamin
1971 The Joyful Community. Baltimore: Penguin Books, Inc.

Zais, Major General Melvin
1968 "The physical and moral stamina of American youth." Annals of the American Academy of Political and Social Science (July): 1-10.

Zetterberg, Hans
1965 On Theory and Verification in Sociology. Totowa, N. J.: The Bedminster Press, Inc.

Zijderveld, Anton C.
1971 A Cultural Analysis of our Time. New York: Anchor Books.

Zinn, Howard
1969 "The Old Left and the New: emancipation from dogma." Pp. 349-360 in Judson R. Landis (ed.), Current Perspectives on Social Problems, 2nd ed. Belmont, Calif.: Wadsworth Publishing Co., Inc.

Name index

Subject index